FOOD CO-OPS IN AMERICA

FOOD CO-OPS IN AMERICA

Communities, Consumption, and Economic Democracy

Anne Meis Knupfer

CORNELL UNIVERSITY PRESS ITHACA AND LONDON

First published 2013 by Cornell University Press
Printed in the United States of America

Library of Congress Cataloging-in-Publication Data

Knupfer, Anne Meis, 1951– author.
  Food co-ops in America : communities, consumption, and
economic democracy / Anne Meis Knupfer.
      pages cm
  Includes bibliographical references and index.
  ISBN 978-0-8014-5114-0 (cloth : alk. paper)
  1. Food cooperatives—United States—History. I. Title.
  HD3444.K68 2013
  334'.6816640973—dc23   2012044701

Cloth printing   10 9 8 7 6 5 4 3 2 1

to Franz Knupfer and Melissa DiRito and to my sisters, Betsy, Jeanne, and Mary

Contents

Acknowledgments

This project originated in part through a grant from the Liberal Arts College of Purdue University. With my American Studies colleagues, Whitney Walton and Nadine Dolby, I organized a series of community panels on food politics. We brought in organic farmers, people from food co-ops, and others who made their living from natural food businesses. I learned a great deal from these conversations, as well as those with other local farmers. I give my thanks to Nadine and to historian Rima Lunin Schultz for reading parts of the manuscript and offering thoughtful feedback, as well as other colleagues who have encouraged me to write this book.

I am grateful to the many archivists who assisted me with historical collections. They include Daniel Meyer, associate director of the Special Collections Research Center at the Regenstein Library of the University of Chicago. The Center had received the Hyde Park Co-operative Society's records several years ago and I was fortunate to be the first person to use them. At the State Historical Society of Iowa in Iowa City, Iowa, I was assisted by Mary Bennett, Special Collections coordinator. I must also thank Janet Weaver, assistant curator of the Iowa Women's Archives of the University of Iowa Libraries, for keeping her own records about the New Pioneer Co-operative Society's unionization conflict. A special thanks to Dr. Mary White, former librarian at The History Center in Ithaca, New York. Mary had lived in Ithaca for many years and gave me a broader understanding of Ithaca's progressive politics during the 1960s and 1970s. Library specialist/supervisor Janet Ness and archivist Nicole Bouche assisted me in locating historical collections at the Special Collections of the University of Washington in Seattle. I am grateful to the staff at Cornell University Library's Special Collections; the Minnesota Historical Society in St. Paul; the Newberry Library in Chicago; the Wisconsin Historical Society at the University of Wisconsin in Madison; the Seattle, Washington Public Library; and the Waukegan Historical Society in Waukegan, Illinois.

There were so many people I visited at food co-ops throughout the country that I cannot name them all. Wherever I traveled, I made it a point to stop and talk to workers, managers, board and co-op members, and eat healthy and delicious food. A very special thanks to Janet McCleod, board president of the Adamant Food Co-operative in Adamant, Vermont. Not only did she provide me with a place at the co-op to examine the records; she also opened her home to me during my stay. I must also mention Lois Toby, local historian who has lived in Adamant for many years. We had a wonderful conversation about the village's history. At North Coast Co-operative in Arcata, California, I met many wonderful and committed co-opers. Thanks to the Membership Director Valerie Davis, who shared her working space with me, and to General Manager David Lippman, who—despite his busy schedule—opened the way for my visit to the co-op. At the Hanover Consumer Co-operative Society in Hanover, New Hampshire, I am most grateful to Eugenia Braasch, board administrator. She was in the process of organizing the co-op's historical materials to transfer to Dartmouth College Library. With her avid interest in history and co-ops, we had long discussions and also visited the co-op's different stores. Thanks to Hanover Co-op's General Manager Terry Appleby, who has had a long history with several co-ops and gave me many insights; to Education and Member Services Director Rosemary Fifield, whose contributions I note in the chapter on the Hanover co-op; and to former board president, Kay Litten, a strong advocate for the Co-op. Marshall Kovitz, a board member of La Montanita Co-op in Albuquerque, New Mexico, introduced me to records there. Also a heartfelt thanks to Robyn O'Brien, general manager of the Putney Food Co-operative in Putney, Vermont. I would also like to thank two people at the People's Food Co-op in Portland, Oregon: Marc Brown, a board member, and board president, Eliza Canty-Jones. It is one of my favorite co-ops and I have fond memories of shopping there with my son. Last, my thanks to Andy Mahler and Debbie Turner, co-founders of Lost River Community Co-op in Paoli, Indiana. I first met them when they came to Lafayette, Indiana to discuss how to start a food co-op. Later, when I traveled to the Paoli co-op, I met them again. Both are active and committed co-opers.

At Cornell University Press, I want to thank Acquisitions Editor Michael McGandy and Acquisitions Assistant Sarah Grossman. They provided encouragement, as well as assistance with matters of production. The two reviewers, Lawrence Glickman and Tracey Deutsch, provided important suggestions for making this a better book. I am grateful for their insights.

Last, many thanks to my family, friends, and others who listened to and encouraged my research and writing of this book. In between my family's camping and hiking adventures, there were always trips to local co-ops. All of these experiences reflect a deep respect for the land and what it offers us.

Abbreviations

AFC	Adamant Food Co-operative
AFCR	Adamant Food Co-operative Records
APP	Annabelle Prescott Papers
BPR	Blooming Prairie, Inc. Records
CAC	Community Activism Collection
CCP	Charles R. Coe Papers
CFLPSR	Chicago Foreign Language Press Survey Records
CTCR	Cooperative Trading Company, Waukegan, Papers
HCCS	Hanover Consumer Co-operative Society
HCCSR	Hanover Consumer Co-operative Society Records
HPCSR	Hyde Park Historical Society, Hyde Park Co-op Records
HSP	Henry C. Simons Papers
ICCS	Ithaca Consumer Co-operative Society
ICCSC	Ithaca Consumer Co-operative Society Collection
ICCSR	Ithaca Consumer Co-operative Society Records
IHP	Irwin R. Hogenauer Papers
IRFC	Ithaca Real Food Co-operative
JRP	Julius Rosenwald Papers
JWC	Janet Weaver Collection
LEC	Lake Erie College Collection
LMC	La Montanita Coop
LMCR	La Montanita Coop Records
MFCR	Minnesota Food Co-operatives Records
NCC	North Coast Co-operative
NCCR	North Country Co-operative Records
NPCS	New Pioneer Co-operative Society
NPCSR	New Pioneer Co-operative Society Records
PFC	Putney Food Co-operative
PFCCR	Powderhorn Food Community Co-operative Records
PFCR	Putney Food Co-operative Records
SC	Sprouts! Collection
SCC	James L. Gibbs, Southside Community Center Collection

FOOD CO-OPS IN AMERICA

A DEMOCRATIC IMPULSE

In the past twenty years, there has been a multitude of books published about healthy foods, nutrition, food politics, and agricultural sustainability. For example, Michael Pollan has noted how many Americans eat "foodlike substances" constituted from food science, not nature; nutritionist Marion Nestle has written about the dangers of "nutritionism," that is, the overuse of additives in foods.[1] Others have critiqued fast foods, genetically modified (GM) foods, and the inhumane practices of agribusinesses. Still others, who have grown their own foods, have chronicled and celebrated the wonders of their bountiful gardens and farms. Documentary films about farming, nutrition, and foods have also become popular.[2] Clearly people are concerned about what they and their children eat.

Readers may think that these are new explorations about food politics. But there has been a long-standing consumer activism around food in the United States. Harvey Wiley, an outspoken critic of the Food and Drug Administration (FDA) warned about "food adulteration" in the early 1900s. During the late 1920s, Ralph Borsodi promoted "organic homesteads" where people were responsible for their own food, clothing, and like, rather than relying on "factory production." F. J. Schlink, who started Consumers' Research in the 1920s, advocated for more accurate food labeling. Interested in organic farming, Jerome I. Rodale started Rodale, Inc. in 1930 and the Rodale Press, which in 1942 started the publication of the magazine *Organic Farming and Gardening*.[3] During the 1960s, many environmentalists and activists documented harmful industrial farming practices and the corresponding poor quality of our food. During the same decade, nutritionist Beatrice Trum Hunter warned us about how corporations interfered with food legislation to protect their own interests, not the consumers'. Wendell Berry, poet and steward of his farmland, has written essays and poetry, which express the deep connections between the earth and what we grow.[4]

Within this history of food politics is the history of food cooperatives. Food co-ops—especially during the twentieth century—advocated for consumer legislation, accurate product labeling, and environmental protection. Concerned with "pocketbook politics," to use historian Meg Jacobs's phrase, members of food co-ops participated in union strikes, boycotts, petitions, and other forms of protests.[5] In their practices of collective ownership and democratic decision making, food co-ops have offered us a viable alternative to corporate capitalism.

Food co-ops are situated within a larger history of the cooperative movement, one that is at least 180 years old in this country. Beginning in the 1830s, laborers started their own producer and consumer cooperatives, of which the latter sold clothing, furniture, coal, and groceries. During the late 1800s in rural areas, farmers too formed producer and consumer cooperatives, which by the 1930s included creameries, fire insurance, telephone companies, electric associations, grain storage elevators, and gas and oil stations. Credit unions, another form of cooperatives, spread nationally during the Great Depression.[6] Even today, the American cooperative movement remains strong, providing services in childcare, finance, farm supplies, electricity, phone, funeral, health care, housing, insurance, agricultural marketing, and, of course, food. One estimate is that as of 2010, there were over 47,000 cooperatives, with 130 million members. According to the International Co-operative Alliance (ICA), one out of four Americans is a member of a co-op.[7] Why have co-ops been such an enduring part of American history?

Food co-ops are stores collectively owned by members who pool their monies and resources, sometimes their labor, and make decisions democratically about their businesses' policies, products, and work structures. Many, but not all, have followed principles practiced by a group of weavers who started their own co-op, the Rochdale Society of Equitable Pioneers in England, in 1844. Historically, the Rochdale principles have included open membership, regardless of ethnicity or religion; democratic control, which allowed each member one vote, regardless of how many shares were bought; a distribution of surplus returned on the basis of each member's purchases; cash purchases only (no credit allowed); the education of members; and political and religious neutrality, that is, not collectively endorsing a political party or denomination. Regardless, some co-ops have not always followed these principles, especially in extending credit, which has sometimes endangered their very survival. Political neutrality, too, has not always been practiced. For example, some Rochdale cooperatives in England formed their own cooperative political party and later affiliated with England's Labour Party.[8] Although most American co-ops have not supported political candidates, they have engaged in some form of political activism.

I argue that this political activism reflects the democratic impulse of food co-ops. But what do I mean by democracy, a term I use throughout the book? As noted, food co-ops that follow the Rochdale principles form a collective ownership, where each member has one vote to deliberate on his or her co-op's policies and practices. Such principles favor a participatory democracy, one that is activated through group discussion and decision making. This model resembles one encouraged by twentieth-century philosopher John Dewey. Using language that mirrored the Rochdale principles, Dewey insisted that people's access to an organization be "equal" and "voluntary," so that they could be "in service of a freedom which is cooperative."[9] Dewey's choice of words was deliberate: freedom is "cooperative" in the interest of a common good, not the individual. Cooperation, then, is both a means and an end. This process of democracy necessarily requires that members participate in discussions about "the means and purposes of policies and [their] institutions." This process is time-consuming and often conflict is inevitable, a process that Dewey believed was not counterproductive but a critical part of democracy.[10]

In fact, many of the first food co-ops engaged in such discussions, what historian Steven Keillor in his description of the first rural coops in Minnesota called "a time-consuming, untidy process." Despite similar ethnic identities and labor concerns, however, there were certainly individual differences among members. To reach political consensus, then, was at best "an approximation," to use philosopher Paul Fairfield's words.[11] Even so, there was and still is the promise of economic and social democracy through these deliberations. And it is through the practices of participatory democracy that "community" takes shape in co-ops.

The word "communities" might better reflect the complexity of food co-ops. For one, there are different "constituents" involved in food co-ops—members, workers, board members, local and even global producers. There are social class differences among members, which means that some have access to foods and products that others do not. Members also vary in their consumer activist practices. Some have favored a participatory democracy where members collectively made decisions about which foods to sell. In some cases, the word community has been ideological, for example, when members have forged ties with exploited workers by boycotting national and multinational food corporations. Clearly, food co-ops are not isolated from the larger politics of local and global producers, regional co-op associations, and national cooperative organizations. To speak, then, of a co-op as a "community" simplifies the complexity of these multiple social and economic relations.

Admittedly, I am a strong advocate of food co-ops that are responsive to a sense of place. That is, they have strong geographic ties to a city neighborhood (or town), and to local growers and producers. Further, I prefer a co-op that has only one store, which provides greater opportunity for participatory democracy because of its smaller membership. This is not to say that small co-ops cannot cooperate or form alliances with nearby co-ops in their towns or cities. I believe they should, as well as establish regional and national affiliations. However, in all the food co-ops that I visited or read about, where there was expansion through multiple stores, especially in different communities, there was a loss of members' interest and participation. Although food co-ops are businesses, they need not follow the corporate model of growth and expansion.

Food co-ops differ from traditional and grocery chain stores in many ways. First, member ownership creates the potential for participatory democracy and community formation. Second, food co-ops have a long history of consumer education, a Rochdale principle taken seriously by members. For example, many women served on their co-ops' committees, testing and rating different food labels, creating recipes, and educating the public about the advantages of joining cooperatives. Although one could argue that these activities reinscribed women's domestic roles, they also indicate that women were not passive consumers.[12] Concerned about the safety and quality of the foods they sold, food co-ops hired nutritionists and educational directors to inform consumers about health, environmental, and agricultural issues. The role of educational specialists enlarged during the 1960s to direct members' attention to environmental problems, such as the overuse of pesticides, the dangers of food additives, and the damage of phosphates to our waterways. Food co-ops, unlike grocery chain stores, advocated for environmental and agricultural reform on behalf of their members, thereby continuing their responsibilities as consumer activists.

Third, food cooperatives have been different from grocery chain stores in their promotion of food legislation. In fact, they have been at the forefront, even ahead of the federal government. During the 1930s, when the FDA dragged its heels in revising the 1906 Food and Drug Act, many food co-ops sold foods with their own co-op labels to ensure high quality. They also rallied for a revised act. Thirty years later, the national organization, the Co-operative League of the U.S.A., spoke out against false advertising and supported the Fair Packaging and Labeling Act. Today, many food co-ops continue to advocate for accurate labeling, whether it involves genetically modified (GM) foods, dairy products with bovine growth hormone, or standards of organic food.[13]

Fourth, food co-ops have been different from grocery chain stores in their long-standing support of local farmers and producer cooperatives. In doing so, they have secured fresh produce for their members and kept money within their communities. For example, the Co-operative Trading Company in Waukegan, north of Chicago, bought fresh milk and cream from nearby dairy farmers before World War I. During World War II, the Ithaca Consumer Co-operative Society bought fresh fruits and vegetables from the local grange, and honey, maple syrup, and Christmas trees from local farmers. During the 1970s and even today, the North Coast Co-operative in Arcata, California has bought fresh fish and local, range-fed and hormone-free beef. Many other food co-ops continue this tradition, ensuring high-quality produce and products.[14]

Here, the reader might question the advantages of food co-ops over other food sources. After all, we can now buy organic and natural food directly from farmers and producers at farmers' markets or through a local community-supported agriculture (CSA). Further, many grocery chain stores, most notably Whole Foods, carry organic food. What advantages, if any, do food co-ops have over these sources?

In the cases of farmers' markets and CSAs, there are the advantages of fresh produce, keeping transportation and thus environmental impact to a minimum, and supporting local farmers, thereby keeping money within communities. However, choice is limited to what farmers grow, which is often seasonal. Given its size and multiple locations, Whole Foods offers more products and produce than CSAs and many food co-ops. Whole Foods has started to develop sustainability practices and policies, which many food co-ops have subscribed to for years. Another practice similar to food co-ops is that Whole Foods stores now offer seminars, classes, and other educational activities. It is clearly an effective marketing strategy by Whole Foods, although this is not to deny its educational value to customers.[15]

However, Whole Foods has been criticized for some of its practices, although these criticisms should be questioned as well. First, its founder has not supported labor unions, although one might counter that its full-time workers receive higher wages and better benefits than most grocery store employees. However, not all food co-ops have supported labor unions, although generally they do pay their workers better than grocery chain stores. Second, as Michael Pollan has argued, Whole Foods "abuses" the term "natural." But "natural" has many meanings in the grocery business because there is no certification process as with organic foods and products.[16] And while it is true that Whole Foods sells organic, "natural," and conventional foods side by side, so do a number of food co-ops and grocery stores.

Pertinent to my discussion of what makes food co-ops unique is that they serve a number of communities. Whereas Whole Foods stores are strategically located in more prosperous metropolitan locations, food co-ops are located there, as well as in smaller cities, towns, and to a lesser extent in poorer rural and urban areas. This means that food co-ops are filling the gap to provide access to healthy foods in communities that Whole Foods would not find profitable. Further, food co-ops provide these community members with opportunities to collectively own and manage their co-op businesses, participate in its decisions, and receive patronage refunds.

My hope is that this book will help rejuvenate a discussion about the economic and democratic ideals of foods. I invite readers to ask what the histories of food co-ops can tell us about our rights as consumers, how we can practice democracy and community, how we might do business differently. What possibilities for change—be they economic, political, environmental, or social—might food co-ops offer to their members, communities, and the globalized world? In contrast to the first worker-organized co-ops, some co-ops today are multimillion dollar businesses. Some of their delis feature freshly made sushi, artisan breads, and imported cheeses. Their beauty and health products are costly, as are their wine collections. Many of their members are middle and upper class; in fact, most working class people cannot afford to shop there. Although most members are concerned about the quality of their organic food and its environmental impact, many do not participate in boycotts or other political activities related to food. In fact, most do not even vote for their co-op board members or attend board meetings. What, then, of co-ops' potential for participatory democracy and consumer advocacy? What has changed since the 1830s and why?

I examine those changes in this history of food cooperatives. I tell their stories, as most historians do, by examining archival records, which include newsletters, correspondence, newspaper coverage, and board meeting minutes. To date, there has been no scholarly book about food co-ops, with the exception of Craig Cox's *Storefront Revolution. Food Co-ops and the Counterculture*, which looks at the Twin Cities during the 1970s. This may well be because of the lack of historical materials about food co-ops.[17] Fortunately, a number of Depression-era cooperatives saved their records. This was not true for many "new wave" food co-ops or "food conspiracies" of the 1960s and early 1970s, so named because the young people who started them envisioned them as revolutionary and antiestablishment.

Although I rely mostly on written documents, I also spent a lot of time at many food co-ops across the country, speaking to managers, board members, workers, and members. As such, this book speaks broadly to the experiences of many food co-ops, while also focusing on specific ones. These experiences include forms of consumer activism alongside the daily operations of food co-ops. As such, this book is both a history of food co-ops as businesses and as sites for food politics. Visiting food co-ops nationally, then, provided me with different perspectives and understandings of both of these aspects of food co-ops. I was especially interested in the "community" of workers, because they were not well represented in archival records, unless they were protesting overcrowded conditions, were starting unions, or asked to speak at board meetings. How well were they paid? Did they join unions? To what extent were they involved in decisions related to their workplaces? Did they buy their food where they worked? Whenever possible, I try to include their stories.

I also wanted to represent food cooperatives across regions, ethnic groups, and various constituencies. Because I am a women's historian, I was especially interested in the roles that women played in the establishment and development of food co-ops. Like workers, women have been under-represented in the historical records. Yet we know that as the primary shoppers for food, they were largely responsible for keeping many food co-ops afloat. Even more so, women were education specialists and nutritionists; they served as board and committee members. And they volunteered in a number of ways, from testing food products and recruiting new members to writing articles for the newsletters, and organizing benefits. In thinking about social class, I have looked at co-op membership, as well as food consumption patterns and products sold. Regarding ethnic representation, I have included immigrants and African Americans who started food cooperatives, especially in the early twentieth century. Unfortunately, there is little information about other ethnic groups, such as Latinos, although we should acknowledge their mutualistas and other collectives.

Today, many food co-ops are located in predominantly white and middle-class neighborhoods, and in college and university settings. But this was not true of the first ones. As will be discussed in chapters 1 and 2, many working-class ethnic neighborhoods organized their own cooperatives from the late 1800s through the 1930s. It was during the Great Depression that a number of native-born white professionals and intellectuals formed cross-class coalitions and helped to establish co-ops in their communities. In some cases, these co-ops were inter-racial. But with the growth of suburbs and residential segregation after World War II, membership in food co-ops became predominantly white and middle class. Why has this been the case? And what might this mean in terms of participatory democracy, food politics, and consumer advocacy?

When a number of food co-ops expanded and relocated to shopping centers during the 1950s, they advocated for a different kind of consumer than the activist ones of the 1930s. Here it is useful to consider the models of consumerism offered by historians. Lizabeth Cohen has spoken of two kinds of consumers: the "citizen consumer," who advocated for consumers' rights, such as fair and accurate labeling, throughout the Depression and World War II; and the "purchaser consumer" who expressed their citizenship and patriotism through individual buying decisions. After the war, many Americans literally bought into the idea of contributing to their country's prosperity by purchasing goods. Charles McGovern has argued that, in exercising their right to vote through what they bought (i.e., brand names), individual choice was privileged at the expense of public good. Lawrence Glickman, however, has cautioned us to think more broadly about how consumer activism was practiced during the 1950s, rather than simply comparing it to the 1930s. As he astutely notes: "The adoption of elements of consumer society should not be seen as a departure from the fundamental nature of consumer activism."[18] It could be argued, then, that even as food co-ops adopted mainstream grocery practices in the 1950s, they still provided an alternative business model through collective ownership, consumer education, and patronage refunds.

During the 1960s and 1970s, consumer activism took another turn when the number of food co-ops mushroomed and many engaged in participatory democracy practices. They eschewed what they believed to be the corporate structure of management of some older food co-ops, formed workers' collectives, and made decisions by consensus. Their mantra, "food for people, not profit," reflected their keen interest in making food affordable for everyone, including the working-class and poor. Young co-opers were also wary of agribusiness and instead nurtured connections with local, organic farmers. They debated about which foods should be sold and many participated in boycotts, including the lettuce and grape boycotts of the 1970s.

Many food co-ops were hit hard by the mid-1970s recession and the Reaganomics of the 1980s. To survive, some became more business-minded and consequently incorporated, elected boards of directors, and hired managers. Concurrently, many continued to engage in environmental activism and agricultural sustainability through their selections of foods and other products. In expanding their organic and artisan food lines, however, these co-ops raised their prices. Consequently, not all members could afford to buy at the co-ops they collectively owned. Or if they did shop there, they might buy cheaper foods, such as rice and grains from the bulk bins. This kind of market segmentation certainly contributed to differences among these co-ops' "communities," even as co-ops rhetorically evoked a sense of collective in their missions and annual reports.

Food co-ops today face many of the same challenges. They must negotiate their multiple identities as business enterprises, collective associations, and consumer educators and advocates, all within local, regional, national, and multinational networks. They follow the Rochdale principles—democratic principles that make co-ops different from other businesses. One of the principles, cooperation among cooperatives, has sparked another round of consumer activism. Older co-ops are participating in an initiative to help poorer rural and urban communities start their own food co-ops. The nonprofit, Food Co-op Initiative (FCI), in conjunction with other cooperative organizations, has launched a program to provide training and consultation to poorer communities to organize their own "grassroots, community-based enterprises."[19] Many of these communities or "food deserts" do not have grocery stores, as grocery chain stores know they will not be profitable in these locations. These activist efforts speak to the promise of participatory democracy within the poorer communities.

Overview of Chapters

Chapters 1 and 2 examine the history of food co-ops from the 1830s to the 1950s. Chapter 1 looks at the ideologies and practices of food co-ops established before the Great Depression. Before the Civil War, most buying clubs (informal arrangements where people pooled their money and bought food in bulk) and food co-ops were formed by workingmen's associations to redress inequitable working conditions and wages, and high food prices. After 1865, labor groups, including the Knights of St. Crispin and the Knights of Labor, renewed their interest in cooperatives. In the case of the Knights of Labor, its vision was larger than the establishment of cooperatives. Hoping to replace capitalism with cooperation, the group called for "the complete emancipation of the wealth producers from the thralldom and loss of wage slavery."[20] The Sovereigns of Industry, too, were utopian in fighting the "evils of the existing industrial and commercial system" through boycotts, protests, and cooperatives.[21] Their working-class solidarity fostered their hope for economic democracy through the creation of co-ops.

With the rise of industrialization and immigration in the late nineteenth and early twentieth centuries, cooperatives flourished. Many were started by immigrant groups in cities, in mining towns, and in farming areas. Further, a confluence of groups promoted food cooperatives: labor unions, farmers, women reformers, philanthropists, colleges and universities, emerging regional and national cooperative organizations, and fledgling consumer advocacy organizations. Not coincidentally, this interest in food cooperatives occurred alongside the growth in grocery chain stores nationally. In many cases, grocery chain stores were able to outsell smaller grocery store and co-ops in ethnic neighborhoods through lower prices and customer selection. But in other cases, members remained fiercely loyal to their co-ops.

Chapter 2 examines a thirty-year period, beginning with the Great Depression. Then there was another swell in food cooperatives, prompted by massive unemployment, concern with food safety and high prices, and a vision of establishing a new social and economic order. New Deal legislation provided loans and other forms of assistance to consumer cooperatives. Colleges and universities, as well as regional and national cooperative organizations, taught classes in management, economics, and consumerism. Despite national concerns, the growth of food cooperatives varied regionally. For example, food cooperatives especially thrived in the Midwest and Northeast because of strong ethnic, labor, and more radical allegiances.

The number of food cooperatives grew during World War II and in some urban areas they were transformed into supermarkets. In fact, a rise in co-op supermarkets, many located in shopping centers, became a postwar trend. Many appealed to suburban housewives who appreciated the conveniences of supermarkets and shopping centers. In addition, changes in household technology, especially household freezer units, opened the door for frozen and convenience foods. Food cooperatives shared in this postwar prosperity, evident in their growth and expansion.

The following four chapters present the histories of food cooperatives started during the Depression and World War II. Chapter 3 focuses on the Ithaca Consumer Co-operative Society (ICCS) in Ithaca, New York. As with many food co-ops, it started as a buying club but incorporated into a cooperative three years later. Like other co-ops, the ICCS grew slowly in membership and waited until it could afford to buy a store in the 1940s. And like many Depression-era food co-ops, its members were active in decision making, including what products to sell. What was unique about the food co-op in Ithaca was its relationship with Cornell University's faculty in agriculture and nutrition. Indeed, many of their faculty served on the co-op's board, gave "expert" advice, and guided the co-op's growth to a supermarket and shopping center. However, during the 1970s, the co-op's finances started to unravel. As I argue, part of its undoing was not being responsive politically to the times. The co-op's staunch refusal to participate in the United Farm Workers (UFW) boycotts led to heated debates, a loss in sales, and members boycotting the store. Alongside the boycotts, a new wave co-op had been formed: the Ithaca Real Food Co-op. In the end, the ICCS could not compete.

In Chapter 4, I explore the history of another university neighborhood's food co-op. The Hyde Park Co-operative Society (HPCS) was started as a buying club by earnest University of Chicago students in Hyde Park. Like the ICCS, the HPCS eventually rented a storefront, then expanded into a supermarket in a shopping center by the 1950s. In fact, the new shopping center had been part of Chicago's "slum clearance," euphemistically called urban development. Nonetheless, the HPCS was a multiracial co-op in its membership, workers, and board of directors. Following the Rochdale principle of mutual cooperation, the co-op assisted other food co-ops, including those in poorer African American communities. At the same time, it continued to grow, opening several other businesses and later a convenience store in Hyde Park. However, during the 1980s, a decade when some large food cooperatives were failing, there were problems with remodeling the store, which led to a loss in business and customer dissatisfaction. Further, grocery profits had declined and some members were displeased with the board, who they thought had too much control. A decade later, it would start another co-op, which would eventually lead to both co-ops' closures.

Chapter 5 looks at the second oldest surviving food co-op today: the Hanover Consumer Co-operative Society (HCCS) in Hanover, New Hampshire. Comprised initially of Dartmouth faculty, their wives, and students, the co-op started small in the 1930s. The co-op's history, though, was one of growth and strong membership involvement, at least through the 1950s. After that, the co-op would face two challenges. One was the UFW boycott, which it weathered, although not all co-op and board members agreed with the decisions. The other was a financial investment: what to do with land that the co-op had bought in nearby Vermont. The suggestions from standing committees, members, and others were various, ranging from starting an organic farm to cooperative housing, to a warehouse. In the end, the decision was a financially conservative but wise one. As of 2012, the HCCS, with its four stores (some with service stations), is one of the fiscally strongest in the country.

In Chapter 6, I turn to the Green Mountains of Vermont, where the oldest and the third oldest food co-ops in the United States are located. The oldest, Adamant Food Co-operative, started in 1935, is in a village with a population of sixty-eight. In many ways, it is reminiscent of an old general store, with its sundry and practical goods, as well as foods. It is also a blend of the old and new. The co-op sells hardware, as well as organic produce and a fine selection of wines. It still has a ledger, where people can write down what they buy and pay for it later. How has it been able to survive? One answer would be "barely." Another answer would be through its rich traditions, the dedication of its members, and an independent spirit that some would say is characteristic of native Vermonters. The co-op recently celebrated its seventy-fifth anniversary, with traditional rituals.

The second Vermont co-op is about 100 or so miles away from Adamant. Putney Food Co-operative belongs to a different kind of community than Adamant. The site of utopias and experimental schools, Putney was a haven for hippies, artists, and other alternative people during the 1960s. In contrast to Adamant's co-op, Putney's was more political, participating in boycotts and deliberating on which foods should be sold. During the 1990s, the co-op relocated to a new building, just off the interstate. It is doing well, in part because of its location and because it has connected regionally with other food and producer cooperatives.

I follow the development of the co-ops discussed in chapters 3 through 6 from their creation during the Depression to the present. With the exceptions of Adamant and Putney Food Co-ops, the other co-ops followed the post–World War II model of supermarkets, many of them relocating to shopping centers. These decisions led to a spiral of continued expansion and the promise of economic growth. As such, these co-ops contrasted with the newly created storefront co-ops of the 1960s and 1970s, which favored collective approaches, participatory democracy, and political activism over financial gain. Unlike the storefront co-ops, the larger co-ops were generally not as responsive to the food politics of the 1970s, which included boycotting agribusinesses and multinational corporations that violated workers' rights nationally and internationally, profited from weapons used during the Vietnam War, and degraded the environment through pesticides and pollutants. Following the trajectory of the growth of larger co-ops allows us to see how their economic models discouraged political activism and participatory democracy.

Part 2 turns to the food cooperatives started during the 1960s and 1970s. Chapter 7 discusses food co-ops as one of many social movements of their time, as well as the challenges the co-ops faced during the 1980s and 1990s. In some ways, these new wave co-ops' initial goals resembled those of the 1800s: to overthrow capitalism, to create communal living, and to eliminate profit. However, most co-op founders and members in the 1960s and 1970s were not workers but college students, many of them from middle-class families. Although they were lean on business know-how, they made up for it with their hard work and idealism.

The 1960s also ushered in the ecology movement. Many Americans had read Rachel Carson's *Silent Spring* and worried about the deleterious effects of pesticides, pollution, and unsustainable agricultural practices. Consumers were also concerned about the prevalence of false advertising and labeling of foods. Then, large food companies lobbied Congress and courted the FDA to prevent fair and accurate labeling of many food products. Food cooperatives responded by advocating for better food labeling, selling natural and organic produce from local farmers, boycotting certain products, and forming alliances with other cooperatives and like-minded organizations. Unbeknownst to many new wave co-opers, these were enduring practices of food co-ops since the Depression.

Chapter 8 takes the reader to Humboldt County in northern California, home of the giant redwoods, a resource that drew much contestation from environmental groups. Like other new wave food co-ops, the Arcata Food Co-op was politically active, evident in their boycotts, their decision to sell mostly local and organic foods, and their interests in workers. By the late 1970s and early 1980s, the co-op, like many others, was forced to make changes in order to survive.

Similar to others, the co-op became more structured hierarchically, with managers and the board making the majority of decisions. By the 1980s, the Arcata Food Co-op's board was talking about "corporate viability." At the same time, many of its members were hipsters, hippies, living-off-the-land entrepreneurs, and the like. There were sometimes culture wars but still the co-op expanded south of Arcata in nearby Eureka and Fortuna. In the latter case, the co-op would face suspicion from timber workers and their families because of the radical reputation of Arcata. Despite these troubles and financial loss, the Fortuna co-op was an experiment in whether a food co-op could survive in a working-class community whose main income relied on the harvesting of old and second growth redwoods.

Chapter 9 looks at the New Pioneer Co-operative Society in Iowa City. Admittedly, I am partial to this co-op since I lived in Iowa City for many years. Again, the co-op started small. I still remember the hardwood floors of the old framed house on a tree-lined neighborhood, where the co-op first started. It eventually moved to its present location, in a neighborhood not far from downtown and within walking distance of the University of Iowa. Like other food co-ops, it faced problems as it tried to expand and open other stores. One of the most controversial issues New Pioneer faced was workers' unionization. Fortunately, older members kept their own archival records, which meant I could flesh out the story beyond the minutes of the board meetings.

I could not exclude the Twin Cities' food co-ops, even though Cox has published a book about the ideological battles among Marxists, Leninists, New Left, and other activists there. Many of these co-ops practiced participatory democracy through discussions, making decisions collectively, relying on workers collectives, and refusing to incorporate. Their battles took many forms: takeovers, bombs, burning a truck, and fistfights. One of the most divisive issues the co-ops faced was what foods they should sell: canned goods, which they claimed the working-class wanted; or natural and organic foods, pejoratively considered the food choice of hippies. Chapter 10 discusses these controversies and the warehouse takeover by looking at a select group of food co-ops in St. Paul and Minneapolis.

The Epilogue looks at food cooperatives that have started in the last ten or so years. Among them are Alberta Food Co-op, located in the gentrified northeast neighborhood in Portland, Oregon; Lost River Food Co-op in a poor, rural community in Paoli, Indiana; co-ops in the South Bronx and in the Bay area, which serve African American communities. How have food co-ops survived in these recent years of economic downturn and how has that fostered the creation of new ones? The establishment of these and other new food co-ops suggests that the cooperative movement remains strong overall.

FOOD COOPERATIVES BEFORE THE GREAT DEPRESSION

When the Frenchman Alexis de Tocqueville visited the United States in 1831, he was astonished at the number of associations formed by Americans. He stated, "I have often admired the extreme skills with which the inhabitants of the United States succeed in proposing a common object for the exertions of a great many men and in inducing them voluntarily to pursue it."[1] Such organizing, in his estimation, provided evidence of a democratic impulse. His visit also coincided with the growth of workingmen's associations, which established some of the first producer and consumer cooperatives. The history of food cooperatives in the United States is an enduring one, one that is at least 180 years old. In fact, the first American cooperatives predate the Rochdale Society of Equitable Pioneers, started in Rochdale, England in 1844.[2]

These first co-ops were created as economic alternatives to industrial capitalism. A working-class and ethnic consciousness fostered members' participation in decisions related to their co-ops' daily operations and utopian ideals. Collectively sharing their money and labor gave them more control over their work conditions, the opportunity to share in whatever profit or surplus they earned, and to reinvest their dollars back into their co-ops. But would their food cooperatives be able to compete with grocery chain stores during the early twentieth century?

By then the vision of food cooperatives had enlarged as middle-class reformers advocated for safe food legislation, educated consumers about their rights, and protested the rising costs of food. As such, consumer activism grew out of various constituencies, ideologies, and political affiliations. These differences sometimes led to heated discussions and debates about the goals and purposes of coopera-tive associations. How should the Rochdale principles of political neutrality and democracy be practiced? How should ideological and political differences be re-solved? Could co-ops be both successful businesses and engage in participatory democracy? These debates reflected the growing pains of an emerging national cooperative movement.

The First Food Co-ops

During the 1830s, laborers organized cooperatives to protect their own economic interests. At one meeting in 1836, where 200 workers discussed cooperatives, a worker sharply asked who was "reaping the profits of your labor"? Later that year, hatters, tailors, saddlers, and harness makers pooled their monies to start their own producer cooperatives,[3] ensured workers' control of labor conditions, wages, and sales. But how to control for the rising prices of food and other necessities, to strengthen their purchasing power? As early as 1829, workers in Philadelphia had opened their own store so that they could buy at cost.[4] In 1832, a group of workers and farmers formed the New England Association of Farmers, Mechan-ics, and Other Workingmen. They, too, were interested in consumer cooperatives and buying clubs. But the Association's goals were larger as well: to reduce the twelve-hour working day; to eradicate the trucking system, through which they were paid in goods, not wages; and to promote education for themselves and their children.[5]

However, it was the Working Men's Protective Union, started in Boston in 1845, that led to the establishment of more cooperative stores. Inspired by the Union, a number of workingmen's associations federated into the New England Workingmen's Association, later named the New England Protective Union. The Union started its own stores where members could buy groceries and other sup-plies.[6] Originally, the Union stores were open only to members of "men of good character," those who did not drink or sell liquor.[7] Later, Union members agreed to open their stores to nonmembers who paid market prices for goods. By 1852, the Union boasted 167 stores, with a capital of $241,000 and sales of $1.69 mil-lion. Five years later, there were at least 800 union stores in thirteen states, mostly in the Northeast.[8]

The union stores were part of a utopian vision to change society. Members were concerned about working conditions, especially the twelve-hour work day. Toward this end, they invited a representative from the women workers of Lowell to their 1845 convention to advocate for the ten-hour work day. At the same time, members did not want to pay higher prices for food and hoped that their union stores would replace grocery stores. Despite its rapid growth, the New England Protective Union did not survive through the Civil War. Labor historian Philip Foner has argued that other grocery stores lowered their prices to undersell the union stores, as well as sold on credit. Another historian surmised the opposite: that many of the union co-ops sold their products at cost and extended too much credit.[9] Both historians were probably right on the issue of credit.

Post–Civil War Co-ops

Following the Civil War, labor groups renewed their interest in cooperatives. From 1865 to 1890, cooperators were "practical utopians," to use historian Steve Leikin's phrase. The nearly 500 producer cooperatives and thousands of consumer cooperatives established then allowed workers to have greater control over their labor and their purchasing power. Workers believed that the democratic practices of cooperatives would grant them their due claim as "citizens of the republic" and that they would no longer be subject to industrial corruption.[10] The National Labor Union (NLU), organized in Baltimore in 1866, encouraged members to form cooperative stores, as they were "the only true protection which the working man has against the over-shadowing influence of capital."[11] Even so, the union was short-lived and no records exist of cooperatives being organized through the NLU.

Two other labor groups—the Knights of St. Crispin (1867–1874) and the Knights of Labor (1869–1890)—supported buying clubs and cooperative stores, although most of those also failed. Loosely organized, the Knights of Crispin was especially concerned with the introduction of machinery into the workplace. One alternative was to start its own producer co-ops, although few workers did so because of little capital.[12] The Knights of Labor's mission was also an economic one: "the complete emancipation of the wealth producers from the thralldom and loss of wage slavery."[13] As Lawrence Glickman has discussed, workers hoped to replace their "wage slavery" with a living wage so that they could contribute to "a democratic political economy." In fact, many hoped that cooperation would eventually replace capitalism. The Knights of Labor organized a number of successful boycotts during the 1880s, which led to a surge in membership of over 750,000 by 1886. However, some of its leaders stymied workers' activism by insisting that workers' education precede boycotts. Despite the leaders and members' interests in producer and consumer co-ops, these co-ops largely failed because of lack of workers' capital, the railroad companies and wholesalers' opposition to them, and technological changes in factories.[14]

When workers in Springfield, Massachusetts organized the Sovereigns of Industry in 1874, they too were determined to eradicate monopolies and the "evils of the existing industrial and commercial system."[15] This group proposed, among other ideas, "to establish a better system of economical exchanges and to promote, on a basis of equity and liberty, mutual fellowship and co-operative action among the producers and the consumers of wealth throughout the earth."[16] Members started buying clubs according to the Rochdale principles. These principles of democracy (one member, one vote) limited buying of shares, and the redistribution of surplus through a patronage refund ensured a collective solidarity. At the height of the movement in 1875, there were over 280 local councils, each with its own buying club. The depression of 1877–1878 forced many clubs to close. Five, though, remained open until 1913, including the Sovereigns Trading Company of New Britain, Connecticut. One of the largest co-ops in New England by 1910, it had 237 members, a real estate value of $470,000, and a surplus of almost $15,000 returned to its members.[17]

Ethnic Co-ops

Not surprisingly, many co-ops during the late 1800s formed along ethnic lines. To be sure, the sharing of language and culture facilitated their establishment within communities. The oldest cooperative in Massachusetts, the German Co-operative Association in Lawrence, was started by cotton and woolen mill operatives in 1874. As of 1890, this association had almost 350 members and over $90,000 in dividends distributed to its members. In Quinsigamond, a suburb of Worcester, the First Swedish Co-operative Store Company started in 1882. Other Swedish cooperatives were established throughout the state, including the Swedish Mercantile Co-operative Company in Worcester (1884), the Scandia Co-operative Grocery Company in Fitchburg (1894), and the People's Co-operative Store in Orange (1901).[18]

Beyond New England, there were ethnic and religious groups who established cooperative stores to ensure their very survival in their westward settlements. Alongside settlements of immigrants and religious sects, cooperatives spread from the Midwest to the West. As early as the 1870s, Mormon women had formed their own co-ops in Salt Lake City under the church auspices. By the end of the 1800s, there were at least 150 cooperatives in Utah, which sold clothing, food, and other goods.[19] In California, the first cooperative was started in San Francisco as early as 1867. More co-ops followed, especially after the passage of a state law in 1894 that required cooperatives to practice the Rochdale principle of the "one member, one vote." The reason for the law is not clear, as many co-ops started by single ethnic groups fiercely protected their members' rights. Finnish immigrants were especially active in forming Rochdale cooperatives in the state; by 1917, they had opened over 140 of them.[20]

Food Co-ops, 1900–1930

That the cooperative movement expanded during the Progressive era was not coincidental. Alan Brinkley and Michael McGerr have argued that "reform" liberals of the early 1900s were opposed to unbridled industrial capitalism. Some of them, Gary Gerstle noted, even advocated for "industrial democracy" in hopes that the disproportionate imbalance of economic and political power would be redressed.[21] One of these reformers was John Dewey, who argued that democracy was both political and economic. As he phrased it, "What does democracy mean, save that the individual is to have a share in determining the conditions and the aims of his own work."[22] Other agreed with him, including Henry Carter Adams, Dewey's colleague at the University of Michigan, who openly favored a "cooperative commonwealth of owner-workers" as early as 1881. For this and other public statements, he was fired from Cornell University and then forced to retract his political views to keep his professorship at the University of Michigan.[23]

Women's Advocacy and Food Legislation

Specific concerns about food safety and consumer protection, as well as ones of labor and agriculture, prompted women reformers, socialists, intellectuals, farmers, immigrants, and labor unionists to advocate for food cooperatives. During the Progressive era, the number of food and other co-ops grew at a tremendous pace, with over 2,500 cooperative societies and buying associations as of 1920.[24] This growth also had been fostered by the establishment of regional and national organizations, especially the Co-operative League of the U.S.A. (CLUSA), founded in 1916. Such organizations, as well as a number of colleges and universities, offered summer institutes and courses to train managers and bookkeepers for co-ops, as well as to widen the public's knowledge about cooperative history, principles, and ideologies. Some ardent co-opers and socialists even believed that co-ops would contribute to a new economic and democratic society. This often led to fierce debates and ideological divides, especially within the CLUSA.

Women had expanded their public roles as municipal housekeepers, arguing that all issues relating to families required their involvement. Women's clubs helped to shape legislation and public policy through their reformist activities. To add to this complexity was women's role as primary consumers for their households, a role that advertisers tried to use to their advantage.[25] Even so, women were a major, although often invisible, force behind consumer advocacy and food cooperatives. For example, the members of the American Home Economics Association, started in 1908 by chemist Ellen Swallow Richards, were interested in food safety. The American Pure Food League was organized by the General

Federation of Women's Clubs (GFWC), the National Consumers League (NCL), and the State Food Commissioners. In 1904, the GFWC organized a Pure Food Committee to interest citizens in food legislation, which resulted in Clean Food Clubs. One of these clubs, the Fifty-First Street Club, along with the Housewives League of Chicago, protested the unsanitary conditions and high prices of retail grocery stores. In 1912, they held an egg sale on Chicago's street corners to break the price of storage eggs that were sold as fresh ones. Other club women joined them and sold eggs at ten cents below store price.[26] The NCL, organized in 1899, was concerned with what Landon Storrs called "ethical consumption." Through networks of women's organizations, such as the GFWC and the Young Women's Christian Association (YWCA), the League encouraged women to buy clothing from factories that followed fair labor practices. The NCL's label indicated those clothes that followed state factory regulations and whose factories were inspected by a League agent.[27]

Many women also participated through the cooperative women's guilds. Similar to women's clubs, these groups engaged in social welfare and educational activities, pointing again to their tremendous esprit de corps, as well as their invisible work. For example, the Women's Co-operative Guild of Minneapolis, in collaboration with other women's auxiliaries and organized labor, gave a benefit program for flood victims in the South in 1927. Through this effort, they donated clothing and $35,000. They also contributed to a striking miners' fund and provided a scholarship for a young local woman to attend the Northern States Co-operative League Training School. At Christmas, they gave baskets of food to poor families. Through the Women's International League for Peace and Freedom, of which the guild was a member, they fought "to see the outlawry of war."[28] And they studied the cooperative movement. As one article encouraged the members: "Women, take your share of the responsibility! Organize, study Co-operation, take up committee work and talk Co-operation every day!"[29]

Women and reformist groups' involvement in consumer issues was critical, as the Food and Drug Administration (FDA) had done little to ensure food protection. As early as 1880, reformers had recommended a national organization to regulate food and drugs but the proposition was defeated. Farmers, too, played an important role in promoting pure food legislation. The Farmers' Alliance, concerned about what happened when they sold their livestock to the stockyards, had pushed for a federal pure food law as early as 1881. Between 1860 and 1906, Congress was presented with over 190 bills for food and drug safety but only 8 passed.[30] Finally, in 1902, Congress appropriated $5,000 to the Bureau of Chemistry (later the FDA) to study chemical preservatives and colors, and their effects. Dr. Harvey Wiley, then head of the Bureau, found evidence of "food adulteration." With the support of women's clubs, he convinced Congress to pass the Food and Drugs Act and Meat Inspection Act in 1906, and the first Certified Color regulations (seven colors suitable for use in foods) in 1907. Perhaps the club women had read Upton Sinclair's *The Jungle* and worried about the quality of meat that they served their families. But Wiley understood that not only would consumers gain from this legislation but so would large food companies, such as Heinz and Kellogg, who could then assure their customers of high-quality products.[31]

There were later attempts to create a national organization to protect consumers. In the late 1920s, reformers in Chicago tried to start the Consumers and Producers Foundation of America, with philanthropist and businessman Julius Rosenwald as its president. Its board of directors included members in labor, business, churches, women's organizations, and former president Theodore Roosevelt. The founders intended to fund a national body of scientists and government officials to create standards in health and food products. Although there is no evidence that this foundation materialized, Rosenwald did invest $10,000 in the cooperative movement through the Co-operative Movement for Production and Marketing of Perishable Commodities. This organization promoted consumer cooperation and education, as well as better working conditions in factories.[32] This group, too, was short-lived.

Clearly the quality and safety of food and health products were on consumers' minds. Here, food cooperatives took the lead in ensuring members of high quality food by establishing their own food labels in the 1920s. Even so, they could not compete with chain stores, which then dominated much of the grocery business. Kroger Grocery & Baking Company, which had started with 40 stores in 1920, had over 5,500 stores by 1930. Safeway Stores had over 2,500 stores by 1931. The largest, though, was the A&P Company, with 16,000 stores as of 1929. Altogether, these chain stores earned 40 percent of all grocery sales as they offered more brand names and at lower prices.[33] As Tracey Deutsch points out, grocery chain stores had other advantages as well, such as their layout and self-service. For example, Piggly Wiggly, a southern grocery chain store, used self-service and an "efficient" and "clean" layout to appeal to middle-class women who had previously had their domestic workers shop for them.[34] In doing so, Lisa Tolbert argues, these stores offered women shoppers "a new cultural and commercial landscape."[35]

Despite such competition, a number of food cooperatives survived and even thrived. By 1935 the sales of 100 cooperatives affiliated with the Central Co-operative Wholesale (CCW) in the Midwest had increased more than Safeway Store, the A&P Company, or Kroger Grocery and Baking Company. Undoubtedly, customers appreciated the co-op labels for over 250 foods, which ensured their high quality.[36] Not only did some co-ops compete successfully against grocery chain stores; in one case, a food co-op used a chain store's lower prices to its advantage. When an A&P store opened next to a co-op at an undisclosed location and undersold sugar, co-op members banded together and bought only sugar at the A&P store so it would lose money. They then did the same with Campbell's products and potatoes. Eventually, they forced the A&P store to close.[37]

Widespread Support for Co-ops

Beyond their volunteerism and buying power, women became professionally involved in the cooperative movement. Initially, co-op boards and employees were mostly men. But over time women became bookkeepers, home economists, and dieticians for food co-ops. Still other women influenced the cooperative movement at the national level. For example, in 1912 Lilian Wyckoff Johnson and Ernestine Noa traveled to Rome to study with David Lubin, founder of the International Institute of Agriculture. Lubin's interest in internationalizing agricultural cooperatives prompted Johnson to bring him to the Southern Commercial Congress's conference that year. The two women then traveled across the United States for five months promoting cooperatives. In 1913, they joined a national commission to study European co-ops and were impressed by the number of cooperatives and credit unions in the nineteen countries they visited. In Denmark alone, there were over 1,500 cooperative societies as of 1914, with almost 336,000 members.[38]

Another female leader known in the cooperative movement was Mary Arnold. A dietician and cafeteria operator at Cornell University, she started a small cafeteria in New York City as a consumers' cooperative in 1919. Membership grew and within a year she opened another branch. Within ten years, the Consumers Co-operative Services had ten branches and almost 6,000 members. At the same time, she helped to establish the regional Eastern Co-operative League and the Eastern Co-operative Wholesale, serving as an officer for both. After seventeen years with the Consumers Co-operative Services, she worked as a co-op organizer in Nova Scotia under known co-op organizer, Father M. McCoady. In 1941, she organized credit unions and other co-ops for Maine lobster fishermen and produced a documentary film about their lives. The following year, she moved to Philadelphia and became director of the Philadelphia Area Co-operative Federation, as well as board member of the CLUSA and the Eastern Co-operative Wholesale.[39]

Some colleges and universities, too, promoted cooperative education, confirming that some professors supported "reform" liberalism. Many taught in land grant institutions whose mission included extension education. For example, the College of Agriculture at Cornell University offered a course on cooperation as early as 1911. In 1913, the University of Wisconsin hired a chair in cooperation. That same year, Hector McPherson, who had studied cooperatives in Europe, offered a course in cooperation at Oregon State College. One nonland grant school, the New School of Social Research in New York City, gave a lecture course on the cooperative movement in the early 1920s. At Columbia University, starting in 1927, philosopher and progressive educator Horace Kallen taught a course on "The Philosophy of Consumption."[40] It appears, however, as if many of these courses were historical and philosophical, rather than how-to ones.

Regional cooperatives and labor colleges pragmatically started their own schools to train managers, bookkeepers, and co-op staff, as well as to instruct them in the history and principles of the cooperative movement. The Eastern States Co-operative League in Brooklyn started its first cooperative training school in 1927. There, native-born and immigrant students—referred to as "a co-operative family of genuine international character"—listened to lectures by the CLUSA president Dr. J. P. Warbasse, Mary Arnold, and other cooperative leaders. They also took courses in the history and principles of consumers' cooperation, cooperative management, and administration.[41] In Minneapolis and Duluth, both strongholds of Finnish immigrants, cooperative schools were attended by students with socialist inclinations, union members, and supporters of the Workers Party. Two other labor schools—Bluefield Institute in Bluefield, West Virginia and Brookwood Labor College in Katonah, New York—taught immigrant and African American students hands-on business skills through their cooperative stores.[42]

Struggles over Political Affiliation

At the national level, organizations such as the CLUSA struggled with those cooperatives whose members were socialist and communist. After all, in subscribing to the Rochdale principle of political neutrality, co-ops were not allowed to favor political parties. Following the Russian Revolution, some co-opers had warned that American communists would "infiltrate" the CLUSA, an umbrella organization for over 330 cooperatives societies, with 50,000 members as of 1924. That year, Warbasse had visited Russian cooperatives, even though he was opposed to communism. At the CLUSA 1926 convention, delegates from the Central Co-operative Exchange (CCE, later the Central Cooperative Wholesale [CCW]) in the upper Midwest wanted to discuss communism. However, Warbasse refused to allow this and wanted the CLUSA to remain nonpartisan. Two years later, at the national meeting, CLUSA members passed a referendum that communism and socialism could not be discussed.[43] Even so, some members of cooperatives in the upper Midwest remained committed socialists and their politics influenced their co-ops' policies and practices.

The question here is whether the principle of political neutrality may have stifled political discussion. On the one hand, Warbasse was worried that one ideological group might attempt to control the discussions and direction of the CLUSA. In effect, that might stifle participatory democracy of all members. On the other hand, not allowing some members to speak about their co-ops and political struggles also inhibited the process of participatory democracy. In shaping the CLUSA's national identity, Warbasse strictly followed the Rochdale principles and was accused by some co-opers of being an autocrat. Some individual cooperatives still subscribed to socialist ideas and remained fiercely committed to them.

Ideological struggles also took place in nonaffiliated CLUSA cooperatives as well. In Chicago, for example, Russian immigrants held varying positions on socialism and communism. The Russian Co-operative Society, organized in 1922, was initially attacked by local Bolsheviks who mocked them and called them "counter-revolutionaries." The Bolsheviks then asked if they could join the co-op in order to gain control. But co-op members worried that the communists would recruit other like-minded people and refused to admit them. In other co-ops, Russian immigrants were more concerned about education and promoting their businesses. The Russian Workers' Co-operative Association of Chicago, formed in 1925, started workers' cooperative restaurants and stores, as well as reading rooms, lectures, and an information bureau. In 1930, another group of Russian immigrants met to establish the Russian American Co-operative Bank of Chicago, the first bank to promote nationwide cooperation of Russians in the United States. This group advocated for cooperative stores, restaurants, dining rooms, and housing cooperatives.[44]

Instead of siding with socialists or communists, many union cooperatives organized directly in response to high prices and low wages. This is not to say that there were no socialist or communist members, only that the co-op did not follow their political ideologies. Workers from the Knights of Labor and other labor groups in Illinois had federated into the Illinois State Federation of Labor in 1884. That year they discussed the eight-hour work day, the promotion of trade unions, safe working conditions, and "equal pay for equal work, regardless of sex." Following their 1904 study of cooperative stores, they decided to create their own. By 1915, they owned two Rochdale stores, as well as worked with the Illinois Mine Workers Union to promote state legislation for cooperatives. By 1918, Illinois had sixty-five co-op stores, most of them owned by railroad brotherhoods and miners.[45] Laborers in other states followed: copper miners in Michigan established co-ops, as did coal miners in Pennsylvania and West Virginia, and gold and silver miners in Nevada and Minnesota.[46]

The Persistence of Ethnic Co-ops

It was the persistence of ethnic solidarity through the 1920s in the Northeast industrial centers that led to the growth of most cooperative societies. By 1926, there were 140 consumers' cooperatives in New England, most organized along ethnic lines. In Cambridge, Massachusetts, there were two Lithuanian cooperatives; in Adams, a Polish grocery and meat store. There were Italian cooperatives in Sagamore and Plymouth, Massachusetts, as well as French and Belgian. The Co-operative Franco-Belge of Lawrence had a membership of 300 families and did $100,000 in business annually in groceries and baked goods. Interested in fair wages and the eight-hour work day, its members participated in the 1911 Lawrence strike and contributed monies for strikers in Belgium and in Lawrence.[47] Clearly co-op members were active in politics, without necessarily subscribing to political parties.

Finnish immigrants in Massachusetts, as elsewhere, had started a number of consumer cooperatives. In 1910, they opened five in Maynard, a textile town with a population of 6,400. One of the largest and most successful of their co-ops was located in Fitchburg. Started in 1910, the co-op also opened a boarding house, a milk distribution cooperative, at least four grocery stores, a men's clothing and shoe store, and a bakery. The total sales for these cooperatives were half a million dollars in 1918 alone. Six Finnish cooperatives—in Maynard, Fitchburg, Quincy, Norwood, Gardner, and Worcester—pooled their capital and properties, and organized the United Co-operative Society of New England for lower wholesale prices. By 1920, however, the Society had closed because of too much infighting about communism. In turn, some of its communist members decided to open their own stores, although these were short-lived.[48]

Those states with strong Scandinavian populations, active labor unions, and liberalism—Wisconsin, Minnesota, and Illinois—had the most co-ops. This led one historian of the cooperative movement to claim that the Midwest was "a center for experiments in co-operative store development," at least from 1897 to 1920.[49] One of the strongest midwestern organizations was the CCE, whose members were mostly first- and second-generation Finns. In 1920, its sales were nearly $410,000; by 1930, $1.77 million. By 1939, the CCE had at least 137 societies, which had over $3.35 million in sales.[50] Ethnic groups in other midwestern states also started their own co-ops. For example, Bohemian Americans formed cooperative stores in the coal mining region of southern Ohio so that they could get food for fair prices through "freedom from the tyranny of the company stores."[51] These cooperatives, which survived through the early 1930s, offered reasonable food prices to members, as well as provided clubrooms for social activities.[52]

Chicago, a city of immigrant neighborhoods, had many non-CLUSA affiliated food co-ops, as well as cooperative housing, restaurants, presses, and banks.

These businesses were a part of the economic networks in ethnic communities. Lizabeth Cohen and Tracey Deutsch have noted that these community businesses were able to thrive not only because of a strong ethnic identity but because most grocery chain stores had not yet located to their communities. As early as 1896, Polish Americans formed the John Sobieski Society of South Chicago and purchased 122 shares of stock (ten dollars per share) toward a Polish co-op store in South Chicago. In order to keep money within their communities, a network of members united into one group, the Alliance of Polish Mercantile Corporation, similar to the CLUSA.[53] In 1905, a group of Bohemians started the cooperative society, Cesky Bazar (Bohemian Bazaar), issuing 10,000 shares at ten dollars each "to enable even the poorest to secure one or more of them and thus become a part-owner of the Bazaar." In addition to groceries, the co-op sold clothing, shoes, and household goods.[54] The Northwest Co-operative Association, a Jewish organization, started a cooperative grocery, as did Lithuanians immigrants on the west side during World War I. However, some of the local grocers and butchers, fearful of losing their customers, tried to persuade customers that the Lithuanian co-op would hurt their businesses. Co-op enthusiasts, however, retorted that customers could be assured of high quality food at their co-ops.[55]

The longest surviving co-op in the Chicago area was the Co-operative Trading Company in Waukegan, north of Chicago. Waukegan's shipping industry hired mostly Finnish and Scandinavian immigrants, as well as German and Slavs. To stretch their husbands' wages, their wives organized a strike in 1910 when milk dealers raised the price of milk from six to eight cents a quart. The women then bought directly from local dairy farmers who delivered milk to their homes. This was the start of the Co-operative Trading Company, which by 1913 had opened a general store and meat market. The co-op was known for its high quality foods, which included smoked meats, milk, cream, co-op-made bread, pastries, ice cream, eggs, milk, buttermilk, potatoes from a farmers' co-op in Wisconsin, and the Co-operators' Best Flour milled by the CCE. By the late 1920s, the co-op, with a membership of over 1,000, owned six grocery stores and meat markets, a dairy and bakery. It survived the Depression through workers forgoing a day's wage and deferring payments to local farmers.[56]

The co-op was also successful because of its women's guild. Guild members compared grocery store prices and quality, and sometimes canvassed house-to-house to recruit more members. To ensure solidarity among co-op members, they organized annual picnics, Christmas parties, bowling leagues, baseball teams (girls and boys), an orchestra, and a drama league. They supervised a youth league, which sponsored dances, sports, and theater events. Although women's involvement in co-ops were not always acknowledged, their activities strengthened the strong ethnic ties within the community, allowing the company to survive until the mid-1950s.[57]

From the Midwest to the West

These examples from the Midwest and especially Chicago demonstrate that many co-ops perhaps fared better when they were independent. Efforts to consolidate, with the exception of the CLUSA and their regional affiliates, were usually less successful. Such was the case with the Right Relationship League, which started from the Associated Merchants USA in Chicago in 1898, then reorganized as the Co-operating Merchants Company of Chicago.[58] The League hoped for a slow revolution in which privately owned stores would become cooperatives. In 1905, about twenty of the 450 member stores of the Co-operating Merchants Company were cooperative. By 1907, for reasons not disclosed, the League broke away from the Company and relocated to Minneapolis. By 1915, twenty-nine cooperative stores opened in Minneapolis. That year, however, the League closed. Four years later, the National Co-operative Association and the Chicago Federation of Labor formed the National Consumers' Co-operative Association, a group of Rochdale co-ops. By 1920, seven stores had opened but were operating at a loss. The following year, that organization also died.[59]

In the Pacific Northwest, especially Seattle, consolidated efforts were short-lived as well. A number of co-ops in Seattle organized not around ethnic solidarity as much as laborers' concern about high prices. As Dana Frank has documented, many of these co-ops grew out of a militant labor movement, especially after World War I. Then two citywide cooperative chains formed: the Seattle Consumers' Co-operative Association, which had 1,600 members, eight branch grocery stores and two producer cooperatives as of 1919; and the American Federation of Labor (AFL)-affiliated Co-operative Food Products Association, with more than 1,000 members. Workers, joined by farmers and women, had decided to establish their own co-ops to strengthen their purchasing power in a time of inflationary prices. Here again, women formed networks throughout the city through their cooperative guilds and engaged in social, charity, and educational work. Nonetheless, by 1921, most of the co-ops had closed for reasons similar to others: poor management and bookkeeping, lack of working capital, noncompetitive food prices, and refusal to extend credit to its customers.[60]

Beyond Seattle, there were other cooperatives in the Pacific Northwest, West, and Southwest. In sparsely populated rural areas, co-ops pragmatically formed along nonethnic lines. When researcher Mabel Cheel traveled throughout the country in 1925, she visited a number of co-ops in Washington, among them one started by a farmers' group of several nationalities that sold dairy products and owned a general store. A co-op store in the town Kennewick had two "well equipped" cars that traveled forty miles a day into the country to sell and deliver food and other goods. Altogether, she documented sixty cooperative stores in the rural areas of Washington.[61] In California, most co-ops initially started in cities, then spread to rural areas. The California Rochdale Wholesale Company, established in San Francisco in 1899, provided groceries at wholesale prices and helped others to start their own co-ops. In 1900 alone, nine stores had opened; five years later, there were fifty-one, with a membership of over 6,000 and $4 million in sales. By 1921, when the Pacific Co-operative League took over the Rochdale Wholesale Company, co-operatives had started not only in California but also in Arizona, Nevada, and New Mexico, with a membership of over 15,000 and sales of over $4 million. But when its administration became too autocratic, the League closed in 1922.[62] Organizing across four states had most likely led to increased centralization of the League.

Laborers were at the forefront in establishing food and other cooperatives from 1830 to the early 1900s. As noted, their concerns were economic: to increase their purchasing power; and to have further control over their working conditions. Immigrants, too, started and supported co-ops for economic reasons, for example, to establish their own businesses and to keep their monies within their communities. In addition, they expanded cooperative educational and social services, such as reading rooms, newspapers, and presses. In all these endeavors, they reinforced ethnic ties within their communities.

In local co-ops and in regional and national cooperative organizations, there were sometimes ideological conflicts. Some members were interested in promoting socialist or communist ideas and practices. In most cases, however, co-ops remained nonpartisan, whether or not they subscribed to Rochdale principles. This is not to say that they were not political. Their discussions—be they about wages, high food prices, or strikes—point to how members conceived of their collectively owned co-ops as sites for participatory democracy.

Other groups participated in the formation of co-ops and consumer politics as well. Women's organizations had formed alliances around the issues of safe foods, accurate labeling, and affordable food prices. In doing so, they both advanced women's political visibility and influence, as well as represented women as shoppers for their families. Not unlike other progressive reforms, women predicated their authority and public engagement on their responsibilities as mothers and wives. More often than not, however, native-born white women's groups did not work with immigrant or labor groups. Instead, as labor historian Shelton Stromquist argued, women reformers put their faith in the state and in experts.[63] Although it is true that middle-class white women advocated for federal legislation and protection, they also protested at the local level, for example, in selling eggs below store price. As such, they did not passively rely on the state or experts.

In teaching about the cooperative movement, university and college professors generated interest within their own communities. As discussed in subsequent chapters, a number of food and other co-ops started in these locations during the Depression, in part because of professors and students' hopes for a new economic order. Regional cooperative associations and labor colleges also hoped to expand the cooperative movement. In some cases, their approaches were both ideological and pragmatic. Students learned the practical skills of bookkeeping and management, as well as different political and historical perspectives. Although it is impossible to know what discussions were like in these classrooms, the very subject of cooperation—with its principles of democracy and collective ownership—probably lent itself to debate among students.

Although the number of small-scale co-ops declined during the 1920s, especially in ethnic communities, the Depression spurred the development of consumer and producer co-ops in both urban and rural areas throughout the country. Labor unionists, intellectuals, and reform liberals of the early twentieth century had organized around the formation of a cooperative movement that took roots at the local level. During the 1930s, they would create alliances to support and protect workers and consumers locally and at the federal level.

Part I
COLLECTIVE VISIONS OF THE DEPRESSION

FOOD COOPERATIVES, 1930S–1950S

During the Great Depression, the number of cooperatives increased because of available federal funding, the need for alternative economies in a time of high unemployment, and the advocacy of many individuals and organizations. As noted by Gary Gerstle and Judith Stein, New Deal liberals—a coalition of government officials, intellectuals, middle-class activists, and labor unionists—hoped to stimulate economic growth and to "tame" unbridled capitalism.[1] By linking consumer activism to labor unions' concerns for higher wages and increased purchasing power, New Deal liberals helped to create a "new Democratic majority."[2] Through their support, President Franklin D. Roosevelt established the National Emergency Council (NEC), the Federal Emergency Relief Administration (FERA), and the Farm Security Administration (FSA), all of which created programs to foster cooperatives. Consumer protection, through the National Recovery Act, was also promoted, although the Act was declared unconstitutional within two years. But how successful were these federal programs in their promotion of cooperatives?

Beyond federal programs, cooperative organizations, women's professional and volunteer groups, consumer advocacy groups, and higher educational institutions rallied for consumer protection and cooperatives through legislation, policy, the development of coursework, and educational outreach. But to what extent did these various groups work together? Did they form a powerful alliance against grocery chain stores and food companies, which continued to lobby against food legislation? How exactly did these activists advocate for the "citizen consumer" and advance consumer rights during the Depression? And if they were successful, why did citizens become "purchaser consumers" and privilege individual consumption after World War II?[3]

The Depression Years

It is difficult to know the exact number of consumer cooperatives during the 1930s because figures sometimes included credit unions, farm supply stores, and other retail stores. One estimate is that as of 1933 there were 2,000 consumer cooperatives and that at least one-fourth of them were grocery or meat stores. One researcher—who included 500 retail stores, 3,600 credit unions, and 1,600 farmers' supply co-ops in his total—concluded that cooperatives in 1934 did $365 million in sales or 1 percent of all retail business in the United States.[4] The Department of Labor reported 3,600 consumer societies by 1936, with a membership of 677,000 and an annual business of over $1.82 million. The Co-operative League of the U.S.A. (CLUSA) reported at least 1,500 cooperative stores in its organization alone as of 1936, although it is not clear how many were food cooperatives.[5] Overall, the number of food cooperatives would have been difficult to tally for many reasons: some were short-lived; there were problems with self-reporting; and the number of cooperatives may have been inflated (or deflated) for legislative or policy purposes. In fact, the Bureau of Labor Statistics noted that from 1933 to 1937, almost 600 cooperative societies had failed or reorganized.[6]

Federal Programs and Co-ops

The Division of Self-Help Co-operatives within the FERA was established in 1933 "to aid in assisting co-operatives and self-help associations for the barter of goods and services."[7] As social scientist Joanna C. Colcord noted of this division: "A new relief era opens, and the co-operative self-help associations, as partners in the new plan, may hope to have their effectiveness vastly increased."[8] However, start-up capital was given mostly to producer—not consumer—cooperatives. The FSA assisted a number of co-operative farms, as well as provided funds for retail shopping centers in rural areas and in planned communities, including three "green towns" established in the 1930s: Greenbelt, Maryland; Greenhill, Ohio; and Greendale, Wisconsin. These communities followed sociologist Clarence Perry's idea of a neighborhood with an elementary school, a community center, local shops, a library, churches, and cooperatives. The first cooperatives started in Greenbelt in 1937, where a local committee decided to establish a credit union, a gas station, a supermarket, a drugstore, a barber shop, and theater.[9] Perhaps it should not surprise us that Greenbelt was an all-white community. In fact, most of the FSA consumer cooperatives were racially segregated: almost 66 percent were largely white, 27 percent African American, and less than .2 percent Native American.[10] Such patterns conformed to the racial segregation of the time period, reinforced by reservations, restrictive covenants, and other housing practices.

In 1934, the Consumers' Division of the NEC was established to coordinate the consumer activities of the National Recovery Act (NRA). The Act had three sections, including the Consumers' Advisory Board, chaired initially by sociologist Mary Harriman Rumsey. Upon her death, Paul Douglas, a former economics professor at the University of Chicago, assumed the position. Douglas established 150 county consumer councils, comprised of a cross-section of members from women's organizations, county agents, farmers, housewives, factory workers, and co-op members. These councils dismantled when the NRA was declared unconstitutional in 1935.[11]

In 1937, Roosevelt commissioned a group of Americans to study European cooperatives. The original commission did not include a woman or farmer until representatives from these groups objected. The commission's report made the following recommendations: that a survey on cooperatives be conducted in the United States; that a special agency be created to disperse research and advice to consumer cooperatives; and that consumer cooperatives be placed on "a parity basis" for financial and banking credit with other types of businesses. Significantly, the report's publication was delayed until Roosevelt was reelected.[12] Little appears to have been done following the publication, prompting historian Ellis Hawley to conclude that Roosevelt was not interested in promoting cooperatives. This was especially true of consumer cooperatives. In fact, Hawley's overall assessment of the Roosevelt years was negative. In his estimation, the consumer was the "forgotten man" during the New Deal and many of the programs were "mostly window dressing."[13]

Although policy analysis is critical, it is also important to look at how the FSA and other New Deal programs changed people's lives. Here I return to the work of Lillian Wyckoff Johnson (see chapter 1), who had not neglected her interest in cooperatives during the 1930s. After underwriting the Highlander Folk School in Monteagle, Tennessee, she turned her attention to Ravenscroft, a nearby mining community. The coal mine had closed in 1937, leaving sixty-four families (with 150 children) starving. Through the FSA, she helped to start a Rochdale agricultural cooperative there. By 1941, the residents had sold over 2,400 bushels of green beans to buyers in six states. The FSA loans also helped improve the living conditions for many families, for example, through electricity, indoor toilets, and other modern amenities. As of 1942, the community had started a grocery co-op, a clothing store, and a community house. By 1945, the agricultural co-op, which had started with only $25, had assets of $25,000.[14]

Leadership in Advocacy and Education

The Ravenscroft example shows how activists worked through federal programs on behalf of disenfranchised communities and consumers, corroborating historian Thomas Sugrue's point about how local grassroots activists enacted federal government policies.[15] Despite their efforts, however, activists were not always able to effect change. Such was the case with food legislation during the 1930s. In 1933, the Food and Drug Administration (FDA) had recommended revising the old 1906 Food and Drug Act. However, food companies and grocery chain stores fought against establishing standards for food because they worried that such standards would "destroy trademarks." They were apparently successful in their lobbying, for in 1935 the bill was amended to exempt "established food products from disclosing a list of ingredients on the labels."[16] It would not be until 1938 when the Federal Food, Drug, and Cosmetic Act was passed, which created standards for canned foods but not grade labeling. Sadly, this Act was passed because of a tragedy: 107 people had died from a new drug called "Elixir of Sulfanilamide."[17]

Regardless of the FDA's tardiness with food labels, many food cooperatives had already established their own. By 1939, the Central Co-operative Wholesale (CCW) had also set up its own testing kitchen and employed a home economist for product control under the co-op labels. Products were graded according to the Department of Agriculture standards with co-op grades of A, B, and C, determined by color, flavor, and consistency. Co-op members clearly patronized the 100 CCW-affiliated cooperatives; by 1935 the CCW's sales had increased more than those of the chain stores of Safeway Store, the National Tea Company, or the Kroger Grocery and Baking Company. Even so, as of 1939, over 90 percent of lower-income people bought their food from grocery chain stores where prices were generally lower.[18]

Women Rally for Legislation and Co-ops

Under the new presidency of E. R. Bowen in 1934, the CLUSA too advocated for co-op labels, as well as federal legislation. By 1938, the CLUSA was a formidable national organization, with twenty-one regional cooperatives and 800,000 members.[19] Bowen's ideology was distinct from his predecessor, J. P. Warbasse. Whereas Warbasse had hoped that the co-operative movement would "replace" the state through a "Co-operative Commonwealth," Bowen pragmatically believed that the state, private businesses, cooperatives, and activist groups could all play a part in economic reform. One example was the passage of a pure food and drug bill "with teeth in it." Bowen rallied multiple constituencies—women's clubs, educational institutions, labor groups, and others—to give their support to such a bill.[20] Women's clubs helped to draft and lobby for consumer legislation, and the Parent Teacher Association (PTA), the League of Women Voters, the National Federation of Business and Professional Women's Clubs, and the League of Women Shoppers were also involved. The American Association of University Women (AAUW) participated as well, forming their own Consumers' Interests Committee to learn about the testing and labeling of foods, drugs, and clothing. These and other examples of women's consumer advocacy during the 1930s pointed to how women eschewed so-called experts and took collective action.[21]

Likewise, at the state and local levels, women organized to consolidate their purchasing power. The Illinois Housewives Association, which organized around consumer issues, held annual state conferences, public meetings and discussions, and protests. At one conference in 1937, women discussed family and home problems, consumers' living costs, food and drug legislation, and community welfare activities. Members emphasized the "need of women realizing their responsibility as consumers and as the world's largest buyers so that they may develop and use their organized strength in the economic world."[22] In 1940, the Association—then 5,000 strong—established a Consumer Day mass meeting for all women's, civic, and social organizations in Chicago. The Chicago Housewives Association, too, was engaged in "corrective" activities against unethical and illegal grocery practices, especially inaccurate weights and measures, and unsafe food. As recourse, they instigated legal action against grocery stores, which engaged in these practices and informed the Department of Health.[23]

In Chicago, African American women were active as consumer advocates in starting cooperatives in their own communities. As Halena Wilson, president of the Chicago Ladies' Auxiliary to the Brotherhood of Sleeping Car Porters, stated: "Consumer education, the feminine complement to worker's education, instructed wives to use their husbands' paychecks to demand union label goods and courtesy from white merchants." The Auxiliary sponsored a lecture series on consumer affairs to educate community members about consumer education, housing problems, and how to select quality products. The organization also created several consumer study groups in the early 1940s, one of which started its own buying club in 1941. Two years later, they opened a grocery co-op that sold mostly canned and dry goods; by 1948, it had over 250 paying members.[24]

Support for Co-ops

Colleges and universities, too, continued to promote the cooperative movement, as well as established their own co-ops. More than likely, this was one reason why a number of food co-ops started in college settings. As of 1934, there were forty-nine cooperatives in colleges and universities, including bookstores, faculty buying clubs, cafeterias and lunch rooms, housing, grocery and gasoline cooperatives. By 1938, there were almost 200 student cooperatives, dormitories, dining clubs, bookstores, with over 104,000 members. Alongside these cooperatives, higher educational institutions taught related course work. By 1935, there were twenty-four college courses in economics and consumption with materials on consumer cooperatives. Three years later, over 130 higher educational courses included the subject of cooperatives.[25] Some cooperative leaders also discussed the idea of starting a cooperative college, although none developed. There were, of course, labor colleges and schools supported by regional cooperatives that trained students and personnel of co-ops in cooperative principles and skills.[26]

Philosophers, theologians, and activists—many of them New Deal liberals— promoted the idea of cooperatives. Progressive educators John Dewey and George Counts supported the ideas of cooperatives through their promotion of community, social action, and creating a new social order.[27] Dewey publicly supported workers' rights, stating in 1933 that he favored "the formation of a genuinely cooperative society where workers [we]re in control of industry and finance as directly as possible through the economic organization of society." Walter Rauschenbusch, a Christian theologian, likewise criticized capitalism and countered that "Co-operation [wa]s the life of the whole economic process." Philosophy professor Horace Kallen agreed, arguing that consumer cooperatives were the "democratic alternative" to capitalism, communism, and fascism.[28] Albert Sonnichsen, in distinguishing between socialism and cooperation, argued that consumers' cooperation was "an anti-capitalist, revolutionary movement, aiming toward a radical social reconstruction based on an all-inclusive collectivism."[29] Pacifists, too, supported cooperatives. Warbasse, a personal friend of Jane Addams, believed that cooperatives led to peace, as did Emily Balch who wrote how cooperatives "struck" against war and greed. Warbasse and Balch were influenced by Toyohiko Kagawa, a Christian socialist and pacifist who popularized co-ops, organized the National Peasants' Union for farmers, and was active in the labor party in Japan. In 1931 and 1936, he visited the United States to promote a worldwide cooperative movement.[30]

The food cooperatives established during the Depression were distinct from those at the turn of the twentieth century. First, with the exception of African American co-ops, most were no longer exclusive to one ethnic group. In fact, some co-ops, such as the Waukegan Trading Company, which had started with mostly Finnish members, now included African Americans.[31] Second, a number of food cooperatives were formed through the efforts of college professors and students. As we will see in subsequent chapters, the University of Chicago, Cornell University, and Dartmouth College played important roles in establishing food co-ops in their communities. Despite these differences, Depression-era co-ops were similar to the earlier co-ops in several ways. First, socialists joined in cooperative efforts, hoping to establish a new social and economic order. During the 1930s, however, they interested not just laborers but many who were unemployed. Second, as with the earlier co-ops, many Depression-era co-ops were short-lived because of a lack of capital.

Co-ops in African American Communities

Lack of capital was certainly a problem in many African American communities. Yet there were historical leaders who had advocated for economic self-determination since the turn of the century. Activist Ida B. Wells and sociologist W. E. B. Du Bois come readily to mind. In his sociological studies of African American communities, Du Bois had documented at least 100 cooperatives in the early 1900s. As he leaned increasingly toward socialism in the 1930s, he continued to advocate for cooperatives.[32] There were, of course, other African American leaders who helped to promote and start cooperatives. Author and intellectual George Schuyler, referring to cooperatives as "the consumer's ballot," started the Young Negroes' Co-operative League in New York City in 1930 with social activist, Ella Baker. Comprised of young members, the League's five-year plan was to train 5,000 cooperative leaders within two years, then establish a wholesale outlet by 1933, and finance a college by 1937.[33] These ambitious plans did not materialize, however. African American educator, Jacob Reddix, was more successful in his plans. Concerned that there were too few "high-end" African American businesses, he started a buying club in Gary, Indiana in 1934. Within three months, the group started a grocery store, the Negro Co-operatives Stores' Association. By the first year, there were over 400 members and the cooperative did at least $35,000 in business. Perhaps part of the co-op's success was because it was advised by the Central States Co-operative League and the Co-operative Trading Company in Waukegan.[34]

One site for the formation of African American food cooperatives were housing projects, built during the late 1930s. In Harlem, the Dunbar Housewives' League bought milk with the "green pine tree" co-op label and set up a milk route. Tenants of the Dunbar Apartments, a low-cost housing project in Harlem, demonstrated that working-class and poorer communities created some degree of economic independence for themselves. In fact, another cooperative in Harlem did so well that it forced the nearby A&P store to close. Strategically, residents bought their food from the cooperative, not the chain store. They then started a second cooperative, the Pure Food Co-operative Grocery Store, which opened in 1934 with 350 Harlem families.[35] Altgeld Gardens, a housing project for wartime workers on the far south side of Chicago, opened "the largest Negro-owned store in America" during the wartime. It later merged with a citywide cooperative, then became independent, but dissolved by 1952. South of downtown Chicago, in the Bronzeville neighborhood, the Ida B. Wells Housing Project also started its own grocery cooperative.[36]

African American churches also were a catalyst for grocery cooperatives. The Open Eye Consumer's Co-operative was started by the Pilgrim Baptist Church congregation in Chicago in the 1930s. However, many people in the neighborhood were too poor to support the store; in fact, most members were unable to spend more than fifteen dollars a month there. Another Chicago cooperative was the Citizen's Non-Partisan Co-operative Organization of Olivet Baptist Church, started by eight unemployed persons in 1936. By 1938, it had sixty-five members, three-fourths of them on relief. As with other co-ops, they purchased their foods from the CCW. The Chicago Baptist Institute offered a course on cooperatives for church workers during 1938 and several ministers decided to start buying clubs at their churches.[37]

Although few food cooperatives were started by African Americans in the South, there were exceptions. Tuskegee College in Alabama, started by Booker T. Washington, had a thriving cooperative store, a smaller one run by students in a nearby grade school, and yet another cooperative started by school children in a neighboring community. Another African American cooperative started in Liberty Square, a suburb of Miami. Members of the Liberty Square Consumers Co-operative Association bought shares at two dollars and their patronage kept the cooperative in business through the war years.[38]

The Growth of Co-ops

Regionally, the South had few cooperatives and the Midwest had many. In Minnesota especially, the socialist leanings of the CCW influenced the growth of co-op stores. In fact, the CCW had adopted a "Resolution on War and Fascism" in 1937, in which it argued that capitalism was on its last legs, and relied on "war and fascism to prolong its existence." As an alternative cooperative, it promised to "build a new, more just social order."[39] As such, the CCW participated in joint conferences with labor unions, producers' cooperatives, and farm organizations. The Cloquet Co-operative Society in Minnesota, one of its member cooperatives, had sales of over $871,000 and employed fifty-one people in 1935, attesting to the CCW's influence. The Virginia Co-operative Society in Virginia, Minnesota—another member co-operative comprised of mostly Finnish members—insisted that their children buy there and not at the other cooperatives in town.[40] In isolated, rural areas, ethnic solidarity still mattered.

The economic situation was especially dire in California, where over 700,000 people were unemployed. (Upton Sinclair had estimated numbers as high as one million, one-seventh of the state's population during his campaign for governor.) Associations or self-help cooperatives were formed for unemployed people to trade labor in exchange for food and clothing. A number of cooperatives were started, mostly in Los Angeles County, where nearly 300,000 persons were out of work. By the spring of 1933, there were 172 self-help cooperatives in the state, with a membership of over 37,000. The End Poverty in California (Epic) campaign of gubernatorial candidate Upton Sinclair further spurred the development of cooperatives in 1934. The EPIC campaign became popular through the radio, as well as the venues of rodeos, parades, and flea markets. Carey McWilliams, then commissioner of immigration and housing, remembered EPIC slogans painted on rocks in the deserts, on the walls of labor camps, and even carved into forest trees. In turn, Epic clubs started their own consumer cooperatives and educational federations, including the Co-operative Education Association of Pasadena and the Northern California Co-operative Council of Oakland.[41] Regardless of this growth in cooperatives, many did not survive the Depression. A study by the California State Relief Administration in 1936 indicated that most co-ops had failed in the state because of small capital, too few members, not enough business, problems with credit and pricing, and a lack of business experience.[42]

World War II and Postwar Cooperatives

By the late 1930s and early 1940s, a number of corporate businesses openly criticized the New Deal and attendant consumer activism. They also targeted a number of consumer groups, such as the League of Women Shoppers, accusing them of communist affiliation. With a membership of 25,000 middle-class women, the League had advocated for accurate labels on consumer products, a higher minimum wage, and equal pay for equal work, clearly siding with laborers and consumers. Regardless, by the early 1940s, the coalition of middle-class activists and workers had started to weaken, as middle-class consumers became more concerned about high inflation and businesses increasingly blamed labor unions for high prices.[43]

Even so, consumer activism persisted through World War II, because food shortages and rationing demanded that American citizens curtail their consumption in the name of democracy. One form of activism was food co-ops' cooperation with the Office of Price Administration (OPA) to ensure price control, accurate grade labeling, and high quality of goods.[44] More than likely, food co-ops' concerns about fair labeling and prices were reasons for their growth. By 1944, there were an estimated 2,810 co-op stores and buying clubs nationally (compared to approximately 500 or so as of 1934), with 690,000 members; collectively, they earned $280 million.[45] Many new co-ops had been formed in rural areas when farm-supply regional cooperatives began selling groceries in rural areas. But food co-ops also started in cities, for example, in New York City, where residents of five boroughs started eighteen cooperative stores, with annual sales from $20,000 to $275,000. At the city's Henry Street Settlement, the education director of Consumer-Farmer Milk Co-operative cooperated with the Eastern Co-operative Wholesale to build a co-op store near three large housing units in 1945. In Harlem, the Harlem Consumers' Co-operative Council and other community organizations continued to promote cooperatives.[46]

Most postwar cooperatives were no longer established along ethnic lines, with the exceptions of Harlem and other African American communities. As such, co-ops upheld the Rochdale principle of open membership, regardless of race and religious affiliation. For example, the Metropolitan Co-operative Council, a group comprised of African American and white consumer cooperatives in New York City, worked together. As noted earlier, membership in the Finnish Co-operative Trading Company in Waukegan, Illinois included immigrants and African Americans.[47] And the New Co-operative Company in Dillonville, Ohio, originally started by Czech coal miners in 1907, accepted members from all ethnicities. As a result, it did a retail business of almost $1.13 million in 1943 through its wholesale and packing plant, ten grocery stores, and a department store.[48]

Postwar Prosperity and Shoppers

Following World War II, food co-ops continued to expand, mostly notably in their size, locations, and choices of foods and other products. These changes occurred alongside those in household technology, demographic shifts, and attitudes that encouraged shoppers to become "consumer purchasers."[49] First, the advent of freezers in the marketplace dramatically influenced grocery stores' food lines, as well as what women customers bought and how they prepared dinner. In 1939, a two-temperature refrigerator was marketed, although it had limited freezing space. By 1944, at least 70 percent of American homes had modern refrigerators with freezer space. In 1946, General Electric manufactured 200,000 household freezers; that number doubled the next year. Certainly, food companies understood the market potential for frozen foods. In fact, General Foods, Birdseye, and other companies had begun to sell frozen foods as early as the 1930s. However, it was during the war and postwar years that their sales skyrocketed, particularly as they advertised their products as "labor saving."[50] By 1956, frozen foods—marketed as "convenience" food—was a $2 billion industry, reaching nearly 4 percent of the total in food sales nationally. As historian Shane Hamilton documented, new refrigerated trucks delivered a multitude of frozen foods to supermarkets, assuring housewives of their families' weekly supplies of fruits, vegetables, and other products.[51]

Second, there were dramatic demographic shifts through "slum clearance," urban renewal, and white flight to the suburbs. Between 1940 and 1958, over 160 metropolitan area suburbs had grown by 77 percent. As Judith Stein noted, as many people resided in suburbs by 1960 as in cities because of newly constructed freeways, mass-produced housing, and the relocation of corporations. Correspondingly, many Americans enjoyed new levels of prosperity; by 1956, more Americans held white collar than blue collar jobs.[52]

Third, population growth in cities and in suburbs resulted in a corresponding growth in shopping centers, some financed through urban renewal funds. By 1957, at least 940 shopping centers were built; by 1960, that number had doubled. Correspondingly, car sales had increased from 27 million in 1940 to over 57 million in 1958. Put differently, 54 percent of families owned cars in 1948; by 1958, 73 percent did. Women were now able to drive to one-stop shopping centers, where they could take care of all of their families' needs at the grocery store, butcher, bakery, drugstore, clothing stores, beauty shop, shoe repair and dry cleaning stores.[53] As Lizabeth Cohen noted: "The first shopping centers were planned with the female consumer in mind."[54]

Fourth, postwar consumer attitudes changed, reflecting a liberalism that favored individual freedom and economic prosperity, what Alan Brinkley has called a "rights-based liberalism."[55] No longer were liberals as interested in labor and the regulation of capitalism as much as in free enterprise, mass consumption, and individual choice. Many consumers were "lured" to buy items they did not need through advertisers who used motivation research. As a number of historians concluded, workers had already started to "los[e] ground" with liberals' retreat from New Deal reforms.[56]

Although Brinkley has argued that postwar liberals were no longer interested in "creat[ing] cooperative associational arrangements," that was not entirely true.[57] Indeed, the growth of cooperatives belies that very claim. As of 1946, there were 2.5 million American families who had joined cooperatives, which did a retail business of $10 billion. This did not mean, though, that the postwar environment was always favorable toward cooperatives. For one, large retailers leveled attacks on co-ops during and after the war, calling them "un-American, subversive and communistic." One newspaper headline, "Retailers Plan Nation-wide War on Co-ops," revealed a new warfront.[58] In 1947, when the US House of Representatives Small Business Committee studied cooperatives, the committee chair stated that cooperatives were "unfair monopolies" and "un-American" because they "stifled competition." The first cooperative to be investigated was the Greenbelt Consumer Services, even though it had been started by the federal government during the Depression. Many residents there testified against the co-op and some even called it "communistic." One source of tension there was between the veterans and pacifists.[59]

Shopping Centers and Grocery Chain Stores

Another problem faced by food co-ops during the postwar years was underselling by grocery chain stores. John Carson, Director of CLUSA's Washington, DC, office, had argued that the "failure" of co-ops in cities was partly due to problems in "compet[ing] against a false price level established by chain stores."[60] Three years earlier, criminal actions had been filed in Danville, Illinois against the Great Atlantic & Pacific Tea Company of New York, eleven of its affiliates, and sixteen of its offices, including one that ran Business Organization, Inc., the A&P's front. These stores had sold below cost and were driving smaller grocery stores, including co-ops, out of business. The A&P stores had also forced manufacturers, canners, and processors to have two price levels, one for A&P competitors, the other for A&P stores.[61]

The reverse problem occurred during the postwar years, when price controls were eliminated. In 1946, with the dismantling of the OPA, wholesale prices rose dramatically, the highest since 1920. Food prices increased by 14 percent and the cost of meat more than doubled. In fact, businesses had lobbied for the discontinuation of the OPA, while at the same time blaming unions for increased food prices and labor strikes. This, in turn, led to President Harry Truman signing the Taft-Hartley Act in 1947, thereby limiting labor unions' choices to strike and boycott. Regardless, some women's groups, such as the American Association of University Women (AAUW) and the League of Women Shoppers, continued to support the OPA and organized a national boycott of meat in 1948.[62]

Despite the problems of high prices, many co-ops prospered during the 1950s. By then there were nearly six million members in 20,000 co-ops, which collectively earned $6 billion annually, 2 percent of the annual retail business in the United States. One reason for their prosperity was that they had started to build supermarkets during and after the war years, some through the financial assistance of the CLUSA. As Tracey Deutsch explained, the CLUSA had recommended more standardization and improved store layout so that food co-ops could compete with grocery chain stores. The United Co-operative Society of Maynard, Massachusetts started the first co-op supermarket in 1941, although it is not clear if it received the CLUSA's assistance. During the 1950s, the largest single co-op was the Greenbelt Co-op in Maryland, with the Palo Alto Food Co-op second. The latter had two shopping centers that earned nearly $6 million in food, drugs, gas, and other products. The Berkeley Food Co-op, whose membership was then one-fourth of San Francisco's population, had opened a second shopping center. The Santa Monica Co-op had built a $250,000 supermarket; the Hollywood Co-op reported sales of over half a million dollars in 1956.[63] In his speech to the CLUSA in 1955, President Dwight Eisenhower proclaimed that these and other cooperatives contributed to the "vital American principles of self-help, mutual assistance, and free enterprise."[64]

Because of the expansion of the automobile industry and urban development, some co-ops changed the way they did business. As noted, some became supermarkets; others "owned" multiple stores; and still others relocated to shopping centers. For example, the grocery co-op in Natick, Massachusetts had annual sales of nearly $2.5 million in 1959 and planned to open two more stores. In Cloquet, Minnesota, a town of only 8,000, a $500,000 shopping center was planned. A whole city block, the center would include a co-op supermarket, a co-op hardware and dry goods store, credit union offices, and an insurance agency. In Eau Claire, Wisconsin, a food co-op that started with 45 members in 1935 had 4,500 family members as of 1955. This cooperative was praised as a pioneer in the development of the shopping center.[65] The co-ops in Hyde Park (Chicago), Ithaca, New York, and Hanover, New Hampshire became supermarkets during the 1950s as well.

The growth of co-op supermarkets occurred alongside that of grocery chain stores, their major competition. For example, in 1956, National Tea Company's annual sales were $600 million; by 1964, the amount was one billion dollars. The postwar growth in supermarkets, however, could not have occurred without the growth in agribusiness. In turn, agribusiness could not have grown to such proportions without increased mechanization, the unregulated use of pesticides, and an over-reliance on migrant workers. Because the war and its industries had drawn many farmers and farm workers from the agricultural sector, there were not enough farm laborers in the Pacific Northwest, California, or Florida. To compound the problem of labor shortage, more food had to be grown to feed American citizens and soldiers overseas.[66] The solution was to bring five million Mexican workers to the United States through the Bracero Program from 1942 to 1964. Transferred from the Farm Security Administration to the War Manpower Commission in 1943, the Bracero program contracted Mexican laborers who worked for low wages, lived in squalid housing, were sprayed with pesticides, and were denied the rights to collective bargaining.[67] In addition, agribusinesses relied on nonunion truck drivers to transport "cheap food" to the supermarkets.[68]

Agribusinesses and Pesticides

During and after World War II, agribusiness relied even more on pesticides to weed and thin crops, as well as to quicken the ripening of fruits and vegetables. Pesticides had been used since the early 1900s, especially lead and copper arsenate, which had prompted Congress to pass the Insecticide Act in 1910 to regulate their use. Nonetheless, lead arsenate was one of the most popular pesticides until 1942.[69] During World War II, synthetic pesticides were also created, including chlorinated hydrocarbons (DDT, heptachlor), organophosphates (i.e., nerve poisons used by Germans, such as malathion and parathion), and herbicides (weed killers).[70] In 1945, American companies, including Monsanto, had produced 10 million pounds of DDT; by 1951, that amount had skyrocketed to 100 million pounds. As of 1947, the United States Department of Agriculture (USDA) estimated that there were close to 25,000 pesticide products; by 1951, that number went up to 30,000.[71]

Farm workers were overexposed to many of these pesticides, especially organophosphates, whether through airplane spraying, contact with sprayed produce, or residue or toxic drift near where they slept and cooked. Yet even when the USDA investigated parathion poisoning of farm workers, the chemical industry continued to advocate for its use. It was only when doctors testified about the link between pesticides and cancer in the early 1950s that Congress passed an amendment requiring the FDA to register all pesticides. Even so, many pesticides were not removed from the market as the USDA had to take companies to court to prove that these pesticides were dangerous.[72] As environmental historian John Wargo has documented, many USDA scientists promoted pesticides, pointing to "government collusion."[73]

During the 1950s and 1960s, agriculture had become increasingly consolidated and industrialized. By 1959, more than 30 million acres of California's 37 million acres of farm land were large "farms" of 500 or more acres, farms that relied on cheap labor.[74] During the 1950s, at least one million Mexicans who had been deported were then "processed" by the Department of Labor and became braceros again.[75] Their poor working conditions and the dangers of pesticides were well kept secrets until the publication of Rachel Carson's *Silent Spring* in 1962. But it would not be until the 1970s when Caesar Chavez organized boycotts on behalf of farm workers that many citizens would join in their protests. And many food co-op members would join in them.

The Depression years witnessed a surge in food and other co-ops. Alliances among government officials, middle-class activists, workers, and other New Deal reformers fostered alternative economic structures to capitalism.

Correspondingly, co-ops started in housing projects, on Indian reservations, in workers' camps, and in small towns. Although many closed, they did provide the immediate benefit of providing food more cheaply for families.

Women played a central role in consumer activism through the 1930s and 1940s. As noted, women's organizations—including the League of Women Voters, the League of Women Shoppers, and the AAUW—worked together to pass federal legislation to protect consumers. At the state and local levels, the Housewives Association organized conferences, held mass meetings, and protested against shopkeepers who cheated them and other customers. In African American neighborhoods, women promoted consumer education, participated in the formation of co-ops, and bought products with co-op labels. During the war years, many women co-op shoppers worked with the OPA to ensure fair prices and labeling. They also boycotted high prices after the war.

Nonetheless, the postwar years witnessed dramatic changes in many food co-ops. Their growth occurred alongside demographic shifts, the rise of the automobile industry, and liberals' retreat from New Deal reforms, with emphases on individual consumer choices and the free market. Although Meg Jacobs has argued that the consumer movement de-escalated, Lawrence Glickman has recommended that we "broaden" how we think about consumer activism, rather

FIGURE 1.   Display of co-op labeled foods, Ithaca Consumer Cooperative Society Records, Division of Rare and Manuscript Collections, Kroch Library, Cornell University.

than simply compare the 1950s to the 1930s.[76] Indeed, even co-op supermarkets continued to provide an alternative economic structure through their collective ownership, patronage refunds, and co-op labeled goods. And they continued to educate their members and advocate for food legislation.

Most histories of grocery stores—be they co-ops or chains—discuss how the growth of suburbs and shopping centers fostered a new kind of consumer. What is not usually considered is how the rise of agribusiness, dependent on cheap labor and the overuse of pesticides, also promoted the "purchaser consumer." In fact, the growth of the food industry relied on liberals' retreat from the New Deal's concern for workers. Here I am not thinking only of labor unions but also migrant workers who were overexposed to pesticides and worked for long hours and poor wages. It would not be until the 1970s that food co-ops would protest migrant workers' conditions and boycott on their behalf.

The histories of the food co-ops discussed in the next four chapters demonstrate that, while some food co-ops adopted supermarket strategies, they still continued consumer advocacy by promoting consumer education and federal legislation to protect shoppers, at least through the 1940s. However, as food co-ops' membership, sales, and investments increased during the 1950s, members' participation in decision making diminished considerably. During the 1970s, however, some members' discontent with what they perceived to be their co-ops' "undemocratic" practices led to a renewed interest in participatory democracy. Members would organize a number of boycotts and protests against multinational corporations, the federal government, and agribusinesses.

ITHACA CONSUMER
CO-OPERATIVE SOCIETY

GreenStar Co-operative Market of Ithaca celebrated its forty-year anniversary in 2011. But more than likely, most of its members did not know that it did not incorporate until 1984 because an agreement could not be reached on whether members or the council should have more power. Nor do most of its members know about GreenStar's predecessors, Ithaca Real Food Co-op and the Ithaca Consumer Co-operative Society (ICCS). Started during the Great Depression, the ICCS was once a strong co-op in terms of membership and finances. It is now left to older residents' memory and to the Cornell University archives. It appears as if no one has examined its records or at least not in some time. Yet the co-op has much to tell us about political conflict, the importance of debate and discussion for ensuring democratic decisions, and the loss of a co-op community.

Like many Depression-era co-ops, the ICCS started as a grassroots initiative to promote economic democracy and consumer education. Initially, members were active in testing food products, recruiting new members, and deciding which products to sell. But over time, as the co-op grew in membership and sales, member involvement declined. Instead, the co-op board and business manager made financial decisions, which included building a supermarket, relocating to a shopping center, and investing in rental properties. The postwar years were prosperous ones for the ICCS and its members must have been pleased with their patronage refunds. But had members become "consumer purchasers," no longer interested in consumer activism and education?

The lettuce and grape boycott of the 1970s would provide a testing ground for the ICCS. Many of the members spoke out against the board's decision to sell union lettuce and to have protesters arrested. In the spirit of participatory democracy, members debated and discussed the issue, putting politics on the front end. But the board was more interested in the co-op's business and how the protests adversely affected sales. Here, the critical questions were: who should make decisions, the member-owners or the board whom the members elected? Should product choice be that of the individual consumer or should co-op members collectively decide? And how do such political decisions affect the co-op as a business enterprise? The lessons learned from this controversy were difficult ones for the ICCS.

The Early Years

Like Hyde Park in Chicago and Hanover, New Hampshire, Ithaca is known for its higher educational institution. Cornell University is both an elite and land grant institution, the latter important because of its historical mission of outreach. Its School of Agriculture, through extension programs, has assisted farmers and cooperatives, including the ICCS. For example, farm marketing professor Howard E. Babcock established the Grange League Federation (GLF) in 1920, a state-wide purchasing association for farmers. In turn, the GLF became "an experimental laboratory for Cornell, putting ideas into business," one of which was assisting the ICCS.[1]

Likewise, Cornell's School of Nutrition worked with the ICCS's educational committee to inform members and the public about the nutritional values of foods. Further, professors of agriculture and nutrition served as co-op board members, while some of their wives served on food and education committees. In the former case, the ICCS relied on the "expert" advice of Cornell professors. Not surprisingly, the early co-op membership drew largely from the Cornell community.

Ithaca is known for its progressive politics, a source of pride for the community. Today, there is alternative currency for goods and services, Ithaca Hours, which keeps money in the community. The community is ecologically proactive.[2] These reform impulses, however, are not new but have drawn from the 1960s and 1970s and even from the early twentieth century. Then, much of the social reform was instigated by women's clubs, which opened a Women's Community Building in 1921, used by community organizations, including the ICCS. There was also a small but active African American community that established a National Association for the Advancement of Colored People (NAACP) chapter and its own newspaper, *The Monitor*, during the 1920s.[3] In 1930, the Southside Community House (later Center), an African American social settlement, opened its doors. One of its executive directors, James L Gibbs, would become board president of the ICCS during the 1960s.[4]

It was during the Depression that the ICCS started. In 1933, four young ministers read cooperative writings, including those of Japanese labor activist Toyohiko Kagawa. Kagawa, known for his advocacy of "brotherhood econom-ics," encouraged churches, cooperatives, and those in the peace movement to collectively create an alternative to capitalism. The Ithaca ministers put a notice in the newspaper about organizing a co-op. Within a year, a group of interested residents started a buying club, the Tompkins County Consumers' Club.[5] By 1935, its membership had grown to fifty-seven and included a cross-section of working class and professionals. The club, however, was not only interested in food costs. As former history professor and club member, Paul W. Gates, re-marked: "We were doing something for society. We were going to make people aware of the problems of the consumer."[6] By 1936, when the club had incor-porated, its membership had doubled and its weekly sales had increased from $100 to $600.[7]

One of the cooperative's foremost activities was to recruit new members. One older member attended the men's forum of the local Presbyterian Church to discuss the co-op and the movement at large. When a manager of a fraternity asked if they could join, the co-op invited the managers from all the fraternities to its director's meeting. The co-op also invited representatives from other buying clubs. Strategically, they organized a social in 1937, at which they served some of the co-op products. Alongside these recruitment efforts were educational ones. The co-op formed a neighborhood discussion group to study cooperatives and their principles through a correspondence course.[8] In fact, many members did not understand that they were actually joint owners of a business. As one 1938 co-op bulletin advised: "Setting all idealism aside, intelligent self-interest should prompt us to safeguard our investments."[9]

What to Sell and Where

As of 1938, the ICCS sold its goods at the local farmer's market. However, it was not allowed to sell potatoes, lettuce, eggs, and other produce, which competed with local farmers. This meant that it was often limited to canned fruits and vegetables from the nearby Tobey Parish Co-operative.[10] Despite these limited selections, the co-op advised its members to be "faithful" and to buy as much as possible from them so the co-op would flourish.[11] Co-op members realized that the farmer's market was a temporary site and that they needed a more permanent location. Yet they could not relocate the co-op to Ithaca's downtown business district because rent there was too high and the grocery competition too great. Professor Samuel Boothroyd, former vice president of the buying club, recommended relocating to property closer to Cornell's campus.[12] In 1939, the ICCS did move into a store not far from campus and expanded its product selection to include toasters, light bulbs, toilet articles, and cleaning products. It added cheese, fruit, coffee, flour, and honey to its grocery line. Significantly, it advertised that none of its fruits had been sprayed, picked green, or chemically ripened or dyed.[13]

Still, the co-op members wanted to own their own "complete" food store, one that included groceries, produce, and meat. Despite advice from Whiton Powell, a Cornell professor who then taught a cooperative marketing course, to continue renting, the co-op forged ahead with plans to raise enough capital and recruit more members to buy a store. At one meeting, the store location committee pointedly asked co-op members whether they favored selling the entire stock of goods, buying back the capital stock, and disbanding the cooperative. If not, they insisted, then members needed to do their part in recruiting members and raising monies. One effort was reaching out to college student groups, such as the Society of Cornell Dames (a Cornell University female literary and musical organization), to bring in younger members.[14] In 1940, the co-op was finally able to buy property on Seneca Street for its future store.[15]

However, its building plans changed when the GLF offered it the option to rent one of its stores on Fulton Street. This was in both of their best interests, for the GLF had just opened a community freezer locker plant there. The blueprint for this "model" freezer-locker plant had been developed by Babcock and faculty from Cornell's School of Nutrition.[16] Babcock was especially interested in helping farmers sell their livestock. As he explained, "We cannot do the farmer any good in this field until we have learned how to run freezer lockers and how to tie up local slaughter houses with them."[17] This location for the food co-op, then, was in a strategic location near the meat lockers, where customers could pick up frozen goods, which would become especially popular after World War II.[18] Undoubtedly, members enjoyed the convenience of a freezer locker plant and co-op combination. In fact, this was a unique feature, as the only other one in the state was in Batavia.[19]

The new store site served the co-op well. Within six months, over 200 new members joined, many of them faculty and students from Cornell University and Ithaca College. In fact, a profile of co-op members in 1942 revealed that of 375 members, 185 (nearly half) were from Cornell University. Only seventy-five were farmers, forty GLF employees, and seventy-five noncollege affiliated residents of Ithaca. Nonetheless, with commitment from all its members, the co-op's weekly sales increased from $2,500 in the spring to over $5,000 by fall. The following year, weekly sales ranged from $6,200 to $7,500.[20] In addition to members' involvement, the "virile," all-male leadership of its board and managers was cited as another reason for the store's financial growth. Again, many of the board members were affiliated with Cornell University and considered experts in their field.[21] It would not be until the 1950s that women would serve on the ICCS's board.

Consumer Education

During World War II, the co-op continued to sell a number of products, despite food rationing. Co-op brands were especially popular, including the red label coffee. The ICCS bought beans, eggs, flour, cereal, juices, fresh fruits and vegetables from the GLF, and honey, maple syrup, and Christmas trees from local farmers. During one summer season, it trucked in eleven tons of fresh peas, three and a half tons of pitted cherries, and 160 crates of strawberries, sweet corn, tomatoes, green beans, and peaches. In other cases, however, food selections were limited because of the war. One co-op bulletin article advised customers that it was patriotic to buy canned vegetables by the case. Another bulletin recommended that customers buy the utility grade beef, the lowest grade beef sold in markets. In fact, members met regularly to inspect and grade their own meat, a scarce item then. These examples point to the members' support of the goals of the Office of Price Administration (OPA), which included grade labeling, high product quality, and price control.[22]

The Educational Committee was active in these and other efforts. It published articles in the co-op bulletins about food availability and offered nutritional advice, such as baking with less sugar.[23] Yet the committee remained interested in product quality. For example, at one committee meeting, members discussed the quality of various soaps. Several members were wives of professors who taught in the chemistry laboratory at Cornell and had tested different soaps. These chemists claimed that the co-op soap was "tops."[24] Activities such as these reflected how women promoted consumer advocacy as a form of good citizenship during the war. At the same time, the women deferred to experts from Cornell. The committee also cooperated with the School of Nutrition, in particular, Professor Leonard Maynard and Dean Sarah Blanding. Maynard had helped to establish a laboratory for the study of nutrition in small animals and during the war had served as commissioner for nutrition of the Emergency Food Commission.[25] Blanding was then the first female dean at Cornell in the College of Home Economics. Both lent their advice about which co-op foods were the most nutritious.

After the war, the ICCS continued its efforts to recruit new members. Eager to find out why farmers did not buy at the co-op, the co-op started a newcomers' club through the GLF. Undoubtedly, the board president, a graduate of Cornell and a recognized state leader of county agriculture agents, was influential in this effort. Regardless of this outreach, farmers were most likely concerned about higher food prices. Although there had been price controls during the war, prices had dramatically risen once the war ended: food costs had increased by 14 percent and the price of meat had doubled. Even co-op members had heard complaints that prices were too high at the ICCS.[26] One female member had even expressed her displeasure that literature about the Price Control Act was no longer in the co-op store. Clearly, as Meg Jacobs has pointed out, some women continued to support the OPA after the war as a means of "protecting their family income from erosion."[27] Despite the rhetoric of postwar prosperity, then, some women shoppers continued to be consumer advocates.

Debating Economic Models

In renewing their discussions of the co-op's purpose during the postwar years, members asked if the store was primarily a business and only "incidentally" a co-op. This discussion most likely occurred because of the high prices, which kept some residents from joining the ICCS. Certainly members were interested in a "well-run" business but they also wanted to honor the Rochdale principles by working with other cooperatives, promoting services to members and customers, and increasing member participation.[28] The co-op did fulfill some of these responsibilities. For example, it assisted a local grocery store, owned by the Co-operative Associations of Producers, and bought meat, butter, sugar, fresh fruits and vegetables from them.[29] It also helped a group of young veterans start their own food co-op, loaning them $500, buying $500 of their stock, and helping them get supplies. Last, the ICCS, like other US co-ops concerned about the destruction of co-ops in war-ravaged European countries, assisted through contributions to CARE International.[30]

The ICCS renewed its discussions about a new store. Fortunately, it had no outstanding debt and its membership had grown to over 860 families and 146 nonfamily members as of 1947.[31] As with other food co-ops then, the ICCS was interested in opening a supermarket co-op in a shopping center. In Quincy, Massachusetts, for example, a working-class suburb of Boston, a co-op had opened a new supermarket, with a lunch bar and appliance department. In Greenbelt, Maryland—a planned community of 8,000 residents—co-op members had contributed toward a funding campaign of $400,000 for a shopping center with a restaurant, bakery, kitchen, bowling alley, game room, and nursery.

In order for the ICCS to open its own supermarket in a shopping center, it needed $100,000 for the property and the new store. In early 1948, it organized "captains" for each neighborhood to recruit new members and to fundraise.[32]

These members' efforts were successful. In 1949, the ICCS's supermarket opened and its membership correspondingly increased to 2,000. The new store was 65 percent larger than the older one, which meant that more products could be sold. There were also extra facilities such as offices, meeting rooms, a customer reading room, and off-street parking for at least seventy-five cars.[33] Correspondingly, the supermarket co-op did well, with weekly sales of nearly $12,000 and annual sales of over $1 million in 1950. By 1953, its annual sales had increased to $1.55 million, with $37,000 returned to members in patronage refunds.[34]

The Board and the Changing Community

As in earlier years, the co-op board was led by men affiliated with Cornell and agricultural organizations. In 1948, members had elected Dr. Arthur Pratt as board president, who had been director of the Eastern Co-operative League during the war. The board treasurer that year was a professor of marketing from Cornell's Department of Agricultural Economics. In 1949, John Lamb, Jr., a soil conservationist with the US Department of Agriculture, was elected board president. The following year, the new president was a professor in the Vegetable Crops Department at Cornell, whose research was lettuce varieties.[35]

By the 1950s, women began to serve on the co-op board. In 1951, three candidates were wives of Cornell professors. All were involved in community organizations such as the Community Chest, the Red Cross, and the local PTA. These candidates believed that their volunteer experiences provided them with a social capital that could be leveraged into board positions. Only one candidate, Laura Lee Smith, was elected, perhaps because of her affiliation with Cornell as an instructor in foods and nutrition in the College of Home Economics. More than likely, her position gave her more credibility. In 1953, Hinda Neufeld, a professor in the New York School of Industrial and Labor Relations at Cornell, also became a board member. Before then, she had been involved in a number of civic and political activities. In 1942, she had helped set up registration procedures for sugar rationing in New York City; she had also conducted research for the New York State Legislative Committee on Industry and Labor Conditions. In 1959, an African American woman, H. Hortense Gibbs, ran for the board. She had been past president of the Ithaca PTA Council and was active in other community organizations. However, she was not elected, although her husband, James Gibbs, had served on the ICCS board from 1951 to 1957.[36]

It was not clear how many African Americans were co-op members or employees. However, white and African American residents had worked together on earlier community initiatives. In the early 1930s, there had been several interracial boards at the African American social settlement, the Southside Community Center. In fact, the two groups had worked together to establish the Center and in 1932 had raised enough money to buy the settlement house.[37] In 1939, the Center had sponsored an inter-racial week to promote understanding among white and African American residents. Undoubtedly, these efforts were spurred by the Center's director, James Gibbs. With a strong interest in cooperatives, he was director of the Co-op Institute Association, an association of eastern cooperatives, in 1952 and, as noted, an ICCS board member during the 1950s.[38]

Most members rated the ICCS highly. A 1951 survey showed that 95 percent of the customers shopped at the co-op because of its high quality food, the parking facilities, the friendly service, its patronage refunds, and their strong beliefs in cooperatives. Of the 5 percent who did not shop there regularly, the main reason continued to be high prices. Regardless of most members' satisfaction, some still wanted the store to expand to include a bakery, a variety store, a drying cleaning service, a drug store, or gas station.[39] Evidently, customers were interested in conveniences that a shopping center offered. At the same time, some were concerned about the loss of community. In fact, S. L. Boothroyd had cautioned members not to give up the co-op's sense of community as the ICCS grew. He suggested neighborhood meetings, although they do not appear to have been organized.[40]

The Co-op's Growth versus Sense of Community

The tension between a co-op's growth—be it in services offered, membership, sales, or location—and a sense of community was not singular for the ICCS during the 1950s. In relocating to a shopping center, the ICCS was no longer within walking distance or close to many Ithaca's neighborhoods. Increased membership also meant that communication among members probably diminished. The education committee, although a long-standing one, appears to have been less involved in educational outreach, at least in ICCS publications. Perhaps one could argue that the Depression and World War II years had demanded more member involvement. It is also possible that member involvement and consumer advocacy were less visible during the 1950s than in the earlier years. That some members voiced concern about a sense of community, as well as the co-op's adherence to cooperative principles, demonstrated that members thought of their co-op as different from a grocery chain store. That did not mean, however, that members were disinterested in their co-op's financial growth.

Even so, the ICCS measured itself in terms of how closely it followed the Rochdale principles upon which it had been founded. On paper, the co-op appeared to be doing well. Its membership then stood at 2,200, with each member allowed one vote. Members received a yearly patronage refund. Likewise, the co-op practiced political, racial, and religious neutrality. Interestingly, it claimed that it also did not take sides on controversial political matters, a stance that would be vexing later. It was also community-oriented and contributed to community organizations, such as the Community Chest and Red Cross. Last, it provided consumer education about better nutrition in bread and other foods, and better food preparation.[41] The focus on community, however, seemed to be less about the co-op community itself and more focused on the Ithaca community at large. As noted, this was not unique for the ICCS, as most co-ops had lost membership involvement as they became larger and their boards assumed more control.

Still, the co-op took its responsibility to educate its members about food and nutrition seriously. One 1946 bulletin published an article about fortifying white bread other than through synthetic vitamins. The co-op planned to sell white unbleached flour because some members were concerned about flour bleached with agene. Later, the co-op would sell freshly ground whole wheat flour, since most whole grains became rancid and lost their flavor and nutritional value.[42] Faculty from the Cornell School of Nutrition worked with other faculty and extension workers to create recipes using whole wheat flour, which the GLF published. In fact, the co-op became known for its triple rich bread, rolls, and doughnuts, using a formula pioneered by Dr. Clive M. McCay of Cornell that contained more milk solids, wheat germ, and soy flour than most breads. The co-op also set up a display of wheat germ, black strap molasses, yogurt, dry skim milk, soy meal, and bone meal, as well as other demonstrations and parties.[43]

Plans for a Co-op Shopping Center

In 1957, the ICCS drew a blueprint for a co-op shopping center, with multiple stores, and broke ground that September. It is not entirely clear why the co-op decided to expand once again. Perhaps it was because of its increased annual sales. Or perhaps the co-op was thinking of investment beyond its five rental properties. Although there was no record of the membership vote on this issue, as early as 1951 members had been interested in expanding the co-op to include other businesses, such as dry cleaning, a pharmacy, and gas station. In May 1958,

FIGURE 2.   Women shoppers (circa 1950s) at Ithaca Consumer Cooperative Society store, Curt Foerster, photographer, Ithaca Consumer Cooperative Society Records, Division of Rare and Manuscript Collections, Kroch Library, Cornell University.

the co-op opened its new store, at the cost of $245,000, almost $18,000 more than members had financially committed. Over time, the shopping center expanded to include a laundry, a pharmacy, a donut shop, an insurance office, an optical center, a beauty shop, and a liquor store.[44]

Clearly the co-op had to bridge the financial gap. The board made a decision in 1958 that was a controversial but profitable one: to sell beer. Some members were not pleased, however. In one editorial, a member claimed that members were not consulted, a violation of the Rochdale cooperative principles. Further, the writer of another editorial stated that alcohol contributed to "family unhappiness" and had a negative influence on youth. She concluded that the co-op should sell only healthy foods. The following year, members did vote on the issue, with two-thirds in favor of selling beer. However, the board, in asking for a vote, had done so without the authority of its members, thereby making the vote "null and void." A special membership meeting was held in accordance with the bylaws and, again, the majority voted in favor of selling beer.[45]

The ICCS in the 1960s and 1970s

Like other cooperatives, the ICCS faced growth and challenges during the 1960s and 1970s. During the first three years of the 1960s, there was an "excess of withdrawals" of equity capital to finance construction of the store's addition. This addition, the board claimed, would be income-generating, because it would be leased to a laundromat-dry cleaning business.[46] The board was confident about this decision because of increased yearly sales. Although sales in 1961 and 1962 had increased by only 1.5 percent, by 1964 they were almost 4.5 percent. Even though sales increased each year, so did the co-op's liabilities. By 1967, the co-op's asset and liabilities were nearly equal as there had been repeated withdrawals of its equity capital.[47]

Still, the co-op continued to give financial assistance to other co-ops. One Rochdale principle to which the ICCS subscribed had been "to work with other co-operatives in the interests of consumers." In 1968, the co-op pledged $10,000 to support the new Harlem River Food Co-op at the Esplanade Gardens Co-operative Housing Project. The following year, the co-op made a loan of over $2,000 to Bahamas Co-op, even though the ICCS's working capital had decreased markedly the previous year.[48] Perhaps the co-op had been influenced by a Co-op Institute Association conference held in 1968. There, more affluent co-op members had been shocked when they heard about the "exploitation" of poor people by neighborhood grocery stores.[49] Perhaps Jim Gibbs, the co-op's first African American board president, also had a direct bearing on the ICCS's pledges to help poorer co-ops. Acting board president in 1964 and president in 1965, Gibbs was a known civil rights activist in Ithaca as a member of the County Human Relations Commission and the Council for Equality.[50]

The African American Community and the Co-op

During the early 1960s, Gibbs and at least one other African American resident, Winston Gaskin, had served on the ICCS's educational and membership committees. Gaskin, a pharmacist by profession, had run for the board in 1960 but had not won. In all likelihood, his and Gibbs's committee efforts were directed at increasing ICCS membership in the African American community. Unfortunately, there are no records of membership by race so it is difficult to know. In 1969, at least two other African Americans ran for the co-op board. Luella Dixon had been a longtime resident of Ithaca and had served on the Southside Community Center's board. Waldo Blackman was a punch press operator and union member. There were no records, however, on whether either won the election.[51]

Their involvement does, however, reflect an emerging civil rights activism in Ithaca. During the 1960s, there was racial strife in the city, as in much of the country. In April 1961, Martin Luther King, Jr. had visited Cornell University, sponsored by the Cornell Committee Against Segregation and Ithaca Freedom Walk. That very month, members of the Afro-American Society had occupied a building at the university for thirty-six hours to protest racism on campus. That same year, the mayor of Ithaca had initiated discussions with concerned citizens about inter-racial conflict at the Ithaca high school. It is not clear whether these issues were resolved, however. Perhaps not, because in 1967 African American high school students formed their own Afro-American Club in order to learn more about their history. Two years later, African American parents expressed concern about the inferior education that some of their children received when placed in remedial and lower-track classes.[52] Despite this activism, James Gibbs was the only African American elected as president of the ICCS board.

Higher Prices and Food Politics

The co-op remained set in its ways in other areas. Carson's testimonies and publications on the dangers of pesticides in 1963 did not influence the education committee's outreach or policy, as it had at other co-ops. In fact, the ICCS did not discuss or even acknowledge problems with pesticides. This may have been because the board president elected in 1961 was also the manager of the GLF's Pesticide Department.[53] Nor was there any promotion of organic or natural food. Instead, the ICCS continued to sell products with brand names such as Kraft, Mott's, Heinz, and Pillsbury. By the late 1960s and early 1970s, the co-op did publish some articles on biodegradable detergent, organic foods, and food additives.[54] Yet these efforts seemed more incidental than purposeful. Perhaps the board was concerned about being too political in its food selections. In fact, its argument of customer choice was one that privileged the individual shopper, thereby avoiding any discussion and different points of view. This approach would create problems for the board and the co-op in the 1970s.

Even so, the co-op seemed to be doing well financially by the late 1960s. As of 1966, the ICCS owned seventeen pieces of property, whose value was worth over $250,000.[55] By 1970, the ICCS was a $4.25 million dollar business. In addition to the food co-op, it ran a self-service laundry and dry-cleaning store in the co-op shopping center. With such sound financial footing, it decided to build a new store, which opened in the spring of 1973. However, there were several unanticipated problems from the beginning. It was drawn into a price war with a local A&P store, which had gone into a discount phase to regain its place in the grocery market during a time of recession. The co-op's business was also interrupted because of construction and a sprinkler leak. As a result, ICCS sales in 1973 were almost $86,000 lower than the previous year.[56]

These losses were passed on to co-op members through higher prices. Noting the high prices, one long-time member argued that it was "not enough to expect loyalty. Inflation is a problem for everyone." She added: "[The] recent expansion of the store did not result in added shopping conveniences." In fact, she claimed, the store was now too congested.[57] She was not alone in her concerns. Over half of the customers averaged less than $10 in weekly purchases in 1972, most likely because of the co-op's higher prices.[58]

In fact, these were difficult times throughout the country. In 1973, inflation was at 8 percent, prompting a new word, "stagflation," marked by high inflation, weak growth in the economy, higher prices, and increased unemployment. One year later, inflation increased to 11 percent, due to the oil embargo and the high costs of the Vietnam War. President Nixon's resignation in 1974 and the end of the war the next year signaled, in Jefferson Cowie's words, "the end of the post-war boom."[59] In response, some citizen groups boycotted foods, such as meat, milk, and sugar during those years. The year 1975 ushered in a recession, with unemployment at 8.5 percent, compared to 3.5 percent six years earlier.[60] To be sure, the ICCS could not have anticipated these tides of economic change when it decided to open a new store in 1970. If so, it might have sold some of its real estate investments.

The Lettuce and Grape Boycotts

There was a political issue that harmed the co-op more than its high prices. That was the call for a national boycott of nonunion lettuce and grapes during the 1970s. From 1962 to 1965, Caesar Chavez had organized the National Farm Workers Association, later the United Farm Workers Organizing Committee in California (UFWOC). When the Delano grape growers signed contracts with the UFWOC, there were massive strikes throughout California, with over 7,000 farm workers. When a judge ordered the UFWOC to stop boycotting, Chavez refused and was sent to jail. In late 1971, after months of meetings with little progress, the growers had rejected the UFWOC. The UFWOC then planned an international boycott of nonunion lettuce.[61]

Although many food co-ops throughout the country supported the UFWOC, the Ithaca co-op did not. If one considers the political temperature of the Ithaca community, this did not seem to be a wise decision. For example, during the late 1960s and early 1970s, there were close to fifty communes in the area. Activist Paul Glover had helped to start the Medical Co-op, a free clinic. Educational reformists started schools that promoted a sense of community, including one in an old farmhouse with alternative energy projects, a focus on healthy foods, and a respect for nature. A group of cooperatives started, which included the Community Self-Reliance Center, Ecology Action, Ithaca Real Food Co-op and the Grain Store, Coalition for the Right to Eat, Women's Center, Alternative Lifestyles, and the Alternatives Fund. On the Cornell campus, there were antinuclear protests and "take back the night" marches. A grassroots political party, the Citizens' Party, was organized and draft counseling was provided.[62]

In fact, the decision not to support the boycott divided co-op members and damaged their trust in the ICCS. From the beginning, the board did not want to support the boycott, using the argument of political neutrality. Yet the board was not neutral, even though it appeared to approach the issue from both sides. Nonetheless, a look at what they published in their newsletters indicated their position. For example, the board republished an article by a Mexican American worker who was anti-Chavez. There was an advertisement for an herbicide next to the article, ironic since many migrant workers were sprayed with pesticides. One newsletter also published an excerpt from an article by Reverend Richard Humphreys, a priest who claimed to have firsthand knowledge of the farm workers' conditions. He stated that California was one of the "strictest [states] with pesticides" and that "no pesticides [we]re sprayed while workers are in the fields." He also claimed that the Teamsters' health and unemployment insurance, as well as pension plan, were better than the UFW's. He then spelled out the "abuses" of the UFW: splitting up families, fines for missing union meetings, and harassment of workers. What was not mentioned was that this information was sponsored by the Free Marketing Council. There was little to no information on the council but the co-op had a brochure from the organization, which freely quoted from conservatives such as Earl Butz and Ronald Reagan.[63] However, when the board received information from the Farmworkers Boycott Committee and from the Cincinnati Citizens for the United Farm Workers, it was not published.[64]

In fact, the co-op's response to the UFW boycotts differed markedly from Cornell's. Working with the university senate, Cornell officials assured students that Cornell would buy only UFW lettuce. Cornell also invited UFW vice president, Dolores Huerta, to speak in March 1974. But the controversy was not just between Cornell and the co-op, for many townspeople, businesses, and organizations weighed in on the boycott. And many of the protesters of the co-op's policy were students. Although they had initially picketed "peacefully," the co-op board was not pleased with their activities. As the board stated in an article, "Pickets at the Co-op. Why Do They Boycott the Truth?": "The CO-OP is not on strike. Our employees have been unionized for 20 years." This statement clearly misrepresented the issue at hand. The board also argued that California lettuce workers were among the highest paid agricultural workers in the country. Further, the board claimed that the ICCS was not selling nonunion lettuce. In truth, the co-op was selling both union and nonunion lettuce, and letting its customers decide which brand to buy. According to one Ithaca newspaper, the Teamster lettuce outsold the UFW lettuce five to one at the co-op, even though the lettuce from both sold for the same price.[65]

The board became concerned about the picketers when they began to stop customers and ask them to shop at the grocery chain supermarket. Some picketers became more vocal and started calling customers who did not take their flyers "scabs." In February 1974, the police were called to keep the picketers away from the co-op store's entrance and parking lot.[66] After a month of daily pickets, the co-op decided to poll its 5,700 members by mail to see if they approved of the co-op's stand on the lettuce boycott. There was clearly a divide among the members. Some wanted an open forum where the boycott issue could be discussed. Others wanted materials available at the co-op to keep them informed about the issue.[67]

Disagreements with the Board

Although the board appeared to be democratic and responsive to its members, their actions were contradictory. Arthur Pratt, chair of the board, assured members that the policy would change if that was what the majority of members wanted. However, he also "flatly stated that the more pressure for a policy change he receive[d] from customers, the less likely he would be to consider a policy change."[68] This was clearly in violation of the Rochdale principles. The board decided to hold a member meeting in late March. But by mid-March protesters from the Ithaca Friends of the Farmworkers were served a show-cause order, temporarily restraining them from picketing at the co-op. If they wanted to continue picketing, the order cautioned, they would have to appear at the State Supreme Court and show that they had not violated the right of the co-op to do business. In compliance, the picketers moved to the sidewalk. In addition, the board decided to sue the picketers $50,000 to "compensate for the alleged damage [the] Co-op says the boycott has caused."[69] Many co-op members, appalled at this court action, wrote that they would not shop at the co-op until the board dropped its lawsuit.[70] The board defended its actions, claiming that its members had had peaceful discussions with the picketers but that the picketers had retaliated with "explicit threats that its business would be affected or economically destroyed if it did not comply with their demands." The co-op claimed that even though the protesters were nonviolent, this did not "lessen the effect of coercion or intimidating patrons." In fact, the co-op had received some complaints from customers, mostly the "elderly" and "housewives with children."[71]

At the co-op meeting in late March, members engaged in a heated debate. One board member, a Cornell professor of agriculture economics, defended the board's actions. He claimed that 85 percent of members responding to the poll supported the board's decision. (About 2,200 of 5,700 members had responded.) The issue was then brought to a vote. But before the members had a chance to vote, the co-op asked them to read "Points at Issue in the Co-op Boycott," written by the board. In essence, the board framed the issue for the members. To some members, this was an attempt to stifle the debate and influence their vote. With regard to the ballot, many members did not like the wording, which did not refer to the lettuce boycott. Instead, the ballot asked whether members agreed or disagreed with "the board's policy to support the right of the consumer to make a free choice of all commodities offered for sale." The dean of the College of Arts and Sciences, Alfred Kahn, argued that the wording was "dishonest."[72] Indeed it was, for "free choice" obscured the very issue of why there was a boycott. Further, such language privileged the "market" and free enterprise side of the ICCS at the expense of its collective identity as a co-op. Some members threatened to leave the co-op and some in fact did. Still others suggested that there were other ways to communicate with the picketers. For example, why did not the co-op organize a forum for airing grievances and disagreements? Conversely, those in favor of the ballot commented that they believed in free enterprise, that they should have choices as consumers, and that they were more concerned with high prices and receiving a patronage refund.[73]

Comments by those opposed indicated how disappointed they were. One member remarked, "I prefer the co-op take a stand in this social issue." Another was more vehement: "The co-op should *not* support the agri-business pigs by selling non-farm workers' lettuce." Others commented on the wording of the ballot: "This ballot is a farce." Or, "This is a cop-out!!!" Or, "I am hurt and surprised that the co-op has to hide behind such obscenely useless and obscuring generalities." And, "We think it criminal that the policy question was asked in a manner to obscure the basic question." Another aptly observed that the co-op behavior "has not been apolitical."[74] Indeed, the board appeared to be neutral in how it framed the issue. But the circumstances that triggered the vote were the UFWOC boycotts. In the end, the vote supported the board's decision to support individual customers in making their own decisions about food products. But then the board received a letter signed by twenty-six people, all of whom had voted in opposition to the board. They recommended that the picket line be stopped, that the co-op drop the lawsuit, that a study group be created, and that the board address one of its main responsibilities—consumer education—so shoppers could make wise decisions.[75] The board did eventually drop the lawsuit, even as picketers continued to protest on the sidewalks.[76]

Testing Participatory Democracy

The boycott issue raises a number of important questions about the ICCS. Did protesters influence the downward spiral of sales? Did the board over-react in their lawsuit against them? And did the co-op act in accordance with its mission and Rochdale principles in the handling of the boycott? With regard to the first question, it is important to look at the co-op's financial history during the early 1970s. Inflation in 1972 and the subsequent years had certainly affected food costs, not only at the co-op but at all grocery stores. In 1972 alone, co-op sales had dropped and the co-op had an operating loss of $33,000. That year, the co-op had also spent $22,000 on new equipment—a bakery oven, refrigeration, and scales. Despite these losses, the board still decided to pay over $44,000 in rebates and dividends of $13,500, which resulted in a $93,000 loss in capital.[77] Several years later, the recession hit the co-op and many grocery stores. Then, A&P's stock nosedived from $60 to $6.50 a share, leading to the supermarket's decision to close over 1,000 locations. The co-op's sales, too, dropped almost $86,000.[78] In short, the co-op was facing financial losses before, not just during, the protests. It is likely that the picketers influenced some shoppers not to buy at the co-op. But its higher prices, evident in customers' complaints, also influenced how much shopping they did at the co-op. In short, the protesters were accused of financial problems that were more complicated than their actions.

Did the board's actions comply with their mission and the Rochdale principles? This is a more difficult question to answer because different co-ops have interpreted the Rochdale principles differently. Further, as the food co-op's membership grew, the co-op became more centralized and formalized in its structure and decision making. What then of the ideas of "member control" and "democracy" once members give board members the responsibility to set policy? To be sure, there was a member vote, although the ballot skewed the issue. The fact that so many members wrote negative letters to the board indicated that they did not think their points of view had been considered. At the very least, the ICCS could have encouraged free speech, even debate, or have organized a forum to include co-op members, protesters, and other concerned residents. This would have honored the Rochdale principle of educating members and promoting a participatory democracy. Instead, the board and the education committee presented materials to members and customers that reflected only one side of the boycott and discredited Chavez and the strikes.[79]

New Competition

Another important consideration was the establishment of a new co-op in 1971: the Ithaca Real Food Co-op (IRFC). During its first year, at least 1,000 members had joined, most of them students or ex-students, who were younger than ICCS members. In fact, some of the co-op's members had left it because of the boycott issue and had joined the IRFC. Many IRFC members did not think the ICCS was committed to cooperative principles or to healthy food. Indeed, the name of the new co-op, "Real Food," indicated it was an alternative to the ICCS.[80] Curiously, the ICCS board minutes or other records did not mention the new co-op. Perhaps the board did not consider the new co-op a threat to its business. But the IRFC had started to cut into the ICCS's membership and business. Furthermore, the IRFC was not the only competition for the ICCS. There were at least eleven supermarkets in Ithaca then.[81]

Even though the ICCS had lost members after the boycott vote, it was still the second largest food store in Ithaca. In 1975, it had close to 5,000 members, with assets of nearly $1.8 million and sales of close to $4.5 million. That year, the board authorized a $600,000 revitalization campaign to reduce outstanding debts, to buy equipment, to improve the store, and to fund a promotional and educational program. As of mid-1976, the co-op had raised $150,000, although it had been a lean year in sales.[82] In fact, sales continued to spiral downward for the next two years. Part of the problem was that in 1975, Mid-Eastern Co-operatives had cut off trade credit with the ICCS because the latter could not pay them. Co-op labels were then replaced by the Shurefine label, a private company's label, considered by many co-op members to be a "consumer disaster" because shoppers would not buy those products. At the annual meeting in 1977, attended by only twenty members, the general manager warned that the co-op would not survive if its sales did not pick up. But sales were not the only problem. There was a union wage increase, replacements and repairs, and the rising costs of gas, electricity, taxes, and insurance. And a low member turnout at the meeting indicated little interest or perhaps even confidence in the co-op. The general manager's recommendations did not generate much confidence either: immediate liquidation; continuing operations but selling the property and renting the store; or getting out of the grocery business and renting the co-op property. Besides a major grocery store, the co-op then owned a commercial complex with retail space and offices, as well as apartments and vacant land. The board president preferred the last option.[83]

Clearly the co-op's customer base had changed. At least half of the co-op's shoppers now lived downtown and over two-thirds lived in the southside neighborhood, the poorest neighborhood in Ithaca, where many made less than $5,000.

A number of shoppers were walk-ins who spent less than $10. Nearly one-fourth of the co-op shoppers were over fifty-five, nearly one-fifth retired, and another one-fifth students, in other words, on limited incomes. At least one-third of the customers mentioned that they watched for co-op newspaper ads and shopped when there were bargains. Still, there were some long-time members who remained committed to keeping the co-op in business.[84] Without a doubt, there was no longer a sense of community among ICCS members.

A Downward Turn in Finances

As of 1978, the co-op's assets were $178,334, down more than $93,000 from the previous year. But its existing liabilities far exceeded that at over $420,000. Nor was 1979 a good year. Sales had decreased by almost $348,000 from the previous year and expenses had increased.[85] In 1979, the board decided to close the store. Members' responses to the closing varied. Some women had tears in their eyes. One said, "People here are like family. I know them all." Another customer said, "The place has been a way of life with us. We started trading here in 1946 or '47." Another member's mother had shopped there and he had continued the family tradition.[86] But others said that the co-op had become just a regular supermarket, indistinguishable from the grocery chain stores. One of the cofounders noted that when he had returned to Ithaca in 1972, he saw a different co-op than the one he had helped to start.[87]

Some members, though, were determined to keep the co-op alive. The education and membership committees sent notices of a meeting to 3,300 members within a fifty-mile radius. Indicative of members' disinterest, only sixty attended. An ad hoc committee brainstormed ideas for increasing the co-op's business. They contacted the IRFC to see if they needed more space; they also contacted successful co-ops across the country for solutions. Some members of the IRFC questioned the ICCS's commitment to cooperative principles. Still, some "Real Food" members wanted to help out, citing the Rochdale principle of assisting other cooperatives.[88] In the end, Real Food supported the co-op's $250,000 loan application, stating: "We believe that the continued operation of the Co-operative Consumers Society's store is important to the Ithaca community, the neighborhood in which it is located, and the co-operative movement."[89] Real Food Co-op even considered a merger with the ICCS. One of its board members suggested, "The two cooperatives serve a somewhat different constituency, and if we could bring the two constituencies together it would help both of us."[90]

However, the ICCS and Real Food held different expectations. Although both expected some kind of exchange of membership benefits between the two co-ops, the ICCS decided it would not give discounts to Real Food members. Apparently the ICCS was hoping for increased volume from Real Food members but was not interested in an exchange where both co-ops might profit. In the end, the ICCS decided not to rent to the IRFC and withdrew the lease offer. Further, the ICCS began to compete by selling bulk and natural food items. This led the IRFC to target students more as customers.[91]

 The ICCS did reopen. But the loss sustained from its closing was over $200,000. During that time, the co-op had sold some of its property and received a mortgage loan of $380,000 from the National Consumer Co-operative Bank (NCCB). The co-op had also reduced its staff to eight workers and hoped that members would volunteer their labor. It sold by bulk and opened a natural food section, although its ads still featured mostly national brands, such as Folgers instant coffee, Ocean Spray juices, and General Mills' corn flakes.[92] The co-op estimated that it needed weekly sales of $65,000 to survive. However, sales were only half of that. By 1980, the co-op suffered a net loss of over $242,000.[93] During the first quarter of 1981, weekly sales continued to be half of what was needed and its vacant property remained unrented. In May, the NCCB sent accounting, food merchandizing, and real estate consultants to the co-op, then in default of its first loan payment. By June, the board decided that its debt was so large that it had no choice except to sell its real estate.[94] In May 1981, the NCCB informed the co-op that it was in foreclosure for failure to pay interest due on the mortgage.

Clearly, the ICCS had lost its customer base. Its board had to decide whether to sell the land across the street from the co-op or to sell all of its real estate holdings, which would clear the mortgage debts and all accounts payable.[95] In 1982, the board called a member meeting (with a membership then of only 300) to discuss selling its plaza, store, equipment, and apartments. The board planned to close the co-op again and perhaps even file for bankruptcy.[96] This time the co-op closed for good, before it had reached its fiftieth anniversary. In reminiscing, Ithaca residents and members voiced different opinions about why the co-op had closed. Some mentioned competition from new chain-store supermarkets, others the recession and overexpansion. Some said that its "best-known trademark," the year-end patronage refunds, had become a thing of the past. Others questioned if the co-op was different from any other grocery store.[97] Curiously, no one mentioned the co-op's stand on the boycott issue or how it had overextended itself during the 1970s recession.

Real Food, too, was forced to make changes during the 1980s and it would close as well. In 1979, the IRFC claimed to have the lowest prices in town and to sell the most "wholesome" foods without additives, as well as fresh local produce and organic produce. Like the ICCS once had, the IRFC bought directly from wholesalers and farmers' market in Ithaca and Syracuse. But as Real Food grew, it organized a board and hired a general manager. As of mid-1981, there had not been a quorum at any of its meetings; in fact, at its last meeting, only three members attended. In December 1982, its Grain Store, which sold bulk items, had incorporated into GreenStar and had become Ithaca's main co-op. Within two years, GreenStar's assets would be nearly $30,000.[98]

GreenStar Co-op

GreenStar, too, had attempted the difficult balancing act of being both a democratic organization and a successful business. As of 1984, GreenStar had yet to file for incorporation with the state because there was no agreement on its governance. Some members believed in the popular vote, that is, that each member's vote mattered. Others preferred giving more power to the council. Unrestricted voting at every meeting had been unique to the co-op and some had wanted the power to remain vested in the members. One idea was to have meetings every three months at which members could overrule the council. That meant that members would vote on key decisions, such as budget, hiring, loans, and major capital expenditures. Those who favored such ideas were worried that GreenStar was becoming more mainstream and less "alternative."[99] Without a doubt, the co-op was doing well financially. By 1989, its sales were over $1 million. Yet it still nurtured local connections. Like its predecessors, GreenStar offered local produce from West Haven Farm, Stick and Stone Farm, Remembrance Farm, and Blue Heron Farm. It also sold locally made items, such as Ithaca Soy (tofu), Silk Oak t-shirts, and Cayuga Pure Organics (beans and bulk food).[100]

In the end, GreenStar became not only larger but more structured. Member and activist Paul Glover later questioned some of the changes that occurred within the co-op. As with many co-ops, GreenStar largely had served middle class by selling natural foods. He, however, recommended that the store also serve lower-income residents, while continuing to promote local and regional growth. As the co-op faced more competition from corporations who had created their own niche in the natural foods market, GreenStar expanded and increased its prices. This undoubtedly affected the co-op's customer and membership base. As Glover pointedly asked: how did the growth of GreenStar's business affect the democratic principles of cooperatives? In his words, it was important to "keep direct democracy fresh."[101]

The ICCS is a case study that challenges those involved in food co-ops to rethink ideas of community and democracy. In the early history of its existence, the co-op was responsive to its community of members through its education committee, discussions at meetings, and its patronage refunds. Yet from its beginning, its community was a section of the town's residents, drawing mostly from Cornell faculty and their wives, and other professionals. As its membership grew and it sales increased exponentially, members participated less in decisions and relied on a board of seeming experts to guide them in their growth. During the 1950s, the height of its greatest expansion, the co-op became part of a shopping center and became more than a grocery store. Members continued to shop there and receive patronage refunds. The co-op also continued to buy local produce, as well as from local wholesalers and co-ops. As such, it was part of a constellation of local producers and "community" was reconfigured as larger than the co-op.

During the 1960s, the ICCS returned to questions of what it meant to be a co-op. It offered assistance to several co-ops in economically disenfranchised communities. It appears that by the end of the 1970s, many of its shoppers (perhaps not members) were from poorer communities and that many of its members had stopped shopping there. But its largest mistake was stifling the democratic process of exchanging ideas, information, and different points of view among its members. Instead, the ICCS remained conservative politically and did not reflect the positions of many of its members or the younger Ithaca community in the 1960s and 1970s. Nonetheless, the co-op hoped to draw a larger membership from college students without accepting or acknowledging their political activism.

Rather than buying property and starting new businesses, the ICCS might have expanded its product line to appeal to new members. It could have become more involved in environmental issues. If anything, it could have revitalized the education committee's work and the member community at large by engaging in discussions and debates about food politics. Instead, it took a more traditional approach to politics and business. In doing so, it alienated a number of its members and other community constituencies, and failed as a cooperative.

THE HYDE PARK
CO-OPERATIVE SOCIETY

I, among others, was saddened to hear about the closure of the Hyde Park Co-operative Society's (HPCS) store in 2008. I had lived in Hyde Park during the 1990s and shopped there. I remember it as being crowded and lively, with lots of conversations among customers and workers. There were shoppers from the University of Chicago, and from Hyde Park and nearby neighborhoods. One could buy both the *Hyde Park Herald* and the *Chicago Defender*, the African American newspaper published since 1907. In fact, many of its workers were African American, testimony to the co-op's longtime commitment to integration. Even so, the co-op's role in "slum clearance" or urban development—as it was euphemistically called in the 1950s and 1960s—raises questions about those commitments.

From the beginning, the HPCS was concerned with racial injustice. It purposefully set up its first storefront near a "slum" neighborhood, where many African Americans lived. Likewise, it recruited African Americans as members and workers, and helped African American communities in starting their own co-ops. Last, it started a co-op in a predominantly African American neighborhood north of Hyde Park. But how successful could the HPCS be in promoting integration when the Hyde Park community practiced segregation through restrictive covenants and urban renewal? The HPCS provides us with an example of how one co-op navigated issues of racial injustice and inequality.

The HPCS is also a case study in how city politics influenced the co-op's development. Anyone familiar with Chicago politics knows how powerful both mayor Daleys were. But aldermen also exerted enormous influence, including

Hyde Park's Leon Despres. The HPCS had much to gain from these political affiliations. Urban renewal gave the HPCS the opportunity to expand and relocate
to a large shopping center. Later, Mayor Daley, Jr. procured federal monies for
an empowerment zone development so that the HPCS could open a food co-op
in the Kenwood community. Both situations had a profound impact on African
American communities. But did they participate in these decisions?

The HPCS, 1930s–1960s

Chicago had a rich tradition of cooperatives, generally established along ethnic
lines. Although some persisted through World War I, many closed their doors as
they faced competition from grocery chain stores. One of those chain stores was
the Jewel Grocery Store, which had started in Chicago in 1899. Originally selling
only coffee, tea, and spices, the chain store did an annual business of $14 million
by 1931.[1] Regardless, food cooperatives started in and near Chicago during the
Great Depression, and by the end of 1936 there were thirty-five with at least 4,000
members. The Evanston Co-operative, for one, had started in 1935 with twelve
members. The following year, its membership had increased to 183; the next year,
there were over 350 members. The members decided to rent a store where they
sold fruits, vegetables, and other groceries. Later, the co-op established a milk
delivery route, opened a meat market, and established a credit union. The reasons
for their success were committed members, a strong leadership, the social reform
orientation of the community, strong business policies and organization, and
educational outreach.[2] What the records did not mention was the community's
wealth.

Before the establishment of the HPCS, a buying club called the Chicago Consumers Society had opened near the University of Chicago in late 1932. In a
rented apartment above a bookstore, members stored at least forty items, which
they bought and delivered for ten cents. A group of students, enrolled in an economics course taught by Paul Douglas, were determined to turn the buying club
into a cooperative.[3] A committed co-oper, Douglas was deeply involved in economic and social reform. He had helped to draft Illinois legislation for old-age
pensions and unemployment insurance. During the Depression, he had become
a member of the Consumers' Advisory Board of the National Recovery Administration in Franklin Roosevelt's administration. When the students asked him
for advice about a co-op, he said, "Either open a store at once, or liquidate before
you lose the money."[4]

Twelve club members held a meeting to elect a four-person board, draw up
bylaws, and open their first store in October 1933. They asked a young lawyer,
Leon Despres, to assist them. He agreed and would continue to advocate for a

Hyde Park cooperative through the 1960s as a lawyer and alderman. The members proceeded to make several financial decisions: to charge a service fee on all consumer goods to meet operating expenses, with the surplus returned to them; and to sell wholesale groceries, as well as services such as laundry, meals at the Green Shutter Tea Room, and home remodeling. But raising money for all these efforts became difficult and so they limited their co-op to groceries. They then hired a university student to recruit members and paid him a bonus of one dollar per new member. Within a short time, he had signed up over 100 members.[5]

Members Start Their Own Co-op

However, trouble arose when the board of directors decided to stop commissions for membership renewals. One member accused the board of being undemocratic and encouraged members to boycott the cooperative. Not only did many boycott the co-op; they held their own meeting and decided to start a new co-op based on Rochdale principles. They adopted a new constitution and became a member of the Central States Co-operative League. They elected a new board, which in turn hired a manager familiar with cooperatives. They named themselves the Hyde Park Co-operative Society.[6]

By 1935, the HPCS boasted many improvements, including doubling the size of its store, a new display refrigerator and aisle shelves, a delivery system, and more food items, including fresh fruits, vegetables, and cold meats. It decided to rent a storefront "in the slums" where the rent was low. Because the storefront was located strategically where one of the trollies turned around, it attracted many new customers.[7]

However, members were not only thinking of the co-op's financial well-being; they were also motivated by a strong integrationist stand. Then, restrictive covenants, reinforced by white home owners and real estate agents, kept African Americans from residing in Hyde Park. Instead, poorer and even middle-class African Americans lived in overcrowded kitchenettes in Chicago, often competing for substandard housing in nearby segregated neighborhoods. As of 1930, 90 percent of African Americans had lived in census tracts that were over 50 percent African American, even though only 7 percent of Chicago's population was African American.[8] Overall, racial politics were complicated in Hyde Park.

The HPCS recruited and educated its members, both white and African American, through monthly educational bulletins, information meetings, tasting parties, discussion groups, and a speaker series. Recruiting more members translated into more sales and the hope of opening a larger store. With a membership of 276 in late 1935, the co-op had increased its sales three times since its founding. By 1940, its membership had increased to nearly 800; by 1942 to over

1,100. Correspondingly, its annual sales in 1942 had increased to $4,000 weekly.[9] Because of its successful fundraising campaign, the co-op decided to open a supermarket at 1464 East 57th Street that year. As Tracey Deutsch has noted, co-ops in middle- and upper-class neighborhoods such as Hyde Park expanded because of higher pledge commitments by its members and access to bank loans. Although HPCS members wanted a supermarket, they were worried that that expansion would compromise a sense of community. Toward that end, the HPCS set up a club room in its supermarket store and members were encouraged to participate in co-op activities.[10]

Supporting Other Co-op Projects

During World War II, there were further opportunities for members' involvement, as the HPCS was active in supporting the Office of Price Administration (OPA). In fact, the OPA had sought support from food cooperatives to volunteer in checking prices. For HPCS members, this was not only a patriotic responsibility but a way to promote and publicize their supermarket co-op store. Women members were also encouraged to take the Housewives' Pledge and to write their congressmen in support of the OPA. But women members went beyond these suggestions and organized a Public Affairs Committee in 1943 to find out about consumer-related legislation. It is not clear, however, how the committee acted upon its investigations.[11]

Even though the co-op had moved to a larger store, it still assisted other cooperatives, especially those in low-income housing projects. In 1945, an African American cooperative in the Ida B. Wells housing project, north of Hyde Park, asked the HPCS for assistance. When the "Wells Homes" had opened in 1941, it was the largest housing project in Chicago, with forty-seven acres and a population of 6,900. Unlike the other two housing projects established in Chicago then, the Wells Homes accepted both working-class and poorer African American families. At least half of its residents were employed but earned low wages. In fact, nearly 95 percent of the tenants' annual income was less than $1,000. The residents wanted to expand their co-op but did not have enough money to buy land across from its community center, despite their savings of $3,000 and individual pledges of almost $600. They asked the HPCS to loan them $1,500, which they promised to repay within six months.[12] The HPCS also received an appeal from the Altgeld Gardens housing project, built for African American wartime workers in 1944 on the far south side. Unlike the Wells Homes, Altgeld Gardens was physically remote and isolated, located twenty-six miles from downtown Chicago. Both the HPCS and the Central States Co-operative League assisted Altgeld Gardens Homes, although it is not clear if either gave a loan to the Wells

Homes.[13] More than likely, their assistance gave the Altgeld co-op the opportunity to expand in 1947, when it opened a new supermarket with a cafeteria.[14]

The HPCS also collaborated with other cooperative societies in the city. In 1945, the HPCS had joined the Chicago Consumers Co-operative. There is little to no information on this consortium of Chicago consumer cooperatives, although it survived through 1948. What is known is that it was comprised of cooperatives from Hyde Park, North Chicago, and Waukegan, north of the city. As one of its booklet claimed, the leadership and financing for Chicago's new cooperative chain was "from a cross-section of this city."[15] To be sure, this enterprise drew on the Waukegan co-op's experiences and personnel. The Co-operative Trading Company of Waukegan had started in 1910 when Finnish and Scandinavian women started their own buying club to buy directly from farmers. By the 1930s, the Waukegan cooperative not only had a dairy but a bakery, six grocery stores, and meat markets. By 1946, it was a $1 million business. The officers and directors of the Chicago Consumers Co-operative included a cross-section of professionals. Jacob Liukku, its vice president and director, was general manager of Co-operative Trading Company in Waukegan. S. I. Hayakawa, a professor at the University of Chicago, was director of the Central States Co-operative League. Volker Koch-Weser was president of the HPCS. Fraser T. Lane, civic secretary of the Chicago Urban League, was a prominent leader in the African American community. And Mary Bolton Wirth, wife of University of Chicago sociologist Louis Wirth, was a committed social worker affiliated with Chicago public housing.[16]

Certainly the HPCS's collaboration with other co-ops honored the Rochdale principle of cooperation. With the case of the Central States Co-operative League, the affiliation was also a financially wise one. The Hyde Park co-op, as did other midwestern co-ops, carried many food items with the Central States Co-operative League's label and continued to do so through the 1950s. The League's green label promised good quality at low prices; the blue, high quality; and red, top quality. The Hyde Park co-op also bought its dairy products from nearby farmers' cooperatives.[17] In addition, the HPCS worked with co-ops nationally and internationally during the 1950s. In 1955, the board passed a motion to donate two weeks of the general manager's time to the Co-operative League of the U.S.A. (CLUSA). The HPCS also gave $2,500 per year to the Co-operative League Fund, formerly the World Wide Co-op Partners. This allowed one cooperative educator from the Philippines to spend two months at the Hyde Park co-op, learning about its operations.[18]

The HPCS continued to nurture collaboration with other Hyde Park co-ops during the 1950s. For example, it helped to start a credit union. In 1953, the HPCS negotiated to buy a building in Hyde Park for Little Children, a nursery school co-op it opened in 1948.[19] Likewise, the HPCS promoted housing co-ops, including the Pioneer Co-op housing development on Dorchester Avenue and Co-operative Homes of Hyde Park, a new cooperative for low-cost housing on land cleared under "slum clearance."[20] Last, the HPCS supported the establishment of other food co-ops in metropolitan Chicago. In fact, many food stores had closed because of the postwar urban renewal, especially on the south side, prompting the co-op to think beyond its Hyde Park neighborhood. In 1956, the co-op's planning committee proposed five super stores, with gas stations, in the South Shore neighborhood, as well as in the western suburbs, and in Evanston. The board estimated that each super store would cost between $300,000 and $350,000.[21] Although none were started, the co-op would try to develop one in a northern suburb in the early 1960s.

"Slum Clearance"

By 1958, two years after the HPCS had relocated to another shopping center, it claimed to be the largest supermarket in Chicago. Its membership was over 3,100 and its sales had increased by 25 percent. One of its annual reports stated that members could buy food cheaper at the co-op but not at the expense of the workers. In fact, many had joined unions, such as the butchers, who were members of the meat cutters union of the American Federation of Labor (AFL); others were members of local 239 of the Congress of Industrial Organizations (CIO). Because of their union membership, the co-op's workers' wages were 20 percent above the chain stores' average wages, at least in 1955. For example, one Chicago chain store paid full-time workers around $39 per forty-hour week, while at the HPCS, the lowest wage was around $54, although most workers earned at least $60.[22]

In truth, the co-op's growth was the result of urban renewal and "slum clearance" in Hyde Park. The history of race relations in Hyde Park was, as stated earlier, complicated. Indeed, Chicago had its share of conservative whites who had joined restrictive covenant and neighborhood improvement associations to keep African Americans out of their neighborhoods. The first communities to do so were the southside neighborhoods of Kenwood, Oakland, Hyde Park, Woodlawn, and Englewood. Chicago Housing Authority (CHA) administrator Robert Taylor had estimated that as much as 80 percent of Chicago was covenanted by 1939, although that estimate was unquestionably high. Nonetheless, by 1950, two years after restrictive covenants were declared illegal, there were still over 200 neighborhood improvement associations in Chicago.[23] One of the most visible white restrictive covenant associations in Chicago was the Oakland-Kenwood Property Owners' Association, north of Hyde Park.

Some Hyde Park residents feared "encroachment" by African Americans into their neighborhood during the 1930s and 1940s. During the late 1930s, for example, some white restrictive covenant associations had opposed public housing in or near their neighborhoods. When the Chicago Urban League president submitted an application for the Ida B. Wells Homes in 1937, property owners in Hyde Park, Kenwood, and Oakland protested, calling public housing "un-American" and "socialistic" because public housing residents did not have to pay taxes.[24] Hyde Park's population then was less than 1 percent African American. Likewise, during World War II, some residents protested attempts by African Americans to live near their neighborhoods. When fifty-five African American Women's Army Corps (WACs) were to be stationed at Gardiner Hospital in Hyde Park, the Oakland-Kenwood Property Owners' Association recommended that the WACs be stationed instead in Washington Park, an African American neighborhood adjoining Hyde Park. The Chicago chapter of the National Council of Negro Women and the Chicago Council Against Racial and Religious Discrimination disagreed with the association and sent letters to the War Department in support of the WACS. But in the end, the WACs resided at an African American settlement house in the Bronzeville neighborhood, north of Oakland and Kenwood.[25]

The Hopes of Integration

One postwar group involved in "integrating" Hyde Park was the Hyde-Park Kenwood Community Conference (HPKCC), established in 1949 by the 57th Street Meeting of Friends. The HPKCC had set up standing committees, including a legal panel committee, proactive about building code laws, and a planning committee, which advocated for new legislation.[26] The language of the HPKCC reflected both an integrationist approach, as well as concerns about protecting property values. In fact, its goals had been to reverse the "downward spiral" of physical deterioration in Hyde Park neighborhoods, as well as to create a "stable, interracial community of high standards."[27] As a matter of course, there had been illegal conversions of mansions into kitchenettes in the Hyde Park-Kenwood area during the 1940s. In 1948, when restrictive covenants were declared unconstitutional, more African Americans had moved into Hyde Park and nearby neighborhoods.[28]

Even so, by 1950, African Americans constituted only 6 percent of the 72,000 residents in Hyde Park-Kenwood area. Some of Kenwood's neighborhoods, however, had a higher concentration of African Americans who were "jammed into apartments in old buildings." Many long-standing residents of Hyde Park were worried that their neighborhood would become an "extension" of the Kenwood "Negro ghetto."[29] They asked home owners to voluntarily improve their property or neighborhood redevelopment corporations would take over. A group of reform-minded women, who called themselves "the Kenwood ladies," tried to find responsible buyers, instead of slumlords, for the old houses. They and others were concerned that if the old houses were torn down, then many African Americans who could not afford to live elsewhere would be displaced. This led many in the community to agree that they "had to accept integration."[30]

Essentially, the HPKCC's approach to integration was a soft one. That is, it hoped to eliminate overcrowded apartments and upgrade property. This reflected the group members' interest in protecting property values and discouraging lower-income African Americans from living in their neighborhoods. In Kenwood specifically, the HPKCC had tried to legally stop rooming house conversions and to promote Kenwood as a "wonderful place" for upper middle-class African American families. Here, the HPKCC's intention was to encourage the "better element" of African Americans to move there. In effect, Hyde Park remained a "segregated, integrated community," with all-African American, all-white, and a few interracial sections. In fact, when the HPKCC started block meetings, few were interracial because African Americans lived in separate apartment buildings where they were charged higher rents than white tenants. Although the National Association for the Advancement of Colored People (NAACP) demanded that realtors not increase rents, the realtors ignored the request.[31] In the end, the HPKCC held over 300 public meetings and decided on a plan that entailed "slum clearance and urban rehabilitation." Consequently, nearly 20 percent of the older buildings were torn down, although many others were refurbished.[32]

The important question here is the role of the HPCS and its members. As Tracey Deutsch has pointed out, the HPCS was interested in racial cooperation, which corresponded to co-ops' ideals of "a better world, one with greater racial tolerance, greater equality, and greater economic justice."[33] Accordingly, the HPCS had organized social activities at the co-op and at the Circle Pine Camp, where co-op members across races could interact. In 1947, the co-op had hired its first African American female worker. It also was the first retail business in Hyde Park to hire an African American for public outreach. Of its twenty-seven workers in 1953, the co-op claimed, fourteen were from different nationalities and thirteen from different religions. By 1958, two of the eleven board members were African American.[34] Likewise, two new members elected in 1959 were Marian Yoshioka, a Japanese American woman who had been the former chair of the co-op's CARE committee; and Charles Beckett, an African American accountant with his own firm. Beckett had also been chair of the HPKCC.[35] In fact, co-op manager Walker Sandbach argued that the HPCS had "prospered" because it included "people of all races and creeds."[36] But to what extent did the co-op promote integration beyond its internal structure? It publicized meetings about restrictive covenants and encouraged its members to become involved in fair hiring practices during the 1940s. It also considered supporting an inter-racial housing co-op in nearby Kenwood. Yet its members did not wholly condemn restrictive covenants.[37]

The process of slum clearance and development was long-term and a painful one for many African Americans. As early as 1947, the Metropolitan Housing and Planning Council (MHPC) had supported the Illinois Blighted Areas Redevelopment Act, which had created the Land Clearance Commission, which bought land in Chicago's slum areas, then sold it below price to private developers. In 1948, the Land Clearance Commission, in the name of urban renewal, destroyed a number of southside African American neighborhoods. From 1948 to 1956, slum clearance had displaced almost 86,000 people, of whom 67 percent were African American.[38] Many had little choice except to relocate to public housing. Middle-class African Americans, though, had more choices, including the neighborhoods of Washington Park, Woodlawn, Englewood, and even Hyde Park. The University of Chicago and the MHPC, though, were so concerned about Hyde Park that they claimed that an "invasion" would lead to further "blighted" areas. Urban renewal became the ultimate solution.[39]

How, then, did the HPCS benefit from this slum clearance? During the 1950s, the co-op had expanded considerably and had, in fact, become overcrowded. To complicate matters, its store was in an area slated for demolition as part of the city's urban renewal plan. In 1954, Jack Meltzer, an urban planner, had been hired to design a new community. Working with the Land Clearance Commission, he drew up a plan to clear one of the neighborhoods—with seventeen taverns in three blocks—and build a new shopping center, townhouses, and the University Gardens apartment buildings. In 1956, Meltzer and others created the Hyde Park-Kenwood urban renewal plan at an estimated cost of over $100 million.[40] Some residents were concerned that the plan was not about urban renewal but about "Negro removal."[41] Regardless of their concerns, a new co-op store opened in the new shopping center with fanfare. Alderman Robert Merriam cut the ribbon and Mahalia Jackson sang celebratory gospel songs.[42]

A New Shopping Center and Co-op

Not unexpectedly, the new store led to an increased membership of 2,500 by 1956. Yet members still tried to maintain a sense of community and cooperation, especially through participation in committee work. They helped with weekends at Camp Duncan, a YMCA-affiliated camp where co-op families gathered for recreation. They also maintained the library, assisted with consumer information and recreation, and helped with programs to develop leadership skills. The co-op also had a CARE committee, which since 1946 had donated $7,000 worth of food, clothing, and other goods to people in developing countries. There was a "sisters swapping service," used by at least sixty co-op families to exchange child-care for free.[43] A store operations committee helped customers by comparing the co-op's prices with nearby chain stores'. In addition, the co-op organized social activities, such as bridge clubs, guitar classes, folk dances, and folk songs. Here, the intentions were not only to develop community spirit but to recruit more members.[44]

Despite the store's new location, it was still not safe from demolition because of further urban development. Therefore, members became active in raising monies and recruiting more members in order to relocate. Within six months, the co-op raised at least $100,000. Its education director, Linnea Anderson, strategically arranged tours of the Hyde Park co-op supermarket for church and women's groups to interest them in joining. Anderson's connections helped as well. She was active in the League of Women Voters and president of the Woodlawn League during the mid-1940s. In 1947, Robert Merriam had hired her as his office manager after his election as fifth ward alderman. Perhaps her husband's connections to Senator Paul Douglas had also helped: he was in charge of the Chicago office for Douglas from 1948 to 1966. Many HPCS members claimed that her telephone campaign during the mid-1950s alone raised enough money for the new Hyde Park shopping center to open.[45]

In October 1959, the HPCS store relocated to the new shopping center, again with fanfare. Mayor Richard Daley, Sr. spoke, Mahalia Jackson sang once more, and Senator Douglas delivered a dedication speech. As one store advertisement proudly declared: "This store, the largest co-op grocery in the world, is an example of democracy, and of the spirit in this neighborhood."[46] Although the advertisement was hyperbolic, the new store was large, with 46,000 square feet. At the cost of $1.25 million, the store had six information stations, operated by push buttons, for customers to learn about its more than 7,000 items. It claimed to have the largest frozen food section in the country with over 365 items. There was a 200-food self-service and meat counter, the largest in Chicago. A new feature was a "coffee bar," the first one in Chicago, which served thirty-two persons at one time, near the delicatessen. The co-op had two test and demonstration kitchens, with a full-time home economist. During some years, she filled over 35,000 recipe requests. In short, the co-op was modern, convenient, and organized, especially for those women buyers who fit the profile of what women buyers should be.[47]

FIGURE 3.   Mahalia Jackson singing at the Ice House, 1959, Hyde Park
Historical Society, Hyde Park Co-op Records, Special Collections Research
Center, University of Chicago.

The HPCS supermarket and its amenities reflected the growth in supermarkets and shopping centers during the 1950s. As noted in earlier chapters, a
number of food cooperatives had become supermarkets during the late 1940s
and 1950s. In 1959, Natick Co-op had started building a million-dollar cooperative shopping center in Framingham, Massachusetts. Their facilities included a
meeting room, a home economics center, a delicatessen with kitchen, and an
outdoor playground and picnic area. The subleased shops in its store were a barber shop, dry cleaners, drug store, bakery, gift shop, and bank. A cooperative
shopping center in Superior, Wisconsin planned to have a gourmet food section,
pastry section, baby food section, pet and household wares, and a floral shop, in
cooperation with local greenhouses. The Co-op Shopping Center in Hayward,
Wisconsin, with a membership of 1,600, had a supermarket, café, clothing, and
hardware departments in one building, as well as a service station. The Minnesota iron range community of Virginia had a new co-op shopping center for
its 3,000 co-op members, as well as for other shoppers. And the Co-op Center

in Berkeley, California not only had a food store but a pharmacy, coffee shop, children's place, book store, credit union office, insurance offices, and arts and crafts shop. Its membership was by far the largest of all food co-ops at 10,000 families.[48] Clearly, these co-ops followed the model of free enterprise through their expansion. However, some of that expansion did include other cooperative stores, such as credit unions and insurance co-ops.

The HPCS, 1960s–2000

As of 1960, the HPCS claimed to have 6,000 members and annual sales of $3.5 million,[49] and considered expanding to other neighborhoods in the Chicago metropolitan area. In the early 1960s, some residents in the northern suburbs of Evanston and Skokie were interested in starting a food co-op. The HPCS agreed to do a marketing survey for them, provided 500 families pledged to invest a total of $50,000. However, the results of the survey were not encouraging. A 1963 survey of these northern suburbs found that only one in three housewives had heard of a consumer cooperative and six of ten reacted negatively to the idea. Those most interested in cooperatives were less likely to drive, worked outside of the home, shopped at more than one store, had younger children and larger families, and had lived in their communities for only a short time. The HPCS used this information to reflect on their own co-op and did not start one in Evanston or Skokie.[50]

Assisting Other Co-ops

At the same time, the HPCS remained interested in cooperative opportunities on the southside, especially those that might improve the lives of lower-income African American residents. Some southside social settlements and churches had already helped to start co-ops in their neighborhoods. In the North Kenwood-Oakland area, the Abraham Lincoln Center, a social settlement that had started in 1904, formed a buying club that hoped to sell co-op brand products donated by the Central States Co-operative League. At the Henry Booth House, a social settlement started in 1898 by the Chicago Society for Ethical Culture, there were plans to open a food buying club. Father Martin Farrell of the Holy Cross Church worked with the Maryland Avenue buying club. In Englewood, there was a "We People Buying Club," organized by the Christ Methodist Church and the London Towne Housing Co-op. And at Altgeld Gardens Homes, Father Zimmerman of Our Lady of the Gardens Church had helped start a buying club.[51]

The HPCS decided to collaborate with the CLUSA to provide educational and organizational assistance to poorer African American residents in Hyde

Park, Kenwood-Oakland, and Woodlawn. One of their projects was to promote fair employment by offering more products in the HPCS supermarket that were made and sold by minority groups. Here, they worked with Reverend Jesse Jackson, whose "Operation Breadbasket" initiative helped community members to find jobs. Later, Jackson renamed Operation Breadbasket Operation PUSH and relocated its headquarters to Hyde Park.[52] The HPCS likewise continued to assist African American residents who had been displaced because of slum clearance. The co-op's president wrote to the Commissioner of the Department of Urban Renewal in 1964, promoting integrated housing: "We believe that significant racial integration could occur because this housing would be new and available at attractive rentals. These are 'forgotten people'—their incomes are too high for public housing and too low for new housing in city."[53] It is clear that in this instance the HPCS advocated on behalf of working- and middle-class African Americans. In fact, by the 1950s, most public housing in Chicago was reserved for poorer, not working-class, African

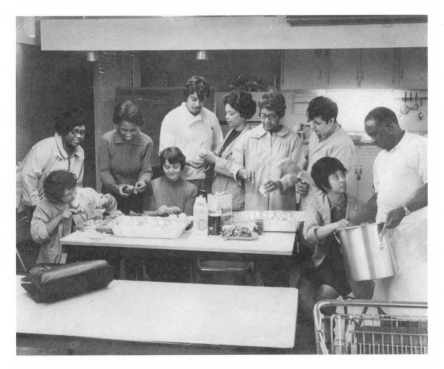

FIGURE 4.   Ethnic dinner, interracial group, Evergreen, 1971, Hyde Park Historical Society, Hyde Park Co-op Records, Special Collections Research Center, University of Chicago.

Americans. Later, in 1968, the co-op worked with local groups to raise money to buy food for persons displaced by the violence following Martin Luther King's death.[54]

Last, the co-op worked with a new organization, the Illinois Federation of Consumers, under the leadership of Jerry Voorhis.[55] Voorhis had a long history of supporting cooperatives. During the 1930s, he had organized them for farmers and ranchers in California. In 1934, he had run for the California legislature and had the backing of Upton Sinclair, a strong supporter of cooperatives. Voorhis was elected to the US House of Representatives in 1936, a position he held for four terms until he lost to Richard Nixon in 1946 because of the latter's accusation that Voorhis was a communist. The following year Voorhis became president and executive director of the CLUSA. In his promotion of co-ops, he argued that they were "islands of economic democracy in a sea of monopolistic oligarchy."[56] Convinced that many co-ops were too conservative and took too few risks, he came before the HPCS in 1966 to encourage the co-op to assist low-income groups in Chicago by helping them start their own co-ops.[57]

To be sure, the HPCS was in a position to do so. As of 1967, the co-op had 10,000 members and annual sales of $6 million. The following year, the co-op grossed $6.5 million; by 1970, its sales had reached $8.4 million. Despite a rise in food prices and inflation during 1973, the HPCS supermarket sales had increased 15 percent from the previous year.[58] The co-op had also been successful during the 1960s with its first FORM store, which sold Scandinavian furniture and gifts, and so decided to open a second one in 1973.[59] However, it would not be until the late 1990s that the HPCS would assist another predominantly African American community, but one that was not poor.

Although the HPCS was doing well financially, this did not mean that it did not participate in boycotts and other political issues. Unlike the food co-ops in Ithaca and in Hanover, New Hampshire, the HPCS supported the United Farm Workers (UFW), especially their lettuce boycott, in the 1970s. In the co-op's estimation, boycotts worked, evident in the earlier UFW grape strike. As twenty co-op members of the HPCS who supported the UFW stated: "As a large, democratically-operated store in an informed community, the Co-op can set a useful and responsible example by promising prompt co-operation with this movement for basic human needs and justice."[60] For a year, the HPCS bought only products with the UFW Black Eagle emblem.

Some of the co-op staff was also concerned about food additives. The home economist wrote an article about them, the long shelf life of products that contained them, and how they might cause hyperactivity in children. She recommended additive-free foods. During the early 1970s, the co-op also discussed whether to carry foods with cyclamate, an artificial sweetener. It is not clear, how-ever, what decision the HPCS made. However, in 1968, the National Academy of Sciences had advised the Food and Drug Administration (FDA) that further studies should be done to determine if there was a link between the sweetener and cancer.[61]

In general, HPCS policies and concerns reflected those of its members, many of whom were educated professionals. A 1974 survey, conducted by the University of Chicago's Sociology School, found that most of the co-op's members lived in the Hyde Park community. In contrast, nearly one-third of its nonmember customers lived west of Woodlawn, a poorer African American neighborhood. Overall, co-op members were more educated and had a higher income than nonmembers. Over 41 percent of its members had an income of over $20,000; almost 26 percent of its members had an income between $10,000 and $20,000. Almost 70 percent of members did 75 percent or more of their shopping at the HPCS, whereas only 28 percent of nonmembers who shopped there bought very much. Those members who did less than 75 percent of their grocery shopping at the co-op usually went to A&P, Jewel, or other grocery chain stores outside the neighborhood. They shopped elsewhere because of the perceived higher prices at the co-op. Last, most members said they would buy more shares so that the co-op could start new businesses.[62]

Expansion and a Financial Roller Coaster

In late 1977, the co-op did open a new business: a convenience store, called Short Stop Co-op, in Hyde Park. The purpose of this store was to "fill a community need, for those members not totally satisfied by the supermarket."[63] It is not clear how the convenience store differed from the supermarket in terms of food items it carried. More than likely, the store sold mostly basic foods, such as bread, milk, and sandwich meats. Nor is it clear who its customers were. But within a year, its sales were more than three times higher than "typical convenience stores." In fact, the store did serve many customers, nearly 8,000 a week but their average purchase was only $2.60.[64]

By 1980, the HPCS had experienced forty-seven years of success. The co-op owned two stores, one a large supermarket with 7,000 different items. An $18-million business, it was one of Chicago area's largest supermarkets in terms of sales, owned by 11,000 members and governed by a nine-member board of directors.[65] Short-Stop Co-op, then in its fourth year, was considered a "proto-type of what a new co-op-market would be."[66] There were problems during the early 1980s as well. The new freezer had not worked well and so the co-op lost a great deal of food. The co-op had remodeled the supermarket and replaced old equipment, which led to loss in business and customer dissatisfaction during the remodeling. Its grocery profits had declined, members were not pleased with the board, and there were problems with the electrical contractor. Part of the problem was that the million-dollar remodeling job did not have the benefit of an engineer or architect. The 1980 annual report claimed that this was one of the worst times since the opening of the supermarket. Two years later, the co-op had lost over $158, 000, with grocery sales down by 10 percent. The co-op decided to divest the furniture division.[67]

The downward turn in sales might have reflected difficult times for some of the HPCS customers. The year 1980, as Bruce Schulman noted, had the "steepest drop in GNP in American history."[68] In 1982, unemployment was at its highest since the Great Depression. At least 17,000 companies had closed their businesses; correspondingly, many workers lost their jobs because of deindustrialization, especially in the Northeast and the Midwest. Spurred by Reagan's neoconservative republicanism that encouraged individual freedom, the economy would begin to slowly grow again.[69] But, as historian Judith Stein argued, the recovery was based on consumption, not wage increases.[70]

Deindustrialization was especially dire in Chicago. In 1979, there were less than one million manufacturing jobs in the metropolitan area of Chicago. Over the next seven years, at least 37 percent of those would be lost, most of them permanently. Sociologist William Julius Wilson pointed out that many African Americans in the city lost their jobs, contributing to a widening gap in racial inequality.[71] It is difficult to say exactly how this job loss directly affected the HPCS as many of its members were middle- and upper-class. However, the fact the co-op's sales had decreased by 10 percent in 1980 suggests that some of its working-class members may have been affected. Or perhaps customers from nearby neighborhoods no longer shopped there or did not buy as much as they used to.

It is possible that reduced sales resulted from some members' dissatisfaction with the direction the HPCS had taken. Some thought that the "innovative" thinking of the past no longer existed. Although they did not mention specific concerns, they wondered if the co-op had grown too large. Some complained that the cooperative no longer belonged to its members but was run by its board members. Still others noted that some services were no longer offered, for example, mothers no longer had free, supervised childcare when they shopped. In fact, the perceived loss of community and of member control were the very concerns that Ithaca co-op members had faced during the early 1980s and even earlier. Unlike the Ithaca co-op, however, many of HPCS members continued to shop there. Their reasons for doing so varied, from its good location to seeing their friends, to the patronage refunds.[72] The board president reasoned: "We're an old-line co-operative—we sell at competitive market prices, and if the year is good, we pass the difference to our customers as cash dividends."[73]

Regardless of his laudatory statements, the co-op continued to have problems through the mid-1980s. In 1984, payroll costs were excessive. The Short Stop store also reported a loss of $63,000, mostly because of labor costs. The co-op reduced its hours at the supermarket, which resulted in long checkout lines and unhappy customers.[74] To be sure, the co-op needed to cut costs to remain viable. Despite these problems, there was still money in its reserves to pay for these adverse years. In 1984, the board decided to divest the Short Stop and to open a new bakery café in the supermarket.[75]

The following year, the cooperative slowly turned around. In fact, 1985 was a year of growth, with more customers whose average purchases were higher than before. Member investment was also growing. The next year was another good one, with a nearly 2 percent patronage refund, which then equaled one week of groceries.[76] The HPCS renewed its membership drive and hired a member services director. The store added new health food items, noting the growth of the natural foods market. Like other co-ops across the country, the HPCS was "regrouping" in order to remain viable. The co-op was well aware of the fate of other large food co-ops in the country. The Palo Alto co-op had recently sold two of its three supermarkets. And the Berkeley Co-op, once the largest in the United States, had "sold out" to a private business.[77]

Like other co-ops, the HPCS stepped up its environmental programs during the 1990s, alongside its promotion of natural products. It formed an environmental concerns committee, which strongly recommended mesh bags and encouraged members to bring their own bags when shopping. The co-op brochures listed less toxic chemical cleaners and different organic home products. There were new recycling containers in the store for paper, glass, metal containers, and plastic jugs. The Hyde Park Environmental Action Coalition, a local environmental group, certified that the co-op was a model environmental community institution. In fact, the co-op had joined with forty-one other businesses in Illinois under the Model Community Program, developed by the Central States Education Center in Urbana, which encouraged recycling, waste reduction, and lowering energy consumption. Last, there were educational programs for customers about how to reduce waste.[78]

By 1995, the HPCS's sales were the highest in its history and at least 65 percent of sales were because of its members. In 1997, there was another all-time high in sales, almost $25.85 million, which was 4.5 percent above the previous year. Clearly its large membership, 22,000 in 1997, contributed to its success.[79] Once again, the HPCS began thinking about a new store, this time in a new shopping center in Kenwood, north of Hyde Park.

The New Co-op Faces Financial Troubles

The Lake Park Pointe Shopping Center opened in the north Kenwood neighborhood in 1999. The over $9 million shopping center's plans included the new co-op supermarket, a bank, real-estate office, drugstore, a dry cleaner, and eye clinic. The supermarket, the developers and the HPCS promised, would provide members with at least a 15 percent savings, compared to the smaller neighborhood grocery stores. Initially, the shopping center was an asset to the community and real estate values increased in the neighborhood.[80] Ultimately, opening the Kenwood store was not a good decision and would lead to the co-op's closure.

Unfortunately, there is little information about what input the Oakland-Kenwood residents or HPCS members had in the decision to build a new co-op supermarket. The HPCS records are conspicuously missing from that time period. Nor it is clear if there was any kind of feasibility study done to confirm whether the community would support a food co-op. It does appear, though, as if the decision was influenced by a windfall of federal monies. In late 1994, Chicago was one of six cities awarded an Empowerment Zone through the federal Department of Housing and Urban Development. There were financial incentives—such as tax and employer wage credits—to open a store in the Oakland-Kenwood neighborhood, then considered a "distressed" area.[81] More than likely, then, city politicians and businessmen were involved in the decision to open a shopping center in Kenwood.

Regardless, one must question the wisdom of starting a store in a community that was economically challenged. As sociologist Mary Pattillo has discussed, the Oakland-Kenwood neighborhoods, although considered middle-class, were pocketed with sub-rosa or illegal activities, including selling drugs. As David Gutnecht confirmed, opening a store an Empowerment Zone redevelopment project led to HPCS's financial problems. In fact, during the store's first five years, the co-op lost money. To add to difficulties, even though the new store closed in early 2005, the HPCS could not get out of its lease with Certified Midwest Grocers, who owned the building. This meant that the co-op ended up paying over $1 million per year for rent for a closed store.[82]

In October 2006, the co-op held a forum about its future. The meeting was attended by only 120 people. Significant disclosures were made to the audience, for example, that the HPCS was paying $90,000 to $100,000 a month for rent for the Kenwood store. Further, the HPCS had a twenty-six year lease that could not be broken. Certified Midwest Grocers also "had a hold" on the HPCS as a vendor, especially for its produce. HPCS leaders said they hoped to have the Kenwood co-op store leased by the next year.[83] That members were told about this situation then and not earlier is alarming. After all, they were the owners of the co-op.

An HPCS board president later admitted that the co-op's financial troubles were due to the Kenwood store and the small convenience store on 53rd Street. There was not enough business at either of them, which meant that the Hyde Park co-op supermarket bore the brunt of supporting all three stores. In addition, the Hyde Park supermarket had its own share of problems, including a major power outage in 2007, problems with cash flow, and not keeping up with paying rent to the University of Chicago, which had owned the building as of 1984. The university offered to forgive the $1.2 million in back rent in exchange for the co-op vacating the building. In late November 2008 there was a referendum to declare bankruptcy, so that the HPCS would not have to pay rent on the Kenwood store.[84]

In 2008, the University of Chicago, which owned the Hyde Park Shopping Center, signed a lease with Treasure Island, which moved into the Hyde Park supermarket location. The co-op closed and its workers were encouraged to interview for jobs at the Treasure Island store. When the HPCS remanded its lease, the university forgave nearly $3 million of its debts and the co-op used what money it had to pay off vendors. The 19,000 members lost any money that they had contributed toward the co-op. But more than that, they lost a long-standing community institution. On January 20, 2008, a New Orleans jazz funeral was held for the co-op, followed by concluding remarks by Leon Despres and the co-op's past presidents.[85]

One year after the co-op's closure, its former employees met at Lil's Kocktail Lounge to reminisce about the HPCS. They hoped to meet annually and keep in touch. As one former employee explained, "We're real good friends, like family, here."[86] As the example of the Hyde Park co-op shows, a sense of community and community making can be fragile. The co-op had a strong membership in Hyde Park. It also had a strong history of consumer advocacy and education, evident in its committees.

So what went wrong? For one, opening a supermarket in the Kenwood shopping center was a bad business decision. But even worse was the decision to sign a long-term lease that would put the Hyde Park supermarket at risk. Like other businesses, co-ops often think in terms of expansion. But expansion plans need to be carefully made. Most important, members need to weigh in on decisions, and co-ops need to examine their histories so that they can make good decisions. Expansion may not always be the best answer, especially if members do not have a say. In the case of the Kenwood supermarket, it clearly was not.

Although it is not clear if and how co-op members were involved in the decision to open the Kenwood supermarket, there is evidence that some members were dissatisfied with how large the Hyde Park co-op supermarket had become. In the late 1950s, co-op members had been proud of their new co-op supermarket, which offered the conveniences of frozen foods, self-service, a delicatessen, and an on-site home economist. In truth, such amenities reflected the prosperity and optimism about economic growth of many co-op supermarkets of the time. But by 1980, some HPCS members realized that expansion had come at the cost of member participation and a loss of community.

In truth, Hyde Park and the HPCS have never been one community. Instead, they have been communities divided by social class, race, income, and employment. The HPCS did provide interracial activities, hire African Americans, and promote integrated housing for middle-class African American residents. However, it also gained much from the displacement of many poorer African Americans. Perhaps the description that best describes Hyde Park and the HPCS is "segregated, integrated."

HANOVER CONSUMER
CO-OPERATIVE SOCIETY

I was fortunate that the Hanover Consumer Co-operative Society's (HCCS) archives were at its oldest store. This gave me the opportunity to talk to the staff, walk around and get a sense of who the shoppers were, and ask workers questions. There were different shoppers, representing at least three generations. Although the store featured organic and natural foods, there were commercial brand names as well. I visited two of its other stores and crossed the Connecticut River into Vermont, where its fourth store later opened. Of those co-ops that started during the Great Depression, the HCCS is the second oldest but largest food co-op in terms of its number of stores, membership, and sales. As such, it has much to tell us about how expansion affects members' participation.

The HCCS is an example of a food co-op whose educational directors have had a significant impact on consumer education. As such, they honored the Rochdale principle of member education by providing individual consumers with information on nutrition, as well as the environmental impact of products. Although this outreach constituted a form of environmental activism, it often precluded collective efforts such as protests and boycotts. This approach raises questions about the range of consumer activism and how it influences co-op members' participation and their sense of community within a co-op.

Like other large co-ops, the HCCS expanded through financial investments and by starting other co-ops. When it bought property in nearby Vermont, the co-op deliberated for almost ten years about how best to use the land. Co-op members, community residents and leaders, and Dartmouth College officials weighed in on the decision. The ultimate decision is indicative of which groups were the most powerful in the community.

Early History, 1936–1960

Like the co-ops in Ithaca and Hyde Park, the HCCS started as a buying club. In 1936, nearly thirty townspeople attended a meeting at the Hanover high school to listen to a short history of the cooperative movement in England and the United States by Roy Chamberlin, chair of a local cooperative buyers' club.[1]

Afterward, people in the audience decided to start a food buying club. The original purposes of this club were "to advance the educational and economic interests of ultimate consumers; to operate in accordance with Rochdale Co-operative Principles; to deal with genuine cooperative societies wherever possible; to practice collective bargaining with distributors or manufacturers for the needs of its members, striving at all times to protect the best interests of the wage earners engaged in industries through their trade unions and of the farmers through their co-operative associations."[2]

The club's interest in workers and union members was important and one not always expressed by many consumer clubs and co-ops. The club also encouraged workers to join, although one might question the language: "Wage earners, housewives, dirt farmers, professional and salaried workers may become members by filing application."[3] In fact, most of its charter members were Dartmouth faculty and their wives, who educated themselves on the principles of cooperation. By late 1937, only 21 of 161 members were not affiliated with the college.[4]

Members Take the Lead

The club's first "store" opened in a member's basement in 1936, where they sold fresh oranges and grapefruit, as well as bread, table wines, and canned vegetables. Customers could also buy gas, fuel oil, and woolen clothes, and have their skates sharpened.[5] Members discussed collectively what products to carry and which local stores and distributors to support. One store they favored was the Hanover Cash Market, whose meats were higher priced than the grocery chain stores but were better quality. Members also recommended the Hanover Baking Company for its white bread. They also patronized a club tailor who offered good prices on overcoats and dry cleaning.[6] Last, there was a German "peddler" from whom they bought "good sausage and pumpernickel."[7]

Club members conducted research and tested the products they considered selling. For example, they compared different businesses that sold firewood. As at the Ithaca Consumer Co-operative Society, women members of the Hanover co-op were especially active in testing various brands of foods. In one case, they tasted ten different brands of canned corn, using scorecards. In another case, they tested thirteen brands of canned peas. After finding dirt in most, they recommended frozen peas. The score for shortening was based on its price, melting point, color, consistency, and, of course, taste. Although the Hanover women did not consider themselves experts, they assumed the role of product testers in order to safeguard the reputation of their store's products and, hence, the store's reputation. In understanding the different grades of products, they followed sociologist Robert Lynd's idea of "effective consumption"—promoting consumer advocacy amid the "barrage of advertising and merchandising."[8]

In addition to publishing these results, the club educated members and the larger community in other ways. In mid-1936, they published and distributed twelve nutrition bulletins, and organized exhibits of materials from the Consumers Affairs Division at nearby libraries.[9] In 1936, they sponsored pacifist Toyohiko Kagawa—who was touring the country to spread the idea that cooperatives were the "economic foundation of world peace"—to speak at Dartmouth.[10] And at least one member surveyed rural churches and granges in 1937 to organize study groups there.[11]

Whenever possible, the club bought in bulk to pass on savings to its members. These items included potatoes, wood, butter, flour, cereals, cheese, shoes, soap, citrus fruit, and maple syrup. Many of these items they bought wholesale from the Windsor County Farmers' Exchange, White River Wholesalers, Co-operative Distributors of New York City, and the Eastern Co-operative Wholesale, then opening a branch in Boston. By 1937, the club had become a member of the Eastern Co-operative League and owned ten shares of stock in Eastern Co-operative Wholesale.[12]

In October 1936, the club had a balance of $187 and outstanding loans of $13.50. Members discussed at length whether they had enough business experience to run a store and, if so, what kind of store, who should be in charge of buying, and how they would raise enough capital. To ensure the club's survival, sixty-two families decided to commit $500 collectively. Club members also decided to hire a manager to assist them.[13] Still the club could not meet all of its financial obligations. Even though the club's average monthly sales were $950 in 1937, the year it incorporated as a co-op, the $1,600 required annually for the manager's salary and rental cost meant that it was not yet breaking even. Another problem was that members did not always pay immediately for their groceries.

Some argued that extending credit was "against the principles of co-operation."[14] Because its 161 members accounted for 90 percent of its sales, it was important that all pay their bills immediately.[15]

Although the co-op was not yet breaking even, members voted to move the store to a larger location on Main Street in 1937 and to hire an assistant manager. Members were asked to recruit new members and to encourage current members to keep buying from the co-op. During 1938, one-fourth of its members had bought more than 50 percent of their groceries there.[16] However, some members disapproved of at least one of the store's items. At one board meeting, "some alarm was expressed by one or two moralists in the audience at Mr. Bristol's' report that 10 percent of the store's total sales [we]re in cigarettes."[17] Despite this concern, overall sales increased, resulting in a net savings of $450 in 1938. Of that, $300 was returned to its members as patronage funds. As Professor Charles R. Bagley, one of the co-op's founding members and first secretary, said of the fledgling co-op: "This was democracy in practice as well as in theory."[18]

"A First Class Store"

By 1940, sales had increased 10 percent from the previous year because of the "timely departure" of the A&P grocery store in town. The following year, sales increased once again, this time by almost 14 percent. Although some members were eager for expansion, the board voted to defer action on moving and expansion because of the war.[19] Instead, the board encouraged members to learn more about cooperative principles. Associating the ideas of cooperation with freedom, the board president stated: "We must educate ourselves in the principles of consumer co-operation in general; but we must also learn the details of the operation of our own business, the grocery business. Our success depends upon it; and it is exciting because in that learning we are forging our economic freedom."[20]

By 1941, members voted to lease property that was formerly the Campus Café to "put in a first class store." However, they needed almost $3,500 more in capital. Sales may not have been as high as expected that year because they were still in a basement location. There were also concerns about competition from another grocery store, First National Store, and with war shortage items such as butter and sugar. The year 1942 was much better, with increased sales of over 63 percent. However, in 1943 there was an 8 percent decrease in store volume, in part because of rationing and the national Office of Price Administration (OPA) price ceilings. Sales had so decreased that the co-op could not afford to pay its manager and he resigned. It is not clear why rationing and prices were problems for the HCCS but not at other co-ops, as most of the records then were damaged. Nor had conditions improved much during the postwar years. By the end of 1948, the co-op carried a deficit of almost $2,500.[21]

Fortunately, the co-op store did much better during the 1950s. By the end of 1954, sales had increased to almost $31,000; 1957 was a record year, with over $500,000 in sales. There were a number of reasons for the upward turn in the co-op's finances. First was the postwar prosperity, which encouraged members and others to buy. Second, the manager, Harry Gerstenberger and his four workers helped to improve store sales through their product selection and marketing. Third, membership had increased. By 1952, there were over 500 members and 34 persons/families had bought co-op stock valued at around $9,000. By 1956, membership had grown to 800 members; by 1958, over 1,000.[22] Clearly the co-op's decision to defer building a new store and to expand the present one had been a wise one.

The HCCS, 1960s and 1970s

The HCCS celebrated its twenty-fifth anniversary in 1961 with speeches from its founding members. Despite its increased membership, however, the co-op felt it still had not reached enough people about the advantages of joining a cooperative. One distinct advantage, the board emphasized, was co-op's truthful advertising. Indeed, the 1960s would alert members to a number of deceptions besides false advertising. Many Hanover co-op members had read Rachel Carson's *Silent Spring* and her articles in the *New Yorker*, which prompted them to start a food safety committee. In 1963, the Hanover Co-op also formed a committee on natural foods to see if members were interested in buying them, to locate sources, and to provide educational information about food safety.[23] Here, the HCCS was distinctly different from the Ithaca Consumer Co-operative Society (ICCS) in its advocacy of consumer safety issues and natural foods. And it was ahead of the Hyde Park co-op in promoting natural foods and environmentally safe products during the 1960s.

Environmental and Labor Activism

In fact, a 1964 survey indicated that members were interested in forming study groups on many health and environmental issues: health costs, nutrition, pesticides, safer car designs, packaging, comparative prices, and consumer counsels. The HCCS responded by publishing articles in their newsletters on dichloro-diphenyltrichloroethane (DDT), food additives, and other related matters. As co-op members became increasingly concerned about such issues, the HCCS began to sell more environmentally safe products, such as biodegradable detergents. The National Co-operatives, Inc., which had started a nationwide distribution of such detergents, claimed that co-ops were in the forefront of this solution. The new co-op detergent, Co-op Controlled Suds, degraded 90 percent in thirteen days and 100 percent in twenty-eight days. The Hanover Co-op sold this product, which was popular.[24]

It is possible that many new members joined during the 1960s because of these environmental concerns. In turn, more members helped to improve sales. In 1957, the co-op had purchased property for a store and asked members to buy more shares. In May 1963, when the new store finally opened, the co-op's sales were over $1 million; the next year, the sales increased by over 16 percent. By 1967, the co-op had reached sales of $1.37 million; the following year, they were up 8 percent to nearly $1.45 million.[25]

Perhaps the most politically contentious consumer issue then for the HCCS, as for the ICCS, was the United Farm Workers (UFW) grape boycott. In late 1968, the co-op had received a request from a member that California grapes be removed from shelves to protest the migrant workers' labor conditions. The board president phoned the member and told him that customers were free to make their own choices.[26] In fact, this had not been the first time that members had wanted the co-op not to sell a product. In 1967, some members had wanted saran wrap removed because it was made by Dow Chemical Company, which also made chemicals used in napalm. Even then, the HCCS board had voted not to take it off the shelves. The grape boycott was different, however, because many younger members protested. In 1969, five younger members asked if they could attend a board meeting. They were part of a group that had been picketing outside the store in opposition to the co-op's stand on selling California grapes. These picketers told customers not to go into the store but to shop elsewhere. One of them even recommended a store in nearby White River, Vermont that had agreed not to sell the grapes. In response to these actions, the board replied that anyone could give out literature to customers. But the young people were asked not to picket until after the membership meeting in a few weeks. The young members refused to comply with this request. The board then decided to place a sign in the store that the co-op believed in the customer's individual choice.[27] In essence, the HCCS took the same stand as the ICCS, which favored the individual consumer at the expense of a collective decision of its members.

At least one board member, however, disagreed with the co-op's stand. Freya von Moltke's involvement with the co-op had started in 1960, when she had moved to nearby Norwich, Vermont. Born in 1911 in Germany, her husband had died as part of the resistance movement against Hitler through the Kreisau Circle. She then moved to South Africa, where she became a social worker. In

1956, she returned to Germany and wrote about her husband's activities. These experiences surely affected her political beliefs. In a letter to the HCCS board in October 1969, she wrote that cooperatives were a "form of democratic selfhelp" and a way to fight "oppression." Now that the HCCS was doing well, she argued, they should help others, such as the UFW.[28] She may have influenced others, for one month later, the managers consulted with the board and the board decided to remove the non-UFW grapes.[29]

Another reason for the board's concern might have been co-op's decreased sales. The opening of two new supermarkets, Purity Supreme and IGA, most likely had an impact on the co-op's downward sales. However, the manager's report in 1969 claimed that: "The effect of the boycott was to reduce sales by approximately $17,000.00 for the period of the picketing."[30] When the boycott ended, he argued, sales returned to normal. Although the board's reaction against the protesters was not as severe as the ICCS's, the HCCS board did not question the impact its decisions had on sales. At one point, the board discussed the possibility of an injunction to keep the picketers away from the store, although that did not occur.[31]

It can be argued that, like the ICCS, HCCS board's reactions to the protesters might have had a negative effect on the co-op's sales and on its members. From the beginning, some board members sought to discredit the boycott. At the November 1969 board meeting, one board member claimed that California workers did not want to organize. Another board member countered that that information was published by a front organization for grape growers. At that meeting, contentious to say the least, the board asked the general manager to tell picketers that they should leave the premises because the co-op store was private property. Further, the board members argued, the co-op should continue with educational programs and not get involved in politics, which they claimed was in violation of the Rochdale principles. This argument, however, seemed disingenuous because other co-ops had been involved in politics and many were boycotting non-UFW grapes. Second, the board's obligation was to represent the members who were collective owners of the co-op. In the end, board members decided to do their own research and to talk to other co-ops, rather than hold further discussions with the members. They met with Art Danforth of the Co-operative League of America, who was also a board member of the Berkeley Co-op that had removed grapes from its store.[32] These discussions, though, did not change their minds about the boycott.

There was another explanation for why the co-op's sales were down. In 1965, most Hanover members spent only $200 to $499 per year on groceries there. If it were not for the 280 families in the top four buying brackets, whose purchases averaged $30 weekly, the co-op's annual sales would have been even lower. In fact, the average member spent less than $14 per week. A 1969 survey corroborated that many members thought the co-op's prices were too high. One member said she used to shop mostly at the co-op but now did only 10 percent of her shopping there because of its high prices.[33] One reason for increased prices was to finance a new bakery in 1970.[34]

But some questioned the decision to add a bakery, including board president and history professor, Charles Wood. He pointedly asked what drove the HCCS's ideas for expansion. Similarly, some members asked the board whether a bakery was really needed or whether it was simply a "nice" idea. On another note, they thought that if the co-op needed more space to bring in new products, there should be a "serious review of goods now stocked."[35] Here, again, members sought democratic input into their co-op store. Yet the board, in hierarchical fashion, assumed control in the decision-making process.

Questions of Activist Leadership

Members continued to weigh in on various issues. A 1971 survey showed that members did not want phosphate detergents sold in the store. Although the education committee's purpose was to provide information to customers, the general manager pointed out that manufacturers could still give false information about products such as phosphate detergents. The chair of committee then urged those concerned to write their congressperson. Another remedy was that through shelving the co-op could highlight differences in detergents. Here, questions remained. Who made these decisions? Was it left up to the members and customers, who would be informed through education? Or did the general manager or the board ultimately decide?[36] Here again, some members sought a more participatory democracy. In fact, they planned to picket unless the board signed a document not to reorder high phosphate detergents. Ultimately, this issue was handled like the UFW grapes. A group was allowed to set up an exhibit and collect signatures in the store. But if they planned to picket, they would have to contact the police department to find out where they could legally do so.[37] In short, the board was curtailing members' democratic right to protest.

As a matter of course, the education committee provided information to members on phosphates, for example, through articles in their newsletters. The co-op had, in fact, recommended a policy on it and planned to present a motion on the issue, although it is not clear how much the motion reflected members' concerns. However, the committee also found that there was no accurate information about phosphates in detergents and little scientific consensus on what level was considered safe. Should the co-op, the committee asked, support legislative action in New Hampshire? There was currently a federal bill about detergent pollution control as well, prompted by congressional and subcommittee hearings. After the hearings, a 1972 congressional report, "Phosphates in Detergents: Government Action and Public Confusion," recommended the complete elimination of phosphate in detergents. The education committee chair decided to ask a Dartmouth chemistry professor if it was possible to find out what the contents of the detergents on their shelves were.[38]

Again, Charles Wood weighed in on the issue. Here he pointed to larger issues: which products should the co-op sell and, most important, how were those decisions made? As he read the history of the cooperative movement, he noted that one purpose of co-ops was to save money for members. But, he warned, that was not the co-ops' only goal; co-ops needed to guarantee the quality of their products as well. This meant that the board should be "a watchdog for their fellow members' interest." When members told him they would not sign a petition because they believed that the board would act in their best interest, this indicated to him that board members would select products with the best price and quality in mind. He hoped the board would consider this larger context because there were no clear policy guidelines about which products to sell.[39] Although he noted the board's responsibilities, he did not include how the board should respond when members disagreed.

Some members were also worried about synthetic hormones and additives in meat. The co-op's meat supplier then was Armour Company after many smaller, local packing plants had been shut down in the early 1970s. But, members asked, were they forced to shut down because their products were underpriced by larger companies? And, if so, what role might the co-op play in supporting these local businesses? In March 1973, when there was a national boycott against meat because of high prices, the board became concerned about being caught "long" on meat if customers did not buy it. Again, some board members suggested making information available to members. The board's vote was a narrow one, with the president breaking the tie. The store continued to sell meat.[40] In the end, it appears as if the members' concerns about Armour Company and local plants had not been addressed.

Discussions were spirited, especially during 1974. One candidate for president, Professor Alexander Laing, said that the co-op should "put the common good above the individual good." One decision was to remove cigarettes from the shelves, an issue that had been discussed in the mid-1930s. As a solution, a no smoking sign was put up.[41] The lettuce boycott resurfaced as well. A letter had been signed by nineteen employees to overrule the board's decision to remove Teamster lettuce. The argument behind the letter was that the daily store operations should be left to the employees, not the board or co-op members. Like some of the workers at "new wave" co-ops, HCCS workers demanded more participation in decision making. Unfortunately, there were no records of the board's discussion about the workers' letter or any other activity. Instead, it appears as if the board members debated about whether the co-op should exert "a moral influence" in their decision not to sell Teamster lettuce. The board voted six to four that all fresh lettuce and grapes of Teamsters would not be sold at the co-op.[42] Here, board members overruled the workers. And their earlier policy of letting the customer decide had changed, perhaps because of the political character of the present board. As board president, Alexander Laing, stated: "The grape issue is a symptom rather than the real cause of trouble. The Co-op has drifted away from the Rochdale principle of co-operative effort to become a competitive supermarket."[43]

Land in Vermont

The most protracted debate was about the 134 acres of land in Norwich, Vermont, which the HCCS had bought in 1973. As early as 1972 there was discussion about the co-op expanding. There were various options discussed: to stay in the present store but add more storage space and parking; to build a smaller satellite store; or to move the co-op to a new site. Different sites were then considered, including the Norwich land.[44] In looking at its options, the board argued that the HCCS was "the strongest co-operative in New England." Indeed, since the present store had opened in 1963, its business had increased by 130 percent. As the general manager stated: "Our sales now are more than twice the national average per square foot for the grocery business."[45] But the HCCS was outgrowing its store. Plus, it did not want to limit its membership, then at 3,300. Very little could be done with the present location because it could not buy land nearby for expansion. Nor could it build a full second story because of the soil conditions under the store's foundation. Some members were interested in building a "village," which might lead to other cooperative ventures. Another consideration was whether the HCCS should only think in terms of just Hanover or think more in terms of a regional co-op.[46]

What to do with the Norwich land was a lengthy decision-making process, with many ideas advanced. Of most concern to many board and co-op members was how the use or sale of the land would affect the HCCS. A group of emeriti wanted the co-op to stay where it was because it had a significant presence in Hanover. They also hoped that Dartmouth College would consider selling a narrow strip of land near the co-op. (Dartmouth rejected this proposal.) Others thought of the Norwich land in terms of an investment. They wanted to hold on to it because its value would increase over time.[47] Still others thought the land could be used for different purposes and that the co-op could be a catalyst in these projects. Former board president Alexander Laing hoped the projects would be nonprofit oriented and cooperative. Accordingly, one of the first uses of the land was a community garden. In May 1974, thirty-one gardeners signed up to use the Norwich plot.[48]

Other ideas followed and included a garden market, a garden supplies store, and a garden and energy center. In typical HCCS fashion, the co-op formed seven subcommittees of the Norwich land committee: agriculture, housing, medicine and health, produce distribution, recreation, retail expansion, and workshops. There was a Norwich land questionnaire, distributed to members in 1976. Some members responded with a proposal for organic fertilization of the land. Perhaps they were inspired by a Vista proposal for a farmers' market and root cellar in the northern part of Windsor County, sponsored by the Upper Valley Food Co-op in nearby White River Junction, Vermont.[49] There was a proposal for berry growing and for a Co-operative Farmers' Market. The board did agree to lease one acre to the Upper Valley Growers Association, a group of farmers who wanted to start a farmers' market. They also leased twenty acres to a local farmer.[50]

Perhaps one of the more interesting proposals was from a Dartmouth student who wanted to know if the co-op could produce food on its own land. He raised fascinating questions. What crops would they grow? Could the co-op get involved in marketing the produce? Could the growing season be lengthened through greenhouses?[51] Unfortunately, his forward-looking ideas did not receive much attention. Another group suggested starting a low-cost cooperative food store on the land. This would extend the co-op's influence regionally and to the state of Vermont. As this proposal suggested, this co-op might assist those with lower incomes as well. Customers could pack bags of food and mark them, thereby eliminating labor costs. Another idea was to build a co-op greenhouse, and have local crops processed in a cooperative cannery—all feeding into the idea of a cooperative wholesale operation to store products and distribute year-round.[52] The board, though, did not act on any of these ideas, which would have honored the Rochdale principle of assisting other cooperatives.

The HCCS, 1980s–2000s

Nor did the board act on another social reform proposal for cooperative housing. The intent of this group was to find an alternative kind of housing that "avoid[ed] . . . the negative images associated with public housing in the public's eye."[53] In late 1979, a special board meeting was held to discuss leasing or selling fifty to fifty-four acres to Twin Pines Co-operative Housing Association. An option to purchase agreement was signed and voted on by HCCS members.

However, Twin Pines was delayed by Vermont Housing Finance.[54] Apparently too much time took a toll on this plan. The chair of the HCCS's business committee recommended that the co-op not "endanger" its health by investing "its resources too heavily in the Twin Pines endeavor."[55] Nor could the HCCS give Twin Pines Co-op permission to develop housing on land because permission had been withheld by the Norwich Planning Commission until there was an overall plan submitted for all of the co-op land. Still the Hanover Co-op board thought that the Twin Pines Co-op could "move forward," although board members wanted assurance that the Twin Pines' development "would not limit its [HCCS's] future development choices any more than necessary."[56]

The Vermont Housing Authority was interested in the project and had set aside rent subsidy money for twenty units of family housing. But the assessment took longer than expected. By February 1982, Twin Pines was at an impasse and did not have money for the Norwich land. In fact, even if the land had been given to Twin Pines, the Association could not afford to build a road, and pay for a sewage system and other infrastructure. By 1984, HCCS interest in Twin Pines was waning. Twin Pines Housing Association decided to look at buildings in White River Junction and finally bought an apartment building to renovate. They did ask the HCCS for matching funds and the co-op agreed to a short-term loan of $5,000.[57]

The Norwich Land Brings Choices

Throughout the negotiations, the Hanover Co-op board realized that the Norwich land was a good financial investment, whether for agricultural or commercial development. And there were short-term developments for renting the land. For example, the First International Co-operative Future Fair was held there in the summer of 1982. Themed "Co-ops and Networks: Economic Alternatives for the 80s," the fair exhibited new products and services, and co-ops' relationships to one another. The organizers, International Future Fairs Co-operative from Thetford, Vermont, thought that co-ops were the solution to food scarcity globally. It was not clear if the HCCS agreed. But one advantage of having the fair on the Norwich land was that it helped to pay for the land's taxes.[58]

Similarly, while interested in Twin Pines Housing Association, the Hanover Co-op did not ignore other options. The co-op was still considering using the land for a cooperative multiservice center, which would provide low prices, quality items, and various consumer goods. This option might include selling Scan furniture (as did the Hyde Park co-op), garden supplies, food, or a pharmacy and optical store. The HCCS was also thinking about a warehouse storage facility to store co-op labeled food, bulk goods, and local produce. At the same time, the board was considering a request from the Cherry Hill Co-operative Cannery for a loan of $6,000. However, the bank had turned down their loan. Regardless, the co-op was making money, at least $26,000 annually, by leasing the land.[59]

In 1983, the Norwich land was appraised at $5,000 an acre. The land review committee still had different ideas about how to use the land. But in 1984, when Dartmouth College expressed an interest in fifty acres of the Norwich land, the board took this option seriously. Dartmouth College owned adjoining land and wanted to ensure that any development was consistent with its vision. The HCCS board met with Dartmouth College officials and museum organizers to develop a joint plan. In 1984, the museum bought forty-nine acres for an undisclosed price. And Dartmouth and the co-op made a deal. Dartmouth gave the HCCS a forty-five foot strip permanent right of way near their Hanover store and $3,000, and the co-op gave Dartmouth twenty acres of the Norwich land.[60]

Without a doubt, buying and holding on to the Norwich land had been sound financial investments. Early on, board members had agreed that if the land was sold, the money could be used for expansion. And, indeed, that is what happened. Despite the various ideas advanced about cooperation—be it housing, an energy center, an organic farm, or a wood co-op—the co-op was fiscally conservative. But that did not mean that the board did not represent the members' best interest. As the board president stated in 1982: "The Board has always felt that the land represented the Co-op's savings account."[61] And, in fact, members had voted to sell the land.[62]

Indeed, the discussion of expansion had occurred alongside the Norwich land debate. In late 1982, a feasibility study on the co-op's expansion had been conducted. In 1985, the co-op bought Park Street Mobil Station, next to the store and renamed it Co-op Service Center.[63] (The co-op still owns it today.) It, too, turned out to be a good investment. The co-op grocery store was also doing well. By 1980, sales were $4.5 million; the following year, they surpassed the supermarket industry in profits. By 1984, net sales were $5.68 million; from 1987 to 1988, the co-op had tripled its sales volume. In 1986, the HCCS started construction at the co-op store.[64]

Expansion in the Upper Valley

The decision to expand had obviously been a protracted and careful one, with feasibility studies, and member questionnaires and surveys. By 1981, most of the co-op's 5,400 members lived in Hanover, Lyme, and Norwich. In fact, nearly 60 percent of the population of Hanover had joined the HCCS. However, the store did only 5 percent of the total food business in the area. This may have been because of the perception that the co-op's prices were higher than other grocery stores'. Yet according to a comparative price survey in 1981, the co-op was the least expensive supermarket in Upper Valley, when the 3 percent patronage refund was taken into consideration. Still, a survey one year later indicated that members did only half of their shopping at the co-op.[65]

This trend remained the same ten years later. A survey in 1991 showed that most of the co-op's members lived in or near Hanover. The median age of members was forty-four and 80 percent of them had households of two to four people. Slightly more than 50 percent held white-collar occupations; another 20 percent were retired. At least 75 percent of the members were college graduates and over 25 percent had an advanced degree. Significantly, the median household income was almost $50,000, much higher than regional median of about $30,000. Nonetheless, the median level of spending at the co-op in 1990 was only $800 per household. Some members also shopped at Purity Supreme, which seemed to be the co-op's main competitor.[66]

Nonetheless, the co-op was doing well. As of 1992, the board oversaw operations of a $16 million food store and an auto service owned by 11,000 members. In 1993, sales were $18.22 million, making the co-op one of the top three food co-ops in sales in the country. To be sure, the co-op was positioned for yet another expansion. In 1995, the board announced that the co-op would open a second service center on Lyme Road and that a second store was just a few years away.[67] In 1996, the board proposed a store in nearby Lebanon, sending out a member survey to find out what services members wanted for "the store of your dreams."[68] The store opened in October of 1997. It was an environmentally friendly store, with almost twice the square footage as the co-op store in Hanover. Together, both co-ops and the two automotive service centers had 250 employees and 19,000 members in Vermont and New Hampshire. In 1998, the two stores grossed over $34.7 million. In the next year, the HCCS converted its second service center into the Co-op Community Food Market, a convenience store/neighborhood market complete with gas pumps.[69]

Nutritional and Environmental Education

The discussion of expansion during the 1980s and 1990s, however, should not obscure other activities, especially those of the education committee. The committee continued to test products and educate members on nutrition, as well as environmental and health hazards. It published articles on the danger of aerosol sprays and food additives. These activities prompted the board to vote unanimously to endorse a proposed federal regulation to change the manufacture of aerosol spray cans. A public forum was held on food irradiation and consumer safety, sponsored by the HCCS, the Upper Valley Food Co-op, and the Montshire

Museum of Science in 1986.[70] Scientific tests had already shown that irradiated food was dangerous.[71]

In fact, during these two decades, one of the key focuses at the co-op was the environment. A large part of the educational efforts was due to Harrison Drinkwater, the education specialist at the HCCS for eighteen years. There was an environmental interest group, concerned with local and international issues, including rainforests. One newsletter published information about the impact Americans had on tropical forests and what co-op members could do. Other newsletters included information about toxic house cleaning products, pesticides, alternative fuel, organic farming, and chemically intensive farming that threatened food safety, water quality, and economic survival.[72] Like the Hyde Park co-op, the HCCS focused on recycling. Since 1983, the co-op had formed a recycling committee to promote awareness about the issue. In 1989, the HCCS won a recycling award from the New Hampshire Association.[73]

Rosemary Fifield became education director in 1998 and was just as active. She reported to the board on various environmental, nutritional, and other relevant issues, such as the overfishing of swordfish. Here, again, several co-op members wanted the co-op to not sell the fish, especially at its lower price. But swordfish made up 25 percent of the co-op's seafood sales. The solution was a familiar one. The fish would be sold and educational information was placed at the store's seafood department so customers could make up their own minds.[74]

During the 2000s, the HCCS continued its environmental advocacy, while also building stronger local and regional alliances. At a 2004 meeting, the board discussed the co-op's weaknesses and strengths. Their weaknesses were typical of many co-ops: the price image (prices were too high), lack of access to capital, and problems with cash flow. But strengths and opportunities included the image of the co-op as a sense of place in the Upper Valley and as a local community institution; collaborations with other co-ops or similar businesses; and a strong tradition of supporting local and regional growers and producers. That year, the HCCS added twenty local vendors to its list of suppliers, which meant that the co-op then sold over 2,000 local products.[75]

Local and Regional Communities

In effect, the HCCS was not only building local but regional connections. In 2004, the Brattleboro, Vermont Food Co-operative called a meeting of board members and general managers from twenty food cooperatives in Vermont, New Hampshire, and Massachusetts. In 2007, they formed a steering committee to facilitate the group, with the National Grocers Association offering support.

Of the seventeen co-ops surveyed, they had a collective membership of 64,000, annual sales of $161 million, and an overall economic impact of $290 million in their states. In fact, these co-ops had collectively bought $33 million in local products.[76]

During the 2000s, the HCCS "measured" community in terms of the number of events, products, customers, and members. Although this data was evidence-based, it appears as if most members' involvement was primarily as consumers. As with other co-ops, members' turnout at board and other meetings was dismally low. Of 27,547 co-op members, representing 18,604 households, only 623 ballots cast their votes on issues about membership and downsizing the board in 2005. That meant that only 2 percent of the members participated in these decisions.[77] Did this lack of voter turnout mean that members were pleased with the HCCS or that they did not care? As with many large organizations, members may not have felt a sense of identity. During the co-op's celebration of its seventy-fifth anniversary in 2010, the board, education director, and others hopefully educated members about the HCCS's history that emphasized its social and environmental concerns, not only its financial progress.

The HCCS, unlike many other food co-ops, did not experience financial difficulties during the 1970s or 1980s. Unlike the supermarket co-ops in Ithaca and in Hyde Park, its investments had been sound ones. Unlike the ICCS, HCCS board's disagreements with members over boycotts did not result in a loss of membership or sales. Why was this the case? For one, there was no competing food co-op in Hanover, as there had been in Ithaca. Second, the HCCS educational director was proactive as a liaison between the board and the members. Finally, the HCCS's expansions included cooperative businesses that the co-op members used, such as a gas station, rather than the ICCS's rental properties.

The HCCS was one co-op I visited where board members expressed concern about members' low participation. As discussed throughout, as co-ops become larger, members generally become less involved. Even in terms of voting turnout, HCCS's has been very low. In 1992, for example, only 112 of its 15,300 members had voted on the question of the main store's expansion.[78] There are, of course, other explanations for lack of member involvement in addition to the co-op's large membership. One might be that members trust that their board will make the best decisions on their behalf. Another explanation might be that the educational directors have "taken on" the political work of members. During his eighteen-year directorship, Harrison Drinkwater was incredibly proactive on environmental issues; his successor remains committed to environmental and nutritional concerns. But that explanation is not entirely accurate, for the HCCS's education committee, working with the educational director, has also been historically involved in outreach and in influencing the board's and man-ager's decisions. During the 1970s, for example, they investigated the negative environmental effects of phosphate detergents. Through the 1980s and 1990s, the committee continued to test products and educate members on nutrition, and environmental and health hazards.

Another explanation is that HCCS approach to member involvement has typically been through committee work. In some cases, members have joined committees, for example, to investigate food safety and natural foods during the 1960s. When considering which decision to make about the Norwich land, the board created seven subcommittees comprised of members. This approach does give some members the opportunity to influence their co-op's decisions and it diffuses the board's centrality. It is possible that such an approach also diffuses other such activities as protests and boycotts. Overall, the HCCS did not have a strong history of consumer activism in terms of protests and boycotts, as other co-ops did during the 1970s and 1980s.

With the exception of low membership involvement, the HCCS is doing well. In fact, it has been doing so well that in June 2010, it opened its fourth co-op grocery store, this time in White River Junction, Vermont. The HCCS was able to do so, despite the national economic downturn. In fact, as general manager Terry Appleby stated: "We stayed profitable despite the recession and growing competition from chain stores."[79] The store is drawing many customers, over 1,000 daily, even though the town is not as prosperous as Hanover. Time will tell, though, whether the store will "hold its own" or rely on the financial stability of the Dartmouth co-op stores. Time will also tell whether the small Vermont town can support two grocery co-ops—one mile from the new store is the Upper Valley Food Co-op. The HCCS hopes that they will be complementary rather than competitive.[80] Thus far, that seems to be the case.

6

ADAMANT FOOD CO-OPERATIVE
AND PUTNEY FOOD CO-OPERATIVE

I am driving to the oldest American food co-op in Adamant, Vermont, a village with a population of forty-eight. I cut through the Green Mountains, thick and full in this rainy summer season. Before traveling, I had tried to locate a history of the village. There was none, other than what I found on the Adamant Food Co-op website and on Wikipedia. The Wikipedia entry intrigued me. It began: "There is no true boundary to define the village, and as such there is great debate as to what constitutes residence. [Adamant is one of five hamlets, including Calais.] This is, however, purely theoretical as there is no legal, governmental or commercial status associated with residence. The debate has given rise to the common aphorism, 'Adamant is a state of mind.'"[1]

I continue reading the village's curious history. It was originally named Sodom, perhaps inspired by the men from Scotland and Canada who immigrated there to work at the granite quarries. The village built Barney Hall in 1893 so the miners had a place to drink, dance, and play pool after work. Because there was no church, they cleaned the hall on late Saturday nights and held Sunday service there. Not surprisingly, some upstanding residents became concerned and requested a change of the village's name from the state legislature. The description ends by mentioning two long-standing community institutions: the Adamant Food Co-operative, a combination general store/post office; and the Adamant Music School.[2]

I then read about Adamant Music School, started by three eclectic people: Edwine Behre, a pianist, known for her pacifist efforts; Alice Mary Kimball, a

106

Vermont journalist and poet; and her husband, Harry Godfrey, also a journalist. All had met and lived together in Greenwich Village in Manhattan. When they visited Vermont, more than likely they stayed at a working farm near East Montpelier, owned by Florence Weed, Kimball's sister. Many artists, musicians, and writers, mostly from New York City, also visited, perhaps because of Kimball's recommendation. In 1942, Weed encouraged her sister to consider converting an abandoned parsonage in Adamant into a music school. After much renovation, the school opened later that year. The school's website notes that it was founded "to promote noncompetitive piano study in an atmosphere of co-operative living, it still lives by these values today." In fact, several of its founders were active in the Adamant Food Co-op and to this day there are close connections between the school and the co-op.[3]

If any co-op invokes its history, it is the Adamant Food Co-op. Determined to keep their co-op open, members have commemorated it through community traditions and celebrations. So how does a co-op survive in an isolated village in the Green Mountains, where the population does not grow significantly, and where some residents struggle to make ends meet? This co-op provides a counterpoint to the historical trajectory of other co-ops started during the Great Depression. The Adamant Co-op has stayed small, sold on credit, and more often than not has been in the red. This smallest and oldest of food co-ops, then, challenges the business model that many other food co-ops have followed. It raises the questions of whether a co-op's sales and product lines need to increase annually, and whether bigger is better. It also teaches us how important a co-op can be in preserving community life.

Adamant Food Co-operative

When I stop in Montpelier for directions to Adamant, which is only nine miles away, the women at the beauty salon have never heard of it, except for one. But even her directions are vague. When I do arrive in Adamant, I find that it is, indeed, a "state of mind." A neighborhood watch sign alerts me to a village but there is no sign telling me if it is Adamant. I drive by local historian Lois Toby's house. There is a road to the left that will later take me to the schoolhouse, built in 1895, which the co-op used for meetings and celebrations. Down the main road is Sodom pond, with a stand of deep purple lupines. On the other side stands the United Methodist Church, once a place for community gatherings, such as fellowship dinners, Lenten Bible classes, and youth and women's group meetings. And there is the music school, with its grand buildings and expanse of land. Dotted throughout the woods are studios with grand pianos.

FIGURE 5.   Adamant Food Co-op, Paul Seaton, photographer, Adamant Vermont.

The Adamant Food Co-op is farther down and is still in the house of Minnie Horr, Toby's aunt. Once a boarding house for the miners, its two stories were built on a local granite foundation, with a wood-framed barn attached. It later became a small store and the village post office. When Horr retired in 1940, the co-op bought the house. Its two original end chimneys still stand but are no longer used.[4] The co-op has been modernized somewhat with a compost toilet and Internet access. A 1999 description has captured its reluctance to lose too much of its old character: "We are quite sure that it is the only co-op in the state that has both an outhouse and a web page."[5] The Adamant Food Co-op continues to have one foot in the present and one in the past.

I step into the co-op and like the feel immediately. It still adjoins the post office so people stop in throughout the day. It is like a general store, with sundry but practical items. The food items include organic products, an impressive selection of wine, and boxed and canned goods. There is artwork for sale, as well as hardware items. I am surprised by how affordable everything is. Off to the side of the co-op is a porch where people enjoy their morning coffee, browse the Internet, and watch the occasional car go by.

Co-op board president, Janet McCleod, meets me and takes me to the second floor, where she has dug out boxes of old records. I sit on a lawn chair and set my computer on an old wooden table, next to a kitchen where one morning a member bakes two peach-rhubarb pies that she will sell at only $2 per slice. In the next room is an art studio, with paintings by McCleod, who rents the space. She is a third-generation co-oper. Her grandfather was a founding member and her mother, also an artist, served on the co-op board. As I look through the records and glance up to meet current members and customers, I step back into a time of seasons, rituals, and sense of place. I read about annual picnics, spring meetings where maple syrup is drizzled on snow, rummage sales, bingo games, bake sales, the kinds of events most people's grandparents would remember. The co-op records both charm and vex me. Some newsletters have no dates, speaking to a kind of timeless quality. Its web of connections was and continues to be economic, social, cultural, and historical. I realize that the bake sales, then and even now, are just as much about community building as fundraising.

The Adamant Food Co-op still fundraises and anchors itself in a sense of community through rituals and celebrations. Each summer, there is the Adamant Black Fly Festival (a pun on the black tie). Black fly sculptures are on display, as are children's crafts. People from Adamant and nearby are encouraged to dress in "creative attire," buy a box dinner from the co-op, and listen to a guest speaker, much like the old Chautauqua circuit. Sometimes music from the 1940s and 1950s drifts through the evening breeze. A silent auction brings in much-needed money for the co-op.[6] That is another enduring history. The Adamant Co-op never seems to have much money. In fact, it barely breaks even, often relying on the goodwill of an anonymous or local donor. Customers still buy on credit, and the store keeps an informal log where names and items are written down. If someone needs help at the post office next door, the clerk stops to assist them. The Adamant Co-op may be short on cash but it is long on tradition.

The co-op is not ambitious. Its dreams of expansion are simple and practical. It does not want to make a large profit nor could it. Members want it to stay open, so it does need to break even. There is almost a kind of thrift, a balance hanging in the air. The co-op still has an old scale. Most of the shoppers live in Adamant or nearby. A paid clerk works part time; the rest of the time volunteers take over. They donate, cut, and stack wood for the hard winters; they also clean, paint, and shovel. In fact, the store's only computer was built from "spare parts by a village college student."[7] It is no surprise, then, that when customers were recently asked why they shopped there, their responses reflected place and community: "a sense of history," "the pulse of the village, to meet your neighbors," "a feel that I live somewhere . . . a sense of place," and "take care of each other."[8]

Perhaps the Adamant Food Co-op has survived because of its very isolation. Native Vermonters have long been characterized as being self-reliant and independent. They are known for having a strong sense of place and seeing themselves as different from newcomers or "uplanders" who have moved to the state.[9]

At one Friday night dinner, co-op members introduced themselves to me according to their nativity. Some were from Connecticut and New York; others had lived on land kept in their families for several generations. Regardless of their origins, the members collectively decided who would cook what food for the Friday night fundraisers.

Trying to Break Even

In 1935, an Adamant minister led discussions about cooperatives, based on literature he had received from the Co-operative League of the U.S.A. (CLUSA). That spring, eleven families invested five dollars each to start a buying club. Of the subscribers who signed their names, at least three were women: Florence Weed and Ella Parker, East Montpelier; and Laura Robinson, Adamant.[10] The purpose of the Adamant Food Co-operative was straightforward: "to render food, fuel, clothing, supplies, and other necessities of life available to members as economically as possible by means of the united fund and united efforts of these members through the method of purchasing, distributing, and producing in common."[11] As such, the co-op sold hardware and household supplies, firewood, clothing, and tools. It bought maple syrup and eggs from farmer members.[12]

At the 1936 annual meeting, twenty-two persons were present. With assets of nearly $825 and liabilities of $812, money was on their minds. Members passed an amendment to the co-op's constitution: "that the highest salary shall be only five times the minimum wage in the organization."[13] There were no records of how much the first co-op manager, Clarence Fitch, was paid. Given the Depression years and the lean finances of the co-op, it is unlikely that it was much. Nonetheless, Fitch financially assisted the co-op whenever he could. In 1937, he loaned the co-op $150 at 5 percent interest. This good will was rewarded by a small increase in his salary. That year, the board also decided to hire a clerk to assist him at $7.50 a week; in 1939, they raised her salary to $10.[14]

One immediate concern to the members was transportation. Because the co-op was not on routes where wholesaler grocers delivered, it had to bring in food and other goods. By necessity, it bought its own truck. The co-op then decided to deliver groceries to those who did not own cars. In 1936, one member gave the names of two families who would patronize the store if the co-op truck delivered to their homes. Members later decided not to include these families on the delivery route, although it is not clear why. More than likely, it was the road conditions, as truck repairs became an added cost for the co-op. In early 1937, the truck brakes needed to be replaced; later that year, two tires had to be patched. Finally, in 1938, members deliberated on whether the old truck should be repaired at $50 or whether they should buy another one. The next year, they exchanged it for a new truck for $240.[15] In late 1938, when the co-op finally got a phone, the members were able to order food and other items directly from New York and drive there in their new truck.[16]

Another solution to ordering food was to work with a food buying club in Plainfield, a nearby village. One advantage was that they could buy in larger volume and at wholesale prices, since both groups had joined the Eastern Co-operative Wholesale.[17] But there was another reason to collaborate with the Plainfield club. It was the home of Goddard College, whose president Royce Pitkin was a strong advocate of cooperatives. Raised on a Vermont farm and mentored by progressive educators at Columbia University, Pitkin believed strongly in college education that promoted community development in Vermont. After consulting with Vermont senator George Aiken and his adviser, Ralph Flanders, he decided that the college should offer courses on cooperatives, as well as on agricultural and community studies.[18] Adamant Food Co-op members were pleased with Pitkin's ideas. One member commended him on the college's possible name change to Greatwood Farm. Referring to the known cooperative site in Antigonish, Nova Scotia, Pitkin and others hoped that Plainfield would become the Antigonish of New England.[19]

Despite these high hopes, the co-op continued to face a number of financial problems, among them extending credit. During the first quarter in 1936, unpaid bills amounted to $38. Members discussed credit at their meetings, for example, whether it should be extended to one customer until her monthly pension check arrived. In her case, they took no action. Certainly, the issue of credit was compounded by the Depression, as well as the cyclical economy of rural Vermont. In 1940, the manager resolved the problem by using some of his own money to cover the shortage. At the same time, he submitted a list of those receiving credit and their amounts due at each monthly meeting. By 1942, he sent letters to those delinquent in their payments, warning them that their credit was limited to two weeks.[20] Regardless of the credit problems, the co-op seemed to be holding its own. The 1936 sales were $8,200; by 1937, they were $11,850. In 1939, the 88 family members received a 2 percent patronage refund.[21]

Political and Educational Outreach

Perhaps because the co-op was in an isolated region, its members wanted to learn more about other cooperatives and the challenges they faced. Some asked that a speakers' program be organized to bring in people from larger cooperatives. Members also wanted to engage in political discussion and action. At the 1939 meeting, a member read a letter from the nearby county unit of the Labor's Non-Partisan League, a labor group organized around Franklin Roosevelt's reelection and progressive politics. They asked the co-op to endorse the work of the La Follette Civil Liberties Committee, which was then investigating how some large industries had skirted collective bargaining with unions. Indeed, the National Industrial Recovery Act and the Wagner Act had encouraged workers to union-ize and fight for their civil liberties. The La Follette Committee actively investi-gated violations of workers to organize unions and bargain collectively, and often worked closely with the Congress of Industrial Organization (CIO).[22]

In early 1939, Harold Ickes asked the president for more appropriations for the committee, to which Roosevelt agreed. Senator Lewis B. Schwellenbach of Washington then introduced a resolution that the committee investigate labor problems in California. The committee had been influenced by John Steinbeck's *Grapes of Wrath* and photographers, such as Dorothea Lange, who documented Depression-era hardships. But they were especially influenced by Carey McWil-liams, whose book *Factories in the Field* had chronicled California's 250,000 farm workers' attempts to organize unions and farm owners' persistent efforts to sty-mie that activism. The phrase, "factories in the field," was not simply rhetori-cal. Because farm laborers were not considered industrial laborers, the National Labor Relations Act had excluded them. At the hearings, the committee learned how agriculture had, indeed, become a large industry. Growers, such as Sunkist, which McWilliams referred to as "Gunkist Orange," had turned their farms into factories. And as agricultural laborers testified, their working conditions were dire. As expected, the committee found violations of workers' rights. At the Ada-mant Food Co-op, members were asked to write to their senators to support this resolution. As such, members advocated for economic democracy not just within their co-op but for others as well. Co-op president Florence Weed proceeded to write two resolutions for the Labor's Non-Partisan League and suggested that one more be written to promote a Credit Union Law in Vermont.[23] Here, again, members acted upon other forms of cooperatives to ensure economic self-determination within their state.

Partly through the co-op members' advocacy, modern amenities arrived in Adamant and other parts of Vermont. The Rural Electrification Act of 1936, cre-ated through an executive order of President Roosevelt, established electricity and telephone services in the region. Prior to this act, fewer than 10 percent of farmers had electricity. Between 1935 and 1939, the number of farms with elec-tricity more than doubled through federal loans to farmers' cooperatives.[24] In 1941, a year after the Adamant Food Co-op bought Horr's house, they installed electricity, and bought electric gas pumps and a refrigerator for the store.[25]

Community Connections

During the 1940s, the co-op's sales increased and its property expanded. In 1940, the co-op celebrated its fifth anniversary. That year, the Adamant Co-op's sales reached almost $22,000. Its sales continued to increase, despite the shortage of sugar during the war and the "substantial raise" of $25 weekly for the manager.[26] In 1944, the board discussed a new venture: buying "Lackey's Store" in Maple Corner, a nearby village. The next year, they bought the store, borrowing $500 from the Adamant Credit Union to make improvements. In 1948, the Adamant Food Co-op cleared almost $2,600 and the Maple Corner Food Co-op nearly $2,300; the next year 1949, those numbers were $2,400 and $2,150, respectively.[27]

During the 1950s, both co-ops' finances continued to improve, albeit slowly. In 1950, the Adamant Food Co-op's annual sales were $67,000; in 1955, $76,000; and in 1959, $81,250. Generally, the Adamant Food Co-op had slightly better sales than the Maple Corner Food Co-op during the late 1940s. But during the 1950s, sales were higher at the latter, perhaps because it sold beer and because more summer residents lived there. After several years of being in the red, both co-ops were in the black by 1953. But they had no reserves, which led the board to discuss how to add to their working capital. One idea was to increase the membership, especially among young people. Toward that end, they hoped to recruit them through more entertainments at their annual meetings.[28] The Adamant Food Co-op newsletter also asked for "large families with hungry children to settle in the Adamant-Maple Corner area." As one member remarked, "On such small changes in the community the success or failure of our store depends."[29] Finally, in 1955, the Adamant Food Co-op retained some of its annual surplus toward a working capital fund.[30]

As in earlier years, community rituals and connections were celebrated at the Adamant Food Co-op throughout the 1950s. At the co-op's quarterly meetings, held at the Adamant schoolhouse, co-op members enjoyed "the appropriate spring tonic"—sugar on snow with pickles and doughnuts—during social hour. Meetings still included an evening of games, cards, dancing and games for the children, as well as adult games and a candy pull. On Arbor Day, the co-op joined Maple Valley Community Center and the Calais Livewires 4-H Club in planting flowers, shrubs, and trees at Maple Corner. The Adamant Food Co-op newsletter also published village news, not just co-op news: who played the fiddle at a square dance festival; who was preaching at the East Village church; whose children had their artwork displayed in Burlington. Such news connected the co-op to the community and vice versa. Last, the co-op supplied customers with seasonal items. For example, they reminded members that with the approaching colder weather it was time to order mittens for the children. Before Thanksgiving, there were notices to order turkeys, dressed the way customers requested.[31]

Co-op members formed a closely knit community but this created some problems, especially with delinquent accounts. In fact, the problem of credit persisted through the 1950s and 1960s. In 1953, the manager again submitted a list of overdue accounts. The board passed a motion that the manager contact those persons and warn them that their bills would be sent to a collector if not paid. The next year, however, he recommended writing off all old bills, $100 at Adamant and $300 at Maple Corner, to which the board agreed. In 1955, the board gave the manager permission to contact a lawyer and settle the debts. Through the 1960s, both co-ops still collected bills through a small claims court. The board recommended setting up a system for advance credit and customer charge accounts. Similar to the Maple Corner Co-op, the Adamant Co-op published an end-of-the-month report on customer charges and advance credits.[32]

Not surprisingly, these credit problems compromised the co-op's profits. At one 1961 meeting, members discussed ways to bring in more money through advertising, weekly specials, charging for deliveries, and selling arts and crafts. Regardless of their ideas, the net profits for Adamant Food Co-op remained low. In 1961, it was only $220; in 1964, $321; and in 1965, $58. To complicate matters, the Maple Corner Food Co-op flooded in the early 1960s. By 1967, the Adamant Food Co-op, with a membership of 200, showed a profit of $978; the net loss for the first half of 1969, however, was $226.[33]

Nor were the 1970s better years for both co-ops. During the winter of 1971, both co-ops were "in trouble." The net loss for the first six months of 1971 was $4,991, plus there was $3,281 in accounts payable. Apparently, unpaid customer bills remained a problem. The co-op asked one member either to pay his bill or to give service to the co-op in some way. On a larger scale, the lack of cash flow meant fewer product selections. In fact, the co-op's survey noted that members were concerned about the low number of items in stock. Receipts for 1970 showed more practical items for sale, such as mittens, caps, socks, batteries, jello, dried beef, coffee mate, sauerkraut, vinegar, and sugar. By early 1972, the consensus was that the Adamant Food Co-op had to change to survive.[34]

Surviving in the 1970s

The co-op turned to one of its friends, Vermont senator George Aiken, who promised to check on small business legislation to see if the co-op could "get relief."[35] Aiken asked the Farmer Co-operative Service (FCS) to act as a consultant to the co-op. The FCS's report noted that the co-op needed more capital to improve its buildings. As it described the Adamant Food Co-op, it had two wood burning stoves but no modern plumbing. Its foundation was not strong enough for upper level storage and storage was important so they could buy in larger quantities and pass the savings on to their customers. Both stores had post offices, which "ha[d] become general meeting and gathering places which give a distinct feeling of belonging and neighborliness."[36] The FCS also reported that most people purchased only some of their groceries from the co-ops. Both co-ops had tried to stock staples but had limited store space. Nearly 40 percent of the items at the co-ops were co-op labeled from Framingham, Massachusetts, which sent a truckload to Hanover, New Hampshire. The Adamant Food Co-op then sent a truck to pick up whatever it needed. Adamant's problems were a lack of space and volume, a decrease in volunteer labor, and an increase in wages. From 1966 to 1971, sales had increased from $84,500 to $124,600. But operating costs had also increased from $13,500 in 1966 to $21,800 in 1971. Clearly the co-op could not compete with the grocery stores in the Montpelier area. The report stated that "at the present level of sales, it [wa]s difficult for Adamant to operate as a viable business."[37] The FCS recommended that both co-ops not stock items that did not sell well; that the Maple Corner Co-op be "modernized"; that both co-ops buy from a nearby wholesale grocer; and that both co-ops start a staff training program.[38]

One financial solution came unexpectedly in late 1972, when someone made an offer to buy the Maple Corner Food Co-op for almost $12,000. Although this might have improved finances for the Adamant Food Co-op, the Adamant community wanted to keep both stores open. More than likely, they thought that both co-ops could weather their financial storms. Still the Adamant Co-op continued to have problems. It was losing customers to Dudley's Store, a general store in East Montpelier. At the 1972 annual meeting, with thirty members present, the board admitted that the profit that year was only $770. The lack of capital, as well as volunteers, persisted. The board told members that the co-op needed $10,000 to expand its storage and display space.[39] One member later wrote a letter to other members, encouraging them to think not just about the future but the past. As she suggested, the two co-op stores "helped us 'put down roots.'" She continued, "Let's help new neighborhoods put down roots—here. Co-op stores started as centers of community and should remain that. [The] question: do we want to sustain these centers of 'community'?" If so, she recommended that 100 people invest in $5 shares.[40] Even that did not seem to have happened.

By the end of 1972, the Adamant Food Co-op was still operating at a financial loss. Several two-party checks of over $800 had been cashed and returned to the store, forcing the co-op to file a civil suit. The board told members that the two co-ops could not compete with larger grocery stores and neither one was viable. A special meeting was called in March 1973 to discuss closing the Adamant Food Co-op. A vote was taken and members approved of the closure. However, a lawyer claimed the decision was illegal because it had not been approved by a vote of two-thirds of all outstanding shareholders. Another vote was taken and members then decided to keep Adamant Food Co-op open after selling the Maple Corner Food Co-op, whose sale was approved at $17,200.[41] The Adamant Food Co-op continued to have financial problems through the late 1970s. Its sales improved somewhat when it decided to sell beer, wine, gas, and tobacco products, all to be paid in cash. But by October 1978, the co-op owed $1,700; the amount that people owed to the co-op was $1,350. Obviously, if people paid their bills, the co-op could have eliminated most of its debt. The next year was not much better, though. In 1979, accounts payable were almost $1,500, some of which were sent to a collection agency.[42]

Financial problems persisted through the 1980s. Accounts payable continued to be "reason for alarm," contributing to a net loss in 1981 of $232. Trips to Hanover were also a problem, for there were never enough funds on hand to buy enough to make the trip worthwhile. Someone suggested that in order to make it through the winter of 1981, the store should be open only part of the week. To complicate matters, a loan with the Adamant Credit Union was delinquent.[43] The board suggested sending letters to all creditors, pointing out the "co-op's frantic need for capital."[44] That year, a co-op member William C. Shouldice came forward and offered to buy the Adamant Food Co-op. He knew that residents wanted to keep it and he promised to still offer case lots and discount prices to co-op members. The board wrote to the Hanover Consumer Co-operative Society for advice. If the Adamant Co-op were sold, the Hanover Co-op reminded them, members would lose their greatest asset. The Hanover Co-op recommended maintaining ownership of the store. The members agreed.[45]

Celebrating History and Traditions

Adamant Food Co-op members decided to step up the fundraisers to bring in more money for the co-op. There was a summer fair (which raised $770), bingo games, and rummage and bake sales. The co-op organized children's events, a parade, and music. The co-op was also encouraged by summer business in 1982. There were orders for supplies by the music school and from its students. The November sales that year were stronger because of the hunting season when the store opened early and held a hunter's breakfast. Still, accounts receivable were over $700. Once again, the co-op sent letters to those customers, warning them they would be denied credit until they paid their accounts. They also reminded the customers that it was one of the few co-ops where a person could still buy goods on credit.[46]

By the mid-1980s, the co-op was making a small profit because of donations and rentals. In 1984, the co-op made $1,800 from renting the second floor; it had also received a $500 gift from Frank Suchomel, director of the music school. At the fiftieth semi-annual meeting of the co-op in 1985, the co-op announced it had made a net gain of almost $3,500 from renting the upstairs and its mail order business. The co-op continued to be patronized during the summer months by the music school and its students. The co-op, however, was concerned that it had become a convenience store for its members, who did not buy groceries there regularly. If they did, the board argued, the co-op would be in less financial trouble.[47]

Despite its fluctuating finances, the co-op and its members continued to celebrate the seasons and holidays, including maple sugar time, Thanksgiving, and Independence Day. The co-op sold fudge for the Fourth of July celebration in East Calais. There was a bake sale, a contest for scarecrows, a harvest bazaar, and dinner. Adamant Apple Works sold homemade cider in the late fall; handmade crafts, such as dried flower wreaths, dolls, and leather belts, were sold before Christmas. During the summer, the co-op sold postcards featuring local scenes, blown glass artwork, homemade strawberry and rhubarb jams, and copies of the Green Mountain Folklore Society's cookbook. In early spring, the co-op advertised its supply of flower seeds.[48]

The co-op newsletter continued to record the history and traditions of the village. Here again, the co-op evoked a sense of history and continuity of village life. One member wrote of her experiences of her first year in the Vermont country. Her memories included picking apples and raspberries, making apple butter, and skiing through the raspberry patch. Alongside historical memories were birth announcements, spring bingo ads, garden news, bird reports, and local events, such as a fiddlers' concert, a flea market, and the annual strawberry festival. In 1988, when the co-op celebrated its fifty-third anniversary, the members organized a parade, Adamant style, with the Plainfield Hobo Band and Adamant Music School Marching Kazoo Band.[49]

Even though the mood was celebratory that summer, by December the board had voted to close the Adamant Food Co-op the following month. But fifteen neighbors objected and promised to donate $450 collectively a month through April to keep the co-op open. The board agreed and decided to vote again at the end of April. To be sure, memories of other hard times had stirred people's determination to keep the co-op store open. They reminisced about the delivery truck, which had broken down in 1976 when there was no money for a new one. They also remembered the credit union failure in the mid-1980s that affected the co-op. Taken over by the Federal Deposit Insurance Corporation, the credit union moved to East Montpelier, thereby severing ties between the co-op and the union.[50]

The recommitment seemed to give new life to the co-op. Sales for 1988 and 1989 were almost $27, 000, with a profit of almost $5,500. In March 1989, an anonymous donor gave almost $800. According to the 1990 Annual Report, sales were slightly over $40,000, with a gross profit around $6,700. Again, there were fundraising efforts for a salary fund (for a manager), a sewage fund, and a building fund. In 1990, the co-op applied to the Preservation Trust of Vermont for a $500 matching grant to study the co-op building. They received an award and hired a consulting architect, who advised that its foundation be prepared. In October 1990, the co-op applied to the Vermont Division for Historical Preservation for a matching grant of $5,200 to repair the roof and foundation. Funding was approved the following year.[51]

The co-op did not keep many records during the 1990s and 2000s. But the March 2006 newsletter was not unlike earlier ones. There was a request for donations for a porch, indoor plumbing, refinishing the second floor, a dishwasher, a water heater, a composting toilet, and insulation. There would soon be running water at the co-op so that it could install an indoor composting toilet and a sink. Janet McCleod had designed a porch overlooking the waterfall. Friday night cookouts were popular. From all accounts, the Adamant Food Co-op was and is still holding its own. It grows slowly, one step at a time. In 2010, it celebrated its seventy-fifth anniversary with fanfare.[52] As one member remarked about the co-op, "It persists in the face of the modern world."[53] It is likely that it will remain the oldest food co-op in this country for some time.

Putney Food Co-op

I am sitting at one of the co-op's tables, near the deli, with a box of historical materials. Folk music from the 1960s plays overhead. There is a long line for lunch and espresso on this Saturday afternoon. The noon hour customers intrigue me. At the table next to me is a youthful-looking man, busy sending e-mails, with a *New York Times* at his side. (In fact, there are many copies of the *New York Times* reserved for customers.) There are some older timers with canes, as well as young children whose parents coax them with healthy food. My immediate thoughts are that Putney is a haven for the independently wealthy, old-time hippies, progressives, entrepreneurs, and perhaps transients. There is even some ethnic diversity here. I have seen a handful of African Americans and wonder if they live here or nearby. Vermont is not known for its ethnic diversity. So who is a flatlander anyway in this state? You can live here for years but if you are not born here, you are an outsider. So some locals tell me. It appears otherwise in Putney.

Community Dreamers

Putney is a different kind of village from Adamant. For one, its population is much larger, slightly more than 5,200 residents. Likewise, Putney has more wealth, with the average income being almost twice as high as Adamant's—$51,201 and $25,625, respectively.[54] Whereas Adamant is somewhat isolated, Putney is right off the interstate, making it a stopover for tourists. Last, Putney's history of utopian communities, progressive schools, arts and crafts industries, and hippy communes marks it as distinct from Adamant's more rugged character. Regardless of their differences, both reflect a kind of Vermont tenacity and independence. The Putney Food Co-op is also a long-standing co-op, the third oldest in the country.

Putney has always drawn dreamers to its community. When John Humphrey Noyes Jr. was expelled from Yale University in the early 1830s for declaring that he did not sin, he relocated to Putney, close to his native town of Brattleboro. Although his license to preach was revoked, he continued to do so, evoking the authority of his own intuition and his personal relationship to God. In 1836, he established the Putney Bible School, which became a communal society in 1844. Like most utopian societies, this one was fraught with contradictions. Members practiced complex marriage (loosely termed "free love" by Noyes, for all men were "married" to all women), male continence, and Perfection (living without sin). But the community became fractured when Noyes was accused of adultery in 1847. The group relocated to Oneida, New York, where it became known as the Oneida Community. With a membership of 300, it survived there until 1879, when Noyes fled to Canada to avoid arrest on the charge of rape. Although most readers have been intrigued by the society's sexual practices, pertinent to the study of cooperatives were the society's economic self-sufficiency and communal labor. Members made silk thread, as well as grew and canned their own fruits and vegetables. Later, they became known for their silver-plated flatware.[55]

By the end of the 1800s, there were fewer than 1,000 residents in Putney. One of those residents was George Aiken. Aiken had joined a grange in high school and later studied horticulture. In 1914, he planted fields of raspberries, which became the Green Mountain Orchards. He was also active in Putney's local government as town moderator for six years and school director for fifteen. In 1931, he was elected to represent Putney in the state legislature. Although Aiken rose to state politics as lieutenant governor from 1935 to 1936 and then governor in 1937, he remained on the Putney school board. While governor, he continued to advocate for farmers and the "common man" by breaking up business monopolies in the state.[56] When he became state senator from 1941 to 1975, he continued to support rural Vermonters, as noted in his involvement with the Adamant Food Co-op.

During the 1930s, despite the loss of many jobs at the mill, Putney became known for its progressive schools, especially the Putney School and the Experiment in International Living. Carmelita Hinton, founder of the Putney School, had worked at the Hull House, a social settlement in Chicago. While there, she had been influenced by progressive educator and pragmatist philosopher John Dewey, who had started a laboratory school at the University of Chicago. In fact, Dewey was himself a native Vermonter, whose concepts of community drew heavily from rural traditions in which he had been raised. Hinton converted the Elm Lea Farm near Putney into a school that emphasized the arts, drama, and manual skills. Faculty included politically liberal professors and artists who believed in progressive education. Among them was Donald Watt, a pacifist from Syracuse, who enrolled his children there. He later established the Experiment in International Living in Putney so that high school students could live with families in Europe and more authentically experience culture and life there.[57]

It was within this context of experiential and experimental living that the Putney Food Co-op was established in 1941. It was also a time when fuel shortages, due to World War II, made it hard to procure some grocery items. Led by Carol Brown, a shopkeeper, a group of Putney residents rented a store building, which they later bought in 1944.[58] The co-op's purposes were initially to "engage in the acquiring, distributing, and exchanging of commodities, goods and services for the primary and mutual benefit of the patrons of this association or their patrons, as ultimate consumers."[59] It is not clear whether the co-op competed with the village general store, which closed in 1949. By and large, most of the businesses that had survived during the 1940s and 1950s were arts and crafts related and catered to tourists: a wood working shop, a basket company, a candy store, tourist cabins and roadside stands.[60]

Communes, Collectives, and Co-ops

Putney changed dramatically during the 1960s when Windham College, originally established in 1951 for foreign students, began to accept American students. In fact, it not only became a haven for students drawn to its arts and music programs but for hippies and draft dodgers. Many of its faculty members were Quaker pacifists, who had established the Putney Preparative Meeting in 1965. Although the practice of preparative meetings had been largely abandoned by the early twentieth century, its informal and egalitarian approach reflected members' attempt to establish a deeper sense of community and perhaps one with utopian sensibilities. However, some townspeople misunderstood them and thought they were communists. Added to this conflict, some townspeople disliked the influx of hippies and threatened them with sheep shears.[61]

In fact, the 1960s witnessed a number of communes and collectives in Vermont, especially in the Putney area. One journalist noted that from 1965 to 1975, nearly 100,000 young people came to the Green Mountains of Vermont, and many stayed and settled in communes. One of those communes was Free Farm, a 150-acres farm bought by artist John Douglas for $18,000 in 1965.[62] Douglas had been a member of Newsreel—a filmmakers' collective in New York City that made documentaries about labor strikes, student revolts, the war, and the Black Panthers. As he explained his reasons for establishing the commune, later called the Red Clover Collective: "I wanted to live a nice country life while making films."[63] In the late 1970, however, the FBI raided the commune, thinking they were harboring Weather Underground fugitive Bernadine Dohrn. As Douglas recalled: "They lined us all up, searched the house and left empty-handed." In 1971, the group made a documentary film about how the police tried to stop them from harvesting vegetables they had planted at Windham College.[64] Another group was Free Vermont, a coalition of groups that started a People's Bank so that wealthier communes could help poorer ones. The group started *Vermont Railroad*, a newspaper published at Franklin County's Earthworks commune. In nearby Brattleboro, there was a worker-owned restaurant, Common Ground, and a car repair shop, Liberation Garage, where women learned how to fix cars. There was a free health clinic in Burlington, a children's collective school in southern Vermont, and forums to protest the war and advocate for environmental issues.[65]

On a larger scale, there were over a dozen food and farm co-ops throughout the state, as well as a cooperative distribution center during the 1960s. As Jim Higgins, a journalist, recalled about the newly created Plainfield Co-op:

> One of our goals was to bring into our co-op network local born adults. It was an energetic effort to reach out with our ideas of co-operative business practices and wholesome food and subverting the system as it were through tremendously reduced prices. There were many co-op discussions about products we would offer that would bridge the gap, so we vigorously pursued non-food products from [wood]stoves to chainsaws, to ball jars, snowshoes, [and] skis; products that generally

had interest to those around us who would not necessarily be interested in brown rice and soy beans. That helped a great deal simply breaking social barriers. They had to come into the co-op to buy it.[66]

What appeared to be missing from these recollections was an understanding of the long-standing traditions of cooperatives, of utopian societies, and of the crafts and arts tradition in the Putney area and in Vermont generally.

Politics and Boycotts

The records of the Putney Food Co-operative are spare. Nonetheless, it is evident that the development and politics of the Putney Co-op were different from Adamant's. For one, the Putney Food Co-op held active discussions about boycotts, one of which was the grape boycott. By 1987, the co-op honored both the grape and tuna boycotts. However, that year someone proposed lifting the ban on the six-year grape boycott since the Brattleboro co-op then sold nonunion grapes. There was a "lively" discussion. Some were concerned that those not present would be upset if nonunion grapes were sold. The rejoinder was that those absent should have been at the meeting. Regardless of the turnout, twelve members voted yes to stop the boycott, ten no, and three abstained. The board then decided that a boycott was not appropriate because it did not follow the Rochdale principle of political neutrality. One must wonder why, then, a boycott had been allowed for six years. Nonetheless, the board presented a bylaw amendment to allow boycotts but that did not get the required two-thirds majority vote.[67]

In 1990, there were two other boycotts. One was against Gillette products because the company did extensive animal testing. The co-op removed their products from its shelves and bought other products to replace them. In response to the question of whether it was fair to boycott one company but not another, the board stated that boycotting Gillette was the first step in investigating other companies who did similar kinds of testing. At the annual meeting, forty-one members voted in favor of the boycott, with none opposed. Another boycott, initiated by members, was against the Putney Food Co-op itself. Although details were not forthcoming, members were pressing the board for a fair termination policy to protect co-op staff from being fired in the manner as one of its managers had. It is not clear whether such a policy was created but the co-op did have a high turnover of employees.[68]

A second difference between the co-ops was that the Putney Food Co-op was more involved in environmental and politics issues than Adamant's. The Putney Food Co-op was active in recycling during the early 1990s. For example, it participated in a pilot recycling program for aseptic packages and paid members to reuse bags. It donated its garbage to a person interested in composting.[69] In terms of politics, the co-op continued to discuss animal rights and considered a ban on Procter & Gamble products. They placed an article on animal cruelty on the shelves so that customers could make informed decisions. Policies related to animal cruelty were also presented at a summer meeting in 1993. Apparently, there was a heated discussion not only about a policy on animal-tested products but the philosophy of the Putney Food Co-op.[70] Clearly not everyone agreed, prompting one board member to comment on the controversy and lack of "co-operative spirit."[71] However, this is the very heart of participatory democracy, where conflict and differences of opinions often co-exist.

The third difference between the two co-ops was that Putney's did not suffer the same financial losses as Adamant's. Here it is difficult to detail the financial development of the Putney Food Co-op from the 1940s to the 1980s because of the lack of records. Financial records from the 1980s, however, indicated that its sales were high. For example, 1987 was a good year, with increased sales of 14 percent over the previous one. In 1987, the patronage refund was diverted to co-op needs, including a kitchen on the second floor, new plumbing, heating and air conditioning, and a new freezer. In 1988, however, a small patronage refund was returned to its members. In 1989, there was another growth in sales of over 14 percent.[72] By 1990, the co-op was in good financial shape, with a net savings of $10,290. A market analysis showed that if the co-op moved into natural foods, it would do well. The consultant also recommended building a new store. This made sense, for the co-op store was overcrowded. In 1989, two committees were set up: a financial one to determine what was financially feasible in terms of renovating, moving, or building a new store; and a planning/building committee for an actual building.[73]

A New Co-op and Village Center

Members were excited about a new store, which they thought might become the "center of village life."[74] The co-op hoped to solicit member loans in the amount of $90,000 to $100,000. In fact, the incomes of many of its members were high enough to support this effort. A 1990 co-op survey ($n = 204$) showed that over 40 percent had incomes above $30,000, almost 20 percent above $50,000. Although most members lived in Putney or the surrounding communities, less than one-third said that the co-op was their primary food store. In fact, just as many considered the Brattleboro Co-op their main source. The consultant concluded that an expansion of the Putney Co-op—that is, a deli, meat department, and bakery—might get customers to shop more at the Putney store.[75]

In 1991, Putney Co-op celebrated its fiftieth anniversary. That year, there was a large turnout of over 400 people at its annual meeting. As one member noted: "I realized just how special the Co-op is when I knew everybody's name. The Co-op does provide a sense of community to our town."[76] The co-op members then voted to move to a new location.[77] Ironically, during 1991, sales had fluctuated greatly and at one point the co-op was in the red. That did not appear, however, to diminish members' enthusiasm for a new co-op. On May 2, 1992, 150 people gathered to break ground for a store that would have more than double the space for groceries, fifteen seats for eating, an expanded deli, a full-length front porch, and a front yard with picnic tables.[78]

As of 2010, the co-op seems to be prospering, despite its small membership. At least 650 or 20 percent of the town residents are members. Its members still enjoy a reciprocal agreement with the Brattleboro Co-op. Both co-ops sell a great deal of local, organic vegetables, fruits, meats, cheeses, and other dairy products. Indeed, the Putney Food Co-op is still the center of village life. In 2009, they started monthly Putney Community Dinners to promote local foods. At least 230 community members attended the first one.[79]

Both the Adamant and Putney Food Co-ops reflect traditions, community, and a sense of place. But they do so in different ways. The Adamant Food Co-op not only celebrates its historical rituals but has created new ones. The Putney Food Co-op remains "alternative," while also catering to travelers off the interstate. Situated within the Green Mountains, both cooperatives draw from local connections to dairy farms and local producers. Most promising to these and other co-ops is a growing cooperation in the state among farmers, producers, and cooperatives. This, too, builds on a strong history. In 1961, there were at least eleven consumer and producer cooperatives in the state, with an annual business of $60 million. By 2009, of the forty worker-owned businesses in the state, 10 percent were organized as democratic co-ops.[80] They would do well to learn from the Adamant and Putney Food cooperatives.

Members of both co-ops have opportunities to grocery shop elsewhere. Adamant is less than ten miles from Montpelier, as is Putney from Brattleboro, which has a larger food co-op. Yet members of the Adamant and Putney co-ops have chosen to support their own institutions. Perhaps that is because both have built on their own community traditions and long-standing history. And, in the case of the Adamant Co-op, it is in the same building as the post office, a place that residents regularly visit. Yet, at the Adamant Food Co-op, many shoppers were middle-age, unlike at Putney, where the young and old came for groceries and lunch. Here, my concern is one that the Adamant co-op historically understood: to ensure its survival, the co-op will need to involve the younger generation. If younger people do not move to the area, will the co-op survive? Isolation can be both a blessing and a bane. It can strengthen a small community but it can also give a community a fragile future. My hope is that there will be Adamant residents in the future who will get their groceries at the co-op and their mail next door.

Part II

FOOD FOR PEOPLE OR PROFIT?

FOOD COOPERATIVES, 1960S–1990S

Many images come to mind when thinking of the 1960s and 1970s: the Whole Earth Catalog, with instructions for building your own geodesic dome; organic gardening; hippies living off the land; the Free Speech Movement; the Vietnam War protests; the Civil Rights movement; free health clinics; psychedelic drugs and music; Caesar Chavez and the lettuce and grape boycotts; Earth Day; the Kent State killings; and flower power. There were, though, other powerful and ominous images: smog and pollution, crabgrass killers sprayed on lawns, more processed foods, the population explosion, gas rationing, oil embargos, DDT, and nuclear power plants.

Those of us who came of age then were full of hope. We actually believed we could change the world through collective, not corporate, approaches. There were food co-ops, as well as bakery, book, and bike co-ops, childcare collectives, artists' colonies, and back-to-earth communes. This was "people power," where members discussed ideas for hours and made decisions together. We were not as interested in profit as much as social and economic exchanges. It was supposed to be a revolution from the bottom up.

So what happened to this revolution? Why were so many co-op and collective efforts short-lived? Were there larger political and economic forces that forced some storefront food co-ops to close their doors and others to adopt a more traditional business model? Another way to ask the question is: What is left of the dream of a revolution? One of the most important consequences was the beginning of the environmental movement. Although there were certainly environmentalists before Rachel Carson, the 1960s and 1970s signaled a growing

concern about the well-being of our planet. How did the environmental movement influence what foods and products co-ops sold and boycotted? And how
did the food co-op movement influence the environmental and organic farming
movements? Perhaps there was a slow revolution in the making.

Legacies and Trends

Historians and political scientists have discussed how liberalism shifted during the 1960s, as the new left focused on the Vietnam War and civil rights,
not the labor concerns of the old left.[1] Nonetheless, in establishing alternative
institutions—food and other co-ops, underground newspapers, organic farms,
free medical clinics, and communes—many young liberals did share an interest
with the old left in dismantling capitalism. What some youth sought, though, was
different. They wanted more direct and immediate experiences, some of which
included drugs and sex. In turn, they were accused of hedonism and narcissism.[2]
In truth, some were escaping from compulsory military service and an imperial
war that made little sense to them.

Although many Americans welcomed the Vietnam War's end in 1974, they
were not prepared for "the end of the postwar boom," to use Jefferson Cowie's words.[3] Even one year earlier, inflation had been at 8 percent, prompting a
new word, "stagflation," marked by high inflation, weak growth in the economy,
higher prices, and increased unemployment. In 1974, inflation had increased to
11 percent because of the oil embargo and high costs of the war. A recession followed in 1975, with unemployment at 8.5 percent. The decade ended with the
Iran oil embargo of 1979, with inflation and unemployment in the double digits.[4]

To be sure, these economic conditions affected people's lives dramatically.
Food and gas prices increased exponentially. Oil prices from 1973 to 1974 had
increased four times and crude oil from 1978 to 1979 by 150 percent. In addition, unemployment was high, the highest in early 1975 since 1941.[5] As political
economist Barry Bluestone explained, at least thirty-two million jobs, many of
them blue collar, had "disappeared" because US businesses had relocated over-
seas and to the Sunbelt, a region known for its antiunionism. By 1977, only 25
percent of workers belonged to a union.[6]

Perhaps the working class had contributed to its own problems by supporting Richard Nixon for president in 1972. However, Nixon had stealthily "forged"
a new American majority, appealing to workers' conservative attitudes toward
protesters and hippies. The Democratic Party, no longer as supportive of labor as
in the past, had become more interested in "posteconomic issues," such as foreign
policy. For example, during democratic Jimmy Carter's presidency, US banks and

corporations increased foreign investments by nearly three times, rather than supporting labor law reform or creating a consumer agency.[7]

The Emerging Environmental Movement

There were other legacies of the 1960s and 1970s. The ones most pertinent to this book were the start of the environmental movement and a return to agricultural sustainability. This is not to say that there were no earlier efforts but Rachel Carson's *Silent Spring* had catapulted a change in US citizens' awareness of pesticides. In turn, this concern influenced many food co-ops to promote local and organic produce, as well as to widen their politics to include issues of agricultural sustainability, recycling, and migrant workers' conditions.

There was, however, a longer history of pesticides in this country, to which Carson only partially alluded. In 1944, seven million pounds of lead arsenate was used in the United States; in 1961, that amount increased to eight million. People were also concerned about radioactive fallout. In 1953, 10,000 lambs in Utah had died and farmers claimed it was because of A-bomb tests, which released clouds of radioactive substances. People were concerned about strontium-90, a radioactive substance found in soil, animal bones, and milk and believed to cause cancer. When the Consumers Union conducted a national study of strontium-90, they found that it was in many foods, not just milk. In 1959, there was a "Cranberry Scandal," which warned Americans not to eat the fruit on Thanksgiving because of pesticide use.[8] In 1962, the year Carson's book was published, over 700 million pounds of insecticides and herbicide were sprayed on US farmland, and even more in urban areas. One estimate was that one of twelve acres in our country was contaminated by pesticides or herbicides.[9]

Carson's book was elegiac, yet also straightforward science. Serialized in the *New Yorker* in the summer of 1962, it was widely read. She documented the use of pesticides in the United States, which had increased from over 1.24 million pounds in 1947 to over 6.37 by 1960. Even though scientists could not agree on safe levels of DDT exposure, Carson found it throughout the whole food chain. She noted the presence of other contaminants as well: chlordane, described by one scientist in 1950 as "one of the most toxic of insecticides"; organic phosphates, including parathion, used on fields and orchards throughout the country; malathion, another commonly used insecticide; and crabgrass killers that contained mercury, arsenic, and chlordane.[10] As several environmental historians noted, Monsanto, as well as other agriculture businesses and chemical societies refuted her findings, discrediting her not only as a scientist but as a female scientist.[11] Perhaps she was vindicated when President John Kennedy appointed a commission that supported many of her conclusions; further, the commission and congressional investigation led to restrictions on the use of insecticides and some pesticides.[12]

Although DDT was banned in 1971, the use of other insecticides and herbicides steadily increased.[13] Ironically, the establishment of the Environmental Protection Agency (EPA) by President Nixon in 1971 did little to stop pesticide use. This was not because the EPA necessarily sided with agribusiness. In fact, from its beginning the EPA insisted that it was not obligated "to promote commerce or agriculture."[14] Rather, the main problem was that the EPA had to review 35,000 registered pesticides but did not have enough staff to do so. Pesticide use continued unabated, increasing from 500 million to over one billion pounds from 1964 to 1994.[15]

Big Business and Shopping Malls

Another recurring theme of the 1960s and 1970s was the ongoing battle against false advertising of food and other products. In 1965, David W. Angevine, public relations director for the Co-operative League of the U.S.A. (CLUSA), testified in Washington, DC, about the number of industries that did not truthfully advertise. At the same time, the National Association of Manufacturers and the Grocery Manufacturers Association lobbied to keep information from consumers. Senator Philip Hart (D-MI) sponsored a bill on truth-in-packaging at least three times. At least one economist, however, claimed that the Hart's bill was not necessary because legislation already existed to protect consumers. The problem, he argued, was that the Food and Drug Administration did not have sufficient funding and staff to enforce these laws.[16] In 1966, the Fair Packaging and Labeling Act, known as the Truth-in-Packaging Act, was finally passed. But in Hunter's estimation, the bill did not "hold a light" to the original one.[17]

The third persistent theme of the two decades was the continuation of the "malling of America." The growth of shopping centers from the 1950s through the 1970s was exponential. In 1960, there were 3,500 suburban shopping centers in the United States and Canada. By 1976, there were over 17,500 shopping centers in the United States alone. And many were large, such as the twenty-eight acre Evergreen Plaza in south Chicago, or the one in Framingham, Massachusetts, a seventy-acre site with forty stores and parking for 5,000 cars. Their size corresponded to the idea of one-stop shopping centers, where people could shop for all of their needs.[18]

Supermarkets had expanded their product lines as well. In 1956, the average grocery store offered 5,000 items; by 1966, there were over 7,000. Ten years later, the average supermarket sold 9,000 products in its store and that number would increase to over 30,000 by the late 1990s.[19] Frozen foods were one product line that expanded considerably, especially after 1967 when the counter microwave became available. By 1975 Americans had bought more microwave ovens than gas ranges; by 1976 nearly 60 percent of American households owned one.[20] For some, simplifying one's life meant living off the earth and escaping technology; for others, these new technologies were a godsend.

Food Co-ops Evolve

As mentioned earlier, some food co-ops started during the Great Depression had relocated to shopping centers. For some, that would be their death knell. In 1970, Greenbelt Consumer Services, renamed Greenbelt Co-operative Society, operated twenty-two supermarkets (nine grocery stores bought from Kroger), ten service stations, five pharmacies, and seven SCAN furniture stores. However, the co-op, then the largest consumer co-op on the East Coast, began a downward turn, losing nearly $8 million over the next thirteen years. It would be forced to close five of its co-op supermarkets and four gas stations.[21] During the 1970s, the Berkeley Co-op had fourteen supermarkets that sold $80 million worth of food and products to its 140,000 members. But by the late 1980s, it had filed for bankruptcy. Other food co-ops, however, continued to thrive. The Eau Claire, Wisconsin, Co-op Center, started in 1938, included grocery and hardware stores, a lumberyard, a hairdresser, and two restaurants as of 1979.[22]

On the federal level, there was limited support for cooperatives. In 1960, President Kennedy stated that co-ops were a "fine expression of U.S. spirit" and pledged to assist farmers' marketing co-ops, rural electric co-ops, credit unions, and housing cooperatives. In some cases, he also linked cooperatives to urban development, arguing that cooperatives could show how "slums could be transformed and blighted neighborhoods redeveloped."[23] Although these ideas were rhetorical, Kennedy did at least establish a Consumer Bill of Rights. President Lyndon Johnson continued this initiative, appointing Assistant Secretary of Labor Esther Peterson as special assistant for consumer affairs.[24] The 1966 Economic Opportunity Act also prompted community action agencies to set up producer and consumer cooperatives. One outcome was that food buying clubs and co-op stores were established in housing projects and on Native American reservations.[25]

Storefronts and Buying Clubs

By and large most co-ops were located in middle-class neighborhoods, not in poor communities. There were exceptions, however. One was Cass Corridor

Food Co-op, which started in 1972 near Wayne State University in Detroit but closed in 2004. At one time, the co-op had annual sales of almost $1 million and 2,000 members, most of whom were poorer African Americans.[26] In Logan Heights, a predominantly poor Latino and African American community of San Diego, twenty-five families started a food buying club in the early 1990s. Two years later, they opened a co-op storefront, Neighbors United, through funding from the city government and San Diego State University. But its members wanted to do more than bring affordable and healthy food to their community: they wanted to encourage other small businesses and community development. Despite community support, it, too, closed.[27]

Many co-ops of the 1960s and 1970s were started by students, college graduates, and professors. In some cases, universities assisted co-ops, as was the case of Boston University providing $10,000 to start the Cambridge Food Co-operative in 1973.[28] A food co-op was started at the University of Maryland in College Park in 1975 in response to the unsavory food served in the dormitories and student union. A member of the North American Students of Cooperation, the Maryland Food Collective (now the Maryland Food Co-operative) still serves natural, vegetarian foods.[29]

Curiously, few of the new wave co-op organizers knew anything about the long history of cooperatives started by workers, immigrants, and socialists in the nineteenth and early twentieth century. Instead, catapulted by the politics of the Vietnam War, the Civil Rights movement, and environmental issues, they engaged in ideological debates. Most notable were the food co-ops in the Twin Cities, which were divided between so-called hippies who preferred natural foods (and so accused of being bourgeoisie) and Marxists, who favored selling canned and less expensive foods in co-ops for working class and poor residents.[30]

It is difficult to know the exact number of food co-ops started during the 1960s and 1970s. The CLUSA reported that between 5,000 and 10,000 consumer co-ops formed during the 1970s alone and that collectively they made over half a billion dollars in sales annually.[31] To be sure, there were many kinds of cooperatives then, ranging from bike to restaurant, housing to book, and health and childcare.[32] Of those, there were an estimated 3,000 food co-ops and food buying clubs as of 1979. Consumer scientist, Anne Hoyt, attributed this growth in food co-ops to rising food costs, as well as an interest in consumer activism that favored a "participatory economic democracy."[33] One outcome of many of these new wave co-ops was a growth in the natural and organic food market. Even so, the organic food business then was a fledgling one, earning $500 million in 1975 compared to the $160 billion in the conventional food industry.[34]

Regardless of the number of food co-ops, it is important to note the differences. First, food co-ops varied in size. Some were small; others were supermarkets;

and still others owned multiple stores. Second, their administrative and staff structures varied. Some eschewed boards and managers, and were collectives; others had various departments and staff; still others relied on volunteer members' labor. Their ideologies ranged from Marxist to liberal, to middle of the road. Some engaged in political protests and demonstrations, while others left political choices up to the customers. Not all food co-ops sold natural, local, or organic foods; some offered commercial brand names as well.

Collective Visions

Many of the food co-ops, however, did start as collectives. Some, however, interpreted the idea of "collective" in different ways. In some co-ops, there were no paid workers. For example, when the Mifflin Street Community Co-op opened in Madison, Wisconsin, in 1969, volunteers stocked the shelves. Ithaca Real Food Co-op in New York, too, relied on volunteers to keep their co-op running. However, eight years later, in 1979, members approved the removal of a bylaw that prohibited paid staff. The affiliated Grains Store Collective in Ithaca also proposed paid staff, arguing that the store was too large and "too complex" to be coordinated by volunteers only. Some members, though, were concerned that this would make co-op less democratic and discourage volunteering.[35] The word "collective" also referred to not being incorporated or having a board of directors or managers, which reflected the hierarchical model of corporations. Last, "collective" referred to the decision-making process. Consensus might take hours, but for those involved this was democracy and community in the making. Many of the Twin Cities co-ops, for example, engaged in long, drawn-out discussions. When the La Montanita Coop started in Albuquerque, New Mexico, in 1976, the 300 family members made decisions collectively. In truth, though, the hard work was often done by a few dedicated members.[36]

Most food co-ops established during the late 1960s and 1970s were small. Many had started as buying clubs, such as two in Portland, Oregon: People's Food Co-op and Food Front Co-op.[37] Later, when more members joined, a buying club often bought or rented a storefront or an old house. For example, Bloomingfoods in Bloomington, Indiana, started in 1975 when the co-op received a $30,000 loan from a local resident. The group found a vacant two-story limestone garage, originally a carriage house. Over the next eight months, nearly 150 people contributed to building the grocery store.[38] Honest Weight Food Co-operative in Albany, New York, started as a buying club in 1976, with members organizing into four "families," each taking turns processing orders. Within a year, the orders had outgrown the basement storage space and members voted to rent a storefront. Seattle's well-known Puget Sound Co-operative League officially started as a buying club in 1961, when fifteen households pooled their money. Members later decided to invest $50 each for a future storefront.[39]

Decisions about what foods to carry were important to members: the amount of sugar or additives, how healthy it was, whether it was local and/or organic, the labor conditions under which it had been harvested or processed, and its cost. Dry goods, oils, and peanut butter were often stored in bins, sold in bulk, and customers weighed and priced them. The early policies of New Pioneer Food Co-op in Iowa City, for example, included selling white organic flour, not flour that had been bleached artificially. Like other cooperatives, New Pioneer formed a committee to research the nutritional values of products. The co-op refused to stock pickles with sodium benzoate, even though its effects were negligible.[40] As early as 1970, the Mifflin Food Co-op in Madison, Wisconsin refused to sell products in nonreturnable bottles because "members believe[d] the items contribute[d] to waste and pollution." At one community meeting, Mifflin members discussed whether to sell more natural foods and whether to get rid of cigarettes, candy, and Coca-Cola. The meeting ended in favor of "purifying" the store.[41] Since its inception, the Honest Weight Food Co-op had been concerned about high quality food. At a members' meeting in 1977, they adopted a policy "to provid[e] the highest quality food at the lowest possible prices. Whenever possible, we shall carry *natural, whole,* and *pure* foods."[42] But not all food co-ops banned so-called harmful foods. The Hanover Consumer Co-op Society in New Hampshire and the Ithaca Consumer Co-operative Society in New York sold brand names products, including Kraft, Mott's, Heinz, and Pillsbury.[43] Both co-op boards argued that food choices should be decided by the customer, not the co-op. Regardless, such decisions were not only political but also financial, as these co-ops did not want to lose their profits.

Many food co-ops linked environmental issues to the products they sold. For example, the Ithaca Consumer Co-operative Society and the Hanover Consumer Co-operative Society, both started in the 1930s, were concerned about phosphates. As noted, Hanover co-op members, after reading Carson's book, decided to start a food safety committee.[44] A 1971 Hanover co-op survey indicated that members did not want phosphate detergents sold or at least wanted them cited as hazardous. Although the education committee's purpose was to provide information to customers, the general manager rightly pointed out that the manufacturers often gave false information. Ultimately, the committee found that that there was no accurate information about phosphates in detergents and little scientific consensus on what level was considered safe. Ironically, a federal bill had been introduced a year before, the Detergent Pollution Control Act of 1970.[45]

Boycotts and Bans

Perhaps the most heated debates in food co-ops surrounded the grape and lettuce boycotts. In 1962, Caesar Chavez had founded the National Farm Workers Association with Delores Huerta, later the United Farm Workers Organizing Committee in California (UFWOC). From 1965 to 1970, Chavez led the Delano grape strike, which brought national attention to the workers' conditions. But Chavez and the UFWOC were concerned with more than just wages. They had set up health clinics, banned pesticides, and provided housing for the workers, as well as started credit unions, provided death benefit insurance, and created education programs. In 1973, when Chavez organized a strike with lettuce growers, many Americans supported him and the UFW. In 1970, at least seventeen million Americans had supported the UFW boycotts and many were food co-op members.[46] When the UFW organized a grape boycott in 1985 to ban five pesticides, including parathion, food co-ops again participated.[47]

Co-ops boycotted other food and products as well. Concerned about the Vietnam War, some co-ops wanted saran wrap removed from their shelves because it was a product of Dow Chemical Company, which also made chemicals used in napalm. In 1979, there was a nationwide boycott on Nestle products because of the corporation's marketing practices of infant formula.[48] The Hyde Park Consumers Co-operative in Chicago and other co-ops called for a boycott of Campbell's soup in 1984. For migrant workers in Ohio, this label meant below minimum wage, substandard living and working conditions, and child labor. In 1978 over 2,000 workers had gone on strike in Ohio's tomato fields.[49] Whole Foods Co-op of Minneapolis (not to be confused with the chain store Whole Foods) discussed the impact of the banana industry on Latin America, citing problems of the overuse of land for growing the fruit, the poor working conditions of workers, and the role of multinational corporations. In 1979, the Wedge Co-op in Minneapolis formed a committee to review new product petitions. Among its standards were that products be minimally packaged and processed, that there be no preservatives or artificial colors, and no bulk sugar be sold.[50]

Clearly many members participated in many political decisions related to food and product selection, and changes in the structure and governance of their co-ops. Even so, not all food co-ops survived. As with earlier co-ops, many had insufficient capital, lack of member consensus or involvement, or inexperience in running a business. Some might say these co-ops failed. But if we look at food co-ops within a larger context, it becomes clear that many provided members with opportunities to engage in grassroots activism. For example, many food co-op members were members of other co-ops and community organizations.

As such, they were part of a constellation of social and political networks, allowing for further change. These food co-ops also provided a sense of community. For example, the early Madison Market in Seattle had a wood-burning stove used for cooking communal food. The co-op, like many others, had its share of community rituals: potlucks, picnics, dances, and other events that brought members together.[51]

The Recession and Re-Invention

Although a number of co-ops did not survive, and that number is not known, many others not only survived but grew. The Food Conspiracy in Tucson, Arizona was the largest new co-op in the Southwest Federation, with sales of $1.2 million in 1979. New Life Co-op in Santa Fe, New Mexico brought in $1 million that year. The People's Food Co-op of Ann Arbor, Michigan, incorporated in 1971, opened its second store in 1975, prompting the startup of four other co-ops on the same block.[52] By 1977, the Puget Sound Co-operative had a membership of more than 14,000 and sales of over $3 million. The largest co-op in the Northwest, it had become a large supermarket, prompting some members to reminisce about the earlier, smaller store when members were more involved in decision making. This prompted the co-op to hire a member relations coordinator in 1976.[53]

By the 1980s, many of these collectives had disappeared and most co-ops had become more hierarchical with boards of directors, teams of managers, and fewer members volunteering. As a result, members became increasingly separated from the operations, finances, and major decisions of the co-ops they "owned." It was not coincidental that these patterns emerged during the early 1980s. The decade had started with the "steepest drop in GNP in American history.[54] Unemployment was at its highest in 1982 since the Great Depression. At least 17,000 companies had closed and many workers had lost their jobs, especially because of deindustrialization. Co-ops, too, were forced to lay off workers or reduce their hours. President Ronald Reagan's neoconservative response was to champion individual freedom, deregulation, and free enterprise.[55] Although the economy would grow the remainder of the decade, that growth, Judith Stein reminds us, was because of consumption.[56]

To be discussed, some food co-ops survived by re-inventing themselves. For example, the board of the Northcoast Co-operative in Arcata, California, decided to focus on "vertical and horizontal expansion in the food industry in order to achieve economies of scale" in order to achieve "long term corporate profitability."[57] Several studies of food co-ops confirmed how their survival depended on the adoption of more business-like structures, which included hiring a general manager and appealing to nonmembers as customers. In turn, this made the work structure more hierarchical, in part by "de-emphasiz[ing] members' work and participation."[58] Once members were removed from their co-ops' daily operations, many became disinterested in the co-ops they collectively owned.[59]

Nonetheless, some co-ops have collectives that have survived to this day. Glut Food Co-op, a workers' food collective, was started in 1969 by conscientious objectors in Mount Rainier, Maryland, outside of Washington, DC. First housed in a church basement, the co-op rented a warehouse in 1971. Today, the collective serves a membership that is largely African American and Latino. It is nonprofit, so there are no members or owners. Its prices are reasonable, as they charge for the cost of food and operating expenses, and any surplus goes back to the store. One worker told me that the co-op is barely breaking even and that workers/managers must sometimes take second jobs. What keeps the co-op strong, she tells me, is its institutional memory and its strong support of social justice organizations.[60]

These examples raise larger questions: How do members' participation and a sense of community change as co-ops become larger? What do members think of their co-op once it becomes a large store or supermarket? Do they feel a sense of ownership? The problem of low member involvement in larger co-ops is not a new one. One strategy was to have members volunteer, for which they would receive member discounts. At Park Slope Food Co-op in Brooklyn, New York, members are still required to work.[61] This not only minimizes labor costs but gives members opportunities to meet other members, to learn about the different foods and products sold there, and to better understand the daily work of their co-op. Although other co-ops might disagree with this approach, it does create membership involvement and community at many levels.

Regardless of a co-op's size and structure, members continued to have several advantages when shopping at their co-ops that grocery chain stores did not offer. Most food co-ops had education departments or educational coordinators, who published newsletters and who alerted customers through store flyers about food additives, nutrition, and other health and environmental issues. Many co-ops offered organic and natural foods, often bought from local sources. Members did have some influence on policy, although that was most often carried out by voting for their boards of directors. Some co-ops gave members working or other discounts, or a patronage fund. How members and boards negotiated and enacted cooperative practices in new wave co-ops is explored more fully in the next chapters.

Some historians have discussed how the new left activism of the 1960s shifted from labor concerns to ecology, women's issues, and ethnicity during the 1970s and 1980s.[62] Such conclusions, though, do not take into consideration how food co-ops continued to participate in boycotts, often on behalf of laborers' working conditions. In some cases, their concerns were both ecological and labor. Further, many young members conceived of their co-ops as alternatives to capitalism in their collective work structures and decision-making process. Members' concern for participatory democracy was reflected in collective decision making, volunteer opportunities, and workers' collectives. Members and workers deliberated on what foods to sell, based on their health value, their environmental impact, and the effects on workers' lives domestically and internationally.

Although many co-ops took on more corporate structures during the 1980s, the next three chapters note how some members continued to advocate for a participatory democracy. And despite what historians think of as a retreat from labor issues, some of the co-ops' battles were labor-related. Northcoast Co-operative in Arcata established a co-op in the working-class timber community of Fortuna. Members of New Pioneer Food Co-op in Iowa City sided with workers there who wanted to start a union. And a number of food co-op members in the Twin Cities fought for working-class inclusion in their co-ops. These examples point to an enduring activism during the 1980s, not a retreat from it.[63]

8

NORTH COAST CO-OPERATIVES
IN ARCATA, EUREKA, AND FORTUNA

There is no place like far northern California. The state has close to ten million acres of old-growth virgin forests, one of the largest in the country.[1] The great amount of rainfall makes the rainforests lush, dense, and towering. The redwoods are majestic, some over one thousand years old. I am traveling along Highway 101, winding my way through the ocean side, coves, and forests to Arcata. I drive through the Avenue of the Giants, referring to stands of giant redwoods, one of its primary natural and economic resources.

After the Gold Rush of the early 1850s, lumber companies moved into the Humboldt Bay area. Overcutting led to a downturn in the lumber industry in Humboldt County. One hundred years later, during the 1950s and 1960s, pulp companies relocated there and brought with them air and water pollution. Alongside deforestation were major floods in the mid-1950s and in Humboldt County in 1964. In the following decades, the forests have been a contested terrain for environmentalists and lumber companies. The protests of tree-huggers and environmental groups such as Earth!First have led to tensions and, in some unfortunate cases, injuries and deaths.[2] And, in the case of one North Coast food co-op, these battles affected its survival. This example shows how closely connected food and environmental politics are, and the difficulties of resolving ideological and political differences when people's livelihoods are threatened.

Humboldt County is known for other alternative groups as well. In the late 1960s, hippies discovered the area and settled in communes. Some grew marijuana, a profitable business. There were also Deadheads (followers of the Grateful Dead), artists, and musicians. To this day, the area celebrates music with four annual festivals: Reggae on the River (started in 1984), the Humboldt Folklife Festival (1978), the Redwood Run (1977), and the Summer Arts & Music Festival (1976).[3] The Arcata Co-op has thrived in this alternative climate. But the co-op, like the town of Arcata, would also be tested by Deadheads, vagrants, and homeless people.

The Arcata Food Co-op (and later the North Coast Co-operative [NCC]) owes a debt to the rich history of cooperatives in Humboldt County. In the late 1800s, there were insurance cooperatives, cooperative creameries, and producer cooperatives, which sold apples, grapes, and berries. In 1930, a credit union opened in the town of Arcata. By 1975, there were at least seventeen co-ops and buying clubs in northern California, including Ruby Valley Warehouse near Redway, the Legget Valley Co-op, and the Arcata Food Co-op. As of the late 1970s, Arcata had an art guild, a dance co-op, a weavers' co-op, and a childcare co-op; the town had also started a farmers' market, which sold only local and naturally grown products.[4] The NCC continues this tradition today: 70 percent of their produce, 100 percent of their beef, and 70 percent of their seafood come from local growers, producers, and fishermen.[5] It is a co-op that teaches us about how the environment can both nurture strong regional connections and create ideological divides.

Arcata Food Co-operative in the 1970s

The Arcata Food Co-operative started as a buying club, the Humboldt Common Market, in 1972. At first, the club stored produce and other food in a member's garage. Later that year, they rented a storefront, which they cleaned and painted, next to the town theater. Only a few people bought groceries from them, however, most likely because customers were never sure what would be available. In one case, one member bought $350 worth of groceries to put on the shelves. Later, members stocked fruit, dairy products, cheese, peanut butter, and flour from a co-op in Richmond, near San Francisco. When sales increased to $1,000 a day, the buying club decided to incorporate, set up a bookkeeping system, and recruit more members through food demonstrations and talks to local clubs and organizations.[6]

By late 1975, at the height of an oil embargo and recession, the Arcata Food Co-op was comprised of seven collectives: the Bulk Food Center, which sold bulk foods at a 10 percent markup; the co-op bakery, which baked whole grain breads; the warehouse, which distributed to other area co-ops and buying clubs at a 5 percent markup; the retail grocery store, which sold many foods (but not meat) at a 20 percent markup; the bookkeeping/accounting department; and a communications/education department. The next year, the co-op started a trucking operation. By late 1976, the co-op's monthly sales were close to $6,000.[7]

Protecting the Environment

Since its inception, the Arcata Co-op sold mostly fresh products. In late 1976, it changed its bylaws so that it would buy locally, whenever possible. Thereafter, the co-op sold fresh fish as well as local, range-fed, and hormone-free beef; it refused to carry any meat with nitrates. Likewise, it carried fresh artichokes, lettuce, squash, broccoli, cauliflower, and apples trucked in from Medford, Oregon. It sold Mexican produce only during the winter but warned their customers about the country's unrestricted use of pesticides. The Bulk Food Center or grains collective offered different kinds of flour, dried fruits, legumes, nuts, and beans, which were color coded according to organic, natural, commercial, treated, or untreated.[8]

The co-op was proud of its products. A 1976 co-op newsletter boasted about the advantages of shopping there: healthy food, education, fair prices, consumer-farmer links, ecological connections, buying in bulk, and excellent consumer services. The co-op educated its members about nutrition through its newsletters, bulletin boards, and a nutritionist who prepared informational labels for foods.[9] Likewise, the co-op continued to educate members about the politics behind food. One article discussed the cereal industry, especially the monopolistic Kellogg Company. The co-op offered its own solution: make your own cereal. The produce department was concerned about bananas grown by multinational corporations because of overuse of scarce land. The co-op decided to sell cashews from Mozambique but only after the country had been "liberated." There were discussions about whether to carry tuna labeled "light meat tuna," which was often yellow fin. In harvesting tuna, porpoises often became entangled in nets and died. Consequently, the co-op asked customers to boycott light meat tuna.[10] Clearly, the co-op linked local consumption to national and worldwide exploitation.

The co-op extended this connection through other environmental activities and through boycotts. At a food day celebration in 1976, members watched a film about the two-and-a-half million farm workers in the United States, as well as one on world hunger. The co-op held a food awareness week, with a symposium and a food fair. Topics included the overuse of pesticides and herbicides, the use of additives in foods, and population growth. With regard to additives, the co-op decided in 1976 to boycott products that contained red dye #2, the most used of all dyes in the food industry. The Food and Drug Administration (FDA), after studying its effects for fifteen years, would ban it later that year. However, the US Court of Appeals would then block the ban because of a lawsuit by the Certified

Color Manufacturers Association of Washington, DC, an industry trade group.[11] The co-op became active in other boycotts as well. In 1975, the board moved to stop selling products "produced by imperialist, multi-national corporations." These included products of Del Monte, a subsidiary of Nestle Company.[12] Nestle was boycotted by many organizations because of its infant formula. In 1978, the board considered boycotting coffee because of its high prices and because it was "a product of poverty."[13] The following year, the membership/education committee considered taking a stand on the national Dow boycott, especially because it involved herbicide spraying in Humboldt County.[14]

The Arcata Co-op was more active in food boycotts than the food co-ops in Ithaca, Hanover, and Hyde Park. There were a number of reasons for this. First, many of Arcata Co-op members were younger, a characteristic of many new-wave co-ops. As noted earlier, those most active in the grape and lettuce boycotts in Ithaca and Hanover, too, were young college students, not older members. Second, Arcata Co-op members were part of the emerging environmental movement. As such, they linked the Dow boycott to the local issue of herbicide spraying. Third, Arcata's community—with its number of cooperative initiatives and small-scale businesses and farms—opposed multinational corporations. Fourth, the Arcata Co-op was a fledgling one and so did not have as much to lose financially, as did the three Depression-era co-ops discussed in earlier chapters. In the cases of the Ithaca and Hanover co-ops, both lost money during the grape and lettuce boycotts.

Food Politics and Policies

The most protracted boycott for Arcata Food Co-op members was to support the United Farm Workers (UFW). Arcata Co-op members were probably motivated by a San Francisco conference in 1975, where some co-opers accused the Arcata Co-op of putting business before politics. It is not clear how Arcata co-opers responded. But three proposals were passed by the conference attendees: to support the UFW; to engage in political organizing; and to educate people about food politics. Apparently, Arcata co-opers honored these proposals for the co-op's UFW boycott shifted from lettuce to wines, mostly those made by Gallo, Paul Masson, Christian Brothers, and Italian Swiss Colony. The co-op also supported UFW boycotts on Sun-Maid raisins, prunes, and diamond walnuts the next year.[15] Alongside these boycotts, the co-op fully supported Proposition 14, a farm workers' initiative that would give them the right to join unions, bargain with employers, and cast secret ballots. This initiative had grown out of talks between Jerry Brown, governor of California, and labor and grower representatives, including Caesar Chavez, to create a collective bargaining law for California farm workers. The co-op sided with the proposition, as stated in one of its 1976 newsletter: "The co-op supports a democratic agricultural union."[16] Although the Agricultural Labor Relations Act would pass, there would still be violations of workers' rights.[17]

One corporation the co-op repeatedly discussed and boycotted was Nestle. As early as 1970, a WHO-UNICEF conference had criticized multinational corporations' marketing practices of infant formula. In 1974, the World Health Assembly published a resolution for regulating their sales. Overall, activists worldwide were concerned about a decline in breastfeeding, as well as the possible misuse of the product, given many developing countries' illiteracy rates. With 50 percent of the market in infant formula worldwide, Nestle was a ready target for boycotts.[18] Joining with other cooperatives, the Arcata Co-op sent a letter to Nestle in the spring of 1978, notifying the corporation of its decision to boycott its products. To be sure, such collective efforts affected Nestle's sales of chocolates, coffees and teas, wines, cheeses, and packaged foods. As Dr. Michael Latham, an international nutritionist at Cornell noted, the Nestle boycott forced the corporation to change its policy. Although the national boycott ended in March 1984, the Arcata Co-op would reconsider it again during the early 1990s.[19]

In 1976, the Arcata Co-op's Products Review Board decided to establish criteria for the selection of new products. First, they should have nutritional value. For that reason, the co-op did not sell soda pop, sugared cereals, and foods which they considered nutritionally unhealthy. Second, they should have little impact on the environment. Consequently, the co-op refused to carry products stored in aerosol cans, over-packaged foods, and to carry yellow fin tuna. Third, products should be affordable; fourth, they should be produced and distributed by cooperatives or collectives. Further, there were "political considerations," as exemplified in the UFW boycott.[20] Although there was no elaboration of "political considerations," it was clear that the review board did not subscribe to political neutrality and that they understood that food choices were inherently political. By 1979, the board adopted a boycott policy and mission statement that supported boycotts supported by "nationally recognized consumer groups." The process for boycotts at the co-op, then, was that the membership/education committee would consider the product, its ingredients, and the producer. They would then collect the members' opinions about a possible boycott through a poll or newsletter. Next, they would identify products related to the boycott and put notices on the shelves. They would then generate discussion about the boycott and make recommendations to the board.[21] Although members participated, ultimately the board made the final decisions.

Regarding the boycotts and other issues, workers did not have as much input as they wanted. If anything, workers were disgruntled about the board's increased power, which they claimed was at the expense of members and themselves. One conflict was the direction of the co-op's growth. In fact, the board had become more interested in finding ways for the co-op to expand, especially since the co-op store had become overcrowded. It discussed buying property, expanding the co-op's product line, and building reserve capital.[22] Yet the board did not want the co-op to grow too quickly, instead seeking a balance where "socialism and corporatism [were] avoided."[23] Some of the workers had also recommended that the co-op relocate to a larger store. As early as 1975, fourteen workers had published a letter about what they called "an unbearable" situation of extreme overcrowding at the store, which led to "overly stressful and inhumane" working conditions.[24] But they wanted members to decide on the direction of the co-op, not the board.[25] Their concern was not unjustified. When the board had discussed members' voting rights in 1974, they argued that co-op members did not have to be informed about all business details. Instead, the board stated, it was its members who made the business decisions.[26]

Growing Pains

Another conflict between the board and the workers was that the board wanted a more professional management. Conversely, workers wanted to eliminate any distinctions between workers and managers. Instead, workers advocated for a system of "worker self-management," which involved collective decision making and shared responsibilities. As the workers explained, they were "struggling" toward "solidarity" to "confront the problems of worker exploitation and consumer manipulation by agribusinesses, sexism, racism, ageism, and classism."[27] As noted, the co-op had been concerned about worker exploitation internationally and the co-op workers used that language to argue on their behalf.

Unfortunately, the recession during the mid-1970s was not a good time for workers at Arcata and across the country. Many were laid off. The national unemployment rate was 9 percent by mid-1975. The recession hit the Arcata Co-op as well and some of their workers were laid off. To cut costs, the board also eliminated overtime, discontinued the food discount program, and reduced the hours of the Bulk Food Center.[28] Some workers became angry about these decisions and resigned. Letters from several of them criticized the power of special interest groups, the board's "manipulation and railroading," and the consequent loss of member involvement. These workers reminded members that the new bylaws had "convert[ed] member representation in decision making to puppetry."[29] One worker also warned that if members were not committed, a few people would take control of the co-op.[30]

Some members, though, must have agreed with the board's direction, for when the board asked members for loans for expansion and improvements, they were generous. In the fall of 1974, the co-op received nearly $11,000 in short-term loans from twenty-seven members to buy their first truck. A second loan, provided by nineteen members, was earmarked for relocating, renovating, and buying new equipment. A third loan, totaling $13,000 from twenty-one members, paid for cash registers and scales. By early 1976, the end of the recession, the co-op was in the black again and able to pay back two sets of these loans.[31]

By 1978, many things had changed with the co-op. Most important, the co-op had relocated to a new store. To pay for new equipment, the co-op had started a fair share membership drive, whereby customers became members by investing $200 in co-op shares. Second, membership had increased dramatically from 425 in late 1974 to almost 3,000 individual and family members by late 1978.[32] In turn, the increase in membership resulted in higher sales. In 1975, sales were $80,000 a month; by 1978, they were $280,000. Third, there were changes in the workers' conditions. Given the store's expansion, the number of workers had increased from fourteen in 1975 to sixty in 1978. This larger number made it more difficult for the once active workers' association to make any decisions collectively. The association's input was further diminished when board hired two general managers so that business decisions could be made more quickly.[33] In 1977, when one worker resigned, she criticized the board's "centralization" as "excessive" and claimed that it had a negative impact on the workers' collective.[34] She was right. By 1978, the Humboldt Workers' Association was no longer meeting.[35] It is difficult to know what members thought about the workers' concerns, given the lack of records on this issue.

Yet we do know that members had considered boycotting coffee and that the membership/education committee deliberated on the national Dow boycott in 1978 and 1979. This was, in fact, consistent with the 1979 board's boycott policy and mission statement that supported boycotts backed by "nationally recognized consumer groups." In directing their attention to national boycotts, had members neglected the politics of workers within their own co-op? Had workers' warnings that the new bylaws reduced "member representation in decision making to puppetry" come true? Conversely, if the Humboldt Workers' Association held meetings for workers only, what were the possibilities for members' involvement and support? As the co-op grew in membership, its number of workers, and annual sales, its power structure become more centralized through its board and general managers. As a result, members and workers had less voice in their co-op.

Despite these criticisms of the co-op's changes, 1979 was a successful year financially. Sales had increased 32 percent over the previous year. The co-op had returned its first patronage refund in its history to members. The five-year capital budget included the purchase of the Arcata store building and consideration of opening a new store in Eureka, about ten miles south of Arcata. Although the management structure had changed, the co-op board was still trying to "interface competent management with workplace democracy."[36] It was not clear, however, what the board meant by "democracy" or how it was to be practiced.

The North Coast Co-operatives, 1980s

In 1980—the "steepest drop in GNP in American history"—Arcata Co-op adopted a new corporate name, North Coast Co-operatives. The board adopted a new mission statement as well: "to encourage the development and growth of various forms of co-operative ownership and to participate in linking them in a co-operative economic system while making available a wide range of goods and services under co-operative ownership and educating members of the community as to the benefits of economic co-operation."[37] The wording spoke to the salience of having several, not just one food, co-op in Humboldt County. In fact, during the 1980s two new food co-ops would be established by the NCC in nearby Eureka and Fortuna. With at least 4,500 members and $5 million in sales in 1980, the NCC was poised for expansion.[38]

Debates about Expansion

But the Arcata members and the board held different positions about a second store in Eureka. Some members wanted the new store to be independent from the Arcata Co-op and start through Eureka's grassroots community. Others disagreed, arguing that because the Arcata Co-op had much more business experience, it should open the new store. Some members' thoughts about a second store reflected broader concerns: that they had little say in the co-op's direction; and that the NCC was becoming too large. Regardless of some members' wish that the co-op remain small and more grassroots, the board was thinking further expansion. In 1980, there were discussions underway about a third co-op, this one in Fortuna, south of Eureka. There, 600 residents had signed a petition for a co-op store. That summer, the NCC board debated whether to make an offer on a vacant Fortuna Safeway building.[39]

When Arcata co-op members had voiced their concerns about expansion, those concerns reflected a grassroots approach not just for their co-op but for the one in Eureka. In fact, the Arcata co-op could have assisted Eureka residents in starting their own co-op and it could have cooperated in other respects. But when a co-op expands to different towns, its "communities" are less well served.

Opportunities for members and workers to collectively organize become weaker, because the constituent co-ops have different sets of members, workers, and perhaps interests. For example, although Eureka was less than ten miles from Arcata, it did not have the radical reputation of Arcata. And Fortuna, a working-class community, was quite different from both Arcata and Fortuna, differences that would create tensions within the NCC.

Even as the NCC decided on expansion, its sales had taken a sudden downward turn in the early 1980s, a time beset by high unemployment and cost of living. In fact, grocery sales nationally had taken a nosedive then. Even Associated Co-operatives, the co-op's chief warehouse supplier, had decreased sales, along with higher costs. The Arcata Co-op store had not met its projections, with sales 1.3 percent lower than the previous year and operating expenses higher than expected. As with the 1970s recession, the co-op eliminated overtime, tightened its inventory, and cut its administrative payroll by 10 percent. Apparently, these measures worked, and by late 1982 the co-op's sales were back up. That year, the NCC opened a second co-op store in Eureka and moved its warehouse and corporate offices there.[40]

Encouraged by the upward turn in sales and its new store, the NCC's board continued to focus on "corporate" growth. As it stated: "Co-op development in the next five years will focus on vertical and horizontal expansion in the food industry in order to achieve economies of scale." The board also decided that "the co-op will aim for long term corporate profitability."[41] These statements were not unique to the NCC, as other food co-ops had adopted similar language. With regard to expansion, the NCC was still deciding on several sites for its third co-op store in Fortuna. With a new general manager eager to open a new store there, the board started negotiations with Safeway in March 1983. It is not clear why the board and general manager were so determined to open another store, given the Arcata Co-op's recent fluctuating finances. In fact, the projection for the summer of 1983 was-$50,000; the winter quarter of 1983 would show losses of over $18,000.[42] At the very least, they might have heeded these financial losses. However, this appears to be a case where the NCC's five-year corporate plan drove its development. What is conspicuously missing from these decisions are the perspectives of the co-op's members and workers.

Several years later, NCC board decided on yet another expansion plan, this time in Arcata. When the general manager notified the board that there were two lots with three houses adjacent to the Arcata co-op store, the board discussed trying to buy one of the lots. The co-op had a "friend of the co-op" who was willing to buy the lot and lease it to the co-op, with the option to buy. A motion was passed to buy the lot. The co-op was also negotiating with the city of Eureka on a possible relocation of its First Street Store. Last, it was considering selling its warehouse or moving it to another location. In 1986, it moved the warehouse to another location in Eureka.[43]

By early 1987, the NCC's sales were one of the highest in its history. In April alone, sales had reached a quarter of a million. One reason was that the co-op in Arcata sold more natural and organic food, resulting in a 3 to 9 percent increase over projected sales. In fact, it claimed that it was selling more organic produce than any other co-op its size in California. The Eureka First Street Co-op's annual sales were close to $620,000. With member investment at over $714,000, the board decided to buy one of the houses and lots near the Arcata Co-op for $64,000. It also renamed the warehouse Wholefood Express and opened a co-op store in Fortuna in 1988.[44]

The Co-op Boycott Policy Reconsidered

Alongside this growth, the board decided to revisit its boycott policy. The NCC had continued participating in boycotts throughout the 1980s, although they deliberately chose which ones they thought important. For example, the board thought that it was not in the best interest of the NCC to take a stand on pro-life versus pro-choice issues. Board members also decided that the best way to fight pesticide use was to build relationships with local farmers and producers, rather than "police" the "existing product line." Although there was much discussion on this issue, the board was unable to pass any motion to change its policy.[45] It did decide, though, that the co-op would carry Libby products from the California Canners & Growers, which was cooperatively owned. They unanimously passed two other motions as well: that the NCC opposed irradiation of food until further research showed that it was safe; and that the NCC would consider consumer- and labor-related boycotts supported by nationally recognized consumer groups.[46]

In 1985, the NCC revisited the grape boycott issue. The board argued that the issue was complex and that it was difficult to decide whether to boycott. But other co-ops did not think so. The Berkeley Co-operative stores had used "in store signs about the grape boycott and carrie[d] UFW grapes when available."[47] Further, 80 to 90 percent of the NCC's members favored the boycott. The NCC's proposed policy was to carry UFW grapes when possible, with positive signs and advertising. When grapes were nonunion, the co-op would still carry them, but with educational signs and not advertise. Ultimately, the board asked the staff to sell both organic and union grapes. If union grapes were unavailable, the co-op would buy nonunion grapes and provide information. The board added a clause to the boycott policy, that it would not "preclude the sale of locally produced grapes."[48]

Here the language of retreat with regard to boycotts resembled that of the Ithaca and Hanover co-ops. However, in the case of the NCC, its members overwhelmingly favored the boycott. Nonetheless, the NCC board played down the issue, essentially selling both union and nonunion grapes, thereby letting the consumers decide. There is some irony to the fact that the 1985 boycott's intent was to ban five pesticides, including parathion. Here, the NCC board had retreated from its earlier activism of banning foods with pesticides as well. Their approach to pesticide use during the 1980s was to build relationships with local farmers and producers, rather than "police" the "existing product line."

The NCC, 1990–2012

In 1992, the NCC had almost 6,000 members: 3,500 at the Arcata Co-op, 1,500 in Eureka, and 800 in Fortuna. The NCC's five- to ten-year plan included developing the Arcata block, expanding its retail bakery sales, increasing storage area, and renting its other spaces. But some of the stores and the warehouse were not doing so well. By 1990, the Whole Food Express Warehouse had a $100,000 loss and was critically short of cash. The Eureka store, too, was having problems, so the board decided on a "facelift," hoping that would improve sales. The Fortuna Co-op was faring the worst, with its 1991 sales down by $150,000. Although a new Walmart store had cut into all of the co-op stores' sales, that did not completely explain the Fortuna store's financial loss.[49]

To complicate matters, the Arcata store was having problems of a different sort. A number of "vagrants" had started loitering in the store's parking lot. In 1989, the board had hired a parking lot attendant following reports of sexual assaults, harassment, public exposures, and drug deals. One person had died, another put in intensive care. Further, some had left their cars and busses behind, including a Hare Krishna bus.[50] The Arcata community had generally been accepting of alternative people, at least during the 1960s and 1970s. But attitudes had changed. Residents now spoke about the problem of homelessness or, as some people called it, "houselessness." In one local newspaper, a resident wrote that Arcata had become the home of "Deadheads." In another article, a resident observed how Conga drum players on the plaza "provoke[d]" complaints.[51] Others were critical of a group of 300 homeless people living near Clam Beach, north of Arcata. A person named Running Deer had been evicted from Arcata by the police and had set up a traveling soup kitchen there.[52]

Earth!First and Fortuna

Fortuna was the most contentious site for the NCC because of Earth!First and other environmentalist groups, who were protesting the clear-cutting of the redwood forests. Local activist Judi Bari and other members of Earth!First had organized the Redwood Summer of 1990 and another in 1991. Thousands of activists rallied in support of the timber workers, the forests, and the protection of endangered species by protesting against Pacific Lumber Company.[53] According to journalist David Harris, when Charles Hurwitz took over the lumber company, he had workers clear-cut the forests, even cutting down second growth trees. To add insult to injury, Hurwitz also borrowed from the workers' pension. Despite the activists' nonviolent protests, Bari's car was bombed in 1990 and she was gravely injured and in constant pain until her premature death in 1997. Rather than fully investigating this crime, the FBI accused her of placing the bomb in her own car and called her a terrorist. But Bari was not the only activist who paid with her life. Later, in 1998, David "Gypsy" Chain and eight other Earth!First activists were protesting logging in the redwood forests of Scotia, California. A logger had threatened Chain; he died soon after when a tree "accidentally" fell on him.[54]

During the Redwood Summer of 1990, Earth!First had organized a march through Fortuna to Pacific Lumber Company's mill. But the activists were not welcome by the townspeople. Workers and other Fortuna residents threatened them, and the Fortuna police and city council of Fortuna made public statements against Earth!First. Some Fortuna residents were suspicious of the protestors, associating them with the NCC. In fact, many did not shop at the Fortuna Co-op because they thought it was "a front for Earth First." The Fortuna Co-op countered this by being more visible in community events.[55]

However, Fortuna residents were not the only ones concerned about the Fortuna Co-op. Arcata Co-op members were worried about its financial losses and how that would have a negative impact on their own co-op. One ad hoc committee stated that the Arcata Co-op "was being squeezed to subsidize the losses of the Fortuna coop." At the same time, the ad hoc committee was worried that the Arcata Co-op was becoming too corporate and losing its "hippie roots." In fact, the board president had been quoted as saying that the co-op had an image of "hippies" and "arrogant liberals." One member retaliated that, "The co-op is becoming less and less responsive to its members." She further claimed, the "counter cultural movement *is not dead.*"[56] When the board president recommended that the co-op not become involved in politics, the ad hoc committee responded with the 1970s mantra, "food for people, not for profit."[57] In turn, the board replied that, although the co-op was founded on political grounds, the issue before them was whether to take political stands on nonfood issues, such as the logging protests.[58] The ad hoc committee decided to survey NCC members. The committee found that members thought that the co-op was more than just a food store, especially for those who saw themselves as environmentalists and progressives. Most were comfortable with the co-op's image and did not want a parking lot guard at the Arcata Co-op. Moreover, most did not want the Arcata Co-op to subsidize the Fortuna Co-op.[59] Here again, members spoke out, yet the board did not listen.

Some board members did agree that closing the Fortuna Co-op would be best for the NCC, which had invested over $100,000 in the store. The bank agreed. But Fortuna members wanted desperately to keep their co-op store open. One brainstorming session led to the ideas of serving buying clubs, and improving community outreach and member education. In March 1992, the board considered shutting down the Fortuna Co-op but the motion to close it failed. Another motion was then made to hire an outside consultant but that motion failed as well. Finally the motion to close the coop was tabled until May.[60] Unfortunately, the next month there was an earthquake. All three co-op stores sustained damage, with most at the Fortuna store, which had no earthquake insurance. Regardless, there were ongoing discussions about keeping that store open, even though its membership had not grown and banks refused to approve any loans for the NCC because of the Fortuna store's losses.[61]

Given these losses, it is incomprehensible why some board members insisted on keeping the Fortuna Co-op open. Perhaps they were sympathetic to those in Fortuna who wanted a co-op. In fact, the Fortuna committee had continued to offer suggestions, including an espresso bar and a yogurt stand. Perhaps some board members hoped that a co-op could survive in the face of hostility. As seen in other chapters, food cooperatives have sometimes compromised their own well-being to open co-ops in other, less fortunate communities. Whatever the reasons, in July the board made the motion to close the store. This time the vote was five "yes" and two "no." The NCC sold the store building for $307,000 to the county for a larger courthouse. Yet they still had to pay off $100,000 on a remaining loan.[62]

Not surprisingly, the sale of the Fortuna Co-op positively affected the NCC. The Eureka Co-op's sales increased by 15 percent and the board decided to expand it. The bakery at the Arcata Co-op was also expanded through local deliveries and later with the additions of espresso, coffees, new breads, and pastries. However, the long-term plans for removing two houses on the Arcata store block were put on hold. Some residents opposed demolishing two historic Victorian cottages for a co-op's truck ramp, offices, and small rental retail shops. The problem was resolved when one couple paid a dollar for one of the houses, took it apart board by board, and rebuilt it; the other was moved.[63]

The NCC faced another challenge in 1994, when a former board member opened the natural food store, Wildberries, in Arcata. The co-op worried that some of its customers were shopping at the new store, reflected in its reduced weekly sales.[64] To add to this problem, there was another earthquake in early 1995 and the Arcata store sustained damages. Sales continued to spiral downward by 14 percent that quarter at the Arcata co-op, although only 2 percent at the Eureka store.[65] The following year, however, both co-ops rebounded, with Arcata sales up by over 7 percent and Eureka's by 8 percent. Encouraged by this, the board decided to relocate the Eureka store to the Fifth and L Market site, scheduled to open in early 1997.[66]

Environmental and Food Justice

Despite its prosperity, the NCC continued to participate in a number of boycotts. The co-op did not carry dolphin-unsafe tuna fish, nonunion grapes, genetically modified foods, Coors beer, and junk food, such as soft drinks and candy. Its Co-operative Affairs Committee had been gathering information on the ongoing boycotts of Nestle and the American Home Products (now Wyeth) Companies. Although no reason was given for boycotting the latter, more than likely animal rights organizations were opposed to the manufacturing of the drug premarin, whose production—they claimed—included cruel treatment of horses. General Electric had also been on some co-ops' boycott lists because they were one of the largest military contractors for the US government during the early 1990s. When they sold their weapons division, they were taken off the many boycotters' lists.[67] In many of these cases, the co-op committee—comprised of active members— reinstituted a number of boycotts.

One of these boycotts concerned the use of the recombinant bovine growth hormone (rBGH). In 1993, the FDA had approved the sale of rBGH to farmers and it did not require dairies to include the hormone use on their labels. Even though Humboldt Creamery, from which the NCC bought many of its dairy products, did not buy milk from dairies that used the hormone, the NCC was considering a motion to participate in the bovine somatotropin (BGH/BST) boycott. In addition, the NCC asked members to write their congresspersons to vote for a federal bill requiring the labeling of all products that contained rBGH.[68]

During the 2000s, the NCC board continued its discussion of whether to boycott Coca-Cola. In July 2003, trade unions worldwide had started a boycott of the corporation. Two years later, co-op members participated in an advisory survey about Coca-Cola products and results indicated that at least two-thirds of them did not want the co-op to carry the soda. Members pointed to a number of concerns. First, there was its high sugar content. Second, the corporation had been accused of antiunion practices. Last, the corporation was purportedly damaging groundwater near its bottling plants. In this case, the board encouraged "an educational campaign" about the company while also "respecting individual buying decisions."[69] As with the co-ops in Ithaca and Hanover, the board recommended individual choice over a collective good.

Throughout the decade, NCC continued to be involved in issues of environmental sustainability. The co-op sponsored a program to raise consumer awareness about choosing sustainable seafood for consumption. They used three categories: best choice (for eating), caution, and to avoid. Similar to the Harvest Co-op Markets in Cambridge, Massachusetts, they "educate[d], rather than dictate[d]" what members should buy.[70] In 2003, the NCC produced a document "Genetically Engineered Foods in the Co-op," based on Greenpeace's True Foods Shopping List of the brand names of over eighty products which had been tested by the organization and found to contain genetically modified organisms (GMOs). At least one North Coast Co-op member requested that the co-op label any products that contained GMOs in the stores so that consumers could make informed decision. Two years later, the co-op did inform the public through green (GMO-free) and red (not GMO-free) dots.[71]

"Genetically Engineered Foods in the Co-op" was timely for another reason. Members of the Humboldt Green Genes and other activists were collecting signatures for a ballot that would ban GMOs in Humboldt County. They hoped to follow Mendocino County south of Humboldt, whose successful Measure H campaign had made it illegal to "propagate, cultivate, raise or grow genetically modified organisms in the county."[72] Although the Humboldt County activists had collected 2,600 signatures, they still needed 1,800 more. Problems arose when several Humboldt State University science faculty noted that the ballot contained scientific errors.[73] That doomed the activists' efforts. Even so, many dairies in Humboldt County were certified organic, thereby ensuring the NCC of non-GMO sources.

Today, the NCC uses a "green dot" program for "all ninety-five to 100 percent certified organic food." The co-op also advises customers "that the best way to avoid eating GMO food is to choose food that has been certified organic." The NCC remains proactive by communicating with certification agencies. As the notice on its website states: "All the certification agencies contacted have a 'no GMO' policy but some do state that they cannot guarantee products are completely GMO free due to genetic drift."[74] Overall, members and shoppers can be assured that their food choices at the NCC are generally healthy ones.

As of 2010, the NCC has almost 13,000 members, 200 employees, and annual sales of $26 million. Its members have been committed to their co-op's growth, contributing over $3 million to its stores.[75] Members' commitment has also been reflected in their outspokenness about political issues, including food boycotts, the corporate image of the co-op, agricultural sustainability, and the safekeeping of the redwood forests. Yet, as its history shows, the NCC board has not always honored its members' protests and other forms of participation. Although members strongly supported a number of boycotts, the board created a policy that often favored financial growth instead. In fact, the decisions to establish two food co-ops in nearby communities were those of the board and the general manager, not the collective of members.

Rather than expanding, the Arcata co-op could have assisted Eureka and Fortuna in establishing their own food co-ops. In that way, each individual co-op could have been more responsive to its town communities and to its members. Instead, the NCC, like many food co-ops, followed the corporate path. To be sure, the disagreements between NCC members and the board have spoken to these very tensions within cooperatives: they are businesses yet they are also collectively owned. This raises the question: Can co-ops be profitable, yet responsive to a collective membership/ownership? I believe they can. However, as the number of co-ops discussed so far has shown, it is less likely the larger co-ops become. Instead, I recommend, food co-ops should capitalize on what makes them different from all other grocery stores: consumer education and advocacy, patronage refunds, cooperation with other cooperatives, member ownership, open membership, and democracy. That seems to be what some Arcata co-op members were saying all along.

NEW PIONEER CO-OPERATIVE SOCIETY

Iowa City is known for the University of Iowa's renowned Writers' Workshop and the International Writing Program. It is considered one of the most literary places in the country; one claim is that it has more poets and fiction writers per capita than anywhere else in the United States. Its municipal policies are progressive and include a human rights ordinance that bans discrimination because of sexual orientation and gender identity. The city council encourages businesses to pay livable wages, as well as protects nearby wetlands and historical landmarks. There are bike lanes and walking trails. It is an oasis of culture and progressive politics.[1] Like a number of other universities in the early 1970s, the University of Iowa was home to a Students for a Democratic Society chapter, Vietnam War protesters, hippies, and unprofitable alternative stores. During the Vietnam War protests, the old Armory building was burned down. Rocks were thrown through the display windows of some downtown businesses and protesters took to the streets. In the spring of 1970, after the Kent State murders, the university closed. As an undergraduate there, I remember those days well.

I also remember the first years of the New Pioneer Co-operative Society (NPCS). Like many other new wave co-ops, New Pioneer had started as a buying club in the late 1960s. Around thirty people shared bulk items, such as brown rice, whole wheat flour, peanut butter, and raisins. It became incorporated in the summer of 1971 through the efforts of two graduate students, a secretary, a Mennonite farmer, and a political science professor.[2] My recollection of the co-op on Bowery Street was that the flour was mildewed and the choices of food were limited. Still, I liked the hardwood floors of the old house in a tree-lined neighborhood. Several years later, it moved above a popular downtown bar.

But how long would the NPCS remain a small, grassroots co-op? How would the recession and economic downturn of the late 1970s and 1980s affect its decision-making process and its members' participation? As discussed, generally the larger the co-op, the less member participation there is. But there are also certain issues that spark and renew members' involvement. With the Ithaca Consumer Cooperative Society, it was the grape and lettuce boycotts. With the North Coast Co-op, it was concern over logging. With New Pioneer, it would be whether the workers should unionize. And this would mobilize some New Pioneer members to ask other questions about the co-op's finances and how transparent the board was in its decision-making. These were catalysts for members to "take back" their co-op and to restore the democratic process. But would they be successful?

The NPCS, 1970s and 1980s

The NPCS's initial goals were to provide low-cost food; to stimulate the local production of and provide a market for organic food; to reject products that "injure[d] the natural environment"; and "to encourage all people to return to the earth, recognize its crucial importance to man and animals and respect the fact that we are but mere guests of this planet, privileged to enjoy its use and responsible for its survival."[3] This was the lofty language of the 1970s, and the co-op's policies reflected these goals. New Pioneer sold organic white flour but not coffee, tea bags, or milk. The co-op refused to stock pickles with the additive sodium benzoate. Its members questioned stocking Hoffman Bars because of their sugar content and Osceola Spruce Root Beer because of its commercial value. Members talked about how to make decisions democratically and formed a committee to research the nutritional values of products. In 1973, four workers formed a staff collective.[4]

During its first year, the NPCS's annual sales reached $35,000; by 1975, its sales had increased to $150,000, with a membership of 300. That year, the co-op opened Stone Soup, which served a cafeteria-style lunch, and Morning Glory Bakery in the basement of a nearby Catholic grade school. However, Stone Soup was evicted from the building for not removing an Emma Goldman Clinic poster from the community bulletin board when a priest asked them to do so. Goldman had been imprisoned for distributing literature and educating American women about birth control choices in the early twentieth century, which the Catholic Church still opposes. In addition, its finances were not well handled. In 1977, the food co-op relocated to the corner of Washington and Van Buren streets, across from city hall. The co-op then opened Blue Parrot Café, a lunch café that promoted foods sold in the store. However, the café lost over $9,000 and closed in March 1982.[5]

A New Management Structure and Board

The early 1980s were a difficult time for the NPCS, as for many others. New Pioneer faced competition from another health food store and its sales fluctuated. After March 1981 its sales picked up, as the co-op worked with Associated Grocers of Iowa as a source for many of its grocery items.[6] In the fall of 1982, the co-op decided to seek input from its members. The survey showed that most members were between twenty and twenty-five years old, held bachelor's degrees, and earned an income under $10,000. Many shopped there at least once a week but also shopped at the town's two grocery chain stores, Eagles and Hy-Vee. Although members did not state why they shopped elsewhere, it may have been the perception of the co-op's higher prices. Members had the option to receive up to 20 percent in discounts by becoming working members.[7] It is not clear how many members did so. What is clear, however, is that member involvement at meetings was low: at least 85 percent did not attend.[8]

The NPCS was faring better than many other co-ops. The Community Consulting Group of Cambridge, Massachusetts noted that the five-year trend of a 30 percent increase in annual sales for many natural foods businesses had dropped to 14 percent in the early 1980s. But New Pioneer had one of the best performances of co-op stores nationally in 1983 and 1984. In fact, the consulting firm thought that New Pioneer was one of the "soundest storefronts in the co-op movement today." But, it cautioned, the co-op could close, along with the estimated one-third of other co-op stores.[9] For the Iowa City co-op to remain vibrant, the firm recommended that it recruit more members and customers, improve its education program, invest in management training, and increase its organic produce. The firm also recommended hiring a general manager to "interface" more easily with the board. Last, they suggested finding ways to appeal to higher-income members who would want convenience and high-quality food.[10]

As with other new wave co-ops—such as the Arcata co-op—the NPCS shifted its management structure during the 1980s, replacing the working collective with a general manager and workers. The general manager worked with a consultant to expand the store's products to include meat, coffee, beer, and frozen foods. As a result, members became increasingly separated from the operations, finances, and major decisions of the co-ops they "owned." Still, some members opposed these changes. They wanted the co-op to continue to participate in national boycotts, such as the Campbell's products boycott.[11] They also did not want the co-op to sell meat. The board disagreed, arguing that "as a pluralistic organization we should meet the needs of the majority."[12] Perhaps New Pioneer was concerned about its bottom line. But there seemed to be little reason to worry. Its inventory had increased almost fourfold and its sales were up 68 percent from the previous year. With the expansion in 1986, membership increased to 1,600. Correspondingly, sales rose from $2.7 million in 1987 to $4.3 million in 1988.[13]

When the NPCS surveyed its members in the mid-1980s, they found that most appreciated the natural, organic, and bulk foods. However, high prices were still a concern, especially for college students. The co-op decided to "build" its product line, as well as improve its pricing. However, these changes did not necessarily mean lower prices. Instead, the co-op promoted local and organic produce, as well as expanded its meat department to include fish and chemically free meat. They also planned to open a delicatessen. Their overall goals were to increase membership by 25 percent and to improve the NPCS's business performance for the next three years. Like the North Coast Co-op, New Pioneer's growth was guided by a long-term business plan, not a collective vision of its members. Specifically, New Pioneer wanted to increase sales from $1.9 million from 1986 to 1987 to $2.3 million the following year, and $2.6 million the next.[14]

The NPCS also decided to start another co-op in Cedar Rapids, Iowa, a city twenty-five miles away. It is not clear whether the board surveyed members about this decision, although there were roundtable talks for members to express their concerns. Nor is it clear if the co-op had hired a consultant about the new store. Apparently, the Good Foods Co-op of Cedar Rapids had approached New Pioneer for financial and managerial assistance. Ultimately, New Pioneer decided to take over the co-op. Perhaps New Pioneer should have asked why Good Foods Co-op was faltering. Instead, construction started in April 1988, with the grand opening in August of the same year. Sales were strong the first week, then slacked. That, along with higher expenses, meant that the co-op did not break even the first year.[15]

Part of the Cedar Rapids store problem was an inexperienced store manager and staff that did not know about the store's products. New Pioneer tried to get out the word through advertisements in Cedar Rapids newspapers and flyers to 5,000 households, presentations to different groups, coupon programs, and gift certificates. To break even, the Cedar Rapids co-op had to make $18,000 in weekly sales. At best, they made between $11,000 and $12,000. One reason was that its membership remained small, at only 800. The Cedar Rapids co-op was not successful, in large part because people were not familiar with the idea of co-ops or their products. Not surprisingly, the store closed in early 1991.[16]

Doing Business a New Way

Like the Arcata Food Co-op, New Pioneer had decided to expand its number of stores, corresponding with the idea of corporate growth. But New Pioneer had other options, as did the Arcata co-op. It could have assisted the failing co-op. If, in fact, the manager and staff did not know much about the co-op's products, New Pioneer could have offered training and consultation. If anything, Cedar Rapids was a very different community than Iowa City. A larger city built on the corn and grain processing industries of Quaker Oats, Cargill, and General Mills, Cedar Rapids had a sizeable working class, which had probably been negatively affected by the deindustrialization of the 1980s. In all likelihood, there was not a large enough market or community for a food co-op in the city. A more viable option would have been the promotion of food buying clubs.

In Iowa City, the New Pioneer Co-op had remodeled and was ready to do business. The co-op now had a deli, meat and fish departments, and had doubled their retail space. They sold over 100 cheeses and many bulk items: 225 food items, 275 herbs, spices, and coffee. There were also more than 100 varieties of wine and beer. According to the general manager, "We perceive ourselves in the marketplace as a neighborhood store."[17] Clearly the products exceeded what any neighborhood store would normally sell. In fact, New Pioneer had taken the advice of the Community Consulting Group of Cambridge, Massachusetts: to appeal to higher-income members.

There were other changes as well. New Pioneer now relied mostly on paid employees, not its members. The newsletter reflected the new attitude: "We are a consumer co-op and we function like a corporation in many respects. Members are shareholders who elect a board of directors, and the board of directors is responsible for providing a general manager."[18] Like the North Coast Co-op, New Pioneer had appropriated corporate language. Members were no longer perceived as collective owners as much as shareholders, whose main responsibility was to elect a board of directors. The hierarchical structure expanded to include managers in marketing, finance, and member services, and five department managers, responsible for customer service, merchandising display, and purchasing and inventory within their areas. New Pioneer was poised for financial growth. In fact, sales did increase, from $1.7 million in 1987 to $2.6 million in 1988.[19] Still, 1989 was a challenging year because of the Cedar Rapids store. By 1990, though, the NPCS made $4.9 million in sales and had a membership of 4,300. Two years later, its sales were over $5 million and its membership had increased to 5,000. In 1993, sales had increased to almost $5.6 million.[20]

Within a twenty-year period, New Pioneer had grown from a storefront that sold mostly bulk goods to a larger store that carried imported cheeses, wine and beer, and other high-end foods. Formerly a workers' collective, New Pioneer now had a general manager, along with a corps of managers. Its membership and sales had increased substantially. But at what costs to its members/owners, who were now considered shareholders? A controversy over unionization in the 1990s would spark New Pioneer's members to engage in participatory democracy.

The NPCS, 1990–2012

In 1991, when the New Pioneer celebrated its twenty-year anniversary, the board discussed expansion yet again. Members, though, held different ideas for how the co-op should grow. Some wanted a bakery added; still others wanted to open a new store. Here, at least, members voiced their preferences and it appears that some approved of expansion. New Pioneer decided to hire a consulting firm to determine the sales potential of various natural food store locations. One outcome was the opening of the Bakehouse in 1995 in nearby Coralville, which made fresh, organic bread with a hearth oven. That year, the Bakehouse served an average of 1,450 customers per day, compared to 850 at most natural food retail stores. The bakery sold $400,000 worth of six types of bread yearly. Although some members had criticized the idea, it was a profitable one.[21]

Expansion Once Again

The NPCS wanted to expand in other ways as well: by opening a co-op store in Coralville, a town next to Iowa City; and by owning, not renting, their own store in Iowa City. At the annual 1993 members' meeting, attended by only seventy members, 87 percent of attendees endorsed the new co-op store. Here, the low level of membership is noteworthy. As noted throughout this book, once a co-op becomes more hierarchical in structure, with a board of directors and managers, members lose interest in their co-op. Perhaps members could have been more involved through committee work or discussions at board meetings. Instead, the co-op, as many others, relied more on consulting firms and market studies to help make decisions about its future direction.

In fact, in 1994 the co-op had another market study done to decide on the issue of expansion or relocation. The study indicated that not expanding would have a negative impact on the co-op, for the consultants predicted growth for other grocery stores in the area. The marketing plan also recommended selling organic foods, frozen foods, vitamins and supplements, and wine to distinguish it from other grocery stores. For the Bakehouse in Coralville, they recommended that it offer breakfast and lunch that would include pastries, soups, salads, and smoothies. The board endorsed expanding the Bakehouse but put the idea of another co-op store on hold.[22]

The Iowa City co-op was also trying to decide whether to own or rent its new store building. Although many members had favored renting, the board made an offer on the site but was outbid. Here, again, it appears as if the board overruled the members. In late 1996, the board was considering a downtown site. But this did not work out either. In early 1997, the board voted unanimously to buy the property on the corner of Washington and Van Buren streets. The landlord had offered to sell the property, rather than renew the lease.[23] But this did not happen either. However, as the board emphasized: "This does *not* alter our previous efforts to pursue new store locations that will better meet the needs of our growing membership and customer base."[24]

In the spring of 1996, there was a Stakeholders' Conference, at which co-op members discussed their core values. Only 50 of the 7,500 co-op members participated, perhaps because they were not comfortable with the business language. Or perhaps they realized that the board had not taken their previous suggestions seriously. Clearly, the NPCS wanted more member involvement. As the board explained, "We are looking for members-owners to participate in our stakeholders conference. The purpose is to involve a broad base of community members in the process of envisioning our future." The board members hoped to reach "a common understanding" of the current external environment and their internal environment of the co-op to identify a "common future vision."[25] Yet member participation remained low; only 1,069 members had voted in the 1997 board elections.[26]

At the Stakeholders' Conference, the core values chosen were food product value and quality; people/community; leadership; commitment to community; cooperative principles; consumer responsibility; support of local food sources; commitment to improve the environment; education and advocacy; and remaining open to new ideas.[27] In fact, the values of improving the environment and supporting local food sources had been in the co-op's original mission. The values of cooperative principles, including education and advocacy, were Rochdale. But those values relating to community were ambiguous. Who was the "community"? Was it the New Pioneer members, the local community, or the larger cooperative community? Again, the small turnout of members at the conference suggests that the member community was often inactive.

Members' Protests

Yet members were active on several issues. One was about which products to boycott. In 1994, members had voted to support the United Farm Workers (UFW) grape boycott. The co-op set up a committee to review its boycott policies and to provide a set of guidelines. Likewise, members organized to resist genetically modified (GM) foods through the Campaign to Resist Genetically Engineered Food. Other advocacy groups then included Greenpeace, which called for a complete ban on all releases of GM organisms into the environment. Likewise, the Pure Food Campaign, founded in 1992, offered practical ways for consumers and retailers concerned about GM foods.[28]

Another concern for members was the co-op's mission statement. In April 1996, the board revised its mission statement to read: "New Pioneer is a co-operatively owned business, fully serving the needs of the natural products consumer. We emphasize high quality, fair prices and product information. We are an environmentally and socially responsible member of the community we serve." As if an afterthought, they added: "We're a business owned and controlled by our members—a Co-op!"[29] The mission statement had previously claimed that the "primary function" of co-op was to "serve the needs of its members."[30] The mission statement had been revised because some members were concerned that the co-op's purposes had been "lost." Their revision was: "The Co-operative is organized on a co-operative basis" and "is dedicated to the purposes incorporated in its founding. Its mission is to serve the needs of its members, stimulate the local agricultural production of organic foods and to provide a market for such foods. The Co-operative fully recognizes the value and dignity of work and shall place the highest priority on the health, welfare, happiness and rights of all its employees. The Co-operative shall strive to set a community standard for the best possible working conditions, training, wages, benefits, and opportunities for advancement of its employees."[31]

The members' intentions were to align the mission statement with its original one. Indeed, members wanted to restore the ideas and practices of cooperative principles. But most telling was their inclusion of workers' rights. Up to this point, there had been little mention of the workers. What had prompted members to add these statements? It was the issue of unionization. This was the issue about which most members were adamant.

Disunity over Unionization

NPCS workers had become interested in unionizing as early as 1990. Then, the co-op had formed a Personal Advisory Committee (PAC), chaired by a human resource manager to listen to the workers' concerns. When the human resource manager left, the committee disbanded but would be "revitalized" in 1996. That year, the board had received a notice from the National Labor Relations Board that the United Electrical, Radio and Machine Workers of America had filed a petition to be a paid representative of the co-op employees. The board replied that they respected the rights of co-op employees to join the union. Management, too, claimed to support the process and the election.[32] But some workers and members were suspicious that the board and management were undermining the process of unionization. One reason was that the board had hired a consulting firm "to guide them through the unionizing process."[33] This firm was known for its union-busting activities. Consequently, some members formed their own organization, Members for an Accountable Co-op (MAC), to support the workers and to reclaim members' "ownership" of co-op decisions. MAC was especially interested in knowing how much the consulting firm had been paid.[34]

When workers voted in early 1997, the vote was split: forty workers against and forty-six workers in favor of unionization. Those in favor noted that part-time workers had no health insurance, sick days, or vacation and holiday pay. Some workers also hoped that a union would bring worker solidarity and create better communication between them and the management. What some workers simply wanted was a voice in the co-op's decisions.[35] According to one employee, the co-op had grown, as had the staff, and many workers had left the co-op "frustrated over a lack of tangible employee input into the daily work decisions and long term policy decisions."[36] Another employee agreed, noting that employees were an important part of the co-op but were not consulted. As he argued, "We need more than just one or two people's input. Unionization is the best way to achieve the ideals of a co-op."[37]

There were charges that several managers discouraged unionism. Some workers said they had been pressured by management to vote against unionization. Other workers stated that the management had handed out antiunion propaganda. When the general manager heard that workers voted to unionize, she cautioned them not to "rush . . . without following fair due process under the authority of the National Labor Relations Board [NLRB]."[38] Another worker thought the union vote had failed because of "six weeks of intimidation" and "union bashing" by the management. At the very least, he argued, management was now more aware of workers' concerns, especially part-time employees'.[39] Ironically, during this time, the board and management had supported the UFW but not a union in their own co-op.

From the general manager's point of view, unionization was an indication that the employees thought New Pioneer was just a business with "no interest in social change." She worried that workers "lack[ed] confidence that the co-op had their best interests in mind." In working for the co-op for twelve years, she noted that the number of staff had increased, making for more difficult communication. For this reason, the co-op had started a staff newsletter, an employee manual, and the PAC. Her main point was that the workers and managers had always "worked through [their] differences" because they were a "partnership." But this was obviously not how the workers saw the situation. Her final statements were clearly antiunion: "While you may get all or more through collective bargaining, you may get less. All of this [a list of their benefits] will have to be negotiated if you choose to have a union represent you."[40] One member responded by stating that management's position was that of "parent knows best."[41]

There is further evidence that the managers discouraged workers from unionizing. One of the in-house newsletters, "A Slice of Pi," published several antiunion statements. There, the store operations manager wrote that she saw no need for a union. A supervisor on duty also wrote that he did not think that the co-op needed one.[42] The associate director of the University of Iowa Labor Education Center countered the so-called factual information presented in the newsletter, arguing that NPCS workers were threatened by management. Disputing the "fact" that "under the law there is no obligation for either party to reach an agreement," he argued that this was "the classic message of the union avoidance consultant." He countered another "fact" that "if the union does not get what it wants, its only option is to strike," stating that it was not only wrong but "emotionally intimidating and scare-mongering." He dismissed another fact as incorrect, that "the union can trade away what you already have."[43] The director of the University of the Iowa Labor Center agreed with workers about management's antiunion sentiments: "I was dismayed to recognize the subtle but pervasive stamp of union avoidance in the document. It is fraught with the spin doctor's delight of partial information and selected interpretation that is designed to cause unease, insecurity and doubt among workers."[44]

Some members accused the board of antiunionism as well. When the board president had weighed in on the issue, he wrote to the employees: "I used to think that unions were like co-ops." But then he saw that there were "good unions and bad unions." He worried that unions would come between management and workers, and so "unionization [wa]s not in the best interests [sic] of New Pioneer." At the same time, he told the workers that, "The decision, of course, is up to you."[45]

"Management Is the Problem"

Some disappointed co-op members returned to the board's earlier decisions to open a store in Cedar Rapids and the Bakehouse. Members wanted to know the amount of financial losses from both ventures. The board stated that any member could make an appointment with the general manager to review the co-op's financial statements. But, it added, the Bakehouse was a success. In response to the question of why it went out of state for a facilitator for the stakeholders' meeting, the board replied that "vendor fees [we]re not disclosed." When asked what the cost of a Chicago attorney was, again the board responded that "vendor fees [we]re not disclosed." It also refused to disclose the managers' salaries. When asked why it did not welcome unionization, the board replied that it wanted to respect all workers' rights. Further, instead of unions it favored a "partnership" among members, management, and staff.[46] In refusing to answer these questions, the board raised members' suspicion. And the board clearly separated itself from the member ownership of the co-op.

MAC reacted by stepping up its protests. Its slogan became: "Management is the Problem, the Board is the Solution." But MAC also thought that the board had forgotten the co-op's mission. MAC president Roberta Till-Retz argued, "Co-ops should be pro-worker, pro-union and pro-local grower."[47] In fact, New Pioneer was "pro-local grower," an issue that was not contentious. MAC not only wanted to discuss unionization with members and employees; it insisted that its rights as members and as shareholders included the right to inspect and copy records. Here, MAC's use of "shareholders" acknowledged that New Pioneer was a business, as did the board. But MAC also clarified what kind of business it was: a co-op that was member-owned. Likewise, MAC argued, members had the right to remove directors and officers, at least through the majority of all voting members. Further, members had the right to look at the list of shareholders. Finally, members could submit issues at board meetings through a petition signed by at least twenty-five members in good standing.[48]

In March 1997, MAC and 325 members signed a petition asking for a special general membership meeting with the board to discuss the management's treatment of the workers. Although this number did not fully represent all co-op members, it was larger than the number of members who had voted at the board elections or who had attended the Stakeholders' Conference. In favoring unionization, MAC thought that management was "wrong" in hiring an attorney in labor management relations. MAC also claimed that the management and board were "secretive" about the co-op's finances. MAC had questions about the board's role in the decision to stall on union recognition and hiring an attorney, as well as opening stores in Cedar Rapids and Coralville. Again, MAC asked about the cost of a "facilitator" for the stakeholders' meeting and the cost of the Chicago law firm and the salaries of top management.[49] The general manager's reply was somewhat evasive: that the co-op's lawyer did not deal with labor issues and that the Chicago firm specialized in this.[50]

MAC was interested in unionization but they used that issue to leverage member interest in other ones. In fact, MAC wanted to return to the original member control structure of the 1970s. That is, the group wanted a co-op where members had more input into major decisions. After all, MAC claimed, it was the

members who owned the co-op.[51] One MAC member claimed that the co-op
made a "mockery" of the idea of cooperation because it was run "like a private
corporation." Further, its members were treated like "absentee shareholders." He
resigned as a member.[52] When another member went to the co-op to see the financial records, she was allowed only fifteen minutes to look at the 1996 financial
statement but not the general ledger. She found that the line item for legal expenses in 1996–1997 was $18,700.[53] In fact, according to the Iowa Code Chapter
499, it was not clear whether members had the right to inspect the co-op's books
and records. This was in contrast to Chapter 490 and 504A, which stated that
stockholders and members had the right to do so with corporations.[54]

The controversy culminated at the September 1997 board meeting, when
the board president ordered that campus security be called to "eject" a co-op
member from a board meeting. The member had a tape recorder but the board
president said the meeting could not be taped, even though the board taped the
meeting. When the member refused to put away his tape recorder, the board
president called for an executive meeting. But no motion had been made for such
a session. When a latecomer arrived and asked what was happening, he, too, was
told to leave. When another member asked what the meeting was for, the board
president replied that "it was none of his business." While the meeting was underway, two security officers entered the room and the board president pointed to
the member that he thought was a problem. When that member refused to leave,
the board president decided that he could stay.[55]

Members became more suspicious of the board when the general manager
resigned at the end of 1997. During her six-year tenure, the co-op's annual sales
had increased from $4 million to $7 million. The number of hourly staff had
increased by 2 percent and full-time staff from 52 percent to 67 percent. The
staff had also become more diverse. Further, she had initiated many benefits for
workers: full-time status was reduced from thirty-five to thirty-two hours; the
hourly-paid staff was given higher wages; and all workers were provided with
health insurance. Members wanted to know why she had resigned. Indeed, it is
difficult to know whether she had been discouraged by tensions with the board
and staff, or whether she might have been asked to resign. Regardless of the reason, MAC continued to argue that the board did not want members involved in
the decision-making process. The board tried to placate MAC by adopting a new
mission statement, clarifying the petition process, and establishing procedures
for removing board members.[56]

Despite these revisions, some members were still suspicious of the board. One
letter in the co-op newsletter accused the new board of hiring its own PR spokes-
person to represent it to members and hiring moderators for the members'
forum at board meetings.[57] Although the truth of these accusations could not be

verified, they did bring back the specter of earlier problems with the board. In fact, letters from members provided an interesting, if sometime unreliable, context for the co-op. For example, one letter noted how many co-ops had changed during the 1980s, as did New Pioneer, to become more like other businesses. This meant that employees "fell by the wayside." Another member wanted to know how much the "facilitator" was paid to "control member input" during the last four meetings. And why was a PR expert paid $50 or more per hour to put a "spin" on the general manager's leaving?[58]

From the "open forum" of the co-op newsletter, former marketing manager gave her opinion of what had happened at New Pioneer: many years of poor employee relations and a board that overspent and "sabotage[d] community and member relations." The good news, she wrote, was that there was enough money so that "even the most amateurish board of directors c[ould] fumble around for quite some time." In her opinion, when the union lost, a "local political machine put their gears of motion" to elect several new board members "with a hidden agenda to fire the general manager as retaliation for the union's loss and to set the stage for the next campaign."[59] There was no evidence of these accusations. However, there seemed to be no reason for the board firing her, unless she was a scapegoat.

A New Business Plan

Despite tensions and disagreements, sales continued to be high at New Pioneer: $6.63 million in 1995, and $7.05 million the following year. Yearly sales for 1997 were $7.56 million (which included Bakehouse's sales of over $713,000). In comparison, the average natural foods supermarket's sales during 1995 and 1996 were around $4.5 million. In addition, the weekly customer count at the NPCS in 1995 and 1996 was over 9,500; the average natural food supermarket's—5,355.[60] NPCS percentage of sales to its members was slightly more than 74 percent in 1997, compared to 55 percent at the average large co-op. However, the average transaction at New Pioneer in 1997 was only $13.66, compared to $22.96 at a natural foods supermarket.[61]

However, another development was brewing in 1998: a business plan for a new co-op in nearby Coralville. Some board members opposed it, citing lack of evidence regarding the consultants' claim of projected growth. Other board members favored the new co-op, arguing that having two stores would not "put our eggs in one basket."[62] A committee was set up to review a business plan, which would then be considered by the board. With a projected completion date in early 2000, the new Coralville co-op would have deli seating, double the space of the first co-op for more product choices, and more members. Although the staff favored another store, not all members did.[63] The NPCS held an open forum in the summer of 1999. But some members thought the new co-op was a "done deal" and there was no "meaningful member participation" with regard to the decision. As one person wrote in the newsletter, "Ain't that democracy. Have a debate on the subject after the deed is done. Nixon's plumbers couldn't have done a better job." Another member wanted the co-op to go back to "food for people not for profit." In the end, the board's vote for a second store was narrow, four to three.[64] A survey, decried by some as confusing, showed that 86 percent of the co-op members approved of a second store.[65] But it was not clear how many members voted. By then, there was no mention of MAC in the co-op records. Perhaps the group has disbanded, for surely they were interested in members' involvement in key business decisions.

In August 1999, the board signed the Coralville store lease. More letters decried this expansion. One member noted that Iowa Cityans were trying to save Iowa City from developers. So why, he asked, was the co-op contributing to urban sprawl?[66] Indeed, a "small" team that included the corporate management team, the project manager, the architect, and some department managers made major construction decisions. There were, however, staff surveys to get workers' input.[67] Nonetheless, some members protested and decided to sue the co-op. In 2000, co-op members Charles and Carol de Prosse sued the co-op to force it to account for all the equity of its members since 1971. They also wanted to stop the building of the new Coralville store until all the equity was accounted for. It is not clear how many members backed their decision or whether they had been part of MAC. The general manager testified that members accounted for 85 percent of the co-op's $8.2 million in gross sales in 1999. And, according to the testimony of the board president, there was a patronage dividend early on but much of that money had been put in the reserve fund.[68]

Regardless of some members' efforts to stop the second co-op, the project moved forward. The Coralville store opened on Valentine's Day in 2001. The store was large, a converted four-plex movie theater with three floors. It had a wine cellar, a meat and seafood department, a juice and coffee bar, a salad bar, two seating areas, the eight-ton stone hearth oven relocated from the former Bakehouse, and a mezzanine for offices and demo/cooking class kitchen.[69] The final cost of the new co-op store was almost $3 million, $1.32 million over costs because the building was difficult to remodel, there were delays in city permits, and there were changes in the plans and in construction supervisors. Its lease was also costly, at $10,000 a month.[70]

The new co-op was beset with problems from the beginning. According to the treasurer's 2001 report, both co-ops had lost $180,000. In early 2002, the two managers of the Coralville co-op resigned, although one was later rehired. In fact, the NPCS had depleted its financial reserves because of the Coralville store. Monthly losses strained NPCS resources, which "threaten[ed] [its] financial vitality."[71] By June 2001, the NPCS had a net loss of $255,000 and a cash balance of only $24,000. The board was considering turning to its members to ask them to participate in a member loan program.[72]

It is interesting that the board finally turned to the members. Board members had not wanted members to play a larger role in decision making, only to financially support the board's decision. To be sure, many members were not pleased about these financial losses. At the 2001 annual meeting they asked about product differences at the two stores, whether the Coralville co-op contributed to urban sprawl, and the issue of buying versus leasing the store building.[73] At an open forum in the spring of 2002, Jim Walters argued that the co-op had misread the market for a Coralville co-op. Walters had been a member since 1972 and a board secretary from 1997 to early 2001. He had, in fact, voted against the Coralville co-op because he did not find the marketing study believable. He called it "a laughable document, replete with errors of census tract populations and absurd estimates of the sales the co-op could expect." As he wrote in an editorial, the NPCS board had made a number of mistakes over the years. The Cedar Rapids co-op had cost the NPCS over $1 million. Similarly, not buying the Van Buren Street building in Iowa City had cost the co-op years of high rent. And then, when the board did decide to buy the property, it did so at ten times the original price. Then it hired a "union-busting Chicago law firm at $36,000." Last, almost half a million dollars of unallocated patronage earnings were used in building the Coralville store. He concluded that it was no surprise that members wanted to take back control of their co-op.[74] Carol de Prosse agreed with Walters, especially about the "poorly reasoned market study by yet another expert."[75]

One of the managers of the Coralville co-op blamed the board for the financial problems. He claimed that New Pioneer had "made progress" toward its financial problems. The management and staff had worked hard to keep the Coralville store afloat. He said that the board, however, was "unwilling" to do anything. Further, the board "had nothing but contempt for its responsibilities" and that no one had experience working with small businesses or managing grocery stores.[76] In the summer of 2002, he resigned over disagreements with the board. He and a former board member then proceeded to write letters to the local newspapers, claiming that the board "lack[ed] leadership" and that it was driven more by ideology than pragmatic needs. The reality was that there was one profitable co-op store and another unprofitable one. Some members thought the Coralville store should be sold. But who would buy it, they asked?[77]

By 2002, the NPCS was $2 million in debt. The board's proposed recovery plan was to charge $60 more per member. Carol de Prosse had another idea. Noting that 6,500 of the members spent $40 or less a month at the co-op, she suggested that its wealthier members give or loan the co-op 1 percent of their gross salaries. In the end, the board decided on cost-cutting measures at the Coralville store by reducing the number of workers by 17 percent and reducing surplus inventories. The workers bore the brunt of the board's bad decisions and the co-op's recovery. These changes did, however, lead to profitable operations by late 2002. By the end of 2004, the Coralville store's sales were close to the Iowa City co-op's sales.[78]

High Prices and Member Discontent

High prices at both co-op stores bothered members. Results of a 2003 survey showed that members wanted lower prices. Still, most members shopped at the NPCS because of its high-quality product selection, especially its organic food, and the locations. Yet 87 percent of the members also shopped at Hy-Vee and even Walmart. The board responded by passing an "affordability policy" to provide food at "competitive" prices in 2004.[79] Unfortunately, there is little information about this or about either co-op for that year. But if one considers the kinds of foods sold at the co-op, it becomes clear that members had to be middle- and upper-class to afford them.

Regardless of the higher prices, the NPCS's 2005 sales were more than 13 percent higher than the previous year. The Coralville co-op had earned a profit for the first time and New Pioneer was now debt free. By 2006, the two stores were a $16 million operation. That year, though, the NPCS faced competition, when a new natural foods store opened in downtown Iowa City. The co-op decided to strengthen its customer service and make products more affordable.[80] The NPCS also faced competition from Walmart. New Pioneer board decided to challenge Walmart on its unfair labor practices, particularly its low wages and lack of full benefits to its workers. In fact, the co-op had joined the Iowa City Stop Walmart Committee but did not join the suit as a plaintiff.[81]

Some members continued to ask the board questions. At an open forum, they asked how the managers chose products to sell at the two co-ops. They were especially concerned about products from China or from any country that violated human rights. They also did not want to support large corporations in the natural food industry. Opposed to irradiated meat served in the local public school lunch programs, co-op members spoke to the school board. In late 2006, members voted on the issue of labeling and decided that if the co-op's produce was not certified organic, it should be labeled "may be heavily pesticided."[82] The members' consumer advocacy was about the products the co-ops carried, not about member control or the co-op's finances. Perhaps they realized that, at the very least, they could exert some influence over these issues.

High prices continued to be a problem for many, especially college students and working-class members. In a 2003 survey, many members again complained about the NPCS's high prices. The co-op suggested that students buy in bulk, buy vegetables, and buy cheaper wines. In late 2009 members continued to complain about high prices. In one 2009 newsletter, a letter from a long-standing member noted how expensive the food was and that the co-op sold food that only middle- to upper-class residents could afford. Her letter had been in response to the last newsletter's recipes for people "feeling" the economic downturn. She countered that even with her 30 percent member discount, she could still only afford a few bulk items. She concluded that the co-op was out of touch with its members. Ironically, she said, people could get more affordable food at Walmart.[83]

Some issues get revisited. In the summer 2010 newsletter's "progress update," the board mentioned two priorities in its three-to-five-year strategic plan. One was to buy the Coralville store; the other was to relocate the Iowa City store, which had flooded in the past because it was in a floodplain. Because of the floodplain, the board claimed, the store had not been able to expand. The present location had also "strained the capacity" of the store and burdened the staff in stocking goods and serving customers. A letter from a long-time member and former board member evoked some of the contentious history behind the co-op's earlier decisions. In the case of the Iowa City store, the co-op had delayed buying the building until the price had risen to almost ten times the original price of $40,000.[84] The decision to open a store in Coralville was fraught with problems: underestimating renovation costs, paying for renovations on a leased building, paying high rent, and not having member support. The Coralville store nearly "did in" the Iowa City co-op.

As of 2012, decisions about relocation of the Iowa City co-op had not been made. Board members and co-op members would be wise to revisit the history of New Pioneer and some of its failed ventures before deciding to relocate. They would learn a number of lessons. First, a co-op board must be responsive to its members, who own the co-op. As New Pioneer's history shows, the board often ignored members who disagreed with its position and, in some cases, tried to stifle their opposition. The board essentially took the members' patronage refund since 1992, put it in reserves, and used it to finance expansion, despite members' disapproval.

Second, the idea of expansion and corporate growth had been a recurring one in the 1980s and 1990s for many co-ops. As with the North Coast Co-op, New Pioneer built two new stores; of those, one failed because it was in a working-class community. A better decision, I believe, would have been to assist the Cedar Rapids co-op and not take it over. In fact, starting new co-ops in Cedar Rapids and

Coralville severely compromised New Pioneer's financial well-being. But beyond that, smaller co-ops, I believe, can be more responsive to their members and to their communities at large. Smaller co-ops can still be "profitable," while also treating their workers fairly and heeding members' concerns. In short, smaller co-ops can better practice participatory democracy because they do not take on a corporate structure that discourages member involvement.

Third, what of the workers? When a food co-op is financially distressed, one of the first things it often does is cut down its workers' hours. New Pioneer was no exception. Beyond that, though, New Pioneer's managers and board members interfered with the process of unionization. Although the board and managers argued for a partnership among members, management, and staff, their actions revealed contrary motives. In fact, underlying some workers' demand for unionization seemed to be an interest in partnership, which for them meant having more influence in the co-op's daily operations. Their concern speaks also to the idea of participatory democracy among workers.

10

COOPERATIVES IN THE TWIN CITIES

Minnesota has historically been considered one of the county's "greatest cooperative states."[1] As early as 1870, there were at least forty cooperatives in Minneapolis alone. Some were started by co-opers, who were immigrants from various countries; one of their co-ops was a store that sold groceries and dry goods. By 1886, native-born white and immigrant laborers from different trades—cigar makers, printers, carpenters, laundresses, painters, and musicians—had organized co-ops as well. However, in rural areas, members of cooperatives, especially creameries, belonged to one ethnic group.[2] Many of these early co-ops, according to historian Steven Keillor, gave communities the opportunity to "use democracy to bring business to them, to control it, and to use it for their benefit." At the same time, he argued, co-ops sometimes "inherited" democracy's "inefficiencies," which included a lack of capital, and members' disinterest and their lack of participation.[3]

Although many of Minnesota co-ops were Rochdale ones and were to follow political neutrality, that was not always the case. The state was populated by Finnish and Scandinavian immigrants, many of them socialists and some members of the Communist Party. In 1917, a number of Finnish American co-ops had established the Central Cooperative Exchange (CCE), predecessor to the Central Cooperative Wholesale (CCW). There were internal struggles over control of funds within the CCE among communists, socialists, and members of a third party, Farmer-Laborites. Finally, in 1929 the CCE split with the communists and changed its name to the CCW. By 1934, the CCW had thirty-three stores in

Minneapolis, among them the Franklin Co-operative Creamery Association, which claimed to be the largest consumer cooperative in the country.[4]

Like their predecessors, the Twin Cities food co-ops of the 1970s were radical and ideological. However, their radicalism was inspired by the New Left. Historian Doug Rossinow has argued that many from the New Left of the 1970s were white college students and members of the Students for a Democratic Society (SDS). In particular, he noted, the SDS sought alliances with the working class through Marxist radicalism.[5] As such, they were critical of hippies whose countercultural practices reflected a middle class "escapism."[6] David Farber, too, has noted that some members of the New Left cynically accused hippies of indulging in drugs and sex until they later became "corporate adult[s]."[7] Van Gosse, however, has enlarged the identity of the New Left, noting that some members from the Old Left of the 1950s joined forces with 1960s radicals. Nonetheless, he too noted that many college students interpreted Marxism as Third World Marxism.[8]

Regardless of these critiques, we should not discredit the social movements and corresponding activism of the 1960s and 1970s. Because the New Left has meant many things, it has been difficult to assess its impact. Nonetheless, there were many social movements then. Much has been written of the women's movement that created shelters for battered women, counseled abused women, and organized "take back the night" marches on college campuses. Most readers are familiar with the Black Civil Rights movement, as well as similar movements for Chicanos, Native Americans, and gays. There were the notable protests against the Vietnam War but also against nuclear power plants and the military-industrial complex at many universities. And there was the emerging environmental movement.[9] It was within these various movements that the food co-ops in the Twin Cities started. As one activist in the Twin Cities' food co-op movement reflected: "I guess they [co-opers] just decided they had to build co-ops in order to stop the war."[10]

To be sure, the co-op wars in the Twin Cities reflected ideological differences among Marxist-Leninist, so-called hippies, and other groups. Further, the issues faced by the co-ops divided many as they disagreed over membership and food choices that reflected social class and community affiliation. Many members organized around working collectives, whereby decision making by consensus enacted participatory democracy and people power, not the corporate structure of most US businesses. However, issues of control were both ideological and personal, sometimes resulting in physical violence, arson, insults, and co-op takeovers. How did various ideologies translate into practice? Did they foster or hinder cross-class and cross-race coalitions? Were the co-ops' struggles a reflection of participatory democracy or the lack of it? Without a doubt, the co-op wars in the Twin Cities were riddled with complexity, contradictions, ideological debates, and sometimes confusion.

The People's Warehouse Takeover

A number of food and other cooperatives had started in the early 1970s in the Twin Cities. In the summer of 1970, Thomas Quinn and Roman Iwachiw, described as "long hairs," started True Grits, which promised "to sell good food to poor people" in downtown Minneapolis.[11] There is little information about what they considered "good food" but more than likely it was natural or organic. The North Country Co-op started in 1970 as People's Pantry on the back porch of four sisters living on the West Bank in Minneapolis. The following year, it became a co-op, whose mission was "to be a working example of participatory democracy in all facets of operation and governance."[12] This spirit was expressed at its potlucks and meetings, "where everybody eats, drinks, talks, smokes, meets, sings, argues, learns, teaches, sees old friends and chooses 12 folks to be on the Board of Directors."[13] The groups decided to sell food that was inexpensive, unprocessed, local, and did not exploit workers. Working collectively, they opened a storefront in 1971.[14] The North Country Co-op also set up a People's Warehouse to distribute foods to various co-ops and buying clubs.

That same year, a number of other co-ops opened. Six blocks from the North Country Co-op was another informally organized co-op—the Seward Community Co-op. Its members wrote down their orders and put money in the old cash register. Similarly, Seward members worked together to build consensus, referring to their co-op as "worker-controlled with community input."[15] But others in the emerging Twin Cities' food co-op movement referred to them as white, middle-class hippies who were "elitist" because they did not want to sell "shit food."[16] The intentions of another new co-op, Ecology Co-op (later the Southeast Co-op), were to not just "feed people" but to ensure that people had access to healthy foods.[17] Whole Foods Co-op (not affiliated with the chain Whole Foods), which started in the basement of St. Steven's Church in Minneapolis's Whittier neighborhood, also promised cheap but healthy food. The Minnesota Health Department thought otherwise, perhaps considering it unsanitary, and closed it down.[18]

Working-Class Alliances

African American and Native American neighborhoods also organized co-ops. As early as 1969, a north Minneapolis African American community had formed the People's Cooperative Union, although it survived less than a year. A south Minneapolis community started Bryant-Central Co-op through the assistance of the Central Neighborhood Improvement Association and the Urban League chapter. They wanted members of the co-op and the community to decide what kinds of food to sell, which might include processed foods, meats, dairy, bulk and produce.[19] Selby Co-op, established in St. Paul in 1970, hoped to build alliances with the working class, especially with the African American community. Part of their democratic plan involved changing its all-white workforce to include African Americans. Toward this end, the co-op set up a new structure, the Co-op Council, which gave the African American working class more say in their store's decisions,[20] including which kinds of food to sell. By including canned goods the co-op thought it "could expand the nature and size of people who support[ed] co-ops."[21] Last, Mill City Co-operative Foods began in the south Minneapolis neighborhood of Phillips, a neighborhood mixed with families, communes, students, senior citizens, and one of the largest Native American populations in an American city. Most residents had incomes of less than $10,000 so the co-op sold mostly bulk and some organic food.[22]

As of 1974, there were at least twelve neighborhood food co-op stores, three co-op book stores, two co-op bakeries, and other types of cooperatives. Some of the food co-ops were on the West Bank of St. Paul, near the University of Minnesota. Others were in the working-class and poorer neighborhoods of Minneapolis.[23] In 1974, yet another co-op opened in a basement apartment in Minneapolis's Whittier neighborhood. Like many others there, the Wedge was interested in selling natural and organic food, mostly in bulk. The following year, Blooming Prairie Warehouse started, serving food co-ops not just in the Twin Cities but throughout Minnesota and other upper midwestern states.[24] Despite the end of the Vietnam War and high inflation nationally at 11 percent in 1974, the food co-op movement in the Twin Cities seemed to be doing well. One reason was that these co-ops were storefronts that kept overhead and prices low, in part through workers' collectives and members' volunteer labor.[25] Because some food co-ops claimed to support the working class, they were determined to keep food prices low.

Those co-ops that sought working-class alliances framed their identities and purposes in Marxist terms. For example, the original mission statements of the 12th Avenue People's Co-op in Minneapolis reflected an anticapitalist, socialist position: "Our volunteer labor is building socialized (in original) property. The value we create doesn't go to a private owner's pockets, but belongs to all working class people." In contrast, its members argued that the profits of Cargill and other corporations were "built on the backs of working people."[26] Accordingly, their four goals were: "to be a weapon in the struggle against the monopolistic profit structure of the food industry"; to reduce the high cost of food; to create jobs "for

the unemployed and foster working class solidarity on the job and off the job";
and to "educate unemployed and working masses about the politics of food."[27]
In their view, their motivations were far different from hippies', who organized
co-ops because of their opposition to the war which, they insisted, did not lead
to class solidarity. Instead, evading the draft was "bourgeois" because the hippy
movement created alternative structures and organizations for themselves alone,
not for the working class.[28] As evidence, the 12th Avenue People's Co-op noted
that many hippy co-ops did not stock canned goods, thereby "st[anding] against
the desires and requests of the poor and working people."[29]

What foods co-ops sold was critical in terms of their identity, social class
alignment, and the communities they served. This led to a struggle simply known
as the canned food and brown rice wars.[30] In some cases, co-ops simply assumed
that working-class residents would not eat natural or organic food but only
canned goods. In other cases, co-ops had working-class members weigh in on the
food issues. For example, the Grass Co-op Grocery, located in a blue-collar working and lower middle-class neighborhood in St. Paul, ordered what its members
requested, including both canned goods and bulk grains. In 1975, North Country
decided to order more canned goods and sugar, after surveying its members.[31]
Food choices, though, would be just one of many reasons for the takeovers of
People's Warehouse and some of food co-ops. Nonetheless, food choice became
a symbol of class struggle.

Alongside food choices, ideological differences in ideas about democracy,
profit, workers' collectives, and labor conditions escalated into the People's
Warehouse takeover in 1975 by the Co-op Organization. In late 1974, different groups emerged among the Twin Cities' food cooperatives. Some were interested in anarchism, some in Marxism-Leninism. Several members from the
North Country Co-op circulated "working" papers in early 1975, claiming that
the Twin Cities' co-ops were too hippie-oriented and had no class consciousness. This study group became known as the Co-op Organization, who espoused
Marxist ideas and claimed that they represented interests of the working class.
Most were members of the Beanery Co-op and the People's Warehouse in Minneapolis, and wanted the warehouse to sell more canned and refined foods.

In March 1975, the study group decided to use the Beanery Co-op as an ideological experiment. One group published the "Beanery Paper," in which they ana-
lyzed the co-op's history and recommended that it could better serve the working
class. In turn, two people at Mill City Foods, under the names of Jeb and Emma,
wrote a critical response to the paper. In turn, the study group responded by referring to Jeb and Emma's "bourgeois-intellectual" attitudes. After this exchange,
two former workers of the warehouse took control of the Beanery Co-op. The
next month, the Co-op Organization attended a Mill City Foods Co-op meeting,

where they accused members of privately owning the co-op and being classist. The Mill City Co-op would be another of the Co-op Organization's attempted takeovers.[32]

Ideological Struggles: Marxists and Hippies

That same spring, Co-op Organization members of the People's Warehouse went to a meeting of the Policy Review Board, which represented various co-ops and the People's Warehouse. In fact, the Policy Review Board was the only mechanism through which all co-ops were represented. Nonetheless, the Co-op Organization wanted to restructure the People's Warehouse, as well as make sure that the warehouse sold canned goods. But the Policy Review Board refused the Co-op Organization's requests. Worried that the Co-op Organization would try to take over the warehouse, some of the warehouse workers spent the night there. When Co-op Organization members arrived, they disconnected the warehouse phones, threatened the workers, and kicked them out. A Co-op Organization member also took $6,000 from the warehouse accounts. The Co-op Organization claimed that it had taken over the People's Warehouse "in the interest of the working class."[33] In turn, ten of the fifteen Twin Cities' co-ops decided to boycott the warehouse and start a new one, the Distributing Alliance of the Northcountry Cooperative (DANCe). The Co-op Organization retaliated by threatening, assaulting, and even bombing the vehicles of co-op members who did not agree to buy from the People's Warehouse.[34]

In May, Co-op Organization members took over another co-op, the Powderhorn Collective. This was not so difficult, as at least half of the sixteen-member collective of Powderhorn was affiliated with the Co-op Organization. The Co-op Organization then decided to restructure the co-op by putting control in the hands of a council and two coordinators. By summer, they had hired Tim Lund as one of the co-op's coordinators.[35] At one meeting, Lund praised the restructuring, arguing that, even though there was now a council and coordinator, most decisions would be made through small groups and referendums.[36] But it was not clear whether this was the case.

In November, there was yet another struggle. This time it was between Bryant-Central Co-op, an African American co-op, and the People's Warehouse, still under control of the Co-op Organization. It was not just a struggle between two co-op organizations but between two people: Bob Haugen, one of the People's Warehouse's representatives, and Moe Burton, an African American community activist who had helped start Bryant-Central Co-op. Haugen thought the African American co-op was under control of the Co-op Organization; Burton thought otherwise. Haugen then challenged Burton to a fight.[37] Afterward, the People's Warehouse refused to sell to Bryant-Central Co-op until Burton was no longer affiliated with the store. Burton responded by calling the Co-op Organization "petty Eva Brauns and Mussolinis."[38]

As evident in the name-calling, the skirmish was a personal power struggle. In an interview with journalist Craig Cox, Burton acknowledged the "deep political grievance" between him and Haugen. But Burton also had a grievance with the Co-op Organization, as did many other co-opers in the Twin Cities. When he first met its members, he found out that, despite their "working-class" talk, they were "really just the same old hippie intellectuals that have been laying a rigid hippie line on everyone before."[39] As Cox conjectured, because so few African Americans were co-op members, Haugen wanted Burton and Bryant-Central Co-op's support to give the Co-op Organization legitimacy. In other words, their support would have demonstrated that the Co-op Organization had, indeed, formed alliances with poorer communities of color.[40]

In January 1976, Co-op Organization members decided to take over Mill City and Seward co-ops by force. At the Mill City Co-op, almost 200 of its members protected the store from Co-op Organization members, whose members retaliated by beating up the co-op's clerks, taking its ledgers, and changing the locks on the

FIGURE 6. Mill City Foods supporters and the Co-op Organization attempted takeover, Pete Hohn, Photographer, Chris Olsen Collection, Minnesota Historical Society, St. Paul, Minnesota.

store doors. Mill City workers decided to call the police, even though the police were part of the "establishment." The Seward Co-op also got a restraining order against those Co-op Organization members involved in the takeover. Later that month, the Co-op Organization filed papers with the state to gain legal control of both Mill City and Seward co-ops. All four signers, including Tim Lund, were from the Powderhorn Co-op.[41]

Trouble was also brewing at the North Country Co-op. In January, nearly fifty people convened to incorporate the co-op, as well as to "flush [the] CO influence out of NCC." In doing so, they insulted Co-op Organization members, calling them phony, shallow, and counterrevolutionary.[42] The next month, however, both groups convened and agreed on six goals for the co-op: to rehabilitate the store, to expand the food products, to organize bookkeeping, to centralize work in the store through a work committee, to set up a delivery service for senior citizens, and to get more neighborhood people involved. Clearly, this alliance was tenuous. When one Co-op Organization member publicly criticized the co-op, calling it "a transformed filthy hippie whole foods store," members became angry and protested the Co-op Organization's involvement.[43] Once again, much of the conflict centered on those who claimed to represent working-class interests versus so-called hippies.

Meanwhile, the Powderhorn Co-op was not doing well financially. Since the takeover by the Co-op Organization, it had lost many of its old customers. In March 1976, there were boycotts and pickets at the co-op, as well as beatings, bombs, and other kinds of violence. Here, the conflict was not just about canned goods or food with preservatives but who ran the store.[44] On March 22, one board member and two Powderhorn bookkeepers went to the bank, closed the accounts, and opened new accounts. They asked that Tim Lund's name be removed from the list of authorized check signers. When Lund went to the bank to protest, the bank froze the co-op's accounts and refused to open them until both sides came to an agreement or obtained a court order. In violation of a court order, which had ordered the co-op closed, the Co-op Organization reopened it one week later. In retaliation, co-op members held a picket and shop-in to protest control of their co-op by the Co-op Organization. Nearly seventy-five men, women, and children marched into the store and set up another cash register. When the managers locked them inside the store, the protestors took the food they had bought and carried it out a back window.[45] The police then came and cleared out the store. In April, there was yet another takeover but this time by sixty members of the co-op. They placed a sign in the window that read, "Powderhorn Co-op—Free at Last!"[46] This takeover had ended the year-long management by the Co-op Organization. By the summer, the co-op wars were largely over. The Co-op Organization's power had diminished considerably. It ran two co-op stores and a bakery. The Policy Review Board had also dissolved.

What do we make of these co-op wars, especially the Co-op Organization's dominance? First, we must ask who were Co-op Organization members? As noted, they were from a number of co-ops, most notably the Beanery and People's Warehouse. Ideologically, as Marxists-Leninists, they were interested in a social revolution, one larger than the co-ops. As one critic of the group noted, the Co-op Organization was not as interested in co-ops themselves as much as in "sharpening their analytical and organizational skill in preparation for the real task, the building of a revolutionary party." The Co-op Organization's first step in the revolution was to take over the People's Warehouse and a number of co-ops because the latter were too "disorganized" to lead a class struggle.[47] Thus, the Co-op Organization branded itself as the one that supported the working class.

But how did the Co-op Organization represent the working class? It was through takeovers of co-ops and the People's Warehouse, and through physical violence legitimized through its Marxist-Leninist ideology. There is little evidence, however, that working-class people participated in these activities. With increased inflation, unemployment, higher food prices, and deindustrialization, what probably mattered most to workers was keeping their jobs, not whether they subscribed to Marxist-Leninist ideology. It is, though, difficult to know how many of the members of the Co-op Organization or any of the food co-ops were working class. If we look at individual co-ops, however, some sold food products that their working-class neighborhoods requested. As such, these co-ops directly represented their communities' interests, not the Co-op Organization. As one critic of the Co-op Organization surmised, the group did not offer viable ways of making "left activity more accessible and meaningful to working people." Instead, he argued, the group alienated itself from the very people with whom they sought alliances: the working class.[48]

After the Takeovers

What happened to the food co-ops and the warehouse after 1976? Although the historical records are uneven, it is clear that some food co-ops did not survive. But that was not just because of the Co-op Organization's takeover. Although the takeovers did discourage some customers from shopping at the food co-ops, there were larger problems that faced all co-ops throughout the country: inflation and corresponding higher food prices. Co-ops adapted in various ways, adopting boards of directors, hiring managers, and expanding their food lines. Could collectives still thrive in this environment?

Collectives, Incorporation, or Consolidation?

Even so, by the late 1970s, the food co-ops in the Twin Cities were reviving. By 1981, there were twenty-seven food co-ops in the metropolitan area. But during the Reagan years, some were forced to make changes in order to remain competitive. One change was that there were fewer worker-managed co-ops.[49] Second, members were not as involved in decisions about their co-ops. Instead, many food co-ops adopted more traditional business practices and organizational structures, such as establishing boards and hiring general managers and bookkeepers. For example, the Whole Foods Co-op reorganized by forming a board of directors, "standardize[ing]" their wages, hiring a bookkeeper, and adopting "a more sophisticated markup system." Some members disliked these changes and thought that the co-op had become "more conservative."[50] By 1981, few members volunteered there and most of the collective membership had left, which led to lower sales and higher labor costs.[51] At the Seward Co-op, the power also shifted from a collective to a board of directors in 1978. In the case of Seward, however, a collective of four had become a management team, which asked the board to consider a general management structure. Instead, the board decided to hire a general manager.[52] The West Bank Co-operative too changed its worker-managed collective and hired a general manager when they realized they needed to improve their finances.[53]

Like these co-ops, the Wedge Co-op faced a transition with its collective. The Wedge collective had been responsible for the co-op's daily operations; further, its co-op members were both workers and managers. Weekly, its thirty-member voting collective met to discuss managerial and philosophical issues about the store's operation. But some thought this management structure did not work well. The co-op held a meeting to discuss different options, which included scheduling management shifts, trying to make the present structure work better or electing representatives for a management team. As early as 1979, the workers' collective and board had met to discuss the co-op's "growing pains." The collective questioned the wisdom of operating through committees, and whether it was too large for policy-making decisions. In 1981, the board eliminated paid time for the voting collective to manage the store and hired a general manager.[54] One bookkeeper resigned, stating, "For the record, I am appalled by recent decisions made by this board of directors which effectively deny Wedge workers power in their workplace."[55]

Even the North Country Co-op, which had resisted the Co-op Organization, struggled with financial growth and "democratic management." During the early 1980s, its planning committee worked on a mission statement that included long-term market goals, criteria for product selection, risks and opportunities, and strengths and weaknesses. When its sales decreased and labor costs spiraled, the co-op hired a general manager. This angered the staff, who were distrustful of the general manager and favored a more democratic management. The board promised to think about the co-op's philosophy, its definitions of workplace democracy, and to look at each worker's job description. In February 1984, the North Country's sales had rebounded. But the workers felt that they no longer participated in the co-op's decisions.[56]

As with other food co-ops, many in the Twin Cities realized that their financial growth depended on incorporating, establishing the formal structures of a board, a managerial staff, and committees, and thinking more like other mainstream businesses. In making these transitions, some of the Twin Cities co-ops struggled financially. In the case of the Seward Community Co-op, it spent much of its time after 1976 "keeping [their] heads above water."[57] It raised $16,000, for its capitalization plan, then put it into the general operating fund for expenses, rather than for remodeling the store. When its bookkeeper stole a large amount of money, it nearly forced the co-op to declare bankruptcy. The co-op was able to survive because five members revitalized the board, wrote a budget and objectives, and got the co-op "running again."[58] The Wedge Co-op, too, faced financial uncertainties. In 1979, it bought and renovated a former 7-Eleven store and relocated to Lyndale Avenue in Minneapolis. It had anticipated some loss associated with the move but had not expected a $10,000 loss in sales the first three months. To complicate matters, the store was robbed at gunpoint and there were problems with spoiled and stolen produce. The co-op became more accountable with more efficient scales and electronic registers. Moreover, the co-op substituted paid for volunteer labor and revised its discount policies.[59]

By the mid-1980s, the Wedge had also changed its food selections, which led to improved sales. The co-op offered more convenience foods, such as frozen dinners and snacks. The acting general manager reinvoked the language of the earlier food wars, but this time with a financial twist. As he stated, "Some [co-ops] haven't realized that you can't just feed the elite brown rice and wheat germ. You have to open the doors and sell food that everyone can eat."[60] Although most members wanted "to keep the food line as pure as possible," the Wedge also wanted to appeal to nonmembers.[61] In fact, a recent survey had indicated that almost 90 percent of its shoppers were nonmembers. Expanding its food lines paid off, for the Wedge grossed more than $1.5 million in sales in 1985.[62]

Seward Co-op finances, too, improved during the mid-1980s. In April 1986, its total sales were over $60,000, a monthly record for the co-op. With continued profits during the summer, the board members began to talk about expansion. A store expansion committee was set up to work on plans and a consultant hired to conduct a feasibility study. Sales continued to climb; for example, daily sales in November were $2,300. The feasibility study revealed that at least 50 percent of shoppers were members and that 45 percent of the co-op customers used Seward as their primary grocery store. However, the average purchase was only $12. The study also showed that 50 percent of the shoppers used the co-op as a neighborhood convenience store but that the other 50 percent traveled there mainly for its organic and bulk foods.[63] The committee then presented three options to the board: to expand the present location, to enhance the present store, or to relocate nearby. In May 1987, the board unanimously passed a motion to include expansion plans in the budget. But the expansion had not gone smoothly. In March 1988, sales were poor because the store was only half completed. Further, the expansion ended up costing almost $20,000 over the budget. Nonetheless, sales rebounded within a few months.[64]

During the 1990s, some of the Twin Cities' co-ops closed. One source claims that by 1991, only sixteen of the thirty co-ops from 1978 were open.[65] During the early 1990s, the Powderhorn Co-op experienced a number of problems and had considered closing. Some workers thought that the reason for little member and community involvement was that the present management system was "oppressive." In 1992, the co-op returned to a collective management and a worker-owned store. The collective of six managers worried that the co-op would only survive for six months. After a year, though, sales became stronger. However, the co-op was beset by other problems: road construction, which affected shopper accessibility, and six burglaries, although in one case the robbers took only fresh brownies.[66]

Two years later, the workers in the collective had completely changed. It is difficult to know whether the workers who left were unhappy with the collective. In all likelihood, they were concerned about the Powderhorn's low sales. In fact, the Powderhorn had been losing customers, although loyal ones still continued to shop there. In the spring of 1993, there were discussions about consolidating five co-ops into one large one. But Powderhorn workers and members were opposed to this. They saw co-ops as "centers for social change" in their communities and thought co-ops should remain small and independent.[67] However, with low sales and profits, the co-op's discussion turned to closing the store. The agenda at the 1994 annual membership meeting included the options of closing the store, declaring bankruptcy, selling the business, or fundraising to keep the co-op store open. In December 1995, after a thirty-seven-year presence in Minneapolis, the co-op closed because of poor sales and a large debt. One explanation was that when other food co-ops expanded during the 1980s, the Powderhorn had become a "second tier of smaller co-ops" with fewer shoppers.[68]

In contrast, the Wedge Co-op, with $200,000 in state and federal monies, expanded its store to include a bakery, a fish department, a natural foods department, and a customer-membership desk. The new store was four times larger, with twice as many workers, and a projected income of $3 to $4 million its first year.[69] But not everyone was pleased with this development. One reporter for the alternative newspaper, *Profane Existence*, called the Wedge Co-op "the Mall of America of co-ops." The author claimed that the co-op was not a "community co-op" but had instead become a "hierarchical, antidemocratically managed institution." As such, he continued, it dishonored the history of cooperatives and its principles. The author argued that even though the Wedge sold natural food, its politics was problematic. Food, he insisted, could not be separated from politics, even though the co-op's general manager had stated, "we promote food rather than politics." Another problem, he added, was the co-op's criteria for membership. The co-op asked for $80 annual membership fee and no longer honored members' working hours or gave members discounts for volunteering. Further, decisions were made by the board, not members. The author concluded that the Wedge was for the upper class.[70] Others apparently agreed with him, for someone spray painted "Capitalist Co-op" on the Wedge's new building; another person wrote "Die Yuppie Scum." Yet others claimed the new store had a "sterile" supermarket feel.[71]

During the 1990s, the North Country Co-op wanted to relocate and signed a lease for a neighborhood building. The co-op hoped to obtain a loan, although it had to raise at least one-third of the total costs. After opening another store, the co-op was forced to close for good in 2007.[72] In early 1991, Seward, too, was considering buying another store in the middle-class St. Louis Park neighborhood. However, its sales were sluggish and so the co-op abandoned its expansion plan. As an alternative, Seward was interested in the idea of consolidating with other co-ops.[73]

In fact, as early as 1989, Seward had approached four co-ops to discuss consolidation. The "Report on the Consolidation Effort of Five Twin Cities Consumer Co-ops" showed that fourteen of twenty-eight co-ops from the past twenty years were still open and most were decentralized. When discussions started again, though, there were many concerns about consolidation. With over 4,000 members in the Twin Cities co-ops, how would all of their voices be heard and represented? Who would make decisions about which stores would close? Who would decide on issues of expansion and new stores? What would happen to employees? As noted, the Powderhorn had bowed out, preferring to remain small and independent. Perhaps its members, realizing the smallness of their co-op, worried that they might be forced to close. To be sure, the other co-ops involved—Lakewinds Natural Foods, Mississippi Market Co-operative, North Country, Valley Co-op, and the Wedge—had differences in the number of members, the sizes of their stores, and their annual profits. For example, Seward had 500 active members, the Wedge 1,200. When a newspaper broke the story about consolidation before the co-ops' members had even heard about the idea, members became angry and voted against it.[74] Given the history of the cities' independent co-ops and their allegiances to their neighborhoods, though, it was unlikely that the consolidation would have occurred.

The Twin Cities Co-ops in the 2000s

Although the Powderhorn had closed during the 1990s, other co-ops grew and even new co-ops started. By the late 2000s, there were at least twelve food co-ops in the metropolitan area: seven in the suburbs and four in Minneapolis but only one in St. Paul. Mississippi Market, which had opened in St. Paul in 1984, had opened another store in 2003. Despite the Seward Co-op Grocery & Deli's most recent relocation, its profit in 2010 had increased by over 6 percent. The Wedge Community Co-op had expanded by doubling its store space in 1997 and opening a bakery in 2001.[75] But the Wedge encountered competition from Trader Joe's in 2009, which wanted to open a liquor store nearby. But it was not just Trader Joe's that the neighborhood was worried about but a larger development project that included a bank and fifty-eight condos. As of June 2012, Trader Joe's had not yet relocated to the neighborhood.[76]

The Wedge has expanded in yet another way: by extending its influence in the organic food market. In 2002, the co-op became the first certified organic store in the state. The next year, when the co-op started a fair trade program, its first project was Native Harvest, the brand name for the White Earth Land Recovery Project. This project supported the Ojibwa tribe's traditional practices of harvesting wild rice.[77] In 2007, the Wedge bought one of the oldest certified organic farms in the Twin Cities area and started Gardens of Eagen, an organic field school "for farmers, educators, policy makers, and the public."[78] The co-op also collaborated with other agricultural organizations, such as the Institute for Agriculture and Trade Policy, on "Sow the Seeds" project which provided education and outreach for farmers in Minnesota, Wisconsin, and Iowa.[79]

Robert Grott has argued that co-ops have historically served two purposes: social and economic. Generally, he notes, they have started in times of "economic need" and when people were interested in establishing a "new social order."[80] This was certainly true for the Twin Cities' co-ops during the 1970s. But what happens when the ideological interests of some take over, when co-op members are no longer represented? How should co-ops resolve ideological differences among the members? Again, I return to what makes co-ops different from all other businesses: member-ownership and the possibilities for a participatory democracy. Certainly there were those types of discussions during the co-op wars of the mid-1970s. However, they often erupted into accusations, threats, and physical violence, in large part because of the Co-op Organization. Further, when the Co-op Organization physically tried to take over individual co-ops, the process of participatory democracy was severely compromised. As one activist explained, "Ultimately, the CO lost its opportunity to influence the direction of the co-ops by disregarding democracy in its campaign."[81] Perhaps the Co-op Organization would have agreed, arguing that it was more interested in a revolution, not democracy.

Coalition building across social class, race, and other differences is difficult. But this is exactly what many of the individual co-ops were doing before the Co-op Organization had organized. As noted, Grass Co-op Grocery, located in a blue-collar working and lower middle-class neighborhood in St. Paul, had asked its members what foods they wanted and then responded accordingly. The North Country Co-op also surveyed its members and thereafter ordered those foods. The Bryant-Central Co-op, too, wanted their members and community residents to decide what kinds of food to sell. And, the Selby Co-op established a Co-op Council where its African American, working-class members would be better represented. All these co-ops did not speak for the working-class, as the Co-op Organization had, but worked together. As such, these activities reflected the hopes of economic democracy and the practices of participatory democracy.

THE AGE OF THE "ORGANIC-INDUSTRIAL COMPLEX"

It is difficult to know the exact number of food cooperatives but one estimate as of 2010 is 350 (not including buying clubs).[1] The good news is that the number of food co-ops is growing. At the 2010 Consumer Cooperative Management Association conference, participants were enthusiastic about those food cooperatives that had opened within the past year. These included Chatham Real Food Market (Chatham, New York), Eagle Rock Co-op (Eagle Rock, Idaho, now closed), Fiddleheads Natural Foods Co-op (New London, Connecticut), Fresh Connections (Algona, Iowa), Lakes Community Co-op (Stone Lake, Wisconsin), Littleton Food Co-op (Littleton, New Hampshire), Local Roots Co-op (Estes Park, Colorado, which has since closed), Mandela Foods Cooperative (Oakland, California), Market Community Cooperative (Spirit Lake, Iowa), South Bronx Food Co-op (Bronx, New York, now closed), and Walsh Community Grocery (Walsh, Colorado). The bad news is that some have been forced to close, pointing to how financially fragile fledgling cooperatives can be in this recession.[2]

Why this rise in new food co-ops? And why are many starting in smaller towns and in poorer urban and rural areas? One reason is that in 2005, food co-ops collectively decided to help "grow" 200 new food co-ops within ten years through a project called Food Co-op 500. Cooperation among cooperatives has always been a time-honored Rochdale principle. But this project, which would bring the total of food co-ops nationally to 500, is truly collaborative and ambitious. Older, established co-ops have committed to assisting new ones through mentoring, directing them to financial sources, and conducting feasibility studies.[3] Indeed, these collaborations have helped jumpstart new food co-ops. For example, Bloomingfoods of

Bloomington, Indiana, has helped Lost River Food Co-op in Paoli, Indiana, a poorer rural town with a population of less than 5,000. Weaver Street Market in Chapel Hill, North Carolina, lent a hand to Chatham Marketplace in nearby Pittsboro, again a town with less than 5,000 residents. And the Ashland Food Co-op assisted the Medford, Oregon, Market Co-op, located in a metropolitan area with a population of over 205,000.[4] Through the Food Co-op 500, food co-ops also have started in poorer urban neighborhoods, such as the South Bronx and West Oakland.[5]

The New Co-ops

Most of these new co-ops, whether in urban or rural locations, offer natural and organic foods, educate their members and other shoppers about environmental and nutritional issues, and promote the local economy by buying from nearby farmers and producers. That many food co-ops started during the ongoing recession may be surprising to some. But the recession may have actually helped trigger the cooperative movement. A number of people on main street who have been un- or under-employed, and have not benefited from the gains on Wall Street, have turned to their communities for small start-up businesses, including environmentally friendly ones. In fact, if one looks at where most food co-ops are located, they are not in cities, as much as in small towns and rural areas. The states with the most food co-ops are Minnesota, Washington, Wisconsin, New York, California, Vermont, Michigan, Oregon, and Massachusetts. In Washington, for example, there are more food co-ops in rural than urban areas. In Wisconsin, there are three times more food co-ops in rural areas; in Minnesota, twice as many in rural regions. Even in New York, there are just as many food co-ops in rural as in urban areas.[6]

In fact, one 2009 report indicated that small businesses are taking the lead in green businesses. Alongside this interest has been a growth in organic farms. According to the United States Department of Agriculture (USDA), organic farm sales have tripled between 2002 and 2007. Correspondingly, the sales of organic foods have tripled from $393 million in 2002 to $1.7 billion in 2007.[7] There are a number of reasons for this. Concerned about large agribusinesses, where animals are caged, penned in, and treated with antibiotics, many Americans choose to buy their foods from organic and natural farmers. They know that their foods will be local, fresh, untreated, and not genetically modified.

Co-ops and Food Deserts

It is here where food co-ops—alongside community-supported agriculture (CSA), farmers' markets, and buying clubs—fill that need. What is especially encouraging about some of the new co-ops is that they have opened in poorer communities, what are called "food deserts." I am not using the USDA definition, in which "33 percent of the population live at least a mile from a supermarket that does at least $2 million in annual sales."[8] This definition favors large chains—including SuperValu, Walgreens, and Walmart—which, with the endorsement of Michelle Obama, hope to open 1,500 new stores in food desert communities in the near future.[9] Instead, I am concerned about poorer rural and urban communities where residents have few choices for where to buy food. In urban areas, they are often forced to buy groceries from convenience or liquor stores, which sell snack and convenience food. And if there is a grocery store in these neighborhood, prices are unusually high and the quality of food often poor. In these communities—often plagued with high rates of hypertension, diabetes, and obesity—residents have begun to take matters into their own hands. They have started community gardens, food carts, and farmers' markets. And some have started food co-ops. All of these activities speak to community-based approaches, not corporate ones.

One co-op that has received much publicity is the South Bronx Food Co-operative (SBxFC), which opened in 2007 but unfortunately closed at the end of 2010 because of loss of funding and low sales. (Some co-op members, though, are determined to reopen the store.) The co-op was started by Zena Nelson, a graduate student in business at Baruch College. She entered a business plan competition and won $25,000. Mentored by Joe Holtz, long-standing manager of the Park Slope Co-op in the Bronx, she opened the co-op in 2009 in a rented community center, near public housing and new condos.[10] The co-op's aims were many: "to provide affordable and nutritious food to all residents of the South Bronx (and New York City) while empowering the local community by encouraging good health, providing relevant job skills and fostering environmentally responsible activities through democratic cooperation."[11] These were ambitious goals not always seen in other co-ops' missions. But for the SBxFC, they were intricately connected. The co-op educated its community members about nutrition and health so that they could better understand the value of what foods the co-op sells. And just as the co-op needed to survive economically, so too did the community. By teaching skills and knowledge, by employing residents, and by linking activism to issues of environmental and economic sustainability, the co-op sought to empower residents. The co-op also widened the circle of economic influence by working with regional farmers and producers, cooperatives, and other community institutions. In this way, community members had access to better foods and did not have to buy poor quality food at high prices. The co-op then carried organic and natural foods but also conventionally grown produce. Concerned about how foods were grown, the co-op refused to sell products that have exploited workers.[12]

In truth, the community knew a great deal of exploitation and poverty. It was crowded, with over 31,500 people per square mile. Most of its residents—98 percent—are African American and Latino. The co-op was responsive to its members' circumstances. It offered free yoga classes and workshops in healthy cooking, recycling, and composting; it held forums where members could ask questions from nutritionists and dietitians. If members were on public assistance, their fees were adjusted. Members worked three hours per month so that they could receive 10 to 20 percent in discounts, which made healthy food more affordable for them. It also meant that they took part in the co-op's decisions.[13]

The South Bronx Food Co-op synergistically worked with other community organizations. One was Nos Quedamos (We're Staying), an advocate of affordable housing in the neighborhood. Another was the health food store and restaurant, the PeaceLove Health Food Store. In fact, the store drew inspiration from the food co-op that opened the same year. Like the co-op, PeaceLove served healthy, not fast, foods.[14] Another community group was Petro-Bronx, which received financial support from Hugo Chavez, president of Venezuela. When Chavez visited the South Bronx in 2005, he promised to help the community. In 2007, CITGO Petroleum Corporation, a Houston-based subsidiary of Venezuela's national oil company, established a program to give $1 million a year for three years to grassroots community organizations in the South Bronx. Petro-Bronx was one such organization, comprised of South Bronx residents who deliberated on which groups would receive funding. Petro-Bronx had assisted twenty organizations, including the SBxFC. Another is the Green Worker Cooperatives, which created environmental jobs through recycling and reusing older building materials that ordinarily would go to landfills. Petro-Bronx has also funded For a Better Bronx program, which educated a youth collective about environmental issues.[15]

The food co-op also worked with communities beyond the South Bronx. One was Corbin Hills Road Farm, a ninety-two-acre farm in upstate New York. Its founder, Dennis Derryck, a seventy-year-old professor at the New School, was motivated to provide healthy food to the South Bronx community. As he noted, "If there is a food revolution, it's not yet including the low income." Derryck started a CSA to give South Bronx residents an opportunity to buy shares in his farm. Some community residents had signed up and the SBxFC had bought twenty-five shares as well. Derryck's CSA differs from others in that he wanted members to help decide what crops should be planted. His plan was to eventually turn over his farm to the members, once he had paid for it.[16]

West Oakland, California is the location of another new food co-op, the Mandela Foods Cooperative. A locally owned grocery store and nutrition education center, it offers nutrition classes and gives residents an opportunity to invest in the co-op at different levels. One of the worker-owners, James Berk, became involved when the executive director of Mandela Marketplace, the co-op's umbrella organization, came to his high school in 2007. Berk helped with a survey, which showed that most West Oakland grocery stores did not carry healthy foods. Mandela Food Coop opened two years later in June 2009. The co-op offers a number of services, for which it received a San Francisco Bay Guardian Small Business Award in 2012: pop-up markets at senior centers, nutrition classes, and produce grown by famers of color.[17] Another food co-op in West Oakland is the Soul Food Co-op. It, too, is located in an African American neighborhood with high unemployment, the usual liquor and high-priced convenience food stores, and underfunded schools. As one cofounder stated: "We know our people have been ridden down with all these liquor stores." The co-op brings all natural foods to the neighborhood. As with other co-ops in poorer neighborhoods, it is collaborating with other community organizations to improve the lives of its residents.[18]

Rural Co-ops Take Root

Not all poorer communities or food deserts are in urban settings. Some are in the rural heartland.[19] Of special note is Lost River Community Co-op of Paoli, which opened in the fall of 2007. Paoli is a rural and relatively poor community, with a population of slightly more than 3,800. It is almost fifty miles south of Bloomington, home to Bloomingfoods Co-op. Lost River grew out of the community organization, Orange County Homegrown, which also started a farmers' market in nearby Orleans and a summer market in French Lick, a local tourist attraction. The hope was that Lost River would be both a grocery store and a community center for Paoli. Situated in an historic building in the downtown, the co-op could also stimulate other businesses there and help create jobs.[20]

In the fall of 2005, sixty people, including staff from Bloomingfoods and Orange County Homegrown, met to discuss opening a food co-op in Paoli. One of those persons was Andy Mahler, an activist deeply committed to protecting the environment. He has been an officer of Orange County Homegrown; Bloomington Cooperative Service; Heartwood, a cooperative group active across eighteen states that is concerned with logging; Protect Our Woods, based in southern Indiana; Shagbark, a nonprofit corporation that runs a center about conservancy and education; and the Indiana Forest Alliance, concerned about nearby Hoosier National Forest, especially off-road vehicle usage.[21] Cofounders Mahler and Debbie Turner worked with different organizations to get the co-op started. Lost River received mentoring from Bloomingfoods, $9,000 in seed money from the Food Co-op 500, and grants from the Indiana Cooperative Development Center and from the Orange County Development Commission. As of early 2010, the

700 members helped to raise $40,000 to reach their goal for the Harvesting the Funds campaign. Members also contributed to reduce the $89,000 loan from the Northcountry Cooperative Development Fund and to start building a reserve. Even so, the co-op has "hit a financial wall," as stated in its August 2012 request for customers to spend at least $25 more in the next six weeks to "close the revenue gap."[22]

In late November 2010, when I visited the co-op, it was thriving. It was nothing short of impressive. Turner was working that day and took me on a tour. The store was small but comfortable. In the front were tables where customers ate deli foods and the talk was lively, at least when I was there. Like most food co-ops, Lost River sells natural, organic, and some conventional foods. Its products include over 150 natural organic bulk items, teas and herbs, local eggs and meats, deli foods, artisan cheese, craft beers and wine, and homemade rugs, baskets, and soaps. They buy from forty or more local vendors and farmers such as Dances with Dirt Farm; Brambleberry Farm, a noncertified organic farm; Kercheval Homestead Farm, which is over 180 years old; and Kenny's Farmhouse Cheese, whose artisan cheese is marketed within 150 miles of their farm. A number of their products—sorghum, maple syrup, popcorn, chestnuts and hickory nuts,

FIGURE 7.   Lost River Community Co-operative, Paoli, Indiana. Courtesy photo.

honey, spelt flour, meats, and produce—come from Amish farmers in the state. In the spring of 2009, the co-op sold over forty-five pounds of morel mushrooms, for which southern Indiana is known.[23]

The co-op reminded me of the Adamant Food Co-op, with its small-town feeling. It was also similar to the Adamant Co-op in how it created community through rituals and local events. At their first year celebration in the fall of 2008, they celebrated with a birthday cake, a barbeque cookout, and free music. The farmers' market and co-op also organized a weekly music jam. They had a summer film series, which featured "Food Matters" and "The Real Dirt on Farmer John."[24] And during the winter months, there was music every Wednesday night. Although located in a small town, the co-op serves residents in five counties, Turner told me. Clearly people drove to the store for more than food.

Paoli is not the only small town that has started a food co-op. In Walsh, Colorado, residents organized to save the town's only grocery store. Almost 300 miles south of Denver, Walsh is an even smaller town than Paoli, with only 723 residents. When the store closed, people had to drive twenty miles to buy groceries. This was a hardship, especially during the snowy winters. How the citizens of Walsh started a co-op was unusual. Rather than hire an economic consultant and pay for a feasibility study, almost half of the residents pooled their money, formed a board, issued 6,000 shares at $50 each, and secured a no-interest loan from the Southeast Colorado Power Association. The grocery store has reopened and is now making a profit. In fact, in 2008, the co-op store grossed $1 million in sales, nearly double the sales of the previous store.[25]

In fact, a number of small towns in rural areas have started food co-ops, largely to build up their local economy and to offer alternative food sources to their residents. In the middle of Iowa is the Fresh Connections Co-op in Algona. The town is small, with a predominantly white population of 5,800 and a median household income of around $32,000. Like other co-ops, Fresh Connections wanted to jumpstart the local food economy and so sells local produce, including popcorn and buffalo meat. Like Lost River, Fresh Connection has received local and state grants: one from the Kossuth County Community Foundation for classes and another from the Iowa Department of Agriculture and Land Stewardship to promote locally grown produce. In 2009, the co-op had almost 200 members and a manager who has had experience as a manager of a farm for 800 families near Madison, Iowa.[26] In Ohio, the Miami Oxford Organic Network of Oxford (Moon) incorporated in 2004; by 2008, its 460 members had pledged over $100,000 toward a co-op store. In fall of 2011, the store finally opened and in the spirit of cooperation has received mentoring from Bloomingfoods Co-op and Good Foods Co-op in Lexington, Kentucky. Although its membership has almost doubled to 900 members, store manager Tana Richards told me that it has been difficult to compete with mainstream grocery stores.[27]

In the Northeast, two rural communities have started food co-ops, again with the aim of helping the local economies. The Chatham Real Food Market Co-op recently opened in Chatham, New York, a small town in the Hudson Valley region with less than 2,000 residents. Like the other rural co-ops, Chatham Real Food received monies through a local nonprofit association, the Community Agriculture of Columbia County. In addition to offering natural and organic produce, the co-op has started two community gardens, one at a middle school and the other in a park. The co-op is slowly growing. In the fiscal year 2011, the co-op actually made a small profit, its membership grew, and it had partnerships with over 180 farmers and producers and over 150 other local businesses.[28] In Littleton, New Hampshire, a town with a population of 6,200, there is the Littleton Consumer Cooperative Society, which serves the north country of New Hampshire and northeastern Vermont. It, too, supports local producers and nurtures regional connections. Its mission statement states that its members are the priority, not "mak[ing] a profit for a large corporation."[29]

Small Town Start-Ups

Other small towns, located near metropolitan areas, have started food co-ops as well. Troy, New York, with a population of 50,000 residents and a median household income of near $30,000, is located near the state capitol in Albany, which has its own food co-op. At least 800 members have joined the Pioneer Food Market, located in downtown Troy. As of early 2010, the co-op had raised $2.5 million and plans to open a store. As with other smaller towns, they have received grants from local and regional sources: private foundations, the city of Troy, and various banks, including the Cooperative Fund of New England. Unfortunately, the co-op was forced to close in fall of 2011 because of lack of cash flow. As with Lost River Food Co-op, its members had not patronized their co-op, perhaps because of its high prices.[30] Another new coop is Fiddleheads Natural Foods Cooperative in New London, Connecticut, a town of 26,000. The metropolitan area of Norwich-New London has a population is 267,000, which is multiracial. Although nearly 55 percent of its residents are non-Hispanic white, 22 percent are Latinos, with Puerto Ricans constituting 13 percent of the overall population. In early 2008, the co-op opened a store, featuring mostly organic and natural foods. That summer, they added frozen foods and bulk items. The co-op continues to grow, with a membership of over 1,100 and increased store sales as of early 2011.[31]

In Idaho Falls, Idaho, there is the Eagle Rock Food Co-op, which opened in the fall of 2008. Again, the co-op community wanted to grow the local economy. With a town population of almost 50,000 and a metropolitan population of nearly 123,000, there was a great deal of interest in the co-op. In fact, the co-op has used some innovative ideas to attract new members. Through a new grass roots movement, they have asked each member to donate one row of garden produce—bring it to the store for exchange or to get a discount. This would ensure that the co-op's produce is fresh and local. Likewise, it would bring people into the store. However, the store appears to have closed, as I could find no current information about the cooperative.[32] Harvest Moon Natural Foods Cooperative, incorporated in the spring of 2006, has also received support from Food Co-op 500, which gave a $10,000 grant and conducted a market feasibility study. The co-op also received assistance from the National Cooperative Grocers Association's Development Cooperative for operational support. Located in the affluent Long Lake/Orono community near Minneapolis, the co-op has received over $900,000 in loans from its members.[33] It appears to be doing well. One last example is Reno, Nevada. When the twenty-five-year-old Washoe Zephyr Food Cooperative closed there, community members were determined to start another food co-op. By the summer of 2006, at least 250 residents helped to locate a place for a new co-op. Members donated furniture, refrigerators, and volunteered their time. By the summer of 2007, the Cooperative Association in the State of Nevada incorporated and was the only food co-op in the state. Unfortunately, this co-op closed as well.[34]

Gentrification Take Hold

Food co-ops have also started in upscale urban neighborhoods. Portland, Oregon is an environmentally conscious city. In an attempt to protect its environment, it has created a network of bike lanes and reduced traffic congestion through trolley and train systems. It has the largest urban forest, lots of city gardens, and environmentally friendly buildings that use natural materials such as cobb. It is a city of neighborhoods, with colorfully painted houses and floribunda, rhododendron, and perennials. The city now has three food cooperatives—Alberta Co-op Grocery, People's, and Food Front—which collectively make nearly $12 million in sales and have 9,000 members. The newest co-op, Alberta Co-op Grocery, started when thirty households started a buyers' club in 1997. When club members decided to form their own food co-op, they started a Founders Fund campaign and 250 households responded by buying five-year memberships. The members also started a member loaner campaign, which netted $70,000. In July 2001, the Alberta Co-op Grocery opened in the Alberta neighborhood.[35]

Historically, the neighborhood had the largest African American population in the city. But within the past ten or so years, it has become gentrified as younger white families have bought houses there. The neighborhood is now known for its art galleries, hipster stores, and upscale cafes. This raises the question of whether the Alberta Co-op Grocery could have succeeded in a poorer African neighborhood. More than likely, gentrification has helped the co-op. Whenever I have shopped there, the customers have been mostly young whites. And the co-op has been doing well financially, with increased sales annually. In 2002, sales were over $980,500; by 2008, they were $2.43 million, up 19 percent from the previous year. In 2009, gross sales were over $2.5 million. Certainly the growth in its membership has helped the co-op's sales, for one in seven of its customers are members. Translated differently, its 737 members were responsible for 24 percent of its 2009 sales. In addition, its working members—12 percent of the members—help reduce labor costs. By 2009, the co-op has paid off all of its member loans and has returned $44,000 to its members through register discounts. The co-op is now debt free and some members would like to have their own store.[36] I hope that they will not relocate, however. Although the store is somewhat crowded, I find it welcoming and small.

In the Bucktown neighborhood of Chicago, there is the Dill Pickle Food Co-op, the only food co-op in the city. The co-op's name hearkens back to the Dill Pickle Club, a group of artists, anarchists, and bohemians who enjoyed jazz, poetry readings and theater, and some illegal activities from 1917 until 1934. Among the known writers who frequented the club was Upton Sinclair, an ardent socialist and advocate of co-ops. Bucktown is a largely young and professional community. The average age is twenty-nine and there are more households without children than with. Most residents have white-collar jobs and the median income is slightly more than $43,000. These demographics reflect the middle-class communities in which many food co-ops are located. Regardless, members are not only interested in their co-op but becoming a community. They hold a monthly potluck, the Dill Pickle Supper Club, so members can get acquainted and discuss ideas about the co-op and community. One of their concerns has been about affordable housing and starting community gardens in the nearby Logan Square neighborhood.[37]

Learned and Unlearned Lessons

The growth in new food co-ops speaks volumes about people's desire for healthy food, local connections, and a sense of community. As some of the food co-op stores discussed in this book demonstrate, they need not be just a place where people shop for food. They can be places where shoppers meet and talk to neighbors, have a cup of coffee or tea with friends, order food from deli workers, look at notices on the community bulletin boards and post questions or comments. But not all food co-ops I visited felt like community. In many cases, board members told me they were concerned about the lack of community among members and membership involvement. Instead, they have tried to evoke a sense of community in their annual reports and policy governance language.

Participatory Democracy and Communities

Members' lack of involvement is an ongoing problem for many co-ops. The common complaints I heard was that members do not attend annual meetings, and they do not vote for their board members, on policy issues, or changes in bylaws. Board members repeatedly asked me how co-op members could become more participatory. This question strikes at the very heart of three common words that co-ops use: "community," "owners," and "democracy." But what do these words mean? More important, how are they enacted? The Park Slope Food Co-op in Brooklyn offers one model of how all three ideas are practiced. The co-op is only open to members who are required to work (2.75 hours per four weeks). There are practical reasons for this. For one, it keeps labor costs down. But this is also participatory democratic, for it requires everyone to work. In terms of ownership, members better understand what is involved in the daily operations and business that they own. Members rotate through various work responsibilities and so learn about all of the co-op's departments. Working alongside others, members get to know one another, thereby building community and purpose. In turn, members are more likely to shop there because of their involvement.[38] Some will argue that most people do not have the time to work in their co-ops. I would counter that Park Slope's time commitment is minimal. Further, if one needs an economic argument, this practice is cost-saving. I would also raise the question: If people do not have time to work in their co-op, would they take the time to attend a board meeting? In terms of building a community, I would emphasize that that takes time and commitment. The Park Slope model offers that.

When food co-ops speak of community, they usually refer to their connections with local, regional, and even global farmers and producers. Certainly, these are important forms of community that have expanded to include small organic farmers; regional warehouses; regional networks where co-ops share ideas, resources, and a sense of identity; and fair trade partnerships and exchanges. What concerns me, though, is that most of these relationships are economic, not political, ones. Is that how we define community: through what we buy, our consumer choices? And is that not how most members even see their board, as those who represent their economic interests? How do we bring social relationships back into the equation?

Food Choices Are Political

Some food co-ops decry political involvement, referring to the Rochdale principle of political neutrality. But, as noted throughout the book, food choices are political. Embedded in every food we eat is someone's labor, working conditions, and wages. Our food choices, as we well know, have an impact on the environment. Sociologist Michael Schudson has argued that we should not separate politics from consumer decisions. Further, he has warned, "The citizen/consumer distinction may itself be damaging to public life."[39] I agree. In writing the histories of food co-ops, I have found that member involvement was often at its highest when food choices were perceived as political. In some cases, there were boycotts and protests; in other cases, heated discussions. But in all instances, members were exercising their rights as citizens and as owners of their co-ops.

Co-op members need to be educated on these issues. They should form discussion and reading groups, and listen to various viewpoints. The impulse to form groups should not come from the board or from an educational director. It should come from the members themselves who choose to come together. However, co-ops can certainly provide a place for members to congregate. Here, I do not mean a board meeting room but a "living" space where you can put tables together, drink and spill coffee, and talk freely. How many co-ops have spaces like that?

There are many issues where members can take the lead. They might consider, for example, what the label "green" means? Are all products advertised as "green" ecofriendly? After all, as one environmentalist tells us, there are "many shades of green."[40] If we accept the premise that the world's resources are finite, then we need to think about where our food comes from and the energy required to bring it to our dinner tables. Members, then, might create food and product labels that inform customers about their environmental impact. Members might also consider labels that include information about the workers' conditions. Although we can be assured when we buy organic produce that workers are no longer sprayed with pesticides, we know little about their wages or working conditions. As geographer Julie Guthman warns, organic farming has become part of what it intended to escape: agribusiness. In California, a state with the most organic farms, those farms have become "capitalist enterprises" or what Michael Pollan has called "the organic-industrial complex."[41] Members might form committees that ask large organic farms such information. After all, we are able to consume because others labor for us.

Another group of the co-op community are the workers. In my research, the voices of workers were noticeably absent in the board minutes and archival records, except when there was conflict. Whenever I visited co-ops, I would talk to different workers and ask them about their work and whether they bought their food at the co-op. It might surprise some that a number of workers simply thought of their work as just that, work. They themselves did not eat organically, perhaps because it was too expensive or they did not believe it was healthier. I am not necessarily arguing that workers feel alienated from their co-ops' missions. But they might not buy into it. What many workers did tell me, though, is that working conditions and pay were often better at their food co-ops than at the grocery stores where they previously worked. The point here is that we should not assume that all workers support green, organic, and natural movements.

Perhaps, then, we might think of co-ops as "communities," not simply one "community." Take co-op membership, for example. Although most members appreciate what their co-op sells, they have different levels of incomes and are from different generations. Not all members have equal access to their co-ops' produce and products. Poignantly, I read in some co-ops' newsletters how people could stretch their budgets during the ongoing recession by buying more bulk items. In the same newsletters, I would see ads for sushi and expensive deli items. Again, most food co-ops fare well in middle-class communities. But what of others? In the cases of the new cooperatives that closed, were prices too high even for members? More generally speaking, how do we make organic and natural foods affordable for all?

This leads me to a word I repeatedly heard and read while visiting food co-ops: "growth." Most food co-ops' expectations were that sales and profits would increase yearly, that their stores would grow and expand in membership, in produce and products, and in physical space. This was true during the postwar years, with the rise of supermarkets and shopping centers. It was also common during the 1980s, a difficult decade for many co-ops. Then, some began to use the word "corporate." In 2010, the National Cooperative Grocers Association set a goal of $3 billion in sales by 2020, which translates to an annual growth in its member food co-ops' sales of 10 percent.[42] Although it is true that food co-ops are businesses, many claim to be community and democratic institutions. Might large-scale capitalism be at odds with practices of democracy and community? In my study of and visits to food co-ops, I found a link between the two. Those co-ops that had grown to supermarkets and had a warehouse usually had less member involvement. In contrast, those food co-ops in small towns and villages, which were often crowded but which also offered space for shoppers to sit and talk, had the most membership and shopper participation. This speaks not just to a store's physical space but more important to how that space is used. Here, I think of the co-ops in Adamant and Putney, Vermont; in Paoli, Indiana; in Arcata, California; in Portland, Oregon; and the New Pioneer Food Co-op in Iowa City. They are small but lively. Unfortunately, New Pioneer is thinking of relocating. I hope not. The present store, although somewhat crowded, has character and has been a part of the community for almost forty years.

Last, as a historian, I want to emphasize how important it is for members to know about their co-ops' histories. I am heartened by those food co-ops that have put their annual reports, some dating from years ago, on their websites. I am also pleased to see posts of old photographs and abbreviated histories. And I appreciate that many food co-ops have a presence on social media websites— Facebook, Twitter, and YouTube—which appeals to younger members.[43] These, too, are venues for outreach and for building community, and for bringing up the next generation of co-opers. But food co-ops are also physical spaces where members and others shop and congregate. Food co-ops should create a physical space where members can look at older photographs, and read about the history of their co-ops. Members would better understand, then, how they stand on other co-opers' shoulders.

WEBSITE SOURCES ABOUT FOOD COOPERATIVES

Food Cooperatives Discussed in this Book

Adamant Food Co-op, Adamant, Vermont: http://www.adamantco-op.org

Alberta Co-op Grocery, Portland, Oregon: http://www.albertagrocery.coop/

Bloomingfoods, Bloomington, Indiana: http://www.bloomingfoods.coop/

Chatham Real Food Market Co-op, Chatham, New York: http://www.realfoodnetwork.org/real-food-coop.html

Dill Pickle Food Co-op, Chicago, Illinois: http://dillpicklefoodcoop.org

Eagle Rock Food Co-operative, Idaho Falls, Idaho: http://eaglerockcoop.org/index.php?section=10

Fiddleheads Natural Foods Cooperative, New London, Connecticut: http://www.fiddleheadsfood.coop/

Food Conspiracy, Tucson, Arizona: http://www.foodconspiracy.org/

Fresh Connections Co-op, Algona, Iowa: http://www.freshconnectionscoop.com/

GreenStar Co-op, Ithaca, New York: http://www.greenstar.coop/

Hanover Consumer Co-operative Society, Hanover, New Hampshire: http://www.coopfoodstore.com/about/hanover-store

Harvest Moon, Long Lake, Minnesota: http://www.harvestmoon.coop/

Honest Weight Food Co-operative, Albany, New York: http://www.hwfc.com

La Montanita Co-op, Albuquerque, New Mexico: http://www.lamontanita.coop/

Linden Hills Co-op, Minneapolis, Minnesota: http://www.lindenhills.coop/

Littleton Consumer Cooperative Society, Littleton, New Hampshire: http://www.littletoncoop.org

Lost River Community Co-op, Paoli, Indiana: http://www.lostrivercoop.com

Madison Market, Seattle, Washington: http://www.madisonmarket.com

Mandela Foods Cooperative, West Oakland, California: http://www.mandelafoods.com

Mississippi Market, Minneapolis, Minnesota: http://www.msmarket.coop/

New Pioneer Consumers Co-operative, Iowa City, Iowa: http://www.newpi.com

North Coast Co-operative, Arcata, Eureka, and Fortuna, California: http://www.Northcoastco-op.com

Park Slope Food Co-operative, Brooklyn, New York: http://foodcoop.com

People's Food Co-op, Ann Arbor, Michigan: http://www.peoplesfood.coop/

Pioneer Food Market, Troy, New York: http://www.troyfoodcoop.com

Putney Food Co-operative, Putney, Vermont: http://homepages.sover.net/~ptnyco-op/

Seward Co-op Grocery & Deli, Minneapolis, Minnesota: http://www.seward.coop/

Soul Food Co-op, West Oakland, California: http://www.flickr.com/photos/bintakinpics/2620366488/

South Bronx Food Co-operative, South Bronx, New York: http://sbxfc.blogspot.com

Upper Valley Food Co-operative: http://www.uppervalleyfood.coop/

Wedge Community Co-operative, Minneapolis, Minnesota: http://www.wedge.coop/

Lists of Food Cooperatives

http://www.coopdirectory.org
http://directory.ic.org/records/coops.php
http://www.dmoz.org/Business/Food_and_Related_Products/Cooperatives/Retail/
http://www.fda.gov/opacom/backgrounders/miles.html
http://www.vtliving.com/healthfoodstores/index.shtml (Vermont only)
http://www.uwcc.wisc.edu/wiscdir/fooddir.html (Wisconsin only)

General and Specific Histories of Food Cooperatives

Davis Food Co-operative: http://www.daviscoop.com/history.html and http://www.niany.com/food.co-op.html

"John Curl, 'History of Work Cooperation in America": http://www.red-coral.
net/WorkCoops.html

Mifflin Street Community Co-op: http://www.waxingamerica.com/2006/05/
history_of_the_.html

Other Food Cooperative Information

Green America: http://www.greenamericatoday.org

National Cooperative Business Association (formerly the Co-operative
League of the U.S.A.): http://www.ncba.coop/about_hist.cfm

Organic Consumers Association: http://www.purefood.org/coopindex.htm

Organic Consumers Association: http://www.purefood.org/coopindex.htm

University of Wisconsin, Center for Cooperatives: http://www.uwcc.wisc.
edu/info/i_pages/prin.html

Notes

INTRODUCTION

1. See Pollan, *In Defense of Food*; and Nestle, *Food Politics*.
2. Among the many books are Pringle, *Food, Inc.*; Ronald and Adamchak, *Tomorrow's Table*, p. 200; Weber, *Food, Inc.*; Kenner, "Exploring the Corporate Powers Behind the Way We Eat," pp. 27–40; Schlosser, "Reforming Fast Food Nation," pp. 3–18; Kingsolver, with Hopp and Kingsolver, *Animal, Vegetable, Miracle*; and Kimball, *The Dirty Life*. Films include "Food, Inc.," "The Future of Food," "What's Organic About Organic," and a new film about food cooperatives, "Food for Change."
3. Coppin and High, *The Politics of Purity*; Borsodi, *This Ugly Civilization*; Sackman, *Orange Empire*, pp. 201–203; and Schlink, *Eat, Drink and Be Wary*. For more on Schlink, see McGovern, *Sold American*, pp. 166–178. Glickman argues that Consumers' Research helped to "broaden" the consumer movement, which had been decentralized. Glickman, *Buying Power*, p. 205. In the 1950s, Rodale wrote *How to Eat for a Healthy Heart*, a title that sounds like many today.
4. Carson, *Silent Spring*; Hunter, *Consumer Beware!*; Berry, *A Continuous Harmony*.
5. Jacobs, *Pocketbook Politics*. Among historians who have written about consumer activism are Deutsch, *Building a Housewife's Paradise*; and Glickman, *Buying Power*, chap. 6.
6. Keillor, *Cooperative Commonwealth*, p. 340.
7. http://www.arroyofoodcoop.com/FAQs, and http://www.ica.coop/coop/statistics.html, accessed Sept. 6, 2011. If one considers that there are over 900 rural electric coops that provide service to more than 42 million customers, 9,400 credit unions, and 10,500 marketing and purchasing coops joined by 1.5 million farmers, these estimates are not unreasonable. http://www.historians.org/projects/giroundtable/Coops/Coops2.htm, accessed Sept. 6, 2011; National Cooperative Month Planning Committee, *Cooperative Businesses in the United States. A 2005 Snapshot* (Oct. 2005).
8. Holyoake, *Self-Help by the People*; Roy, *Co-operatives*, p. 205.
9. Caspary, *Dewey on Democracy*, p. 8.
10. Ibid., p. 101; Fairfield, *Why Democracy?*, p. xiii.
11. Keillor, *Cooperative Commonwealth*, p. 3.
12. Deutsch, *Building a Housewife's Paradise*.
13. Greer, with Logan and Willis, *America the Bountiful*, pp. 121, 130; U.S. Food and Drug Administration, "Milestones in U.S. Food and Drug Law History," http://www.fda.gov/opacom/backgrounders/miles.html, accessed Aug. 12, 2010.
14. Ad for Co-op Foods, 74.155.15 (6), CTCR; Wilson, "Growth of a Co-op Food Store," p. 9; 2010 North Coast brochure.
15. See http://wholefoodsmarket.com/company/corevalues.php, accessed Sept 6, 2011. I have not included in this discussion other large grocery stores and Walmart who also affect food legislation.
16. Shapin, "Paradise Sold," pp. 84–88; Mackey, "Walmart for the Granola Crowd," p. 60.
17. In the case of the Palo Alto Food Co-operative, there are over forty boxes of records but they are housed upstairs in an old warehouse where there is no electricity.

18. Cohen, *A Consumers' Republic*; McGovern, "Consumption and Citizenship in the United States," pp. 37–58; McGovern, *Sold American*; Glickman, *Buying Power*, pp. 257, 260, 272.

19. See http://www.foodcoopiniative.com, accessed Sept. 6, 2011. I am grateful to Stuart Reid of the FCI for sending me information about this important project.

20. Foner, *History of the Labor Movement in the United States*, vol. 2, p. 436.

21. Ford, *Co-operation in New England*, p. 21.

CHAPTER 1

1. Tocqueville, *Democracy in America*, p. 106.

2. See Holyoake, *Self-Help by the People*.

3. Commons, Phillips, Gilmore, Sumner, and Andrews, *A Documentary History of American Industrial Society*, pp. 59–60; Untitled, in ibid., p. 63.

4. Angevine, "The Roots of Consumer Co-operatives in the U.S.," p. 20.

5. Commons et al., *A Documentary History of American Industrial Society*, p. 185; Ford, *Co-operation in New England*, p. 14; Darling, "The Workingmen's Party in Massachusetts, 1833–1834," p. 82.

6. Cowling, *Co-operatives in America*, p. 81; Ford, *Co-operation in New England*, p. 14; Foner, *History of the Labor Movement in the United States*, vol. 1, p. 181.

7. Ford, *Co-operation in New England*, p. 15. It is quite possible that this was an exclusionary requirement against recent Irish immigrants.

8. Ibid., p. 15; Cowling, *Co-operatives in America*, p. 100; Leikin, *The Practical Utopians*, p. 2.

9. Foner, *History of the Labor Movement in the United States*, vol. 1, pp. 182, 198–199, 203, 211; Whelan, "The Growth of Consumer Co-operatives in the United States," p. 45.

10. Leikin, *The Practical Utopians*, p. 33. Even so, Leikin argues, this democratic impulse excluded African American, women, and unskilled workers. Leikin, *The Practical Utopians*, pp. xviii, 32–33, 158.

11. Foner, *History of the Labor Movement in the United States*, vol. 1, p. 417.

12. The Knights of Crispin was especially concerned about the Blake-McKay sewing machine, which threatened shoemakers. Angevine, "The Roots of Consumer Co-operatives in the U.S.," p. 20; Hall, "The Knights of St. Crispin in Massachusetts, 1869–1878," pp. 163, 170, 171; Leikin, *The Practical Utopians*, p. 17.

13. Foner, *History of the Labor Movement in the United States*, vol. 2, p. 436. See also Voss, *The Making of American Exceptionalism*; and Fink, *Workingmen's Democracy*. Neither Voss nor Fink fully discusses the role of cooperatives in class formation.

14. Glickman, *A Living Wage*; Foner, *History of the Labor Movement in the United States*, vol. 2, pp. 48, 54, 75–77, 81–82; Ford, *Co-operation in New England*, p. 27; Leikin, *The Practical Utopians*, pp. 71, 158. Leaders instead recommended lecture series, reading rooms, and libraries for workers. The emphasis should not be on the failure of the early co-ops. Rather, we might think of how their efforts led to the formation of other cooperatives. Further, many small businesses, not just cooperatives, were short-lived. Although there are no exact numbers on how many failed then, a later report by the US Department of Agriculture documented that 1,353 of 12,000 co-ops from 1911 to 1925 failed, nearly 11 percent. One study in the early 1920s showed that most small grocery stores did not last more than seven years. Cohen, *Making a New Deal*, p. 118.

15. Ford, *Co-operation in New England*, p. 21.

16. Ibid., p. 22.

17. Ibid., pp. 22, 23–24. In some New England states, laws discouraged the formation of co-ops. Both Connecticut and Massachusetts had special laws for incorporating co-ops, requiring a minimum of seven people and $1,000 minimum capital. The laws also

stipulated that there could be no distribution of profits before at least 10 percent of net profits were applied to a savings fund. Both states also required annual statements of accounts. Ibid, pp. 60–61.

18. Ibid., pp. 35–36.

19. Wallis, "The Women's Co-operative Movement in Utah," pp. 316, 318, 319–320.

20. Randall, *Consumers' Co-operative Adventures*, p. 150; Harris, *Co-operation*, p. 288; Conover, "The Rochdale Principles in American Co-operative Associations," p. 118.

21. Brinkley, *The End of Reform*, p. 9; McGerr, *A Fierce Discontent*, p. xv; Gerstle, "The Protean Character of American Liberalism," pp. 1054–1055.

22. Westbrook, "Schools for Industrial Democrats," p. 413.

23. Ibid., p. 406.

24. Over two-thirds were in eastern and northern states, mostly supported by farmers and in small towns. Knapp, *The Rise of American Co-operative Enterprise*, p. 417.

25. Although much of the scholarship has focused on native-born white women, immigrant women should also be acknowledged. In Chicago, for example, Croatian women were interested in the socialist movement but did not want a separate women's branch. As one newspaper article stated: "A woman like a man becomes a real revolutionary only then, when she is confronted with capitalism. But a housewife also may become a good fighter for Socialist rights." "The Women's Movement," *Radnicka Straza*, Mar. 4, 1914, I E, I K, box 8, FLSP. Lears's casting of women as "victims" by advertisers does not capture women's agency or resistance during the early twentieth century. Lears, "From Salvation to Self-Realization," p. 27. For a thoughtful collection of essays about gender and consumerism, see Scanlon, *The Gender and Consumer Culture Reader*.

26. Sorenson, *The Consumer Movement*, pp. 6–7. On the home economics movement, see Stage and Vincenti, *Women and the History of a Profession*.

27. Storrs, *Civilizing Capitalism*, pp. 18, 36; "Founder's Day," *Lake Erie Record* 16, no. 1 (1901–1902): 193, Lake Erie College Clippings file, Lake Erie College.

28. Northern States' Co-operative League, *1928 Yearbook*, pp. 121–122. The Women's Co-operative Guild in Minneapolis, affiliated with the Franklin Co-op Creamery Association, was also active in educational and charity work. The Association's radical character was reflected in the Guild's goals: "'to cheer and to urge the men on' in their 'industrial struggle' toward the 'ultimate goal of the co-operative commonwealth.'" Northern States' Co-operative League, *1925 Yearbook*, pp. 61–62.

29. Cheel, "A Journey of Four Weeks to Some Co-operative Centers in the U.S.A.," p. 46.

30. Kane, "Populism, Progressivism, and Pure Food," pp. 161–162.

31. However, when the Supreme Court ruled on food additives in 1914, it argued that in order for bleached flour with nitrites to be banned, the government had to show a relationship between the additives and human harm. Bloodworth, *Upton Sinclair*, pp. 58, 66; US Food and Drug Administration, "Milestones in U.S. Food and Drug Law History," http://www.fda.gov/opacom/backgrounders/miles.html, accessed Mar. 12, 2010; Levenstein, *Revolution at the Table*, pp. 30, 40; Hawthorne, *Inside the FDA*, pp. 39, 41. Harvey Wiley, head of the Bureau of Chemistry, warned that food in the United States was in a "sorry state" and he had ample evidence for this statement. Alongside food packaging, which had started in the late 1800s, was the use of preservatives. In his crusade against food adulteration, Wiley opposed saccharin, which resulted in President Theodore Roosevelt forcing him to resign. Strasser, *Satisfaction Guaranteed*, pp. 256, 259, 260. Kane has noted that the research of chemists who worked in agricultural experiment stations has been omitted in the scholarship about pure food advocacy. Kane, "Populism, Progressivism, and Pure Food," p. 162.

32. Letter from E.R.E., Jan. 13, 1928 to JW, Series I, box 12, folder 10, JRP; Letter from William McCarroll, Chair of Board, Consumers and Producers Foundation of America,

Nov. 19, 1927 to JR, Series I, box 12, folder 10, JRP; HW to JW, "Consumers and Producers Foundation of America," n.d., Series I, box 12, folder 10, JRP; Memorandum, Sept. 4, 1929, Series I, box 12, folder 12, JRP. I have not found any other information about these organizations. Letter from Henry C. Simons to Co-operative Distributors, Inc., Dec. 12, 1934, Series I, box 2, folder 18, HCP; Letter from E. J. Lever, President of Board of Directors, Co-operative Distributors, Dec. 19, 1934, Series I, box 2, folder 18, HCP. The founder of the Consumers' Research, the first product testing organization established in 1929, published the book, *Eat, Drink, and Be Wary*, which advised consumers to "follow your grand-mother's instincts—back to the ante-bran, pre-crisco days." Sorenson, *The Consumer Movement*, p. 46; Glickman, *Buying Power*, p. 195.

33. "Letter from the Acting Chairman of the Federal Trade Commission," in *Chain Stores. Final Report on the Chain-Stores Investigation*, pp. 9, 10; Buder, *Capitalizing on Change*, p. 237; "Do the A. & P. Stores Make Money?" pp. 145–146; Greer with Logan and Willis, *America the Bountiful*, p. 52; Deutsch, *Building a Housewife's Paradise*, p. 58. There is a long history of chain stores undercutting prices. See Strasser, *Satisfaction Guaranteed*, p. 228.

34. Deutsch, *Building a Housewife's Paradise*, pp. 53–54; Tolbert, "The Aristocracy of the Market Basket," pp. 181, 183, 184. By the mid-1930s, supermarkets added florescent lighting and displays to create, in Adam Mack's estimation, a new aesthetic to appeal to women shoppers' senses. Mack, "'Speaking of Tomatoes': Supermarkets, The Senses, and Sexual Fantasy in Modern America," pp. 815–816.

35. Tolbert, "The Aristocracy of the Market Basket," p. 195.

36. Most labeled goods were canned vegetables, fruits, milks, cereals, coffee, and flour. See *Consumers' Co-operation* 21 (Feb. 1935): p. 23; "Co-operative Supersedes Private Business," p. 111. It is difficult to know how many grocery cooperatives there were. By 1920, there were 2,600 cooperative buying societies. Of 1,009 for which data was collected, only 728 were consumer societies. Knapp, *The Rise of American Co-operative Enterprise*, p. 416.

37. "How One Co-operative Closed A Chain Store," p. 210.

38. Johnson was the first women to receive her doctorate in history from Cornell University; Noa was a graduate of the Women's College in Baltimore. Knupfer, "The Urban and Rural Reform Activities of Lilian Wyckoff Johnson," pp. 13–14; Howe, *Denmark*, pp. 76,130,131. Danish farmers had been inspired by their visits to English cooperatives in the early 1870s. Another influence was the Danish folk schools, called "people's colleges," which promoted agriculture, as well as citizenship participation and cultural history. In 1933, 42 percent of all Danish households were members of a consumer cooperative. Howe, *Denmark*, pp.102, 103–104, 133.

39. Knapp, *The Advance of American Co-operative Enterprise*, p. 173; Woodcock, "Mary Ellicott Arnold—Creative Urban Workers," pp. 39–41. Arnold was also involved in the Women's League for Peace and Freedom, evidence of women's social networking. Woodcock, "Mary Ellicott Arnold," p. 41. There were three regional federations: the Northern States' Co-operative League, headquartered in Minneapolis and organized in 1921; the Eastern States League, started in 1924; and the Central States Co-operative League headquartered in Bloomington, Illinois, which started in 1926. Cowling, *Co-operatives in America*, pp. 110–111. By 1938, two regional leagues in California were added. Daniels, *Co-operation*, p. 353.

40. Knapp, *The Rise of American Co-operative Enterprise*, pp. 164–165, 169, 175; *Consumers' Co-operation* 23 (Feb. 1927), p. 29.

41. Northern States' Co-operative League, *1927 Yearbook*, pp. 36, 37. The Co-operative Central Exchange of Superior started a school in 1918. By 1925, 175 graduates had become cooperative store managers and employees. This was an alternative education for them, as many had only completed elementary school. Northern States' Co-operative League, *1925 Yearbook*, pp. 22, 23.

42. Henderson, "The Co-operative Training School," pp. 24, 25; "Negro Co-operative Store," p. 212.

43. Cowling, *Co-operatives in America*, p. 108; Knapp, *The Advance of American Co-operative Enterprise*, pp. 179, 180, 183–184; Knapp, *The Advance of American Co-operative Enterprise*, p. 172.

44. "In the Russian Co-operative Society of Chicago," *Rassivet*, Aug. 17, 1929, I D 2 b, II A 2, box 49, FLSP; Extracts from Constitution of Russian Workers' Co-operative Association of Chicago, July 17, 1925, I D 2 b, II A 2 box 49, FLSP; "The Russian-American People's Co-operative Bank in Chicago, Illinois," *Russkove Obzronie*, Mar. 22, 1930, I D 2 b, II a 2, box 49, FLSP.

45. Staley, *History of the Illinois State Federation of Labor*, pp. 141, 156, 340.

46. It was only in Illinois and Pennsylvania that cooperative stores were organized by unions. Angevine, "The Roots of Consumer Co-operatives in the U.S.," p. 21.

47. Many of these areas were liberal strongholds. Gerstle, "The Protean Character of American Liberalism," p. 1047. They also sold bread at cost price to the strikers and provided a free hall for them to meet. *Co-operation* 12 (July 1926), pp. 122–124; Ford, *Co-operation in New England*, pp. 37–39.

48. Ford, *Co-operation in New England*, pp. 25, 43; Savele, *The Story of a Co-operative*, pp. 25, 28–29, 31; Knapp, *The Rise of American Co-operative Enterprise*, p. 395; Sonnichsen, *Consumers' Co-operation*, p. 162. Ford has estimated that at least half of the Finnish cooperative members were socialists. Ford, *Co-operation in New England*, p. 44.

49. Gerstle, "The Protean Character of American Liberalism," p. 1047; Knapp, *The Rise of American Co-operative Enterprise*, p. 396.

50. As of 1926, Minnesota had 1,300 co-op associations alone. Cowling, *Co-operatives in America*, p. 95; "Minneapolis and Its Many Co-operatives," p. 182; Knapp, *The Advance of American Co-operative Enterprise*, p. 173. The Cloquet Co-operative in Cloquet, Minnesota was the largest co-op society in the North Central States as of 1926. Nearly two-thirds of its 560 members were Finnish. "1,000 Co-operators at Cloquet," p. 142. In addition to selling groceries, the stores sold shoes, clothing, hardware, furniture, feed, seeds, and farm machinery. *Co-operation* 10 (Apr. 1924), p. 70.

51. Cowling, *Co-operatives in America*, p. 95.

52. Ibid., p. 96.

53. Deutsch, *Building a Housewife's Paradise*; Cohen, *Making a New Deal*, pp. 64, 76, 80–83, 110; "Poles Organize Co-operative," *Dziennik Chicagoski*, Jan. 16, 1896, I D 2 b, box 42, FLSP; "Alliance of Polish Mercantile Corporations," *Dziennik Zwiazkowy*, Sept. 14, 1918, I D 2 b, II D 2 b, box 42, FLSP.

54. "Co-operative System Gains among Chicago Bohemians," *Denni Hlasatel*, June 8, 1905, I D 2 b, II A 2, box 1, FLSP; Untitled, *Jewish Daily Forward*, Aug. 2, 1920, I D 2 b, box 30, FLSP; "West Side L. Plan a Co-operative Food Store," *Naujienos*, Apr. 26, 1916, I D 2 b box 35, FLSP; "The Cicero Lithuanian Co-operative Society" by A. Ciceronian, *Naujienos*, Apr. 15, 1916, I D 2 b, I D 1 b, box 35, FLSP. In Cleveland, Bohemian socialists started the Workingmen's Co-operative Company in 1912, which opened seven grocery stores. The company had 1,100 members and employed twenty workers. "The Bohemians in Cleveland," p. 142.

55. Co-operative Trading Company, *Twenty Years of Co-operative Trading in Waukegan, Illinois, 1911–1931*, pp. 7, 9, 14, 30; Arra, trans. Andrew I. Brask, *The Finns in Illinois*, pp. 151, 156, CTCR.

56. Ad for Co-op Foods, 74.155.15 (6), CTCR; Northern States' Co-operative League, *1927 Yearbook*, p. 137. With the rise in urbanization, farmers looked to cities for marketing, which led to more producer cooperatives. In 1920, there were almost 3,000 creamery associations. Knapp, *The Rise of American Co-operative Enterprise*, p. 101.

57. Co-operative Trading Company, *Twenty Years*, pp. 36, 43; Arra, *The Finns in Illinois*, p. 156.

58. Knapp, *The Rise of American Co-operative Enterprise*, pp. 397.

59. Ibid., pp. 398, 400; Warne, "The National Consumers' Co-operative Association," pp. 230, 236, 244.

60. In 1904 and 1908, the Labor Union Co-operative Company and the Producers' and Consumers' Association, respectively, were formed. Little is known about either co-operative. Frank, *Purchasing Power*, pp. 41–42, 46, 50, 52, 146–148; Knapp, *The Rise of American Co-operative Enterprise*, p.411; Cowling, *Co-operatives in America*, pp. 106–107. In 1896, the new American Federation of Labor had recommended "the Rochdale system of co-operative distribution and production." Angevine, "The Roots of Consumer Co-operatives in the U.S.," p. 21.

61. Cheel, "A Journey of Four Weeks to Some Co-operative Centers in the U.S.A.," pp. 44–45.

62. Randall, *Consumers' Co-operative Adventures*, pp. 151–154; Cowling, *Co-operatives in America*, p. 100. Consumer cooperatives lagged in the South. The only example of co-operatives I have found for Latinos was in Tampa, Florida. After a long strike in cigar factories in 1914, Gregorio Chavez promoted community stores. Within three years, there were seven cooperative buying clubs in West Tampa and Ybor City, with 450 members. By 1919, the number of clubs had increased to twenty-one, with a membership of 1,500. Sonnichsen, *Consumers' Co-operation*, p. 164.

63. Stromquist, *Re-inventing "The People,"* pp. 2, 9, 34, 71, 117.

CHAPTER 2

1. Gerstle, "The Protean Character of American Liberalism," p. 1045; Stein, *Pivotal Decade*, p. 4; Stein, *Running Steel*, p. 311. See also Brinkley, *The End of Reform*.

2. Jacobs, "Pocketbook Politics. Democracy and the Market in Twentieth-Century America," in *The Democratic Experiment History*, Jacobs and Zelizer, p. 261; Jacobs, *Pocketbook Politics*, pp. 124–131.

3. See Cohen, *A Consumers' Republic*; Weems, Jr., *Desegregating the Dollar*. For a discussion of the history of labeling, see Strasser, *Satisfaction Guaranteed*, chap. 2. See also Schudson, *Advertising*. Grocery chain stores had three advantages over food cooperatives. First, they could buy more volume directly from suppliers and eliminate markup. Second, they were able to expand their product lines to include meat and nonfood items, all under one roof. Third, grocery chain stores used advertising to maximize their profits. Greer, with Logan and Willis, *America the Bountiful*, pp. 11, 15. This meant that customers, who were overwhelmingly women, were seen as "a bundle of sales possibilities." Bowlby, *Carried Away*, p. 144. For a discussion of advertising and its effect on consumers, see Charles McGovern, "Consumption and Citizenship in the United States, 1900–1940," pp. 37–58.

4. Crews, *Can We Establish A Consumer Society*, p. 43; Cooley, *Behind the Bricks and Mortar*, p. 25.

5. Cowling, *Co-operatives in America*, p. 158; Central Co-operative Wholesale, *1937 Year Book*, p. 15.

6. Lewis, "A Critique of Consumer Co-operative Theory and Practice," p. 192. By 1932, there were 1,700 credit unions in the United States. Angevine, "The Roots of Consumer Cooperatives in the U.S.," p. 26.

7. Knapp, *The Advance of American Co-operative Enterprise*, pp. 289, 291. The Division of Self-Help Co-operatives ceased in 1937.

8. Colcord quoted in Knapp, *The Advance of American Co-operative Enterprise*, p. 290.

9. One was at Casa Grande, Arizona in 1936. Originally an 80-acre farm, it grew to a 5,000-acre cooperative. Baker, "Self-Help Co-operatives and the Consumer Movement," p. 67; Knepper, *Greenbelt, Maryland*, pp. 14, 16, 19, 41. See also Cooper and Mohn, *The Greenbelt Cooperative*.

10. Parker, *The First 125 Years*, p. 137. Parker was first employed by the US Bureau of Labor Statistics, then became involved in union issues, pension plans, and welfare laws. She later became president and director of the Rochdale Co-operative in Washington, DC, and director of the CLUSA. Angevine, "Florence C. Parker—A Beacon Light," pp. 379–382. Another communal farm of Native Americans was Pembroke Farms in North Carolina. See Anderson, "Lumbee Kinship, Community, and the Success of the Red Banks Mutual Association," pp. 39–58.

11. Indeed, the NRA had been highly controversial and some had even likened it to fascism. Warbasse, "Consumers' Co-operatives and the National Recovery Administration," p. 64; Sorenson, *The Consumer Movement*, p. 17. For more information about Rumsey, see Jacobs, *Pocketbook Politics*, pp. 67–69.

12. See the *Report of the Inquiry on Co-operative Enterprise in Europe, 1937*; Rodgers, *Atlantic Crossings*, p. 458; Central Co-operative Wholesale, *1937 Year Book*, p. 15.

13. Hawley, *The New Deal and the Problem of Monopoly*, pp. 201, 203; Rodgers, *Atlantic Crossings*, p. 409.

14. Knupfer, "The Urban and Rural Reform Activities of Lilian Wyckoff Johnson," pp. 22–23. In 1933, there were nearly 12 million unemployed workers; 20 percent of them subsisted through private charity or public monies. Warbasse, "Consumers' Co-operative and the National Recovery Administration," p. 63.

15. Sugrue, "All Politics Is Local," p. 307.

16. Greer, with Logan and Willis, *America the Bountiful*, pp. 121, 130.

17. Ibid., p. 123; Hawthorne, *Inside the FDA*, p. 42; US Food and Drug Administration, "Milestones in U.S. Food and Drug Law History," http://www.fda.gov/opacom/backgrounders/miles.html, accessed Mar. 3, 2009.

18. Central Co-operative Wholesale, *1940 Yearbook*, p. 72; *Consumers' Co-operation* 21 (Feb. 1935), p. 23; Cohen, *Making a New Deal*, p. 237; Deutsch, *Building a Housewife's Paradise*, p. 71. A new co-op green label was introduced to cut costs for lower-income families. The red co-op label promised the highest quality, then blue and green. "Consumer Co-op Progress in 1941," p. 12. The use of labels and testing kitchens confirmed Deutsch's idea that co-ops, while adopting some chain store strategies, "did not challenge the *idea* of mass retailing itself." Deutsch, *Building a Housewife's Paradise*, p. 122. The Central Co-operative Wholesale supported labor rights, reaffirming their rights to organize into unions and bargain collectively with their employers. Central Co-operative Wholesale, *1943 Yearbook*, p. 29.

19. Whelan, "The Growth of Consumer Co-operatives in the United States" p. 60; Sorenson, *The Consumer Movement*, p. 142.

20. Campbell, "Growth of Co-operatives," p. 33; Knapp, *The Advance of American Co-operative Enterprise*, pp. 379, 380; "General Co-op History," *Co-operation* (Nov.–Dec. 1934): 180–181, box 1, HPCSR.

21 Sorenson, *The Consumer Movement*, pp. 13, 84–85, 93, 96, 127. Here I am thinking of Lawrence Glickman's two models of consumer organizations during the 1930s: those that privileged experts, such as advertisers and product testers; and those that collectively organized on behalf of consumers and producers (or laborers). Glickman, "The Strike in the Temple of Consumption," p. 100.

22. "Living Costs to Be Viewed by Consumers," *Chicago Defender*, Oct. 16, 1937, p. 17. As Stuart Chase claimed: "The consumer is really not a man but a woman, an Amazon

with great power over the economic future. Women buy at least three-fourths of the goods that go to the ultimate consumer. She is, indeed, an Amazon, towering portentous and blocking the whole economic horizon for the years before us." Chase quoted in Crews, *Can We Establish A Consumer Society?* p. 11.

23. "Illinois Housewives Group Plans Big Mass Meeting," *Chicago Defender*, Apr. 27, 1940, p. 18; "Lola M. Parker Main Speaker at Exposition," *Chicago Defender*, Aug. 31, 1940, p. 18; "Hilliard and Berry to Address Audience," box 1, file 2, APP.

24. Chateauvert, *Marching Together*, pp. 96, 107, 143–144.

25. The Institute for Consumer Education at Stephens College, a women's college in Columbia, Missouri, had the first consumer education department established in the country in 1937. Knapp, *The Advance of American Co-operative Enterprise*, pp. 389; *Consumers' Co-operation* 21 (Mar. 1935), p. 87; Houston, "The Teaching of Co-operation in the Public Schools," p. 103.

26. Sorenson, *The Consumer Movement*, p. 76; Angevine, "The Development of Consumer Education in the Classroom," pp. 259–264; Henderson, "The Co-operative Training School," pp. 24–25. William Zeuch, director of the labor Commonwealth College, recommended establishing a co-operative college. Zeuch, "Rochdale College," p. 64; Jacobson, "Shall We Establish a Co-operators' College in the Northwest?" pp. 104–106. Various states passed laws about co-operative education during the 1930s, including Wisconsin, Minnesota, and North Dakota. Knapp, *The Advance of American Co-operative Enterprise*, p. 385; "Wisconsin First State to Require the Teaching of Consumers' Co-operation," *Consumers' Co-operation* 21 (Dec. 1935), p. 181. Some states—including Washington, Pennsylvania, Kansas, Wisconsin, and Minnesota—introduced cooperative legislation but it was not passed. "Co-op Legislation Killed," *Consumers' Co-operation* 23 (Sept. 1937), p. 140.

27. See Bowen, *The Co-operative Road to Abundance*.

28. Ibid., pp. 81–82; Kallen, "The Philosophy of Co-operation," p. 3; Westbrook, "Schools for Industrial Democrats," p. 415. See also Kallen, *The Decline and Rise of the Consumer*. Gerstle notes how during the late 1920s, Kallen changed from an ethnic to an economic approach, thus his interest in cooperatives. Gerstle, "The Protean Character of American Liberalism," p. 1065.

29. Sonnichsen, *Consumers' Co-operation*, p. 185.

30. Warbasse, "Co-operation, A Way of Peace," pp. 154–157; Balch, "Why Co-operation Is Not Enough," p. 208; Topping, "Kagawa and Co-operation in Japan," p. 20; Knapp, *The Advance of American Co-operative Enterprise*, p. 383; Saunders, "Toyohiko Kagawa: The St. Francis of Japan," pp. 314–315.

31. Co-operative Trading Company, *Twenty Years of Co-operative Trading in Waukegan, Illinois, 1911–1931*, p. 8.

32. Parker, *The First 125 Years*, pp. 308–310; Gorman, "W.E.B. DuBois and His Work," pp. 80–86. See http://www.marxists.org/history/etol/newspape/fi/vol11/no03/gorman.htm, accessed Mar. 9, 2009.

33. Ransby, *Ella Baker and the Black Freedom Movement*, pp. 82–83, 84; Schuyler, "Consumers' Co-operation, The American Negro's Salvation," pp. 144–145. In Los Angeles, Clayton Russell, Jr., minister of the People's Independent Church of Christ, set up five cooperatives in the community, which lasted for at least five years. The Virtual Oral/Aural History Archives, http://salticid.nmc.csulb.edu/cgi-bin/WebObjects/OralAural2.woa/wa/interview?ww=1280&wh=610&pt=109&bi=1&prj=a1101&col=a1001&ser=a1012, accessed Sept. 8, 2012.

34. Reddix, "The Negro Finds A Way to Economic Equality," pp. 174–175; Weems, Jr., *Desegregating the Dollar*, pp. 58–60. The Educational Committee had published a pamphlet, "A Five Year Plan of Co-operative Action for Lifting the Economic Status of the Negro in Gary." See also Reddix, *The Negro Seeks Economic Freedom Through Co-operation*.

35. Bolles, *The People's Business*, p. 115; "350 Harlem Families Operate Grocery Stores," *Pittsburgh Courier*, July 6, 1935, p. 2.

36. Parker, *The First 125 Years*, p. 310.

37. Drake, *Churches and Voluntary Associations Among Negroes in Chicago*, p. 212.

38. Bolles, *The People's Business*, pp. 120–121.

39. *Consumers' Co-operation* 21 (July 1935), p. 135; Central Co-operative Wholesale, *1937 Year Book*, p. 30.

40. Central Co-operative Wholesale, *1939 Yearbook*, p. 27; Lewis, "A Critique of Consumer Co-operative Theory and Practice," p. 193; Kercher, Kebker, and Leland, Jr., *Consumers' Co-operatives in the Northern Central States*, pp. 355, 360, 361.

41. Sinclair, *The Autobiography of Upton Sinclair*, p. 268; Randall, *Consumers' Co-operative Adventures*, pp. 155ff.; Sackman, *Orange Empire*, pp. 187, 194. Another estimate for unemployment in California in 1933 was 29 percent for nonagricultural workers. Gregory, *American Exodus*, p. 13.

42. Campbell, "Growth of Co-operatives," p. 31; Cowling, *Co-operatives in America*, p. 151; Whelan, "The Growth of Consumer Co-operatives in the United States," p. 87.

43. Jacobs, *Pocketbook Politics*, pp. 9, 11, 170, 171. See also Glickman, *Buying Power*, p. 280.

44. Jacobs, *Pocketbook Politics*, pp. 174, 213.

45. Nilsson, "Get into Groceries—Why and How?" p. 91; Whelan, "The Growth of Consumer Co-operatives in the United States," Appendix 2. Another estimate of co-op members in 1944 was even higher, at 1.5 million; Deutsch, *Building a Housewife's Paradise*, p. 116.

46. *Consumers' Co-operation*, 27 (Mar. 1941), p. 141; "Food Co-operatives' Operations Expanded by Opening of 5 Additional Outlets in East," *New York Times*, July 2, 1944, p. S8; "Lower East Side Consumer Council Votes to Set Up Its Own Co-operative Store," *New York Times*, Apr. 11, 1945, p. 20; "Harlem Consumers Hold Conference," *Chicago Defender*, Nov. 16, 1940, p. 21.

47. Myers, *Labor and Co-ops*, p. 21. James Myers was industrial secretary of the Federal Council of the Churches of Christ in America. He was also on the board of directors of CLUSA and was a member of its Committee on Organized Labor and Consumer Co-operation.

48. Ibid.

49. Cohen, *A Consumers' Republic*, p. 119.

50. Anderson, Jr., *Refrigeration in America*, pp. 198–199, 213, 276–278, 299.

51. Hamilton, *Trucking Country*, pp. 122, 125, 126.

52. Stein, *Pivotal Decade*, p. 2; Jacobs, *Pocketbook Politics*, p. 249.

53. Feinberg, *What Makes Shopping Centers Tick*, pp. 15, 16, 20; Cohen, *A Consumers' Republic*, pp. 258, 272. Feinberg was a featured columnist for the *Women's Wear Daily*.

54. Cohen, *A Consumers' Republic*, p. 278.

55. Brinkley, *The End of Reform*, p. 10.

56. Ibid., pp. 265, 270, 271; Jacobs, *Pocketbook Politics*, p. 257; see also Packard, *Hidden Persuaders*; and Schulman, *The Seventies*.

57. Brinkley, *The End of Reform*, p. 265.

58. Savele, *The Story of a Co-operative*, p. 45; Consumers Co-operative of Walworth County, Elkhorn, Wisconsin, *Co-op News* 8 (Dec. 11, 1943), n.p.

59. Knepper, *Greenbelt, Maryland*, pp. 82, 83.

60. Letter from John Carson, Director, Washington Offices, The Co-operative League of the U.S.A. to Managers, Educational Directors, Editors, Oct. 4, 1948, Scrapbook, HCCSR. There were exceptions. When a large co-op store opened in Detroit in 1949, its prices were 8 percent below those of chain stores. *HCCS Co-op Bulletin* (June 1948), Co-op Bulletins file, 1944–1954, HCCSR.

61. "Justice Dept. Story: How A&P Has Hold on Food," Apr. 1, 1945, Scrapbook, HCCSR.

62. Cohen, *A Consumers' Republic*, pp. 106, 107; Jacobs, *Pocketbook Politics*, pp. 10, 239, 241.

63. Conover, "The Rochdale Principles in American Co-operative Associations," pp. 111–113; Harmer, "The Amazing Co-ops," *Frontier* (Dec. 1957): 5–8, box 1, HPCSR. One advantage they had over chain stores was that the income tax statute of 1951 exempted co-ops from income tax if they were "strictly Rochdale." Again, this meant that co-ops did not make a profit but a "surplus saving" and gave back patronage dividends.

64. The Council for Cooperative Development also encouraged coops to "consolidate authority" and become more like mainstream stores. Deutsch, *Building a Housewife's Paradise*, pp. 148–150; *HPCS Co-op News* (Jan. 1955), Co-op News-1950s file, HPCSR; Whelan, "The Growth of Consumer Co-operatives in the United States," Appendix 2.

65. *HPCS Co-op News* (Sept. 1959), Co-op News-1950s file, HPCSR; *HPCS Co-op News* (Nov. 1959), Co-op News-1950s file, HPCSR; "Your Co-op Handbook," box 1, HPCSR.

66. http://encyclopedia.chicagohistory.org/pages/2790.html, accessed Oct. 7, 2011; Deutsch, *Building a Housewife's Paradise*, p. 187; Gamboa, *Mexican Labor and World War II*, p. 125.

67. Gamboa, *Mexican Labor and World War II*, p. 39; Nahmias, *The Migrant Project*, pp. 104, 105, 120. The term "agribusiness" was coined during the New Deal by the then secretary of agriculture Ezra Taft Benson. Hamilton, *Trucking Country*, p. 9. Consolidation of farm land, especially in California, led to specialized, labor-intensive crops, such as wine grapes and strawberries that had to be handpicked. Lopez, *The Farmworkers' Journey*, p. 94. Borsodi claims that specialization had started as early as the 1920s, as had plane spraying of pesticides. Borsodi, *This Ugly Civilization*, p. 275; Wargo, *Our Children's Toxic Legacy*, p. 69.

68. Hamilton, *Trucking Country*, p. 2.

69. Valdes, *Al Norte*, p. 202; Daniel, *Toxic Drift*, p. 7; Wargo, *Our Children's Toxic Legacy*, p. 67.

70. Daniel, *Toxic Drift*, 2. There is less documentation of the effects of pesticides on farm workers before World War II. But organic phosphate and other pesticides were used on the fields. See Galarza, *Merchants of Labor*, p. 196; Lopez, *The Farmworkers' Journey*, pp. 130–139.

71. Wargo, *Our Children's Toxic Legacy*, pp. 70, 72, 80.

72. Daniel, *Toxic Drift*, pp. 8, 122; Wargo, *Our Children's Toxic Legacy*, pp. 74–75.

73. Daniel, *Toxic Drift*, pp. 5, 6.

74. Hamilton, *Trucking Country*, p. 9; Galarza, *Merchants of Labor*, p. 107.

75. Nahmias, *The Migrant Project*, p. 105.

76. Jacobs, *Pocketbook Politics*, p. 252; Glickman, *Buying Power*, pp. 257, 260.

CHAPTER 3

1. Milliman, with Sage, *The GLF Story, 1920–1964*, pp. 33, 63, 73.

2. Kammen, *Ithaca*, p. 118.

3. Dieckmann, *A Short History of Tompkins*, pp. 147–148; Kammen, *Ithaca*, p. 99.

4. http://www.thehistorycenter.net/news/AAH_timeline.html, accessed Mar. 17, 2009.

5. Letter from Mark Rich to Professor Paul W. Gates, Cornell University, Dec. 27, 1948, box 1, folder 9, ICCSR.

6. "Co-op: A Success Story Comes to a Bewildering End," *Ithaca Journal*, Dec. 29, 1979, box 1, folder 3, ICCSR; ICCS Members' Guide brochure, n.d., box 1, folder 3, ICCSR.

7. "Co-op: A Success Story Comes to a Bewildering End."

8. ICCS, Minutes of Meeting, Feb. 2, 1937, box 1, folder 8; ICCS, Minutes of Meeting, Feb 16, 1937, box 1, folder 8; ICCS, Minutes of Meeting, Mar. 2, 1937, box 1, folder 8; ICCS, Minutes of Meeting, May 4, 1937, box 1, folder 8, ICCSR.

9. *ICCS Bulletin* (April 1938), box 5, ICCSR.

10. Sometimes the co-op sold dairy products from the Dairymen's League. ICCS, Minutes of Meeting, Oct. 10, 1938, box 1, folder 8; *ICCS Bulletin* (April 1938), box 5, folder 8; ICCS, Minutes of Meeting, Nov. 22, 1938, box 1, folder 8, ICCSR.

11. *ICCS Bulletin* (April 27, 1938), box 5, ICCSR.

12. *ICCS Bulletin* (May 1938; Feb. 1946), box 5, ICCSR.

13. ICCS, Minutes of Meeting, Sept. 14, 1938, box 1, folder 8; *ICCS Quarterly Bulletin* (Feb. 1939), box 1, folder 9; ICCS, Minutes of Meeting, Mar. 7, 1939, box 1, folder 8, ICCSR.

14. ICCS, Minutes of Meeting, Feb. 13, 1940, box 1, folder 8, ICCSR. The store location committee strategically recommended a site near a local meat market so members could shop at both places. It was during the 1930s that grocery chain stores started selling a combination of foods, including meats. See Greer with Logan and Willis, *America the Bountiful*, p. 154.

15. ICCS, Minutes of Meeting, Feb. 4, 1941, box 1, folder 10; ICCS, Minutes of Meeting, Feb. 13, 1940, box 1, folder 8, ICCSR. Whiton also advised them that their annual expenses should not exceed 15 percent of their gross sales and that they should not sell meat, because they could not compete with the town butchers.

16. Milliman, with Sage, *The GLF Story*, pp. 256–257. By 1941, there were over 3,600 locker plants nationally; by 1946, over 8,000. By 1946, nearly 3.3 million families, most of them farmers, used locker plants. Anderson, Jr., *Refrigeration in America*s, pp. 288, 298.

17. Milliman, with Sage, *The GLF Story*, p. 259.

18. The GLF also installed new equipment in their store and hired a bookkeeper for the ICCS. "History and Growth of the Ithaca Co-op," n.d., box 6, ICCSR. 18; Shapiro, *Something from the Oven*, p. 10. Shapiro noted that, as of 1952, most families who owned freezers either lived on farms or had access to one at a locker plant. Shapiro, *Something from the Oven*, p. 16.

19. Wilson, "Growth of a Co-op Food Store," pp. 9–11, ICCSR.

20. ICCS, Minutes of Meeting, May 12, 1942, box 1, folder 10; Wilson, "Growth of a Co-op Food Store," pp. 9–11; *ICCS Bulletin* (May 1944), box 5, folder 9; ICCS, Minutes of Meeting, Jan. 4, 1943, box 1, folder 10; *ICCS Bulletin* (Spring 1945), box 1, folder 11; Letter from Store Expansion Committee to Members, Oct. 2, 1941, box 1, folder 10; Analysis of Store Sales and Margins, box 1, folder 11, ICCSR.

21. Wilson, "Growth of a Co-op Food Store," p. 9. This pattern, which persisted until the 1960s, also confirms Tracey Deutsch's observation that the co-op movement generally did not challenge gender relations. Deutsch, *Building a Housewife's Paradise*, pp. 131, 175.

22. Wilson, "Growth of a Co-op Food Store," p. 9; Jacobs, *Pocketbook Politics*, p. 213.

23. Wilson, "Growth of a Co-op Food Store," p. 9; *ICCS Bulletin* (Winter 1945), box 5, ICCSR.

24. ICCS, Minutes of Meeting, Jan. 16, 1941, box 1, folder 10, ICCSR.

25. ICCS, Minutes of Meeting, Mar. 2, 1942, box 1, folder 10, ICCSR; Cohen, *A Consumers' Republic*, p. 83.

26. ICCS, Minutes of Meeting, May 21, 1945, box 1, folder 11; *ICCS Bulletin* (April–May, 1946), box 5; ICCS, Minutes of Meeting, June 21, 1945, box 1, folder 11, ICCSR; Cohen, *A Consumers' Republic*, p. 106.

27. Letter from Alice Mack to Emma Lokken, Aug. 16, 1945, box 1, folder 11, ICCSR. Some women's groups were involved nationally in price controls after the war, such as the American Association of University Women and the League of Women Shoppers. They were also part of a national boycott of meat in 1948. Cohen, *A Consumers' Republic*, p. 106–107; Jacobs, *Pocketbook Politics*, p. 218.

28. "What Is the Fundamental Philosophy of the Ithaca Co-op?" July 18, 1945, box 1, folder 11, ICCSR.

29. Report of the Operating Committee of the ICCS, Inc., Mar. 13, 1946, box 1, folder 11, CCSR; *ICCS Bulletin* (Dec. 1946), box 5, ICCSR.

30. Cornell University also assisted through a loan of $1,500. The ICCS was interested in the veterans' store becoming a branch store of theirs. But for reasons not disclosed, the veterans wanted their own store. In 1945, the ICCS's annual sales were $330,000, with weekly averages of $8,600. This was more than double the weekly averages in 1942. Report of the Operating Committee of the ICCS, Inc., Mar. 13, 1946, box 1, folder 11, ICCSR; *ICCS Bulletin* (Jan. 1946; Jan. 1947), box 5; *ICCS Bulletin* (June 1945; Oct. 1947), box 1, folder 9, ICCSR.

31. *ICCS Bulletin* (Oct. 1947), box 1, folder 9, ICCSR.

32. Ibid.; *ICCS Bulletin* (Jan. 1947; Jan. 1948), box 5, ICCSR.

33. ICCS Members' Guide brochure, n.d., box 1, folder 3, ICCSR; "History and Growth of the Ithaca Co-op"; *ICCS Bulletin* (Feb. 1948), box 5, ICCSR.

34. By 1956, sales had reached $1.67 million. "Co-op: A Success Story Comes to a Bewildering End"; ICCS, Examination of Accounts for Year Ended Dec. 31, 1951; Examination of Accounts for Year Ended Dec. 31, 1953; Examination of Accounts for Year Ended Dec. 31, 1956, box 5, folder on Operating Statements, ICCSR.

35. *ICCS Bulletin* (May, 1948; July–Sept., 1948; May 1, 1949; June 1, 1950), box 5, ICCRS.

36. *ICCS Bulletin* (Feb. 15, 1951; Apr., 1953), box 5, ICCSR.

37. Diedre Hill Butler, "The South Side Community Center of Ithaca, New York: Built Through 'Community Mother,' 1938," box 72, folder 1, p. 82, ICCSR: Viola Marshall, "The Southside Community Center," 1942, SCC.

38. Allen B. Jones had joined the co-op's education committee in 1949. *ICCS Bulletin* (Aug. 1952; Oct. 1, 1949; Feb. 1959), box 5, ICCRS. During the war, a graduate of Cornell University taught African American history classes there. Butler, "The South Side Community Center of Ithaca, New York," p. 85. The Co-operative Institute Association started in 1929 and was sponsored by the Eastern Co-operatives, Inc. Co-op Education Institute, 1951–1955, Catalogue of the Twenty-Seventh Annual Co-op Institute, July 22–28, 1956, box 1, HPCSR.

39. *ICCS Bulletin* (Dec. 1951), box 5.

40. *ICCS Bulletin* (Oct. 1, 1949), box 5.

41. *ICCS Bulletin* (Nov. 1952), box 5.

42. *ICCS Bulletin* (Jan. 1946; Jan. 1948; June 1956), box 5, ICCSR. Agene was used through the 1950s. Hunter, *Consumer Beware!* p. 294. During the 1920s, Borsodi had written about how white bread was "made." Borsodi, *This Ugly Civilization*, pp. 84–87.

43. The ICCS sold 1,000 loaves of bread a week. Milliman, with Sage, *The GLF Story*, p. 99; *ICCS Bulletin* (Sept. 1953), box 5, ICCSR; Cosline, *An Adventure in Co-operation*, p. 46. In 1950, its bulletin printed the bread recipe developed at Cornell University. In 1951, the Messing Brothers of Brooklyn baked and sold the bread under the name "Cornell Loaf." Other special foods were soy flower, kelp tablets, wheat germ, and sodium-free foods. The FDA refused to approve the Cornell Formula Bread for sale "because it had more nutritional elements than were called for in the standards then in force!" The co-op had its own name for the bread, "Triple Rich." For a recipe, see http://www.motherearthnews.com/Real-Food/2005-02-01/Dr-McCays-Miracle-Loaf.aspx, accessed Mar. 19, 2009. See also http://www.isga-sprouts.org/history.htm, accessed Mar. 18, 2009.

44. *ICCS Bulletin* (Nov. 1957), box 1, folder 4; Examination of Accounts for Year Ended Dec. 31, 1957, box 5, folder on Operating Statements, ICCSR; *ICCS Bulletin* (Dec. 1951), box 5; Examination of Accounts for Year Ended Dec. 31, 1958, box 5, folder on Operating Statements, ICCSR; Report on Co-operative Consumers Society, Inc., prepared by Mid-

Eastern Co-operatives, Inc., Mar. 1977, box 6, no folder, ICCSR. At the same time, the ICCS continued to buy from local producers. In 1953, the co-op bought at least $97,000 worth of food from local farmers, mostly dairy, poultry, fruits and vegetables, and herbs. *ICCS Bulletin* (June 1953), box 5, ICCSR.

45. Editorial Letter from Three Former Members of Board of Directors of Co-op, n.d., box 1, folder 3, ICCSR; Letters re. Beer file, Sequence of Events Concerning the Possible Sale of Malt Beverages at the Co-op Shopping Center, 1958; Letter to Stockholder from Harold G. Smith, Pres. to Ruth Deabler, Sec., June 11, 1959; "Store Votes Beer, 81–76," *Ithaca Journal*, June 26, 1959, box 6, 1958–1959 Letters re. Beer file, ICCSR.

46. ICCS, 1961 and 1962 Operating Statements, box 5, folder on Operating Statements, ICCSR.

47. ICCS, 1964 and 1965 Operating Statements; Examination of Accounts for Year Ended Dec. 31, 1967, box 5, folder on Operating Statements, ICCSR.

48. http://www.time.com/time/magazine/article/0,9171,838451,00.html, accessed June 2, 2010; article (no source), Apr. 3, 1968, box 7, Newsclippings folder; ICCS, Examination of Accounts for Year Ended Dec. 31, 1969, box 5, folder on Operating Statements, ICCSR.

49. "Co-op Employee News," Aug. 28, 1968, box 5, Newsclippings folder, ICCSR.

50. *ICCS Bulletin* (Oct. 1964; May–June 1965; July 1966; May 1968), box 5, ICCSR; Kammen, *Ithaca*, 102. The first two female board presidents followed Gibbs: Seymour Bulkley in 1966 and Ruth Polson, a high school teacher and community activist, in 1968.

51. *ICCS Bulletin* (Feb. 1960; May 1961; Feb. 1969), box 5, ICCSR.

52. Bradwell, "Always Room at the Top: Black Students and Educational Policy in Ithaca, NY," pp. 216–217; http://www.news.cornell.edu/stories/April09/StraightRevisited.gl.html, accessed Oct. 15, 2011; see also http://www.news.cornell.edu/releases/Jan04/King.Jr.Talk.fac.html, accessed Oct. 15, 2011.

53. *ICCS Bulletin* (May 1961), box 5, ICCSR.

54. *ICCS Bulletin* (Dec. 1967; Feb. 1969; Oct. 1970; Feb. 1973), box 5, ICCSR.

55. ICCS, 1970 Annual Report, box 1, folder 2, ICCSR; Proposed By-Law Changes to be voted on Mar. 16, 1971, box 1, folder 2, ICCSR; Cosline, *An Adventure in Co-operation*, 14; ICCS, Examination of Accounts for Year Ended Dec. 31, 1970, box 5, folder on Operating Statements, ICCSR.

56. *ICCS Bulletin* (Apr. 1973), box 5, ICCSC; ICCS, Examination of Accounts for Year Ended Dec. 31, 1973, box 5, folder on Operating Statements, ICCSR.

57. Letters to Editor, *Ithaca Journal*, Mar. 24, 1973, box 7, Newsclippings folder, ICCSR.

58. *ICCS Bulletin* (Feb. 1974), box 5, ICCSR.

59. Cowie, *Stayin' Alive*, pp. 12, 163, 222; Schulman, *The Seventies*, pp. 7, 129.

60. Cowie, *Stayin' Alive*, p. 72; Friedman, *Consumer Boycotts*, pp. 78–80.

61. "UFWOC and the Lettuce Growers," ICCS box, file 3, ICCSC.

62. "Our Kind of Town," pp. 47–50; Paul Glover, "Quit School as Soon as You Can"; Glover, "Starting your own School"; Hoffman, "In Defense of Independent Schools," in *An Ithaca Schools Book. Toward Real Learning Within the System Without the System*, Educational Activism, 1970 file, CAC.

63. Rev. Richard Humphreys, "Facts about the Lettuce and Grape Boycott from a Priest Who Lives with It," *Ithaca Sunday News*, July 28, 1974, box 7, ICCSR; Untitled brochure, box 7, ICCSR.

64. "We Want to be Free!" Oct. 6, 1973; "Don't Buy Lettuce Without this Label," n.d., box 7, Newsclippings folder, ICCSR.

65. "Bureau Condemns Lettuce Boycott," *Ithaca Journal*, Jan. 11, 1971; "Co-op vs. the Picketers …," *Ithaca Journal*, Feb. 13, 1974; "Is That Social Justice?" n.d., box 7, Newsclippings folder, ICCSR.

66. "Pickets Help Lettuce Sale?" *Ithaca Journal*, Feb. 15, 1974, box 7, Newsclippings folder, ICCSR.

67. "Co-op: Poll Membership on Lettuce-Picker Issue," *Ithaca Journal*, Feb. 26, 1974; Letter from Nancy and Phil Bereano to Robert Brill, General Manager, Feb. 18, 1974, box 7, Newsclipping folder, ICCSR. A book, *Little Caesar*, by Ralph Toledano, a known conservative journalist, was displayed on the checkout counter of the ICCS. This book was an exposé of the UFW and Caesar Chavez's leadership. Several members objected. ICCS, Co-op Board Meeting Minutes, May 20, 1971, box 1, folder 5, ICCSR.

68. Bill Farmer, "On the Line at the Co-op," *Tompkins County Bulletin* (Feb. 22–Mar. 7, 1974), box 7, ICCSR. For more information on Pratt, see "Arthur Pratt, 1905–1994," *American Journal of Potato Research* 72 (Mar. 1995): 191–192. See also http://www.springerlink.com/content/lm05145g163q7760/, accessed June 14, 2010.

69. Farmer, "On the Line at the Co-op"; "Co-op Boycotters Served with Show Cause Order," *Ithaca Journal*, Mar. 12, 1974, box 7, Newsclippings folder, ICCSR.

70. Letter from a Member to the General Manager, Mar. 14, 1974; "Hearing Set for UFW Backers to Defend Picketing of Market," *Cornell Daily Sun*, Mar. 22, 1974, box 7, Newsclippings folder, ICCSR.

71. Hearing in Sixth Judicial District, Courthouse, Ithaca, Mar. 1974 Decision on Case *CCS, Inc. vs. William Farmer et al.*—representative of the Local Supporters of the UFW of America and Ithaca Friends of the Farmworkers, box 7, ICCSR.

72. "Points at Issue in the Co-op Boycott," n.d., ICCS box, file 3, IHC; "Co-op Members Split over Lettuce Policy," *The Cornell Daily Sun*, Mar. 27, 1974, box 7, Newsclippings folder, ICCSR.

73. "Co-op Members Split over Lettuce Policy," *The Cornell Daily Sun*, Mar. 27, 1974, box 7, Newsclippings folder, ICCSR.

74. Index cards with votes and opinions of members check source, box 7, ICCSR; "Co-op Picketers Deny Harassing Shoppers," *Cornell Daily Sun*, Apr. 3, 1974, box 7, ICCSR. At least twenty-five members expressed their disapproval of the co-op's actions.

75. To the Editor, *Ithaca Journal*, Apr. 22, 1974, ICCS, box 1, file 3, ICCSC.

76. They decided not to advocate a secondary boycott, although "they reserve[d] the right to secondarily boycott stores not unionized." UFW protesters, information sheet, Apr. 19, 1974, box 7, ICCSR.

77. "Co-op Debenture Drive under Way," *Ithaca Journal*, May 20, 1976, box 1, folder 4, ICCSR; ICCS, 1972 Operating Statement, box 5, folder on Operating Statements, ICCSR.

78. Report on Co-operative Consumers Society, Inc., prepared by Mid-Eastern Co-operatives, Inc.; *ICCS Bulletin* (Spring 1975), box 1, folder 4, ICCSR; Ithaca Friends of the Farmworker, flyer, n.d., box 7, ICCSR.

79. Report on Co-operative Consumers Society, Inc., prepared by Mid-Eastern Co-operatives, Inc.

80. IRFC/ICCS Relationship, n.d., box 1, folder 7, ICCSR.

81. A pharmacy, located in a rental above the ICCS, sold health and beauty products that competed with the co-op. Report on Co-operative Consumers Society, Inc., prepared by Mid-Eastern Co-operatives, Inc. See also http://www.blnz.com/news/2008/05/13/Food_co-op_staple_Ithaca_community_8331.html, accessed Mar. 17, 2009.

82. Facts You Should Know about the 1976 Reinvestment Revitalization Campaign of the ICCS, box 1, folder 1; "Co-op Debenture Drive Under Way," *Ithaca Journal*, May 20, 1976, box 1, folder 4; Peter H. May, "Marketing Strategy for the Co-op," May 28, 1981, box 6, ICCSR.

83. ICCS, Examination of Accounts for Year Ended Dec. 31, 1977, box 5, folder on Operating Statements, ICCSR; *Co-op Newsletter* (Apr. 1977), box 1, folder 4, ICCSR.

84. Peter May, "CCS Market Survey Analysis," June 1981, box 6, no file, ICCSR.

85. ICCS, 1978 Annual Report, box 1, folder 1, ICCSR; ICCS, Examination of Accounts for Year Ended Dec. 31, 1978, box 5, folder on Operating Statements, ICCSR.

86. "Shareholders angry at supermarket closing," *Ithaca Journal*, Dec. 27, 1979, box 7, Newsclippings folder, ICCSR.

87. "A New Brand of Co-op," *Ithaca Times*, Apr. 17, 1980, box 7, Newsclippings folder, ICCSR.

88. "A New Brand of Co-op."

89. "Resolution of Support for Co-operative Consumers' Society," n.d., ICCS box, file 3, ICCSC; "IRFC/CCS Relationship."

90. "Shareholders Angry at Supermarket Closing," *Ithaca Journal*, Dec. 27, 1979, box 1, file 3, ICCSR.

91. "Co-op Chief Resigns Over Reopening Plan," *Ithaca Journal*, July 8, 1980, box 7, Newsclippings folder, ICCSR. One comparative study of the two food co-ops in 1980–1981 confirmed how different their approaches and customers were. The ICCS sold food at market price but had returned patronage funds each year. Real Food, in contrast, gave discounts to its working members and had lower shelf prices. Real Food attracted younger people, whose educational level was generally higher than the ICCS's. But the ICCS attracted more minority customers than Real Food or the local commercial supermarkets. Customers stated that they shopped at ICCS because of convenience, its low prices, and its Rochdale philosophy. Sommer, Becker, Hohn, and Warholic, "Customer Characteristics and Attitudes at Participatory and Supermarket Cooperatives," pp. 136–137, 141, 143–144.

92. "Strategy for Co-op Survival Planning," n.d., box 6, ICCSR; "President's Report," 1980s, box 1, folder 3, ICCSR.

93. ICCS, Minutes for Special Meeting of ICCS, Dec. 1980, box 1, folder 3, ICCSR.

94. ICCS, Minutes for Special Meeting of ICCS, June and July 1981, box 1, folder 3, ICCSR.

95. ICCS, Minutes for Special Meeting of ICCS, Mar. 15, 1982; ICCS, Examination of Accounts for Year Ended Dec. 31, 1982, box 5, folder on Operating Statements, ICCSR.

96. Letter from Board President to Members, Mar. 1, 1982, box 1, folder 3, ICCSR.

97. "An Assessment of Our Economic Situation," 1981, box 1, folder 3, ICCSR.

98. "Co-op: A Success Story Comes to a Bewildering End."

99. *Sprouts!* (Feb. 1984; June 1984), IRFC, Newsletters, box 1, SC.

100. *Sprouts!* (May 1984; Sept. 1984), IRFC Newsletters, box 1, SC.

101. Paul Glover, "GreenStar's Green Future" (April 2001), http://www.ithacahours.com/archive/0104.html, accessed Mar. 17, 2009.

CHAPTER 4

1. "Lunding Is Giant of the Jewel Story," *Chicago Daily News*, Aug. 27, 1959, Newsclippings file, box 1, HPCSR. According to the same source, as of 1931, Jewel trucks operated in urban areas in thirty-eight states.

2. *Consumers' Co-operation* 22 (July 1936) 111; *Consumers' Co-operation* 21 (Dec. 1935): 212; Barclay, "Cooperation Advances in a Mid-West Community," pp. 56, 58; Stickney, "The Consumers' Cooperative Movement in Chicago," p. 226; Deutsch, *Building a Housewife's Paradise*, p. 119. There was also the Roseland Co-operative Association, which in 1923 had sold $89,000 worth of groceries and $83,000 in meats. "Roseland in Chicago," p. 123. As early as World War I, club women in Hyde Park and Woodlawn had tried to interest people in a food co-op. Another attempt was the National Consumers' Cooperative Association, a group of Rochdale co-ops headquartered in Chicago in 1919, which started with the National Co-operative Association and the Chicago Federation of Labor. Short-lived, the Association started seven stores, although they operated at a loss. In 1921, the Association closed. Warne, "The National Consumers' Cooperative Association," pp. 230–244.

3. Angevine, "The Roots of Consumer Cooperatives in the U.S.," p. 22; Letter from Dwight H. Ferguson to Gladys Scott, Apr. 3, 1972, box 1, HPCSR.

4. See http://www.co-opmarkets.com/history.htm, accessed July 16, 2010.

5. Angevine, "The Roots of Consumer Cooperatives in the U.S.," p. 22; Letter from Paul Douglas to Gladys Scott, Mar. 20, 1972, box 1, HPCSR. Despres had lived in Hyde Park since he was a child. "Leon Despres—artful dissent in City Hall," *Chicago Daily News,* May 23, 1970, n.p., box 1, HPCSR.

6. Davis, "How Success Followed Failure," pp. 56–57.

7. Letter from Paul Douglas to Gladys Scott, Mar. 20, 1972, box 1, HPCSR.

8. Wirth and Furez, *Local Community Fact Book, 1938,* n. p.

9. Davis, "How Success Followed Failure," 58; "Conversation with a Founding Father," *Spectrum,* Dec. 22, 1978, box 1, Newsclippings file, HPCSR; Report on Consumers' Co-operative Services Inc., July 1, 1934 to July 31, 1935, box 1, Consumers Co-operative Services Audits file, HPCSR; 1940 Audit, box 6, 1940–1941 Financial Statements file, HPCSR; 1942 Audit, box 6, 1942–1943 Financial Statements file, HPCSR. The co-op started a radio repair store in 1945; the following year, it moved into a store next to the co-op, with the electrical appliance store that was an independent but an affiliated store. The appliance store closed in 1948. Ruth Sumner, "From 'Play Store' to Success," *Hyde Park Herald,* Oct. 13, 1959, box, 20, Misc., Newsclippings file, HPCSR.

10. Deutsch, *Building a Housewife's Paradise,* pp. 124, 152.

11. Ibid., pp. 174, 175.

12. There was a cooperative nursery school, started in 1948, affiliated with the food co-op. "Progress Report, 1932–1953," box 6, 1950s Annual Reports and Progress Reports file; Knupfer, *The Chicago Black Renaissance and Women's Activism,* pp. 121–122; Ida b. Wells Consumers Co-operative, Inc., Letter, June 26, 1945, box 10, HPCS Board of Director Minutes file, HPCSR.

13. HPCS, Minutes of Board Meeting, July 2, 1945, box 10, Board of Director Minutes file, HPCSR. In 1945 the co-op had joined the South Park Improvement Association. Founded in 1901 by the Chicago Woman's Club, the Association was historically concerned with improving neighborhoods through garbage collection, flower plantings, and lawn care. In truth, many improvement associations functioned as restrictive covenant associations, designed to keep neighborhoods white. HPCS, Minutes of Board Meeting, Feb. 4, 1946, Board of Director Minutes (Jan. 8, 1945–July 8, 1945) file, box 10, HPCSR. For more about these efforts, see also http://www.archive.org/stream/neighborhoodimpr00hofe/neighborhoodimpr00hofe_djvu.txt, accessed Oct. 21, 2010.

14. Deutsch, *Building a Housewife's Paradise,* p. 119.

15. "Let's Try Co-operation in Chicago" booklet, n.d., box 1, Chicago Consumers' Co-operative file (1946–1948), HPCSR; Parker, *The First 125 Years,* p. 72.

16. Cowling, *Co-operatives in America,* pp. 96–98; Parker, *The First 125 Years,* p. 313; "Let's Try Co-operation in Chicago" booklet. Despite his more liberal leanings then, Hayakawa became a Republican senator from California in 1976. As a professor at San Francisco State University, he had opposed student activists on campus.

17. HPCS, "Progress Report, 1932–1953," box 6, Annual Reports, Progress Reports file (1950s), HPCSR; HPCS, 1956 Annual Report, box 6, Annual Reports, Progress Reports file (1950s), HPCSR.

18. "Then and Now Hyde [*sic*] Co-operative Society, Inc.," box 20, History of the Hyde Park Co-op file, HPCSR.

19. HPCS, 1954–1955 Annual Report, box 6, Annual Reports, Progress Reports file (1950s), HPCSR; "New Co-op Opens Tonight," *Hyde Park Herald,* Oct. 13, 1959, box, 20, Misc., Newsclippings file, HPCSR.

20. HPCS, 1956 Annual Report, box 6, Annual Reports, Progress Reports file (1950s), HPCSR. Two other cooperatives, the Co-operative Fuel Association and the Pioneer Co-operative, were also formed. The latter owned buildings and leased apartments to member families, perhaps becoming one of the first housing cooperatives in the city. The United Co-operative Projects was an incorporated federation of housing cooperatives at the University of Chicago. In 1945, individual housing cooperatives at the university joined together. "Progress Report, 1932–1953," box 6, 1950s Annual Reports and Progress Reports file, HPCSR.

21. Ad, *The Hyde Park Herald*, 1954, box 1, Co-op Ads file (1950s), HPCSR; "Then and Now Hyde [*sic*] Co-operative Society, Inc."; HPCS, 1956 Annual Report.

22. HPCS, 1956 Annual Report.

23. Sugrue, "Crabgrass-Roots Politics," pp. 551–552; Plotkin, "Deeds of Mistrust: Race, Housing, and Restrictive Covenants in Chicago, 1900–1953," pp. 21, 96; *Chicago Defender*, Jan. 14, 1939.

24. Mikva, "The Neighborhood Improvement Association," pp. 29, 31, 32.

25. *Chicago Defender*, July 7, 1945, p. 6.

26. Muriel Beadle, "The Hyde Park Kenwood Urban Renewal Years," 1964, box 1, Hyde Park Information (1960–1964) file, HPCSR, 10, 12. Beadle's husband was president of the University of Chicago.

27. Hyde Park-Kenwood Community Conference, p. 5.

28. Ibid.

29. "The Hyde Park Kenwood Urban Renewal Years," pp. 3, 6.

30. Ibid., p. 17.

31. Mikva, "The Neighborhood Improvement Association," p. 17; Fields, *Integration on Trial in the North*, pp. 4–5.

32. Hyde Park-Kenwood Community Conference, *Hyde Park-Kenwood*, p. 5.

33. Deutsch, *Building a Housewife's Paradise*, pp. 122–123.

34. Ibid., p. 123; "Members Control Policy Through Elected Board," *Hyde Park Herald*, Oct. 13, 1959, box, 20, Misc., Newsclippings file, HPCSR; Voorhis, *Cooperative Enterprise*, p. 225; HPCS, 1958 Annual Report, box 6, Annual Reports, Progress Reports file (1950s), HPCSR.

35. In 1959, the co-op would receive an award from the National Conference of Christians and Jews for its interracial efforts. "Members control policy through elected board."

36. As Paul Douglas spoke of the co-op: "In the co-op, people of all national and racial stocks, all religions, found a growing sense of community, the feeling that they were all brothers and sisters together. They learned that mutual co-operativeness and helpfulness form the basis on which life should be lived." Angevine, "The Roots of Consumer Cooperatives in the U.S.," p. 23. Sandbach would continue to be active in the cooperative movement. He was executive director of Consumers Union, a nonprofit and noncommercial organization founded in 1936 to provide consumers with information and advice about goods and services. As of the early 1960s, it was the largest consumer testing and reporting organization in the world and its magazine, *Consumer Reports*, had a readership of two million. Sandbach had also been chair of the board of the Co-operative League of the U.S.A. in 1961 and 1962. Biographical Sketch, Walker Sandbach, n.d., box 1, HPCSR.

37. Deutsch, *Building a Housewife's Paradise*, p. 128.

38. Satter, *Family Properties*, pp. 47–48. Satter has documented how at least 85 percent of homes purchased by African Americans in Chicago were bought "on contract." What this meant was that these homes were overpriced and that the sellers made up to a 75 percent profit. Satter, *Family Properties*, pp. 4, 11.

39. Pendleton and Heller, "The Relocation of Families Displaced by an Urban Redevelopment Project," pp. 47, 48, 55, 57–64, 70; Stampley, *Challenges with Changes*, p. 3; Satter, *Family Properties*, pp. 50, 52.

40. See http://www.co-opmarkets.com/history.htm. The Land Clearance Commission planned to buy several areas near the area, with Hyde Park considered a "test area" for re-development in other parts of Chicago. Letter from Seymour Banks, President to Campaign Worker, Oct. 26, 1953; Eloise Lushbough, Chair, Telephone Campaign, Open letter, n.d., box 1, New Store (1954) file, HPCSR.

41. "Co-op," box 1, Herald's 100th Anniversary file, HPCSR.

42. News release draft on opening of supermarket, n.d., box 1, New Store (1954) file, HPCSR.

43. HPCS, 1956 Annual Report, box 6, HPCSR; "Co-op Enterprise Gives Life, Hope to Area," newspaper unknown, July 9, 1953, box 1, Newsclippings file, HPCSR; HPCS, Progress Report, 1932–1953.

44. HPCS, 1956 Annual Report.

45. "New Store," 1954, box 1, HPCSR; "Linnea O. Anderson," *Evergreen* (Sept., 2001), box 8, Linnea Anderson file, HPCSR, 19. The Evergreen was the Hyde Park Consumer Society's newsletter.

46. Ad, *Hyde Park Herald*, Nov. 5, 1958, box 1, Co-op ads file (1950s), HPCSR. A developer conducted a survey to decide which grocery chain food store should be in the center. The cooperative members campaigned to have theirs there. The new store had 100 grocery items and three checkout counters. Angevine, "The Roots of Consumer Cooperatives in the U.S.," p. 22. Its sales volume would jump 400 percent in ten years. "New Co-op Opens Tonight."

47. See http://www.co-opmarkets.com/history.htm; "New Co-op Opens Tonight"; News Release Information, 1954, box 1, New Store file (1954), HPCSR; HPCS, 1956 Annual Report; News release draft on opening of Hyde Park Consumer Society supermarket. The Hyde Park Co-op's home economist prepared twenty to thirty recipes during a two-week special. There were foods from nearly fifteen countries in the store. Home delivery was available, for a small fee of less than one dollar. "The Co-op Calls Itself Typical Grocery, but 19,000 Customers Know Otherwise," n.d., box 20, Misc., Newsclippings file, HPCSR. Kroger's, too, had a home economist during the 1930s. Deutsch, *Building a Housewife's Paradise*, p. 143.

48. "Co-op Supermarkets Come of Age," box 1, Educational Materials on Co-operatives file (1937–1957), HPCSR.

49. PCS, 1960 Annual Report, box 6, Annual Reports, 1960s file, HPCSR.

50. HPCS, 1963 Annual Report; 1962 Annual Report, box 6, Annual Reports, 1960s file, HPCSR; "A Report to the Hyde Park Co-operative Society, Inc., July, 1963," box 1, Expansion, North Shore file (1963), HPCSR.

51. "Progress Report of the N. Kenwood-Oakland and Woodlawn Development Cooperative Development Project," box 20, 1960 file, HPCSR; "Five Month Progress Report of the North Kenwood-Oakland and Woodlawn Demonstration Cooperative Development Project," box 6, HPCSR; HPCS, 1963 Annual Report, Annual Reports, 1960s file, HPCR. The Henry Booth Settlement was in the ninth ward, as was the Hull House.

52. HPCS, 1967 Annual Report; 1968 Annual Report, box 6, Annual Reports, 1960s file, HPCSR; http://www.encyclopedia.chicagohistory.org/pages/934.html, accessed Oct. 18, 2010. One of the co-op's policies was giving preference to suppliers and producers who engaged in good practices in labor and race relations. "Policies of the Hyde Park Cooperative Society," 1969, box 1, Basic Rules of Hyde Park Co-op file (1969–1981), HPCSR.

53. Letter from Joel Seidman, president, HPCS, to John Duba, Commissioner, Department of Urban Renewal, Jan. 6, 1964, box 1, Correspondence file (1934–1980), HPCSR.

54. Knupfer, *The Chicago Black Renaissance and Women's Activism*, p. 119; "Policies of the Hyde Park Co-operative Society."

55. HPCS, 1968 Annual Report, box 6, Annual Reports, 1960s file, HPCSR.

56. Voorhis, *Cooperative Enterprise*, p. 190; Jacobs, *Pocketbook Politics*, p. 230.

57. *HPCS Co-op News* (May 1959), box 6, Co-op News—1950s file; 1966 Annual Report, box 6, Annual Reports, 1960s file, HPCSR. As with the Ithaca co-op, the women members of the Hyde Park co-op served as committee members and volunteers. A group of housewives helped the shoppers. There was also a consumer information committee, advised by the home economist, who answered questions about freezing food, the best buys, how to fix cuts of meat, and who also helped lower-income members "stretch" their dollar. The committee had already opened an educational library, set up comparative product displays, and gave out product information. "Consumers Themselves, They Aid Baffled Shoppers," *Chicago Daily News*, May 15, 1968, box 20, Misc., Newsclippings file, HPCSR.

58. "The Co-op Calls Itself Typical Grocery, but 19,000 Customers Know Otherwise"; 1974 Annual Report, box 6, Annual Reports, 1970s file, HPCSR. In 1977, the co-op expanded its supermarket, adding a wine and liquor department. HPCS, 1979 Annual Report, box 6, Annual Reports, 1970s file, HPCSR.

59. HPCS, 1972 Annual Report; 1973 Annual Report, box 6, Annual Reports, 1970s file, HPCSR; "Then and Now Hyde [*sic*] Co-operative Society, Inc."

60. HPCS, 1972 Annual Report. In 1984, the cooperative called for a boycott of Campbell's soup. "Campbell's Soup Not Good Food to Strikers," newspaper article, unknown source, box 20, Misc., Newsclippings file, HPCSR.

61. "Consumers themselves, They Aid Baffled Shoppers." As of 1957, there was concern about chemical additives at various food co-ops. Berkeley's public relations committee urged Congress to appropriate more funds for the FDA and asked that the law be changed to put the burden of proof of safety of a new additive on the manufacturer. The committee wrote other cooperatives, asking them to take the same stand and for all members to write their congressperson. Betsy Wood, "Consumer Education, Everyone?" *California Co-op Leadership* 1 (Mar. 1957), box 1, Education Materials file, HPCSR. In 1985, the National Academy of Science published a report that cyclamate was not carcinogenic. See http://www.flavored-waters.com/Sweeteners/Cyclamane.asp, accessed Oct. 18, 2010.

62. "The Hyde Park Co-operative Society—Present and Future: A Report on A Survey of the Hyde Park Community," Oct., 1974, box 7, HPCSR.

63. HPCS, 1976 Annual Report, box 6, Annual Reports, 1970s file, HPCSR.

64. HPCS, 1978 Annual Report, box 6, Annual Reports, 1970s file, HPCSR.

65. "Board Seeks Cure for Co-op," *Hyde Park Herald*, Dec. 3, 1980, box 1, Newsclippings, file 1, HPCSR; Angevine, "The Roots of Consumer Cooperatives in the U.S.," p. 23.

66. Letter from G. Scott to Mendell Hill, National Consumer Co-operative Bank, Aug. 11, 1980, box 20, HPCSR. Howard Bowers was the new associate manager of the co-op in 1982. He believed in participatory management and involving the staff in the decision-making process. He had thirty years of working with cooperatives, including twenty-three years with the Consumers' Co-op in Eau Claire, Wisconsin, where he had been a grocery manager, supermarket manager, and had been responsible for the security, marketing, promotion, and advertising divisions. "Bowers Settles into Hyde Park, Co-op," *Evergreen* 36 (May 11, 1983), box 1, HPCSR.

67. HPCS, 1980 Annual Report, box 6, Annual Reports, 1980s file, HPCSR; *Evergreen* 34 (Oct. 18, 1981) and *Evergreen* 36 (Nov. 16, 1983), box 6, HPCSR.

68. Schulman, *The Seventies*, p. 142.

69. Ibid., p. 218; Stein, *Pivotal Decade*, pp. 145, 265, 267; Cowie, *Stayin' Alive*, pp. 228, 235.

70. Stein, *Pivotal Decade*, p. 268.

71. Doussard, Peck, and Theodore, "After Deindustrialization," pp. 187, 193; Wilson, *The Truly Disadvantaged.*

72. "Hyde Park Co-op: Food for Thought, but Not for Profits," *Chicago Sun-Times*, Jan. 13, 1983, box 1, Newsclippings file, HPCSR. During the first twenty years, $153,000 in patronage funds had been returned to members. "Co-op Notes Progress of 20 Years Names Miller," box 1, Co-op Ads, 1950s file, HPCSR.

73. "Hyde Park Co-op: Food for Thought, but Not for Profits."

74. See *Evergreen* 36; HPCS, 1985 Annual Report, box 6, Annual Reports, 1980s file, HPCSR.

75. Ibid.

76. HPCS, 1986 Annual Report; 1987 Annual Report, box 6, Annual Reports, 1980s file, HPCSR.

77. HPCS, 1988 Annual Report, box 6, Annual Reports, 1980s file, HPCSR.

78. HPCS, 1997 Annual Report, box 6, Annual Reports, 1990s file, HPCSR; Hyde Park Environmental Action Coalition, Press Release, n.d., box 1, HPCSR.

79. HPCS, 1997 Annual Report.

80. "A Suburbiascape Grows in Inner-City Chicago," *New York Times*, Oct. 20, 1999, box 6, HPCSR.

81. See http://www.channelingreality.com/SBA_Corruption/Chicago_Empowerment_Zone_Program.pdf, accessed Oct. 20, 2011.

82. See Pattillo-McCoy, *Black Picket Fences*; Dave Gutknecht, "Hyde Park Co-op Closes After 75 Years," *Cooperative Grocer* 135 (March–April 2008), see also http://www.hyde park.org/hpkccnews/co-op.htm, accessed Oct. 18, 2010.

83. http://www.hydepark.org/hpkccnews/Co-opforum06.htm, accessed Oct. 18, 2010.

84. Gutknecht, "Hyde Park Co-op Closes After 75 Years." For residents' viewpoints, see http://hydeparkprogress.blogspot.com/2007/08/heralds-chicken-herald-balks-at.html, accessed Oct. 21, 2010.

85. See *Hyde Park Herald*, Oct. 22, 2008.

86. See http://www.facebook.com/note.php?note_id=64677123880, accessed Oct. 18, 2010.

CHAPTER 5

1. "Organization of the Hanover Consumers Club," Jan. 6, 1936, Co-op History Project file, HCCSR.

2. *Co-op News Bulletin* 12 (Apr 2, 1936), 1930s file, HCCSR.

3. Ibid.

4. Hanover Consumers Club Minutes, Oct. 26, 1937, 1936–1942 HCCS Board Minutes folder, HCCSR.

5. Hanover Consumers Club, *Bulletin* 1 (Jan. 13, 1936), HCCSR

6. "Organization of the Hanover Consumers Club."

7. Hanover Consumers Club Minutes, Feb. 26, 1936, 1936–1942 HCCS Board Minutes folder, HCCSR.

8. *Co-op News Bulletins* 10 (Mar. 2, 1936), 11 (Ides of Mar, 1936), 12 (Apr. 2, 1936), 1930s file, HCCSR; Fox, "Epitaph for Middletown. Robert S. Lynd and the Analysis of Consumer Culture," p. 126; Lynd, "The Consumer Becomes A 'Problem,'" p. 6. For further information about Robert Lynd, known sociologist who was a member of the Consumers' Advisory Board of the National Recovery Act, see Horowitz, *The Morality of Spending*, pp. 148–153. In June 1975, the federal trade commission made nutritional labeling of all processed foods mandatory. But some of the co-op label brands had already used this system. The co-op tested and published results for food items, using scoreboards, through the 1980s. By 1981, there were over 700 products packaged under the co-op label. *HCCS*

Co-op Newsletters (Apr. 1976; June, 1977; Feb., 1988; Feb./Mar., 1981), HCCSR. The co-op also tried to keep packaging to a minimum.

9. Report of Secretary on Activities of Executive Committee, Hanover Consumers Club Minutes, Feb. 26, 1936; Committee Report, Aug. 18, 1936, 1936–1942 HCCS Board Minutes folder, HCCSR.

10. *Co-op News Bulletin* 14 (Apr. 28, 1936), 1930s file.

11. Hanover Consumers Club Minutes, May 31, 1937.

12. Hanover Consumers Club Minutes, Committee Reports, Aug. 18, 1937, Mar. 15, 1937, HCCSR.

13. Hanover Consumers Club Minutes, Oct. 12, 1936, Oct. 28, 1936, HCCSR.

14. Hanover Consumers Club Minutes, Annual Report of Business Committee, Mar. 15, 1937, HCCSR.

15. Ibid.

16. Hanover Consumers Club Minutes, HCCS Reports of Committees, 1938, 1936–1942 HCCS Board Minutes folder, HCCSR.

17. Hanover Consumers Club Minutes, Jan. 23, 1940. Several co-op leaders weighed in on the issue, for example, J. P. Warbasse, who thought it was both a matter of ethics and business. "Should Co-operatives Sell Beer?" pp. 131–132.

18. Daniels, *Cooperation—An American Way*, pp. 3–4; *Co-op News* (May, 1960), 1960–1965 folder, HCCSR.

19. *Co-op News* (Mar., 1940; May, 1941; May, 1940; June, 1940), 1940s folder, HCCSR.

20. Quarterly Meeting of HCCS, Oct., 1940, HCCSR.

21. Letter to Dear Fellow Co-operator from Arthur E. Jensen, President, HCCS board, June 11, 1941; Hanover Consumers Club Minutes, Apr. 30, 1941; "A Report on the Society's Business for the War Year, 1942," 1936–1942 HCCS Board Minutes folder; HCCS Co-op News (Jan. 1944; Dec. 31, 1943; Oct. 1944), Co-op Bulletins file, 1944–1954; HCCS Balance Sheet, Dec. 31, 1948, Scrapbook, HCCSR. The co-op was also trying to raise $5,000 to increase its investment in the Eastern Co-operative Wholesale, which they and other co-ops owned. HCCS Co-op News (Sept. 1946). Unfortunately, most of the records from the 1940s were being treated for mold and so were unavailable to me.

22. HCCS Co-op News (Jan. 1955; Jan. 1952; Feb. 1956; Feb. 1958), 1950s file; *Hanover Co-op Bulletin* (May 1950). In 1957, the co-op had bought a parcel of land, for which they had to negotiate with four separate owners: the Hanover Associates for the freezer-locker plant; a resident for her apartment house; Dartmouth College for a lot; and the Socony Mobil Oil Company. The store's final design had been delayed until all negotiations were finished. HCCS Co-op News (May 1962), 1960–1965 file. In 1965, manager Harry Gerstenberger retired, as did his wife, Sally. He had started in May 1949. In 1948, the co-op's assets were slightly less than $25,000 and the store had a net loss of $5,478. But in 1949, the co-op slowly started to turn around with a small net savings of $101. As of December 31, 1964, his last full year as manager, assets were $497,470, twenty times greater than in 1948 and sales were $1.18 million. HCCS Co-op News (Nov. 1965), 1960–1965 file. His nephew replaced him as manager.

23. At the anniversary celebration, Mrs. H.R. Sensenig, one of the original founders and the only past female president (1954–1956), spoke. HCCS Co-op News (Jan. 1961; Apr. 1963); Ida Gallant Delaney, "Consumer Education Will Build Consumer Co-ops," *Canadian Co-operative Digest* (Apr. 1961), Scrapbook, HCCSR. Some farmers were concerned about the dangerous levels of radioactive iodine in some areas because of fallout from atomic testing. Officials advised farmers that they could cut grass, which had been contaminated, but should wait twenty-one days to feed to their cattle. HCCS Co-op News (Sept. 1962).

24. *HCCS Co-op News* (Apr. 1964; June 1964). Residents had formed the Upper Valley Committee on Environmental Hazards, which was concerned about air and water pollution, soil and food contamination. *HCCS Co-op News* (Dec. 1964; Mar. 1965).

25. *HCCS Co-op News* (June 1962; Apr. 1963; Feb. 1964; Apr. 1964; Mar. 1965); Envelope with Hanover Consumer Co-operative Society information, Adamant Co-op; Board Minutes, Jan. 14, 1969, HCCSR.

26. HCCS Board Minutes, Dec. 9, 1968.

27. HCCS Board Minutes, Oct. 8, 1969. A group, called "Vermonters for the Grape Boycott," had been picketing the store. At a meeting of almost 400 of the 2,200 members on Oct. 29, the co-op decided to keep all grapes on the shelves and allow customers to make decision. "Co-op Management Halts Sale of Boycott-Provoking Grapes," *Valley News*, Nov. 8, 1969, Activities file on Grape Boycott, HCCSR.

28. HCCS Board Minutes, 2008 Allen and Nan King Award Nominations, Oct. 25, 1969.

29. HCCS Board Minutes, Oct. 25, 1969.

30. "Co-op Management Halts Sale of Boycott-Provoking Grapes."

31. HCCS Board Minutes, Manager's Report, 1969, Nov. 4, 1969, Activities folder.

32. HCCS Board Minutes, Nov. 17, 1969; Oct. 29, 1969.

33. *HCCS Co-op News* (July 1965); HCCS Board Minutes, Oct. 14, 1969. Even though sales were down, the co-op had a strong history of patronage refunds. In 1961, for example, it was 4 percent, in 1963, 2.8 percent. Some of the highest were in the 1972 at 4.7 percent and 1973 at 4.2 percent. HCCS Board Minutes, Financial Data for Five Years, 1973. Some members had expressed concern about the co-op's rising prices, which prevented poorer people from shopping there. In 1965, Jerry Voorhis, then president of the Co-operative League of the U.S.A., urged co-ops to study efforts to help poverty areas, both urban and rural. *HCCS Co-op News* (Mar. 1965). At one 1969 meeting, some members thought something should be done to attract lower-income people to the store. HCCS Board Minutes, May 12, 1969.

34. HCCS Board Minutes, Feb. 25, 1970; Sept. 10, 1968.

35. Letter from Charles Wood to Harry Gerstenberger, May 1, 1970, HCCS Board Minutes, May 19, 1970; Nov. 9, 1970.

36. HCCS Board Minutes, Dec. 10, 1970.

37. Letter to James Rodes from Charles Wood, HCCS Board Minutes, Mar. 4, 1971. In 1995, the co-op management called police to interrupt a small demonstration commemorating the bombing of Hiroshima. It was quiet and not disruptive. One outraged co-op member wanted an apology. Apparently, customers complained and so the manager called police. Letter from college professor to Co-op, Aug. 9, 1995, Activities folder, On Hiroshima Protest.

38. Letter from Joan Erdman, Chair, Education Committee to Board Members, HCCS Board Minutes, Mar. 9, 1971. For a complete history of the phosphate issue, see http://www.colorado.edu/conflict/full_text_search/AllCRCDocs/94-54.htm, accessed Oct. 15, 2010.

39. Letter to Board Members from Charles Wood, Letter from Joan Erdman, Chair, Education Committee to Board Members, HCCS Board Minutes, Mar. 12, 1971.

40. HCCS Board Minutes, Dec. 10, 1970; Mar. 21, 1973. Board members debated grain-fed meat, when people were starving in other countries. HCCS Board Minutes, Apr. 1975. There was also the possibility of another grape boycott in 1973. The co-op's policy, according to the general manager, was to carry only United Farm Workers grapes. No consensus was reached about boycotting lettuce or grapes. The grape boycott resurfaced again in 1978. There were point-of-sales notes in the store that discussed the boycott. HCCS Board Minutes, Apr. 25, 1973; Mar. 20, 1974; Jan. 25, 1978; Sept. 21, 1978. See also http://www.

nader.org/index.php?/archives/800-The-Lessons-of-the-Meat-Boycott.html,   accessed Oct. 15, 2010.

41. HCCS Board Minutes, Apr. 17, 1974. There also continued to be discussions about which products to sell, including cigarettes. A resolution was brought forward that no product that was dangerous to anyone's health be sold at the co-op, which was aimed at cigarettes. But the resolution was defeated. HCCS Board Minutes, Feb. 14, 1973.

42. HCCS Board Minutes, Feb. 27, 1974.

43. "Members Petition Co-op," *Dartmouth*, Nov. 4, 1973, Untitled folder.

44. HCCS Board Minutes, July 26, 1972; Dec. 11, 1972.

45. HCCS Board Minutes, Feb. 12, 1973.

46. Ibid.

47. Ironically, in 1968, the co-op could have bought property near the co-op store but did not. Report of the Task Force to Study Land Capability of the Proposed Co-op Purchase in Norwich, HCCS Board Minutes, Mar. 8, 1973; Mar. 23, 1973.

48. HCCS Board Minutes, Apr. 16, 1973; Alexander Laing, "Questions for the Co-op," "The People's Forum," *Valley News*, Feb. 21, 1975; HCCS Board Minutes, May 15, 1974.

49. HCCS Board Minutes, Feb. 24, 1975; Nov. 10, 1976; Jan. 19, 1977; Feb. 2, 1977.

50. HCCS Board Minutes, Feb. 16, 1977; Apr. 20, 1977; Sept. 17, 1975. Another suggestion was to establish the American School of Luthiery, a professional training facility for craftsmen of stringed musical instruments, on a small acreage of the land. An owner of a Wooden Shoe Farm was also interested. Letter from School of Guitar Research & Design Center, Strafford, Vermont to Board of Directors, Sept. 20, 1979, HCCS Board Minutes; Letter from Wooden Shoe Farm to Board of Directors, Sept. 26, 1979, HCCS Board Minutes.

51. HCCS Board Minutes, June 15, 1977.

52. Steven Flanders, Chas. Baker, "Proposal: "A 'No-Frills' Co-op Food Store," HCCS Board Minutes, Sept. 17, 1977.

53. Letter from Vermont State Housing Authority to Board of Directors, Nov. 19, 1979.

54. HCCS Board Minutes, Dec. 3, 1979; Apr. 16, 1980; "Option to Purchase" agreement, n.d, Untitled folder; "Norwich Sites Offered by Co-op for Housing," *Hanover Gazette*, Nov. 15, 1979.

55. HCCS Board Minutes, Mar. 11, 1981.

56. Letter from Board of Directors President to Twin Pines, June 18, 1981; Letter from HCCS to Twin Pines Co-op, May 8, 1981.

57. HCCS Board Minutes, Feb. 10, 1982; HCCS Board Minutes, Feb. 17, 1982; Apr. 13, 1982; June 28, 1984; July 18, 1984; Nov. 28, 1984.

58. HCCS Board Minutes, Feb. 20, 1982; Feb. 4, 1982; Feb. 24, 1982.

59. HCCS Board Minutes, Aug. 19, 1980; Sept. 29, 1980.

60. HCCS Board Minutes, Feb. 16, 1983; Mar. 3, 1983; Mar. 12, 1984; June 13, 1984; June 15, 1984.

61. HCCS Board Minutes, "Co-op Board Votes to Sell Norwich Land," Press release, n.d.

62. June 1984 letter, HCCS Board Minutes.

63. HCCS Board Minutes, Dec. 1, 1982; Nov. 17, 1982; Jan. 3, 1985; May 15, 1985.

64. HCCS Board Minutes, Mar. 17, 1980, "Planning for Directing the Hanover Consumer Co-operative Society, Inc., Into the Next Century," HCCS Board Minutes; HCCS Board Minutes, Mar. 11, 1981; Balance Sheet, Dec. 29, 1984, HCCS Board Minutes; HCCS Board Minutes, Jan. 15, 1986.

65. *HCCS Co-op Newsletter* (May 1981); HCCS Board Minutes, Nov. 13, 1982.

66. "Member Profile and Analysis, 1991," HCCS Board Minutes, 1991.

67. GM ad, HCCS Board Minutes, Dec. 10, 1992; Apr. 6, 1994; *Co-op Newsletter* (Dec., 1995).

68. *HCCS Co-op Newsletter* (Jan. 1996). When Terry Appleby was hired as general manager in 1992, he was quickly included in the discussion of expansion. A building committee was set up for the proposed expansion. HCCS Board Minutes, Sept. 16, 1992; Nov. 5, 1992; Jan. 20, 1993; "Hanover Co-op Approves Expansion," n.d., HCCS Board Minutes.

69. HCCS Board Minutes, Oct. 1997; "Lebanon Co-op Getting Ready," *Valley News*, Sept. 27, 1997, Pressclippings folder.

70. *HCCS Co-op Newsletter* (Oct. 1978; Nov.–Dec. 1978); Harrison Drinkwater, "Hanover Co-op Joins Call for Aerosol Control," n.d., HCCS Board Minutes, May 29, 1986.

71. Hunter, *Consumer Beware*, p. 72. In 1963, irradiated canned food was given to soldiers in Vietnam, even though studies at Cornell University showed how "lethal" irradiation was. Hunter, *Consumer Beware!* pp. 75, 76. On dangers of irradiation, see also http://www.truehealth.org/nukedfood.html, accessed Aug. 25, 2011.

72. Letter to General Manager from George Economy, June 14, 1989; HCCS Board Minutes, July 5, 1989; *HCCS Co-op Newsletter* (Sept. 1987; Sept.–Oct. 1989; Aug.–Sept. 1989); "25 Years Since Silent Spring: Are We Any Better Off," HCCS Board Minutes, Education Committee, Aug. 8, 1990.

73. *HCCS Co-op News* (Mar. 1983; Dec. 1989). The co-op noted that the Willy Street Co-operative in Madison, Wisconsin recycled all their cardboard, glass, aluminum, and plastic as of 1990. A "Year in Review Report," CCMA Conference 1990 HCCS Board Minutes.

74. HCCS Board Minutes, Sept. 16, 1999, Education Department Report to Board of Directors, HCCS Board Minutes, May 19, 1999. The Food and Nutrition Subcommittee of Education Committee read about GM foods and created a display on bioengineered foods. They also asked members to sign a petition for federal labeling legislation. This was an important consideration since the USDA's standards on organic food production then included genetically engineered foods, ionizing radiation, and sludge on farmland. HCCS Board Minutes, Food and Nutrition Subcommittee of Education Committee, May 1, 1997; Rosemary Fifield, Education Department to Board of Directors, Jan. 14, 1998, HCCS Board Minutes.

75. "Annual Business Plan, Fiscal Year 2005," HCCS Board Minutes, Dec. 2004; Jan. 2005.

76. Deluca, with Nilan, Nolan, Crowell, and Howard, "Planning in Collaboration," pp. 10–14. Regional cooperation arose in part from fear of Whole Foods and Wild Oats as competition. Ruth Sylvester, 1993 CCMA Short Summary, HCCS Board Minutes, HCCS.

77. HCCS Board Minutes, 2004; *HCCS Co-op Newsletter* (May–June 2005).

78. HCCS Board Minutes, Sept. 16, 1992; Nov. 5, 1992.

79. http://www.cooperativegrocer.coop/articles/2010-10-05/hanover-co-op-opens-fourth-store, accessed Nov. 9, 2010.

80. Ibid.

CHAPTER 6

1. http://en.wikipedia.org/wiki/Adamant,Vermont, accessed July 14, 2010.

2. Ibid.

3. See http://www.adamant.org/history.htm, accessed July 14, 2010; http://www.vtsunlight.net/emhouse/historicalnotes.htm, accessed Sept. 24, 2010; http://www.adamant.org/founders.htm, accessed Sept. 24, 2010. Biographical information on the three founders is spare. For Kimball, see "Alice Mary Kimball," in *These Modern Women*, ed. Showalter, pp. 52–57. Florence Weed was president in 1939; Kimball was head of an auditing committee. AFC Meeting Minutes, Oct. 10, 1939, Co-op Meeting Minutes, 1936–1945 file; AFC Meeting Minutes, Sept. 25, 1953, 1952–1960 file, AFCR.

4. Lois Toby, "History of South Calais, Elbridge and Lois Toby," Lois Toby file, AFCR; Letter to Nat Frothingham, Manager of Co-op, from Thomas F. Keefe, architect, State of Vermont, n.d., Historical Preservation Communication file, AFCR.

5. Application for Historical Preservation Grant, Oct. 29, 1999, AFCR.

6. For the 2010 festival, see http://7d.blogs.com/stuckinvt/2007/05/black_fly_festi. html, accessed July 7, 2010.

7. "The Adamant Co-op, Adamant, Vermont" booklet, AFCR.

8. Ibid.

9. Freidel, *The New Deal in Vermont*, p. 41; Bathory-Kitsz, *Country Stores of Vermont*, p. 73. When the co-op started in 1935, the state was reported to have more cows than people. Freidel, *The New Deal in Vermont*, p. 7.

10. Letter to Nat Frothingham, Manager of Co-op, from Thomas F. Keefe, architect, State of Vermont, n.d.

11. Toby, "History of South Calais, Elbridge and Lois Toby."

12. Ibid. They discussed buying maple syrup and potatoes from the nearby Maple Sugar Co-operative. AFC Meeting Minutes, Mar. 8, 1938, Co-op Meeting Minutes, 1936–1945 file, AFCR.

13. AFC 1936 Annual Meeting Minutes, Co-op Meeting Minutes, 1936–1945 file.

14. AFC Meeting Minutes, Mar. 9, 1937, May 21, 1937, May 24, 1937, Oct. 10, 1939, Co-op Meeting Minutes, 1936–1945 file.

15. "Sketches about the Adamant Co-operative, Inc. and the Adamant Credit Union, 1947," Adamant Co-op file, AFCR; AFC Meeting Minutes, Nov. 11, 1936, Jan. 12, 1937, Aug. 10, 1937, Sept. 13, 1938, May 26, 1939, June 13, 1939, Co-op Meeting Minutes, 1936–1945 file.

16. AFC Meeting Minutes, Nov. 8, 1938, Co-op Meeting Minutes, 1936–1945 file.

17. AFC Meeting Minutes, Oct. 14, 1936, Mar. 9, 1937, Co-op Meeting Minutes, 1936–1945 file.

18. Benson and Adams, *To Know for Real*, pp. 14, 22, 23, 28, 29. In 1935, Pitkin, a graduate of Goddard Seminary, became president of the new Goddard College. Cappel, *Utopian Colleges*, p. 100.

19. AFC Meeting Minutes, Mar. 19, 1938, Co-op Meeting Minutes, 1936–1945. When the college moved to the Greatwood Farms estate, it was a 200-acre campus. Cappel, *Utopian Colleges*, p. 101. For more information on Greatwood Farms, see http://www.nps.gov/history/nr/travel/centralvermont/cv36.htm, accessed July 16, 2010. Goddard College, too, had a summer music camp and some Adamant children took art classes at the college. Giles and Adams, *To Know for Real*, p. 128.

20. AFC Meeting Minutes, Nov. 11, 1936, Aug. 13, 1940, Mar. 9, 1942, Co-op Meeting Minutes, 1936–1945 file. One CLUSA document noted how in rural areas, many cooperatives had to extend credit. Co-operative League of U.S.A., *Reading Between the Lines. For Study and Action*, pp. 6–10.

21. AFC Meeting Minutes, Oct. 14, 1936, Nov. 11, 1936, Dec. 9, 1936, July 27, 1939, Sept. 29, 1939, Co-op Meeting Minutes, 1936–1945 file.

22. AFC Meeting Minutes, Mar. 19, 1938, June 14, 1938, Sept. 13, 1938, May 26, 1939, Co-op Meeting Minutes, 1936–1945 file. Auerbach, "The La Follette Committee," pp. 435–459.

23. Sackman, *Orange Empire*, pp. 281–282, 286; McWilliams, *Factories in the Field*, pp. 212–214, 230–239; AFC Meeting Minutes, May 26, 1939. In 1942, the first state-chartered credit union in Vermont started in Adamant. Floersch, "Adamant Co-operative Store Celebrates 50 Years," p. 24.

24. Floersch, "Adamant Co-operative Store Celebrates 50 Years," pp. 22–25. Aiken told 225 members of the Electric Co-operative that he had attended almost all of its co-op

meetings since it started in 1939. "Aiken: Don't Give Up Co-op," unknown newspaper, n.d., Adamant Co-op file. Aiken, as well as governors in New York, Wisconsin, and Minnesota, promoted cooperatives. "Four Governors Endorse Consumer Co-operatives," p. 46.

25. AFC Meeting Minutes, Mar. 12, 1940, Apr. 30, 1940, Co-op Meeting Minutes, 1936–1945 file; Toby, "History of South Calais, Elbridge and Lois Toby."

26. AFC Meeting Minutes, July 31, 1946, AFCR; "Sketches about the Adamant Cooperative, Inc. and the Adamant Credit Union, 1947"; AFC Meeting Minutes, Jan. 9, 1940, Sept. 27, 1940, Jan. 12, 1942, Co-op Meeting Minutes, 1936–1945 file.

27. For more information on the history of Maple Corner, see http://www.central-vt.com/towns/history/HstCala2.htm, accessed July 14, 2010; AFC Meeting Minutes, Sept. 11, 1944, June 1, 1945, Aug. 13, 1945, Co-op Meeting Minutes, 1936–1945 file; Financial Statements, Nov. 1948, Mar. 1949, 1946–1951 file, AFCR. In 1947, when a fire destroyed the Calais Co-op, the Adamant Co-op board voted to house a temporary store and post office at the grange hall in Maple Corner. Such a decision points to the cooperative spirit of co-ops. AFC Meeting Minutes, Oct. 13, 1947, 1946–1951 file, AFCR.

28. "Sketches about the Adamant Co-operative, Inc. and the Adamant Credit Union, 1947"; AFC Financial Statement, Feb. 1950; AFC Newsletter (Christmas, 1954), 1952–1960 file; AFC Meeting Minutes, Jan. 2, 1953, Sept. 25, 1956, 1952–1960 file, AFCR.

29. AFC Newsletter (Nov. 1953), AFCR.

30. AFC Newsletter (Sept. 1955); AFC Meeting Minutes, Feb.–Mar. 1956, 1952–1960 file; AFC Newsletter (Mar. 1955). They used this money to buy a new glass display case and refrigeration unit for the co-op.

31. AFC Meeting Minutes, Jan. 9, 1960, 1952–1960 file; AFC Newsletter (Mar. 1952, Apr. 1952, and Nov. 1953). The Adamant Food Co-op continued its interest in other cooperatives, following the Rochdale principles. AFC Newsletter (Feb.–Mar. 1955); AFC Meeting Minutes, Mar. 23, 1951, 1946–1951 file.

32. AFC Meeting Minutes, Dec. 14, 1953, Sept. 13, 1954, Aug. 8, 1955, 1952–1960 file; Audit Report to Directors of Adamant Co-op, Inc. (1965?); AFC Meeting Minutes, Nov. 10, 1965, 1964–1965 file, AFCR.

33. AFC Meeting Minutes, Oct. 14, 1961, 1960–1963 file; Nov. 14, 1964 AFC Meeting Minutes, 1964–1965 file; Adamant Co-op Income Statement for Year Ending Aug. 1, 1961, 1960–1963 file; Adamant Co-op Balance Sheet, July 31, 1964 and Adamant Co-op, July 31, 1965 Balance Sheet, 1964–1965 file; AFC Newsletter (Spring, 1962); AFC Meeting Minutes, May 12, 1962, 1960–1963 file; Adamant Co-op Information Sheet (1966?), Adamant Co-op Balance Sheet, July 31, 1966, July 31, 1967, 1965–1968 file; Balance Sheet, July 31, 1969 for Adamant Co-op, 1968–1973 file, AFCR.

34. AFC Meeting Minutes, Mar. 15, 1971; Balance Sheet, Adamant Co-op, July 31, 1971, 1968–1973 file; Letter from Polly Holden to Bob, Oct. 15, 1972, Co-op Education Committee file; Receipts from 1970s; AFC Meeting Minutes, Apr. 11, 1972, 1968–1973 file, AFCR.

35. Letter to Senator Aiken from Polly Holden, Feb. 4, 1972, Co-op Education Committee file.

36. Letter from Aiken to P. Holden, Feb. 10, 1972, Letter from Jim Temple to Dr. Eric Thor, FCS, May 5, 1972, Co-op Education Committee file, AFCR.

37. Letter from Eric Thor, USDA, Farmer Co-operative Service (FCS) to Senator George Aiken, Sept. 28, 1972, Co-op Education Committee file, AFCR.

38. Management Study of Adamant Co-op by Raymond Williams, Aug. 1972, 1968–1973 file, AFCR.

39. AFC Meeting Minutes, Apr. 28, 1972, June 9, 1972, Oct. 20, 1972, 1968–1973 file, AFCR. See http://www.central-vt.com/towns/history/HstEast2.htm, accessed July 14, 2010, for information about the history of the Dudley store.

40. Letter to Friends from Margaret Liff, Oct. 22, 1972, Adamant Co-op file.

41. AFC Meeting Minutes, Dec. 12, 1972, Mar. 15, 1973, 1968–1973 file. In 1972, a new line of natural foods was added at both stores. AFC Meeting Minutes, Apr. 28, 1972, 1968–1973 file, AFCR.

42. Notice/Letter, Oct. 26, 1978; AFC Meeting Minutes, Dec. 20, 1979, Mar. 20, 1980, Balance Sheet, 1978, 1977–1981 file, AFCR.

43. AFC Meeting Minutes, Aug. 28, 1980, Jan. 8, 1981, 1977–1981 file; AFC Meeting Minutes, Dec. 8, 1981, 1980–1983 file.

44. AFC Meeting Minutes, 1977–1981 file, Feb. 12, 1981.

45. Letter from Wm. C. Shouldice, III to David Thurber, Chair of Board, Adamant Co-op, June 10, 1981, 1977–1981 file; Letter from Harrison Drinkwater, Education Director, Hanover Consumer Co-operative Society to Board of Directors, Adamant Co-op, June 11, 1981, 1977–1981 file.

46. AFC Meeting Minutes, Aug. 28, 1980, 1977–1981 file; *Adamant Life* (Jan. 1982, Feb. 1983, July 1983); AFC Meeting Minutes, Sept. 14, 1982, Nov. 10, 1982, Dec. 14, 1982; *Adamant News* (Jan. 1983), 1980–1983 file.

47. Statement of Income and Expense, Aug. 1, 1983–July 31, 1984, Adamant Co-op file: *Adamant News* (Aug. 1984, May 1985), List 1984–1985; AFC Meeting Minutes, July 7, 1986, Sept. 9, 1986, Oct. 24, 1986, *Adamant News* (Feb. 1984), 1983–1986 file, AFCR.

48. *Adamant News* (June 1988, July 1984, Fall 1984, Mar. 1985, Nov. 1985), 1983–1986 file.

49. "First Christmas in Adamant," *Adamant News* (Mar. 1984, June 1984, Jan. 1985, Aug. 1985), 1983–1986 file.

50. "Adamant Co-op Store Struggles to Survive," *New York Times*, 1988.

51. 1990 Annual Report, Aug. 1, 1989-July 31, 1990, Treasurer Records, 1988–1990 file, AFCR.

52. "Convenience, Community, Cordiality; "The General Stores of Calais," *Calais Backroads*, n.d., 6–7. For information about the seventy-fifth anniversary events, see http://www.adamantco-op.org/calendar.php, accessed July 14, 2010.

53. Preservation Grant Application, p. 52.

54. http://www.zip-codes.com/city/VT-ADAMANT.asp, accessed July 7, 2010. The 2000 census showed 2,634 residents. *Putney*, 149.

55. *Putney*, 22, 25–27; Kern, *An Ordered Love*, pp. 207, 208, 213; Parker, *A Yankee Saint*, pp. 11, 89.

56. *Putney*, pp. 31, 35, 43; http://www.putneyvt.org/history.php, accessed July 14, 2010; Freidel, *The New Deal in Vermont*, pp. 60–61.

57. *Putney*, pp. 43, 52, 53; Lloyd, *The Putney School*, pp. 21, 26, 101.

58. *Putney*, 67; http://www.ncga.co-op/node/936, accessed July 14, 2010.

59. "Putney Consumers' Co-operative, Inc.," Corporate Documents file, PFCR.

60. *Putney*, 38, 80–81.

61. Ibid., 98, 99–100, 107–109, 122. The college is now Landmark College for students with ADHD.

62. Ibid., p. 110.

63. http://www.anarkismo.net/newswire.php?story id=7248, accessed July 16, 2010; http://www.7dvt.com/2008hippie-havens, accessed July 14, 2010.

64. http://www.7dvt.com/2008hippie-havens.

65. Ibid.

66. Ibid.

67. PFC Annual Minutes, Nov. 9, 1989; Dec. 3, 1992, Minutes file; "To Boycott or Not to Boycott? A Little History on the Matter," Oct., 1987, History file, PFCR.

68. PFC Annual Minutes, Dec. 13, 1990, Minutes file; Letter to Mike Mross from Ryland White, Jan. 7, 1990, Controversy file, PFCR.

69. *PFC Newsletter* (Apr. 1991, Aug. 1, 1991), Newsletters file; PFC Minutes, July 1991, Minutes file, PFCR.

70. PFC Annual Minutes, Nov. 14, 1991, Oct. 24, 1993, Minutes file; *PFC Newsletter* (June 1993, Aug. 1993), Newsletters file; Annual Minutes, June 17, 1993, PFCR.

71. PFC Annual Minutes, Nov. 18, 1993, Minutes file, PFCR.

72. PFC Annual Minutes, Nov. 12, 1987, Nov. 29, 1988, Nov. 9, 1989, Minutes file, PFCR.

73. PFC Annual Minutes, Nov. 9, 1989, Minutes file, PFCR.

74. PFC Annual Minutes, Dec. 13, 1990, Minutes file, PFCR.

75. PFC Annual Minutes, Aug. 1, 1991, Minutes file; "Report and Recommendations. Putney Food Co-op," Renovations Consulting, Dec. 1990," FmHA Loan Application file, PFCR.

76. PFC, Manager's Report, Apr. 11, 1991 and Aug. 1, 1991, 1991 and 1992 file, PFCR.

77. PFC, Manager's Report, June 5, 1991, 1991 and 1992 file, PFCR.

78. *PFC Newsletter* (May 1992, Sept. 1992), Newsletters file, PFCR.

79. See http://www.putneyco-op.com/about.html), accessed July 14, 2010.

80. PFC Annual Minutes, Sept. 29, 1961 1960–1963 file, PFCR; *The Beet Newsletter* (June 2009), http://www.social-ecology.org/2009/05/toward-food-sovereignty-in-vermont-and-northern-new-england/, accessed Mar. 20, 2009.

CHAPTER 7

1. Stein, *Pivotal Decade*, pp. 17, 18; Gerstle, "The Protean Character of American Liberalism," p. 1073.

2. Schulman, *The Seventies*, p. 9; see also Lasch, *The Culture of Narcissism*.

3. Cowie, *Stayin' Alive*, p. 12.

4. Schulman, *The Seventies*, pp. 7, 129; Cowie, *Stayin' Alive*, pp. 72, 163, 222, 301. See also chapters in Schulman and Zelizer, eds., *Rightward Bound*.

5. Regarding food, a Thanksgiving turkey, for example, that cost thirty-nine cents a pound in 1972 cost ninety cents a year later. Stein, *Pivotal Decade*, pp. 10, 74, 121, 211, 219; Schulman, *The Seventies*, p. 131.

6. Bluestone, "Foreword," ix; Stein, *Pivotal Decade*, pp. 38, 175, 182; Schulman, *The Seventies*, xiii.

7. Cowie, *Stayin' Alive*, pp. 122, 165; Schulman, *The Seventies*, pp. 38, 39, 40; Stein, *Pivotal Decade*, xi, p. 204. Stein noted that Reagan favored "financial services and real estate," rather than manufacturing. Stein, *Pivotal Decade*, p. 262.

8. Since 1867, lead and arsenic had been used in farming. Lutts, "Chemical Fallout," pp. 211–215. Between 1967 and 1973, at least twenty-five consumer and environmental regulatory laws were passed. Cohen, *A Consumers' Republic*, p. 357. But court intervention also influenced environmental policy. See O'Leary, *Environmental Change*. For a transnational and historical perspective on ecology, see Bramwell, *Ecology in the 20th Century*.

9. Wargo, *Our Children's Toxic Legacy*, p. 83.

10. Carson, *Silent Spring*, pp. 25, 30, 32, 35, 37, 38, 79. In 1957, ornithologist Robert Cushman tried to get a court injunction to prevent DDT spraying on Long Island. The case even went to the Supreme Court but it would not hear the case. Carson, *Silent Spring*, p. 144.

11. Smith, "Silence, Miss Carson!" pp. 733–752; Hazlett, "'Woman vs. Man vs. Bugs': Gender and Popular Ecology in Early Reactions to Silent Spring," pp. 701–729; Hunter, *Consumer Beware*, p. 41.

12. Smith, "Silence, Miss Carson!" pp. 743, 747.

13. Wargo, *Our Children's Toxic Legacy*, p. 89; http://pubs.usgs.gov/circ/circ1225/html/sources.html, accessed Mar. 7, 2011.

14. Hynes, *The Recurring Silent*, p. 143.

15. Ibid., p. 149; Wargo, *Our Children's Toxic Legacy*, p. 94.

16. *HPCS Co-op News* (July 1965), 1960–1965 file, HPCSR; Mayer, "Requiem for the Truth-in-Packaging Bill?" pp. 1–5; Hunter, *Consumer Beware!* p. 26. The National Consumers League, the only consumer organization to span the entire history of the consumer movement in the twentieth century, was also concerned with truth in packaging and labeling. Angevine, with Newman, "The National Consumers League," p. 361.

17. In 1965, Senator Thomas McIntyre (D-NH) cosponsored a bill to establish a new government agency, a consumers' office. *HPCS Co-op News* (July 1965), 1960–1965 file, HPCSR; http://www.fda.gov/opacom/backgrounders/miles.html; U.S. Food and Drug Administration, "Milestones in U.S. Food and Drug Law History," accessed Aug. 12, 2010; Hunter, *Consumer Beware!* p. 26. George Lipsitz argues that the discussion should include transnational corporations. See Lipsitz, "Consumer Spending as State Project: Yesterday's Solutions and Today's Problems," pp. 127–148.

18. Cohen, *A Consumers' Republic*, p. 258; Feinberg, *What Makes Shopping Centers Tick*, pp. 3, 6, 15.

19. Deutsch, *Building a Housewife's Paradise*, p. 187; Waldman, "The Tyranny of Choice," p. 360.

20. http://www.eatmedaily.com/2010/04/natural-history-of-the-kitchen-the-microwave/, accessed Mar. 7, 2011; http://www.gallawa.com/microtech/history.html, accessed Mar. 7, 2011.

21. Knepper, *Greenbelt, Maryland*, p. 165; "Co-operative to Close Food, Gas Services," *Washington Post*, Jan. 4, 1984, HCCS.

22. In 1988, the Berkeley Co-op had three full service supermarkets. Margo Robison, a board member, thought that the co-op was not prepared for the expansions from 1962 to 1975. See Neptune, *California's Uncommon Markets*; and Gutknecht, "Development Directions Part 1"; Hunter, *Consumer Beware!* pp. 18, 19, 20. Correspondingly, the Eau Claire Co-op had spent over $1 billion a year in advertising, at least during the 1960s.

23. *HPCS Co-op News* (Dec. 1960), 1960–1965 file, HPCSR.

24. http://www.consumersunion.org/aboutcu/estherp.htm, accessed Mar. 2, 2009; *HPCS Co-op News* (Feb. 1964), 1960–1965 file, HPCSR.

25. Willett, "Consumer Education," p. 291. As of the mid-1960s, there were twenty-one Native American cooperative associations, with 12,500 members, for which the Office of Indian Affairs in the Department of Interior was responsible. Roy, *Co-operatives*, p. 140. There were earlier Native American cooperatives, started during the 1930s and 1940s in Red Lake, Minnesota; Belcourt, North Dakota; Black River Falls, Wisconsin; Ethete, Wyoming; Gallup, New Mexico; and in Alaska. But little is written about them. Parker, *The First 125 Years*, pp. 307–308.

26. See http://www.cooperativegrocer.coop/articles/2004-01-07/detroits-cass-corridor-food-co-op, accessed Nov. 12, 2010. Another study of food co-ops in metropolitan Boston in 1974 noted that there were fewer co-ops in the city and more in the suburbs. Many of the urban co-ops had been started by young activists who were not from the communities. In the end, community members did not control their food co-ops or buying clubs. When there is no government or philanthropic support, these urban co-ops faltered. Curhan and Wertheim, "Consumer Food Buying Cooperatives Revisited," pp. 23–24, 30–31.

27. See http://home.earthlink.net/~rflyer/nucoop.html, accessed Nov. 12, 2010; http://www.startwhereyoulive.com/profiles/blogs/logan-heights-story-overcoming, accessed Mar. 7, 2011; and http://www.cooperativegrocer.coop/articles/2004-01-09/can-we-help-build-inner-city-co-ops, accessed Mar. 7, 2011.

28. See http://home.earthlink.net/~rflyer/nucoop.html, accessed Nov. 12, 2010; http://www.startwhereyoulive.com/profiles/blogs/logan-heights-story-overcoming, accessed

Mar. 7, 2011; and http://www.cooperativegrocer.coop/articles/2004-01-09/can-we-help-build-inner-city-co-ops, accessed Mar. 7, 2011.

29. See http://marylandfoodcollective.org/history.php, accessed Mar. 6, 2011. For current information, see http://collegepark.patch.com/articles/an-hour-with-the-mary land-food-co-op, accessed Mar. 6, 2011; and http://www.energystar.gov/index.cfm?c=sb_success.sb_successstories_umd_food, accessed Mar. 6, 2011.

30. Ed Felien, "What's Happening in the Co-op Movement, Nov. 19, 1975," box 4, COP, MFCR.

31. Zwerdling, "The Uncertain Revival of Food Co-operatives," p. 90; Roy, *Co-operatives*, p. 119.

32. Roy, *Co-operatives*, p. 119. The *Food Co-op Handbook* listed around 1,200 existing food co-ops. See the Co-op Handbook Collective, *The Food Co-op Handbook*. The handbook also provided information on how to start and run a food co-op.

33. Hoyt, "The Renaissance of Consumer Food Cooperatives," pp. 1, 2, 7. Another study noted an estimated 3,000 buying clubs and co-op stores in the United States and Canada. Most were located in the West, where 41 percent of households were members. Sommer, Becker, Hohn, and Warholic, "Customer Characteristics and Attitudes at Participatory and Supermarket Cooperatives," pp. 134–135.

34. Ibid., pp. 22–23; Belasco, *Appetite for Change*, p. 111.

35. Bodden, "People's History," http://www.waxingamerica.com/2006/05/history_of_the_.html, accessed May 5, 2006; *Sprouts!* (Mar. 1979), Sprouts! Newsletters, box 1, SC.

36. LMC, Untitled, History file, 1989, LMCR. Not all decisions were made through consensus, at least in the Twin Cities cooperatives. There were also physical assaults, bombs, and other forms of violence because of ideological differences among some St. Paul/Minneapolis co-ops. See chap. 10 in this volume.

37. http://www.foodfront.co-op/AboutUs/OurHistory/tabid/130/Default.aspx; http://www.davisco-op.com/history.html, accessed May 8, 2010; see also Brown, "Building an Alternative," pp. 298–321.

38. http://www.bloomingfoods.co-op/index.php?option=com_content&task=view&id=34&Itemid=89, accessed May 8, 2010.

39. However, many of these households had been active in buying clubs since 1953. See http://www.hwfc.com/about_history.html, accessed Oct. 9, 2009; *PCC Program Report in Developments in Consumer and Worker Democracy* (Seattle: Board of Trustees, PCC, July 1999), 5. During the 1940s, there were a number of cooperatives in Seattle, including the Cascade Co-op League, at least three food co-ops, a cooperative insurance agency, health cooperative, a credit union, and cooperatives that sold gas, tires, and hardware. See "Climb Aboard" brochure, #3697-3 and "Evergreen Co-operatives," n.d., #3697-3, IHP. Many activists in Seattle linked cooperatives to democracy and social justice. See for example, "America's Answer = Consumer's Co-operation," #341, CCP. As of 1999, the co-op had over 35,000 members. Touart, "The Nation's Largest Natural Food Co-op," pp. 23–24.

40. *Co-op Newsletter* (April, 1975?), box 17, file 5, BPR.

41. Bodden, "People's History."

42. http://www.hwfc.com/about_history.html, accessed May 8, 2010.

43. *ICCS Bulletin* (Feb. 1969), box 5, ICCSR.

44. *HCCS Co-op News* (Sept. 1962; Sept. 1963), 1930s–1965 file, HCCSR.

45. HCCS, 1970 Board of Director Minutes, Dec. 10, 1970; HCCS, 1971 Board of Director Minutes, Jan. 13, 1971; Letter from Joan Erdman, Chair, Education Committee to Board Members, Mar. 9, 1971; Letter to James Rodes from Charles Wood, Mar. 4, 1971, HCCSR. For information about the federal legislation, see http://www.colorado.edu/conflict/full_text_search/AllCRCDocs/94-54.htm, accessed Mar. 9, 2009.

46. Ithaca Friends of the Farmworker, flyer, n.d., box 7, ICCSR; "UFWOC and the Lettuce Growers," file 3, ICCSR. For more about Chavez's advocacy of cooperatives, see David Thompson's article, http://www.cooperativegrocer.coop/articles/2004-01-09/cesar-chavez-his-lifelong-links-cooperatives, accessed Nov. 12, 2010. For more information on Delano and the grape industry, see Cowie, *Stayin' Alive*, pp. 49–54. Schulman argues that Chavez ran the UFWOC like a mutualista, not just a union. Schulman, *The Seventies*, p. 65.

47. Hynes, *The Recurring Silent Spring*, p. 125; Lopez, *The Farmworkers' Journey*, pp. 102–106. For a list of different pesticides used today, see Lopez, *The Farmworkers' Journey*, Appendix A. A photo-documentary study on migrant workers that greatly moved me was Rothenberg, *With These Hands*.

48. HCCS, 1969 Board Minutes, Oct. 8, 1969; HCCS, 1978 Board Minutes, Sept. 21, 1978, HCCSR. For information on the Nestle boycott, see http://en.wikipedia.org/wiki/Nestl%C3%A9_boycott and http://scholar.google.com/scholar?q=Nestle+boycott&hl=en&um=1&ie=UTF-8&oi=scholart, accessed Jan. 10, 2010.

49. HPCS, "Campbell's Soup Not Good Food to Strikers," unknown source, box 6, HPCSR; NPCS, Quarterly Member Meeting Minutes, Feb. 12, 1985, box 17, file 3, BPR. For information on this boycott, see http://en.wikipedia.org/wiki/Farm_Labor_Organizing_Committee, accessed Mar. 9, 2009.

50. Whole Foods Co-operative, "The Banana Committee's Report for the March 25 Community Meeting," Mar. 29, 1979, box 6, MFCR; The Wedge Food Co-operative, Recommendations of Product Standards Committee, Aug. 23, 1979, box 5, MFCR.

51. *PCC Program Report in Developments in Consumer and Worker Democracy*, 30.

52. It is not clear if all of the Ann Arbor co-ops sold food. The Consumers Co-op of Berkeley, which had opened during the Depression, had thirteen stores in 1979, with 86,000 families as members. P. C. Kreitner, Congress Watch Report # 2, July 30, 1979, box 32, file 4, BPR; http://www.peoplesfood.co-op/about/history.php, accessed Mar. 12, 2010; Zwerdling, "The Uncertain Revival of Food Co-operatives," pp. 106, 107. In 1979, Congress set up a National Consumer Co-operative Bank to provide technical and financial assistance to consumer cooperatives. Consumer Co-operative Bank Act passed in 1978.

53. Board of Trustees, PCC, Inc., July 1999, p. 8; *Seattle Times*, June 20, 1976, p. G6; *PCC Program Report in Developments in Consumer and Worker Democracy*; *Seattle Times*, June 19, 1985, p. G1, G11.

54. Schulman, *The Seventies*, p. 142.

55. Ibid., p. 218; Cowie, *Stayin' Alive*, p. 228; Stein, *Pivotal Decade*, pp. 145, 265.

56. Stein, *Pivotal Decade*, pp. 267, 268.

57. NCC Board Minutes, Mar. 15, 1982, Dec. 20, 1982, NCCR.

58. McEvily and Ingram, "The Organization Is the Political," http://apps.olin.wustl.edu/faculty/conferences/oesc/pdf/mcevily_ingram_paper.pdf, accessed Oct. 29, 2011, p. 2.

59. Curhan and Wertheim, "Consumer Food Buying Cooperatives Revisited," p. 32.

60. See http://glutfood.org.history.htm, accessed Mar. 6, 2011. Demographic information is from http://en.wikipedia.org/wiki/Mount_Rainier_Maryland, accessed Mar. 6, 2011.

61. Lewis, "A Critique of Consumer Co-operative Theory and Practice," p. 196; http://www.co-operativegrocer.co-op/articles/index.php?id=153, accessed May 5, 2010.

62. Schulman, *The Seventies*, p. 13.

63. Some historians have discussed the conspicuous consumption of yuppies and other young professionals during the 1980s. Food co-ops, I argue, provide evidence of consumer activism then. Lasch, *The Culture of Narcissism*, p. 73; Schulman, *The Seventies*, p. 219.

CHAPTER 8

1. Dasmann, *The Destruction of California*, p. 97.

2. Ibid., pp. 86, 88, 181, 182; Beach, *A Good Forest for Dying*, p. 3.

3. For information about marijuana growers in the California backcountry, see Raphael, *Cash Crop*. Two personal accounts of communes in Humboldt County are Anderson, *Whatever Happened to the Hippies*; and Anders, *Beyond Counterculture*. 2010 census data show that Arcata has slightly over 16,650 people, with a median age of 25.8, compared to the national average of 35.3. Almost 85 percent of its residents are white, 7.2 percent Hispanic. See http://www.americantowns.com/ca/arcata-information, accessed Sept. 24, 2010. For thoughts on how hip and alternative Arcata is, see comments on http://www. hippy.com/php/review-14.html, accessed Sept. 24, 2010.

4. *NCC Newsletter*, Aug. 1, 1975, Dec. 1978, June 1979, Oct. 1979, NCCR.

5. 2010 North Coast brochure.

6. NCC, *Orientation Manual*, 2009, 41; *NCC Newsletter* (Dec. 1980), NCCR.

7. *NCC Newsletter* (Oct. 1975). The bakery also sold granola made by Redwoods United Workshop, which hired people with disabilities. *NCC Newsletter* (Apr. 1976). The bulk food center was opened by the co-op to "get food cheaper to people by cutting out the conveniences that a supermarket offers." Students were a large part of its success because they "were not afraid of the co-op idea as the general public might be." *NCC Newsletter* (Feb. 1975). In 1974, the co-op had trucked collectively with thirty-four stores. In 1976, the co-op bought a truck trailer because renting a truck was too expensive. NCC Board Minutes, Aug. 19, 1974, Oct. 20, 1975; *NCC Newsletter* (Jan. 1976), NCCR.

8. NCC Board Minutes, Nov. 1, 1976, Nov. 7, 1976; *NCC Newsletter* (Jan. 1975; Summer 1976; Dec. 1, 1976), NCCR. Early on, employees had suggested a new position, a community action coordinator, to organize member-volunteers to work on a community newsletter, to organize buying clubs and a membership drive, and to start a recycling program. The community coordinator held workshops with two nutritionists to "provide consumers with pertinent information, including speakers, bulletins, demonstrations, articles, newsletters, and co-operative with other interest groups." NCC Board Minutes, June 26, 1974; *NCC Newsletter* (Jan. 1975), NCCR.

9. *NCC Newsletter* (Apr. 1976); NCC Board Minutes, Feb. 25, 1974, NCCR. In a comparison of prices of the co-op, Purity, and Safeway, the co-op had the cheapest produce, dairy, and grains. The co-op made these comparisons every three months. *NCC Newsletter* (Jan. 1975), NCCR.

10. *NCC Newsletter* (Aug. 1975; Oct. 1975; Jan. 1976), NCCR. Blue fin tuna is still a controversial fish today. See http://green.blogs.nytimes.com/2010/10/13/a-showdown-on-bluefin-tuna/?hp, accessed Oct. 13, 2010; and Kolbert, "The Scales Fall," pp. 70–73. The co-op was also a pioneer in its concerns about phosphates, like the HCCS. As early as 1976, the newsletter published an article on phosphates in laundry detergents. *NCC Newsletter* (Nov. 1976), NCCR.

11. *NCC Newsletter* (Jan. 1976; Mar. 1976; Apr. 1976; May, 1976), NCCR; "Regulation: Death of a Dye," *Time Magazine*, Feb. 2, 1976. There was an article in the co-op newsletter about pesticides and organophosphates. One FDA official in 1969 testified that there were 80,000 pesticide poisonings a year and 800 deaths. See "food for people, not for profit," edited by people from the "Berkeley Bark," in *NCC Newsletter* (Apr. 1976), NCCR. There was also an article on harmful aerosol sprays and alternative natural remedies. See *NCC Newsletter* (Summer 1976), NCCR.

12. NCC Board Minutes, Oct. 30, 1975, NCCR.

13. *NCC Newsletter* (Dec. 1978), NCCR.

14. *NCC Newsletter* (June 1979), NCCR.

15. NCC Board Minutes, May 17, 1976; *NCC Newsletter* (Jan. 1976), NCCR.

16. *NCC Newsletter* (Apr. 1976), NCCR.

17. *NCC Newsletter* (Summer 1976), NCCR.

18. Baker, "The International Infant Formula Controversy: A Dilemma in Corporate Social Responsibility," pp. 181–182.

19. *NCC Newsletter* (Apr. 1978; Mar. 1979); NCC Board Minutes, Mar. 19, 1984; Dec. 9, 1992; Mar. 23, 1993, NCCR.

20. *NCC Newsletter* (Jan. 1976), NCCR.

21. *NCC Newsletter* (Feb. 1978); NCC Board Minutes, Dec. 17, 1979, NCCR.

22. As of 1974, no funds had been set aside for a patronage refund and the co-op's taxes had eliminated its reserve. NCC Board Minutes, May 20, 1974; June 5, 1974, NCCR.

23. NCC Board Minutes, Dec. 4, 1974, NCCR.

24. *NCC Newsletter* (Oct. 1975), NCCR.

25. Ibid.

26. *NCC Newsletter* (Jan. 1976); NCC Board Minutes, Sept. 3, 1974, NCCR.

27. NCC Board Minutes, Oct. 30, 1974; Jan. 8, 1975; *NCC Newsletter* (Oct. 1975), NCCR.

28. *NCC Newsletter* (Nov. 1975), NCCR.

29. *NCC Newsletter* (Jan. 1976), NCCR.

30. Ibid.

31. *NCC Newsletter* (Apr. 1976; Jan. 1976); NCC Board Minutes, Oct. 31, 1975, NCCR.

32. *NCC Newsletter* (Mar. 1978; Apr. 1979); NCC Board Minutes, Oct. 7, 1974, NCCR.

33. *NCC Newsletter* (Feb. 1978), NCCR.

34. NCC Board Minutes, Oct. 10, 1977, NCCR.

35. *NCC Newsletter* (Apr. 1978), NCCR.

36. *NCC Newsletter* (Apr. 1979; May 1979), NCCR.

37. *NCC Newsletter* (Apr. 1980; June 1980), NCCR. There were no 1988, 1989, or 1990 board minutes. Also, for most of the 1980s, there was little information about the coop's financial situation.

38. *NCC Newsletter* (Nov. 1980), NCCR.

39. NCC Board Minutes, July 28, 1980; *NCC Newsletter* (June 1980), NCCR.

40. NCC Board Minutes, Dec. 21, 1981; Feb. 15, 1982, NCCR; http://arcata.north-coastco-op.com/website/strategicplan2009.pdf, accessed Jan. 15, 2010.

41. NCC Board Minutes, Mar. 15, 1982; Dec. 20, 1982, NCCR.

42. NCC Board Minutes, Nov. 22, 1982; Mar. 28, 1983; May 23, 1983; Dec. 19, 1983; Sept. 10, 1984, NCCR.

43. NCC Board Minutes, Feb. 18, 1985; Mar. 18, 1985; Apr. 15, 1985; Aug. 19, 1985; Sept 16, 1985, NCCR; http://arcata.northcoastco-op.com/website/strategicplan2009.pdf. Local stores did not buy from the warehouse because of its close association to the Arcata Co-op. But the co-op needed to "crack" the local market. NCC Board Minutes, Feb. 26, 1987, NCCR.

44. NCC Board Minutes, Apr. 20, 1987; June 16, 1987; Aug. 17, 1987, NCCR.

45. NCC Board Minutes, Mar. 17, 1986, NCCR.

46. NCC Board Minutes, Aug. 16, 1982; June 16, 1986, NCCR.

47. NCC Board Minutes, Sept. 16, 1985; Nov. 18, 1985, NCCR.

48. NCC Board Minutes, Dec. 16, 1985; June 16, 1986, NCCR.

49. NCC Board Minutes, Nov. 19, 1990; Dec. 17, 1990; Jan. 14, 1991; Feb. 7, 1992; May 14, 1991; Merchandising Committee Minutes, Nov. 13, 1991, NCCR.

50. Letter from John Corbett to Tim McKay, c/o North Coast Environmental Center, Oct. 15, 1991; "Arcata co-op is out to bolster its own image," *Times-Standard*, Aug. 25, 1991, NCCR.

51. Arcata retained its entrepreneurial spirit during the 1990s. People made and sold jams, wines, sauces, honey, roasted coffee, beer, noodles, and breads. There was still the

annual Reggae on the River in French's Campy in Piercy in the summer. However, the group, Taxpayers for the Environment and Its Management (TEAM), was concerned about the festival's environmental impact and thought the music might disturb spotted owls nesting nearby. This was a critical habitat for owls, listed as a threatened species. "Humboldt Home Grown (It ain't weed)," newspaper unknown; NCC Board Minutes, Jan. 28, 1991; "Action Toward Music Fests Confuses Justice, Revenge," *North Coast's Daily Forum*, June 9, 1991, NCCR.

52. "Forest Campers Migrate North," *Union*, Sept. 17, 1992, NCCR.

53. See Bari, *Timber Wars*. For an update on Bari's court case, see http://www.judibari.org, accessed Oct. 8, 2010.

54. See Harris, *The Last Stand*; and Beach, *A Good Forest for Dying*.

55. Harris, *The Last Stand*, pp. 78, 102, 338; NCC Board Minutes, Dec. 17, 1990, NCCR. The Fortuna Co-op needed to make $25,000 a week. One person said that if the co-op would not associate with Earth!First and the Sierra Club, its business would come back. When a Walmart store opened, the co-op's sales dropped $300 to $500 a day. NCC Board Minutes, July 16, 1991, NCCR. For information about Earth!First history in Humboldt County, see http://www.North Coastearthfirst.org/NCEF_History.htm, accessed Sept. 25, 2010.

56. Letter from Member, NCC Board Minutes, Oct. 31, 1991, NCCR.

57. Ad Hoc Committee, "Save Our Co-op," n.d., NCCR.

58. "Co-op's Drive to Clean Up Seen as Try to Abandon Roots," *New York Times Sunday Supplement*, Nov. 24, 1991; NCC Board Minutes, Nov. 19, 1991, NCCR.

59. Ad Hoc Committee, "Save Our Co-op."

60. NCC Board Minutes, July 9, 1991; Nov. 14, 1991; Mar. 17, 1992; Letter to NCC, Sept. 26, 1991; Managers' Letter to NCC Board of Directors, Mar. 5, 1992, NCCR.

61. John Corbett to NCC, May 15, 1992; Letter about Analysis of Fortuna, n.d.; Memo to Board of Directors from Janelle, n.d., NCCR.

62. NCC Board Minutes, May 12, 1992; July 21, 1992; Nov. 17, 1992, NCCR. The general manager thought that the board's decisions were influencing management's ability to manage the co-op's assets. More directly, he said, "The Fortuna decision has impacted profitability." NCC Board Minutes, Nov. 6, 1991.

63. NCC Board Minutes, Mar. 12, 1992; July 16, 1992; Sept. 1992; June 6, 1993, NCCR.

64. Letter on Customer Service Project, June 17, 1994; NCC Board Minutes, Mar. 22, 1994; Nov. 8, 1994, NCCR. The board discussed making a bid to buy Wildberries. NCC Board Minutes, Dec. 2, 1998, NCCR.

65. NCC Board Minutes, Mar. 28, 1995; July, 5, 1995, NCCR.

66. NCC Board Minutes, May 13, 1996; May 21, 1996; Aug. 19, 1996, NCCR.

67. NCC Board Minutes, Dec. 9, 1992; Mar. 23, 1993; July 27, 1993; Nov. 1, 1993, "NCCR; Boycott Is Working, Group Says," *New York Times*, June 13, 1991, http://www.nytimes.com/1991/06/13/business/company-news-ge-boycott-is-working-group-says.html, accessed Dec. 30, 2010. For a history of Monsanto, see http://www.saynotogmos.org/monsanto_1.htm, accessed Oct. 10, 2010.

68. NCC Board Minutes, July 14, 1993; Apr. 13, 1994; Nov. 25, 1995, NCCR. The BGH remains controversial. In 1993, the FDA approved Monsanto's BGH Posilac. For information, see https://hfa.org/campaigns/dairy.html, accessed Oct. 15, 2010. In the mid-1990s, four states refused to let companies label milk that was BGH-free. Ben & Jerry's Homemade, Stonyfield Farms Yogurt, Whole Foods Markets, and Organic Valley Family of Farms filed a suit against Illinois and Chicago. See http://findarticles.com/p/articles/mi_m0820/is_n230/ai_18696318/, accessed Oct. 15, 2010.

69. "Handout on Coca-Cola Boycott Alternative: Consumer Education," Feb. 28, 2006; Handout, Oct. 18, 2005, NCCR. As of 2007, the NCC still sold Coca-Cola. See http://www.northcoastjournal.com/062107/cover0621.html, accessed Jan. 15, 2011.

70. Article on "Seafood Watch," July 23, 2002; e-mails from various co-ops about meat sales, NCC Board Minutes, May 2, 2002, NCCR.

71. NCC Board Minutes, Oct. 11, 2003, Email Handout; NCC Board Minutes, Aug. 23, 2005, NCCR. For current information about Greenpeace and GMOs, see http://www.greenpeace.org/international/en/campaigns/agriculture/problem/genetic-engineering/, accessed Oct. 8, 2010.

72. E-mail to Board of Directors, Mar. 22, 2004; NCC Board Minutes, Mar. 23, 2004; e-mail, Feb 23, 2004, NCCR; http://voiceoftheenvironment.org/gmos/, accessed Jan. 15, 2010. In 2004, the NCC had over 10,000 members for a county population of 126,000. Its annual sales were nearly $18 million. Its community fund donated up to $30,000 yearly to nonprofit organizations. See Web Design Information, NCC Board Minutes, Apr. 24, 2004, NCCR.

73. http://www.northcoastjournal.com/100704/cover1007.html, accessed Jan. 15, 2010.

74. http://www.northcoastco-op.com/healthy.htm#greenDot, accessed Oct. 10, 2010.

75. *Orientation Manual*, 2009, 45; *NCC Newsletter* (Spring 2010), NCCR.

CHAPTER 9

1. "Our Kind of Town," p. 55.

2. "New Pioneer's Co-operative Society, Articles of Incorporation," box 17, file 2, BPR; "A Brief History of New Pioneer Food Co-op," http://www.mewpi.com/AboutUs/History/aspx, accessed May 16, 2009. In 1973, the co-op and several food retailers formed Blooming Prairie Co-operative Warehouse that served Midwest buying clubs and other co-ops. The warehouse cooperative was inspired by the then defunct People's Warehouse in Minneapolis, discussed in the next chapter. There was also Frontier Co-operative Herbs, based in Norway, Iowa, about sixteen miles from the Cedar Rapids-Iowa City area, which is still in business. Notes on an Audit, n.d., box 17, file 1, BPR.

3. "New Pioneer's Co-operative Society, Articles of Incorporation."

4. *NPCS Co-op Newsletter* (April 1975), box 17, file 5, BPR.

5. John Higgins, "Financial History of New Pioneer Co-operative Society," box 17, file 5, BPR; Morning Glory Bakery, Annual Report, October, 1979, box 17, file 3, BPR. In 1979, the board's role was to act as a facilitator to the community and to provide continuity and long-term directions. It did not make decisions but "formulate[d]" what decisions were needed. That would change with the hiring of a general manager. "New Pioneer Co-operative Society Policies," Dec. 12, 1979, box 17, file 3, BPR.

6. "Subtle Sabotage at the Co-op," box 5, file 1, BPR; Higgins, "Financial History of New Pioneer Co-operative Society"; New Pioneer Balance Sheet, Mar. 31, 1982, box 17, file 3, BPR.

7. Results of New Pioneer Shopping Survey, Nov. 15, 1982, box 17, file 5, BPR; New Pioneer Interview Checklist, Dec. 3, 1982, box 17, file 3, BPR. Working members were required to work three hours per month and could join committees. They could work in the general store as cashiers or at the Blooming Prairie warehouse. "How to Be a Working Member," June, 1981, box 17, file 5, BPR.

8. "Long Range Planning Committee Survey," Fall 1982, box, 17, file 5, BPR. By 1982, there were eighteen buying clubs in Iowa City. Of those, four were religious organizations, one political, one a day care, and one a housing co-op. "Buying Clubs in Iowa City Area," July, 1982, box 17, file 5, BPW.

9. Community Consulting Group, Cambridge, Massachusetts, "A Report on the Technical Assistance Delivered to New Pioneer Co-operative, Iowa City, Iowa," July 1984, box 17, file 3, BPR.

10. Ibid.

11. See http://en.wikipedia.org/wiki/Farm_Labor_Organizing_Committee; NPCS, Quarterly Member Meeting Minutes, Feb. 12, 1985, box 17, file 3, BPR.

12. NPCS, Board of Director's Report, May 14, 1985, box 17, file 3, BPR.

13. Notes on Financial Statement, Dec. 31, 1985, box 17, file 3, BPR.

14. Stapenhorst & Associates, "New Pioneer Co-operative Market. Market Analysis and Estimates of Sales Volume Potential," Jan. 1986, box 27, file 1, NPSCR; "Proposed Goals and Objectives," Mar. 10, 1986, box 17, file 3, BPR.

15. *Catalyst* (May 1987; Oct. 1987). The location in Cedar Rapids for the New Pioneer's co-op was the very building where Frontier had started. "New Pioneer Tracks Sales of $2.3M," *Natural Foods Merchandiser* (January 1988) box 17, file 4, BPR.

16. Carbrey and Chevalier, "New Pioneer Co-op Closes Its Second Store; *Catalyst* (Mar./Apr. 1991).

17. There were 1,800 family members, although half of their 740 daily customers were nonmembers. "New Pioneer Tracks Sales of $2.3M.," *Natural Foods Merchandiser* (Jan. 1988.

18. Ibid.

19. "New Pioneer Tracks Sales of $2.3M."; NPCS, 1988 Annual Report & Board Election, box 37, file 2, NPCSR; *Catalyst* (June 1988).

20. NPCS, 1989 Annual Report & Board Election; *Catalyst* (Nov./Dec. 1991; Oct. 1992; Oct. 1993).

21. *Catalyst* (Jan./Feb. 1992; July/Aug. 1995); "A History of New Pioneer's Bread," Series 2, box 33, History folder, NPCSR; *Catalyst* (Dec. 1996).

22. *Catalyst* (Nov. 1993); Marketing Plan, 1996–1997, box 27, file 6, NPCSR; *Catalyst* (Dec./Jan. 1994).

23. *Catalyst* (June 1996; July/August 1996; Dec. 1996).

24. *Catalyst* (Mar. 1996).

25. *Catalyst* (Dec./Jan. 1997).

26. *Catalyst* (Nov. 1996). Rick Stewart asked members to vote because a very unhappy group of members want to "*turn back the wheels of time.*" Form letter to "Co-op Friend" from Rick Stewart, Sept. 15, 1997, New Pioneer file, JWC.

27. *Catalyst* (Mar. 1996).

28. *Catalyst* (Sept. 1994; Jan. 1995; Dec./Jan. 1997). For more information on the Pure Food Campaign, see http://www.foet.org/past/biotech-century.html, accessed Aug. 2, 2010.

29. *Catalyst* (Apr. 1996). That motion passed 789 to 195.

30. 1997–98 Business Plan and Operating Budget Draft, box 27, file 7, NPCSR.

31. Ibid.

32. *Catalyst* (Oct. 1996); "Labor Board to Supervise April 4 Co-op Union Vote," newspaper unknown, n.d., JWC; *Catalyst* (Mar. 1996).

33. Letter from Jim Walters to Rick, Board of Directors, and General Managers, Feb. 19, 1997, box 32, file 19, NPCSR.

34. MAC, Questions for the Board and General Manager, n.d., New Pioneer file, JWC. There were "union" songs, with lines such as "This Pi is your Pi, This Pi is my Pi"; "Solidarity Forever"; and "You gotta go down." It is not clear who sang them but probably MAC members did. Union Song, n.d., JWC.

35. "We Make the Union" and "Protect Our Benefits!" *New Pioneer Co-op Voice* (Mar. 27, 1997); box 32, file 20, NPCSR; handwritten letter from Chad Clark, n.d., box 32, file 20, NPCSR; "Labor board to supervise April 4 co-op union vote," *Icon*, Mar. 6, 1997, box 32, file 20, NPCSR.

36. "Prioritize Employees!" *New Pioneer Co-op Voice* (Feb. 25, 1997), box 32, file 20, NPCSR. One staff member, who supported the union, compared the situation to "'a sort

of business equivalent of a peyote ceremony,' complete with fasting, purging, and praying." That is, the process opened up issues. *Catalyst* (May/June 1996).

37. "Prioritize Employees!"

38. "Labor Board to Supervise April 4 Co-op Union Vote," *Icon*, Mar. 6, 1997, box 32, file 20, NPCSR; James L. McCurtis, "Close Vote Ends Co-op Workers' Union," *Press Citizen*, April 5–6, 1997, box 32, file 20, NPCSR.

39. "New Pioneer Co-op Nixes Union Representation Plan," unknown newspaper, n.d., box 32, file 19, NPCSR.

40. Letter from Rochelle, General Manager to Staff, n.d., box 32, file 19, NPCSR.

41. Letter from Laurie Clements to Sondra Smith, Board Members, Mar. 9, 1997, box 32, file 19, NPCSR.

42. "New Pi Union Organizers Vow, 'We still Have a Union,'" *Icon*, April 17, 1997, New Pioneer file, JWC.

43. Associate Director, The University of Iowa Labor Education Center, "Response to 'Factual Information,'" *A Slice of the Pi*, 434, box 32, file 19, NPFCR.

44. Comments of Laurie Clements, Prepared for March 12 Meeting of Co-op, New Pioneer file, JWC.

45. Letter from Rick Stewart to New Pi Friends, n.d., box 32, file 19, NPCSR

46. From Members to Board of Directors and General Manager, Question and Answer, Mar. 14, 1997, JWC.

47. "Co-op Members to Discuss Unionizing," *Daily Iowan*, Mar. 11, 1997, 3A, box 32, file, 20, NPCSR.

48. "Our Rights as Members under the Co-op's By-Laws and Articles of Incorporation, and Under Iowa Law," n.d., JWC.

49. MAC, Questions for the Board and General Manager.

50. Form, "What Exactly Is MAC Saying and What Do They Want?" n.d., New Pioneer file, JWC; "Co-op Members Want Meeting on Union," *Iowa City Press Citizen*, n.d., box 32, file 20, NPCSR.

51. Form, "What Exactly Is MAC Saying and What Do They Want?"

52. Letter from Robert Lewis To Whom It May Concern, Apr. 13, 1997, box 32, file 19, NPCSR.

53. Memo from Carol Dieterle re. Co-op Finances, Mar. 28, 1997, New Pioneer file, JWC.

54. Clip from Opinion of Secretary of State's Office in Des Moines, July 25, 1997, New Pioneer file, JWC.

55. "Board President Stewart Threatens New Pi Member," *One Slice of the Pie*, Sept. 12, 1997, JWC.

56. From Denise Chevalier, Store Manager, New Pioneer file, JWC; *Catalyst* (Feb. 1998).

57. *Catalyst* (Apr. 1998).

58. *Catalyst* (May/June 1998).

59. *Catalyst* (Oct. 1998).

60. *Catalyst* (Sept. 1996). In 1996, sales for New Pioneer were up, especially in wine, supplements, dairy, and deli foods. The Bakehouse's sales were over $700,000, up $100,000 from the previous year.

61. *Catalyst* (Sept. 1996); Information on Business Plan Committee Meeting, June 19, 1998, box 27, file 11, NPCSR.

62. Confidential Memorandum, Nov. 26, 1997, box 27, file 7, NPCSR. In 1998, there were amendments to the bylaws: that members could access certain financial information amendment to bylaws, important for making informed votes; that members had access to a member list; that members had a right to submit issues for decisions sixty days prior to a meeting and signed by twenty-five members in good standing; that members could call for

a vote for removal of a board member through a petition signed by 50 percent of members who voted in the last co-op election. To remove a director, 65 percent of members had to vote in the affirmative. Information on Business Plan Committee Meeting, June 19, 1998, box 27, file 11 (1998), NPCSR.

63. Information on Business Plan Committee Meeting, June 19, 1998, box 27, file 11, NPFCR; *Catalyst* (Oct. 1998; July 1999).

64. *Catalyst* (July 1999).

65. *Catalyst* (May 2000).

66. *Catalyst* (Aug./Sept. 1999). Interestingly, the same year the board endorsed the new co-op in Coralville, it also passed new resolutions that included supporting the rights of workers to join organizations of their choosing. It also directed the management team to work with a legal team to research and report to the board about ways that would "shelter the Van Buren Store from risk assumed by the Coralville venture." And it devised a plan on a living wage if the county passed this ordinance. "Board Welcomes Second Store," *Catalyst* (Oct./Nov. 1999). Human Rights Iowa City wanted the board to endorse their campaign for a local "living wage" ordinance. Iowa City mayor, Ernie Lehman, had proclaimed the city a Human Rights Community. The board voted to endorse this campaign. Jim Walters, NPCS Board Report, 1999(?), box 37, file 13, NPCSR.

67. "New Pioneer Opens Coralville Site," *Co-operative Grocer* (May–June 2001), p. 5, Series 2, box 33, file 14, NPCSR.

68. "Co-op: Privacy of Membership List Vital to Its Business," *Cedar Rapids Gazette*, Feb. 18, 2000; Depositions Pertaining to DeProsse Lawsuit, 2000, box 33, file 12, NPCSR. In 1994, eligible members received a patronage dividend for the first time. In 1996, the co-op returned almost $75,000 to members as patronage dividend. *Catalyst* (Nov. 1994; Oct. 1996). Rick Stewart and his wife had started Frontier Herbs in 1976. By 1988, Frontier had 3,500 members, served over 550 accounts in eight midwestern states, and had yearly sales of $6.5 million. "New Pioneer Tracks Sales of $2.3M." As of 1992, Frontier Herbs had 5,500 members in the U.S. and Canada, including bakeries, restaurants, and college campuses. It was the largest buyer and seller of certified organic plant products in the United States. Untitled information, n.d., New Pioneer file, JWC. For further information on its history, see http://www.answers.com/topic/frontier-natural-products-co-op and http://www.frontierco-op.com/company/history.html, accessed August 4, 2010.

69. *Catalyst* (Mar. 2001; May 2001). The Coralville co-op offered classes in cooking, yoga, and floral design.

70. *Catalyst* (Oct. 2000); Financial Questions and Answers on Store Finances, Dec. 31, 2001, box 27, file 20, NPCSR; *Catalyst* (Nov. 2001).

71. *Catalyst* (Nov. 2001; Jan./Feb. 2002). According to the 2002 treasurer's report, the new store was 50 percent over budget, in large part because they built a basement, even though they did not own the building. *Catalyst* (July/Aug. 2002). The Iowa City co-op's sales dropped by 29 percent with the opening of the Coralville store. Still, New Pioneer was operating at twice the national average of sales per square foot for a store this size. *Catalyst* (Apr. 2001).

72. "New Pioneer Unveils Finances," *Press Citizen*, June 1, 2002, box 33, file 24, NPCSR; *Catalyst* (Jan./Feb. 2002).

73. *Catalyst* (Dec. 2001). By mid-2001, the Coralville store brought in nearly 1,000 customers a day; the Iowa City co-op—almost 1,300. The Coralville store had a staff of ninety-three, the Iowa City co-op—eighty-seven. Dennis Maclearn, Ben Mauman, and Jennifer Masada, "New Pioneer Opens Coralville Site," p. 5.

74. Jennifer Masada, Marketing Manager, "Ten Ways to Help Your Co-op!" *Catalyst* (Mar./Apr. 2002); Jim Walters, "Pros Don't Always Know Best," *Press Citizen*, June 5, 2002, box 33, file 24, NPCSR.

75. Carol de Prosse, "New Pioneer Member Says Bad Board Has Been Replaced," *Press Citizen*, June 8, 2002, box 33, file 24, NPCSR.

76. Ben Nauman, "Sharp Divides at New Pioneer," *Press Citizen*, June 8, 2002, box 33, file 24, NPCRS.

77. *Catalyst* (July/Aug. 2002).

78. Ibid.; "Lean Diet Restoring Health," *Cedar Rapids Gazette*, Jan. 18, 2003, Series 2, box 33, file 24, NPCSR; *Catalyst* (Sept./Oct. 2004).

79. "About the Proposed Research," n.d., box 33, file 12, NPCSR; *Catalyst* (Jan./Feb. 2003).

80. *Catalyst* (Sept./Oct. 2005; Feb. 2006; Mar./Apr. 2006;). Sales for 2005 were 13 percent above the previous year. The Coralville co-op store sold 17 percent more than in last year's third quarter. Sales in Iowa City were 14 percent higher than in third quarter of 2004. *Catalyst* (May/June 2005).

81. Press Release, Oct. 3, 2005, Series 2, box 33, file 23, NPCSR; *Catalyst* (May/June 2006).

82. *Catalyst* (Feb. 2004; May/June 2006).

83. (Mar./Apr. 2004); "Organic for Everyone," *Catalyst* (Sept./Oct. 2006) ; "join us!" brochure, 2009; *Catalyst* (Spring 2009). On the efforts to stop the growth of Walmart, see http://dkosopedia.com/wiki/Iowa_City and http://www.dailyiowan.com/2009/11/09/Metro/14229.html, accessed Aug. 3, 2010.

84. *Catalyst* (Summer 2010).

CHAPTER 10

1. Cowling, *Co-operatives in America*, p.154.

2. Leikin, *The Practical Utopians*, pp. 31, 119, 123, 127–128, 134.

3. Keillor, *Cooperative Commonwealth*, pp. 4, 16.

4. Cowling, *Co-operatives in America*, p. 154; "Minneapolis and Its Many Co-operatives," p. 182. The Women's Co-operative Guild in Minneapolis, affiliated with the Franklin Co-op Creamery Association, was also active in educational and charity work. The Association's radical character was reflected in the Guild's goals: "'to cheer and to urge the men on' in their 'industrial struggle' toward the 'ultimate goal of the co-operative commonwealth.'" Northern States' Co-operative League, *1925 Yearbook*, pp. 61–62.

5. Rossinow, "'The Revolution Is About Our Lives,'" pp. 101, 110.

6. Ibid., p. 110.

7. Farber, "The Intoxicated State/Illegal Nation: Drugs in the Sixties Counterculture," p. 18. See also Anderson, *The Movement and the Sixties*.

8. Gosse, *Rethinking the New Left*. Christopher Lasch concluded that most college students were not interested in classical Marxism but in "an ideology of intense activism aiming at the violent overthrow of colonialism by a guerilla elite." Lasch, *The Agony of the American Left*, p. 179.

9. Gosse, *Rethinking the New Left*, pp. 200, 201, 210.

10. Cox, *Storefront Revolution*, p. 39. Cox was president of the interim board of the Bryant-Central Co-op and also a journalist. "Food Co-op Struggle Explodes in Violence," *Minneapolis Star*, Jan. 14, 1976, box 4, Food Co-operatives: Bryant-Central Co-op (Minneapolis, MN), 1970–1996 file, KOP, MFCR. Kris Olsen, an activist and employee at Seward, collected and preserved this and other co-ops' records. See also Annie Young and Shirley Krogmeier, "History," Dec. 18, 1985, and Seward Community Café, box 2,

Histories, Undated and 1989, SSCR. Young was hired in membership development in 1981, when Seward nearly closed.

11. "Food for Freaks," *One Hundred Flowers*, Aug. 21, 1970, box 5, True Grits (Minneapolis, MN), 1970 file, MFCR.

12. "North Country Co-op," brochure, n.d, box 7, North Country Co-op, Flyers & Brochures, Undated and 1973–2000 file, NCCR. On the vague definitions of "natural foods," see Belasco, *Appetite for Change*, pp. 220–225.

13. "Food Conspiracy in the North Country," *Changes* 21 (July–Aug. 1972), box 7, Newspaper Clippings, 1975–1997 file, NCCR.

14. Ibid. The co-op even milled its own flour.

15. Letter from Dave Speidel to Kris Olsen, Sept. 25, 1991, box 2, Seward Community Café, Histories, Undated and 1989 file, SCCR. Seward Community Café started in 1974 and was managed by a worker collective. Its menu offered natural food, including affordable local and organic foods. It later expanded with an outdoor eating area, a new kitchen, a parking lot, and green space. Seward Café, n.d., box 2, Seward Community Café, Histories, Undated and 1989 file, SCCR.

16. Young and Krogmeier, "History"; Estep, "The Effect of Interorganizational Ties on the Contemporary Consumer Cooperative Movement in Minnesota," p. 26.

17. *Ecology Co-op Newsletter* (Oct. 28, 1971), box 4, Ecology Co-op (Minneapolis, MN), 1970–1972 file, MFCR; Cox, *Storefront Revolution*, p. 45.

18. The co-op would help open another co-op, the Beanery, in south Minneapolis. "History," box 6, Whole Foods (Minneapolis, MN) file, MFCR; Cox, *Storefront Revolution*, p. 42.

19. Cox, *Storefront Revolution*, p. 37; Pledge Announcement, n.d.; and "Grocery Cooperative Proposed for South Minneapolis Corner," *Minneapolis Spokesman*, May 23–29, 1996, box 4, Bryant-Central Co-op (Minneapolis, MN), 1970–1996 file, MFCR.

20. "The Selby Food Co-op," *Changes* 21 (July–Aug. 1972), box 5, Selby Co-op (St. Paul, MN), 1972–1975 file, MFCR; "A Report About Transformation at Selby Food Co-op by Its Co-op Council," n.d., box 5, Selby Co-op (St. Paul, MN), 1972–1975 file, MFCR; Dave Gutknecht, "A Report on Selby," *Scoop* (Aug/Sept. 1975) box 5, Selby Co-op (St. Paul, MN), 1972–1975 file, MFCR.

21. Mimoed Paper, n.d., box 5, Selby Co-op (St. Paul, MN), 1972–1975 file, MFCR.

22. "Mill City Foods," *Changes* 21 (July-Aug. 1972), box 4, Mill City Co-operative Foods (Minneapolis, MN) file, MFCR; Survey, 1976, and "Mill City, Food News and Notes" (late 1974), box 4, Mill City Co-operative Foods (Minneapolis, MN), Correspondence, Flyers, Etc., 1972–1978 file, MFCR. There was also the Indian Nutrition Store on the southside of Minneapolis. "An Indian Nutrition Store (Economic Development # 1)," n. d., box 4, Indian Nutrition Store (Minneapolis, MN), 1974 file, MFCR.

23. North Country Co-op, Co-op Work Study Project Flyer, 1974, box 7, NPCSR; "Food Co-ops," n.d., box 33, file 14, NPCSR.

24. "Food Co-ops," NPCSR; http://www.wedge.coop/about-the-wedge/, accessed Oct. 22, 2010.

25. Cowie, *Stayin' Alive*, p. 12.

26. *12th Ave. People's Co-op Newsletter* (Mar. 1976), box 4, 12th Avenue People's Co-op (Minneapolis, MN), 1976–1978 file, MFCR.

27. Ibid.

28. *12th Ave. People's Coop Newsletter* (July 1978), box 4, 12th Avenue People's Co-op (Minneapolis, MN), 1976–1978 file, MFCR.

29. Ibid.

30. Ed Felien, "What's Happening in the Co-op Movement," Nov. 19, 1975, box 4, Beanery (Minneapolis, MN), 1972–1976 file, MFCR. Eddie Felien, a Marxist scholar from the

University of Minnesota and later member of the Minneapolis City Council, had started an underground newspaper, *Hundred Flowers*, to encourage other people to open their own neighborhood stores. For a response to Felien's criticism of the Co-op Organization, see "Learn from the Political Mistakes and Move Forward. A Response to Eddie Felien's Criticism of the CO," n.d., box 4, The Beanery (Minneapolis, MN), 1972–1976 file, MFCR.

31. Excerpt from *Green Grass Gazette*, Apr. 22, 1975, box 4, Green Grass Co-op Grocery (St. Paul, MN), 1975 file, MFCR; "What's Happening at North Country Co-op?" (Dec. 1975), box 7, North Country Co-op, "Co-op" Wars, Flyers, Statements, & Manifestoes, 1975–1976 file, NCCR.

32. Jeb Cabbage and Emma Evechild, "A Response to the Beanery Paper," Mar. 1975, and Kris, Judy, Michael B., "A recap on 'Jeb' and 'Emma's' response to the beanery paper," n.d., box 4, The Beanery (Minneapolis, MN), 1972–1976 file, MFCR; "Should Our Leaders Subvert Other Coops?" *Powderhorn Food Community Co-op Newsletter* (Jan. 1976), 1973–1994 file, PFCCR. Often the insults bordered on ideological parodies. For example, Jeb and Emma were accused of "thr[owing] a nasty bourgeois-intellectual stone from the unsanitary cesspool of anti-communism." See 'A Recap on 'Jeb' and 'Emma's' Response to the Beanery Paper."

33. *Powderhorn Food Community Co-op Newsletter* (May 5, 1975), box 1, 1973–1994 file, PFCCR. The Policy Review Board (PRB) operated through representatives from each co-op that bought from the People's Warehouse. The All Co-op Assembly would replace the PRB. Estep, "The Effect of Interorganizational Ties on the Contemporary Consumer Cooperative Movement in Minnesota," p. 53.

34. *Powderhorn Food Community Co-op Newsletter* (Sept. 27–28, 1975) and (Jan. 10, 1976), box 1, 1973–1994 file, PFCCR; "What's Happening at North Country Co-op?" Dec. 1975, box 7, North Country Co-op, "Co-op" Wars, Flyers, Statements, & Manifestoes, 1975–1976 file, NCCR.

35. "Should Our Leaders Subvert Other Coops?," *Powderhorn Food Community Co-op Newsletter* (Jan. 1976), box 1, 1973–1994 file, PFCCR. Unfortunately, I have found no biographical information about Lund.

36. Ibid.

37. The People's Warehouse sent trucks of food to the Bryant-Central Co-op in the spring of 1975. Bob Haugen was one organizer on the food truck who accused Moe Burton of self-serving interests in the Bryant-Central Co-op. *Powderhorn Food Community Co-op Newsletter* (Nov. 1975), box 1, 1973–1994 file, PFCCR; "Press Release from People's Warehouse in response to Moe Burton's Running to the Bourgeois Press" and an interview with Linda Janssen of the People's Warehouse and John Ryan of KMSP-TV, Jan. 7, 1976, box 4, Bryant-Central Co-op (Minneapolis, MN), 1970–1996 file, MFCR.

38. *Powderhorn Food Community Co-op Newsletter* (Nov. 1975), box 1, 1973–1994 file, PFCCR.

39. Cox, *Storefront Revolution*, p. 102. Embarrassed by Haugen's antics, the Co-op Organization later "purged" him.

40. Ibid.

41. "Area Co-ops Become Uncooperative; Violence Could Bring Legal Actions," *University of Minnesota Daily*, Jan. 12, 1976, box 4, Mill City Cooperative Foods (Minneapolis, MN) file, MFCR; Cox, *Storefront Revolution*, p. 107.

42. "Note to the Community" and "Meeting Announcement," Jan. 1976, box 7, "Co-op" Wars, Flyers, Statements, & Manifestoes, 1975–1976 file, NCCR.

43. Cox, *Storefront Revolution*, p. 112.

44. "The Co-op Organization in Action; The Subjugation of Powderhorn Co-op," Mar. 19, box 1, Powderhorn Food Community Co-op, Newspaper Clippings, 1975–1995 file;

"Picketing Focuses Co-op Turmoil on Powderhorn Store," *Southside Newspaper*, Mar. 10, 1976, box 1, Powderhorn Food Community Co-op, Flyers (Co-op Wars), 1975–1976 file, PFCCR.

45. Captions from two photographs, *Southside Newspaper*, Apr. 7, 1976, box 1, Powderhorn Food Community Co-op, Newspaper Clippings, 1975–1995 file, PFCCR.

46. *Powderhorn Food Community Co-op Newsletter* (May 1976), box 1, 1973–1994 file, PFCCR.

47. Cox, *Storefront Revolution*, p. 122.

48. Ibid., pp. 122, 124.

49. "Facing Debts, Powderhorn Co-op Seeks Neighborhood Support," no source, n.d., box 1, Powderhorn Food Community Co-op, Newspaper Clippings, 1975–1995 file, PFCCR. By 1985, there were sixteen food co-ops in the Minneapolis area: Anoka Food Co-op, East Calhoun, Harvest Pantry Co-op, Linden Hills Co-op, N.B.C. Foods, North Country Food Co-op, Northside Food Co-op, Park Pantry Co-op, Powderhorn Co-operative Grocery, Rainbow Community Co-operative, St. Luke's Co-operative, Seward Community Co-op, Valley Community Food Co-op, Wedge Community Co-op, West Bank Co-operative, and Whole Foods Co-op. In St. Paul, there were four: Capitol City Co-op, Mississippi Market Co-op, St. Anthony Park Food Co-op, and St. Anthony Park Food Co-op II. List of Food Co-operatives, *Minneapolis Star Tribune*, Mar. 27, 1985, box 5, The Wedge Co-op (Minneapolis, MN) file, MFCR.

50. "History," box 6, Whole Foods (Minneapolis, MN), Board of Directors, 1979–1984 file, MFCR.

51. Whole Foods Board Minutes, Oct. 26, 1981 and Jan. 18, 1982, box 6, Whole Foods (Minneapolis, MN), Board of Directors, 1979–1984 file, MFCR.

52. Board of Directors Report, 1978–1979, box 1, Board of Directors, 1975–1984 file, SCCR; Young and Krogmeier, "History."

53. "Struggle to Survive Pushes Co-ops Closer to Supermarkets," *Minneapolis Star Tribune*, Mar. 27, 1985, box 5, The Wedge Co-op (Minneapolis, MN), Correspondence, Reports, Newspaper Clippings (1976–1996) file, MFCR.

54. Gail Graham, "Collective Management," n.d., box 5, The Wedge Co-op (Minneapolis, MN) file, MFCR; The Wedge Co-op Board Minutes, Oct. 13, 1979, box 5, The Wedge Co-op (Minneapolis, MN), Board of Directors' Minutes, Oct. 1979–June 1981 file, MFCR; Proposal for Wage and Benefit Contract—Fiscal Year, 1981–82, box 5, The Wedge Co-op (Minneapolis, MN), Correspondence, Reports, Newspaper Clippings (1976–1996) file, MFCR.

55. Nancy Mosier, Resignation Letter of Senior Bookkeeper, Mar. 17, 1981, box 5, The Wedge Co-op (Minneapolis, MN), Correspondence, Reports, Newspaper Clippings (1976–1996), MFCR.

56. *Newsletter* (May 29, 1983), box 1, Board of Directors, 1975–1984 file, SCCR. Some workers at the North Country received management training, the co-op secured a bank loan and made structural changes. Then the co-op began to do well. In 1991, the North Country had 225 active members, as well as sixteen coordinators, who all received the same pay and benefits. "People's Bakery, North Country Celebrate 20 Years of Co-operation," *Phillips Community Newspaper*, June 1991, box 7, Newspaper Clippings, 1975–1997 file, NCCR.

57. Young and Krogmeier, "History."

58. Ibid.

59. "Wedge Co-op Has Plans to Expand—Again," *Whittier Globe*, Aug. 1996; "So What's Happening with Wedge Finances?," n.d.; State of the Store Address, Jan. 31, 1980; Board of Director Minutes, Oct. 13, 1980, box 5, The Wedge Co-op (Minneapolis, MN file, MFCR.

60. "Struggle to Survive Pushes Co-ops Closer to Supermarkets," *Minneapolis Star Tribune*, Mar. 27, 1985, box 5, The Wedge Co-op (Minneapolis, MN), Correspondence, Reports, Newspaper Clippings (1976–1996) files, MFCR.

61. "Struggle to Survive Pushes Co-ops Closer to Supermarkets."

62. "Co-op: Customer Base Has Changed," *Minneapolis Star Tribune*, Mar. 27, 1985, box 5, The Wedge Co-op (Minneapolis, MN) file, MFCR.

63. Board Minutes, June 2, 1986, box 1, Board of Directors, 1985–1986 Minutes file, SCCR.

64. Board Minutes, Mar. 1, 1988, box 1, Board of Directors, 1985–1986 Minutes file, SCCR.

65. "People's Bakery, North Country Celebrate 20 Years of Co-operation," *Phillips Community Newspaper*, June, 1991, box 7, North Country Co-op, Newspaper Clippings, 1975–1997 file, NCCR.

66. "Powderhorn Food Co-op Returns to Collective Management," *Southside Pride*, Mar. 1992; "Co-op Takes Steps to Keep Doors Open," *Powderhorn Paper* (Aug. 1994, box 1, Powderhorn Food Community Co-op, Newspaper Clippings, 1975–1995 file, PFCCR. In early 1993, the co-op met with the Minnesota Small Business Development to draft a business plan for long-term goals. In December 1993, it planned to develop a financial committee to work on the budget for operations and for long-term development. Its finances were more stable but the co-op needed more cash flow. By late summer of 1994, sales were steadily declining. Gentle Strength Co-op, "Co-operative Strategic Planning Toward an Evolving Organization," box 2, Board of Directors, 1992, Minutes, Notes, Correspondence file, PFCCR.

67. "Coalition for Co-op Democracy," Announcement, Mar. 1993, box 1, Powderhorn Food Community Co-op, Flyers and Pamphlets, 1985–1994 file, PFCCR.

68. "Powderhorn Co-op Closes After 20 Years," *Southside Pride*, Jan. 1995, box 1, Powderhorn Food Community Co-op, Newspaper Clippings, 1975–1995 file, PFCCR; May 7, 1994 Minutes, box 2, Powderhorn Food Community Co-op, Annual Membership Meetings, 1975–1994 file, PFCCR.

69. "City Food Co-op Outgrows Store," *Minneapolis Star Tribune*, July 1, 1991, box 5, The Wedge Co-op (Minneapolis, MN), Correspondence, Reports, Newspaper Clippings, 1976–1996 file, MFCR. It is not clear how the Wedge Co-op was able to receive state and federal funds.

70. "Sifting the Crap from the Co-op: Sledging the Wedge Pt. 2 and *Profane Existence*, 17 (Sept./Oct. 1992), box 5, The Wedge Co-op (Minneapolis, MN) file, MFCR.

71. "For the Record: 'Granola Wars,'" *City Pages*, Sept. 30, 1992, box 5, The Wedge Co-op (Minneapolis, MN) file, MFCR.

72. Letter to Kris Olsen from North Country Co-op Community, Apr. 25, 199, box 5, North Country Co-op, Correspondence, 1971–1997 file, NCCR; http://www.northcountrycoop.com, accessed Dec. 12, 2010; http://www.starttribune.com/local/minneapolis/11549521.html, accessed Dec. 12, 2010. The DANCe, after serving eleven years as an alternative to the People's Warehouse, was sold to Blooming Prairie Foods of Iowa City. *Co-op Corner* 22 (Jan./Feb. 1989), box 4, East Calhoun Co-op (Minneapolis, MN), 1977–1990 file, MFCR.

73. "Seward Co-operative—Future Planning—Can We Ignore the Future Any Longer" and Jan. 3, 1991 Minutes, box 1, Board of Directors, 1987–1991 Minutes file, SCCR.

74. Gail Graham, "Co-operative Natural Foods. A Report on the Consolidation Effort of Five Twin Cities Consumer Co-ops," (1992?), box 1, Board of Directors, Consolidation Issue, 1989–1993 file, SCCR.

75. http://www.lindenhills.coop/store/history, accessed Dec. 10, 2010; http://www.seward.coop/history, accessed Dec. 10, 2010; http://themix.coop/?q=node/104, accessed Dec.

12, 2010; http://www.msmarket.coop/pdf/AnnualReport2010.pdf, accessed Dec, 12, 2010; http://www.wedge.coop/history/, accessed Dec. 10, 2010; July/Aug. 2010 Report, http://www.themix.coop, July/Aug. 2010, accessed Dec. 10, 2010. http://www.msmarket.co-op/, accessed Dec. 12, 2010. For more about the history of Mississippi Market, see Carolee Colter, "Expansion Case Study: A Near Miss at Mississippi Market," *Cooperative Grocer* 92 (Jan.–Feb. 2001).

76. http://heavytable.com/the-wedge-co-op-wants-fair-fight-regarding-liquor/, accessed Oct. 26, 2010; http://www.tcdailyplanet.net/article/2009/04/14/wedge-vs-trader-joe-minneapolis.html, accessed Oct. 26, 2010; http://www.minnpost.com/cityscape/2012/06/conflicted-over-trader-joes-minneapolis, accessed Sept. 9, 2012.

77. http://www.cooperativegrocer.coop/articles/2003-12-02/Minnesota-fair-trade-wild-rice, accessed Oct. 25, 2010.

78. http://www.wedge.coop/about-the-wedge/, accessed Oct. 22, 2010; http://en.wikipedia.org/wiki/Wedge_Community_Co-op, accessed Oct. 26, 2010; http://www.organicfieldschool.org/about-ofs/vision-and-goals-of-the-organic-field=school, accessed Oct. 26, 2010.

79. http://www.sowthe seedsfund.org, accessed Oct. 26, 2010.

80. Grott, "Why Co-ops Die," p. 1.

81. *Cox, Storefront Revolution*, p. 124.

EPILOGUE

1. The numbers vary; see http://reic.uwcc.wisc.edu/groceries/, accessed Mar. 4, 2011.

2. http://www.cooperativegrocer.coop/aticles/2009-10-06/celebrating-excellence-and-new-co-ops.

3. http://www.cooperativegrocer.coop/articles/2009-01-19/mentoring-startups, accessed Nov. 7, 2010. For assistance on how to start a co-op, see http://www.cooperativegrocer.coop/articles/2009-01-21/500-co-ops-10-years, accessed Dec. 2, 2010.

4. http://medfordfoodcoop,com/minutes-of-the-5-24-2010-board-meeting/, accessed Nov. 23, 2010. For more information about the new co-op, see http://medfordfoodcoop.com; information on the Ashland co-op is available at http://www.ashlandfood.coop/about/about.php, accessed Nov. 30, 2010. Demographic information is found at http://en.wikipedia.org/wiki/Pittsboro,_North_Carolina, accessed Sept. 9, 2012; and http://en.wikipedia.org/wiki/Medford,_Oregon, accessed Sept. 9, 2012.

5. http://www.cooperativegrocer.coop/articles/2004-01-09/can-we-help-build-inner-city-co-ops, accessed Nov. 7, 2010.

6. These calculations rely on the food co-ops affiliated with the National Cooperative Grocers Association.

7. http://www.openforum.com/idea-hub/topics/lifestyle/article/small-business-are-the-green-growth-engine-jen-van-der-meer, accessed Nov. 29, 2010; http://www.grist.org/article/Soybean-counting, accessed Nov. 29, 2010.

8. Huber, "Walmart's Fresh Food Makeover," p. 24. For information about consumer practices of low-income families regarding major durables during the early 1960s, see Caplovitz, *The Poor Pay More*.

9. Huber, "Walmart's Fresh Food Makeover," p. 24.

10. http://www.foodsystemsync.org/interview+zena+nelson, accessed Nov. 6, 2010; http://bookstore.icma.org/Case_Study_6-2_The_South_Bron_P2121.cfm?UserID=49 24097&jsessionid=4e30d263dfed3b767332, accessed Nov. 7, 2010. For more on Zena Nelson, see http://www.womenmakingmoves.org/2009/03/zena-nelson.html and http://www.womenandbiz.com/2007/12/21/south-bronx-food-cooperative/, accessed Dec. 2, 2010.

11. http://www.sbxfc.org/about_mission.htm, accessed Dec. 2, 2010; http://www.dai lygotham.com/blog/mole333/south_bronx_food_co_op, accessed Dec. 2, 2010; http:// www.nytimes.com/2007/11/11/nyregion/11co-op.html?_r=1&ref=park_slope_food_ coop, accessed Dec. 2, 2010.

12. On its closure, see http://motthavenherald.com/2010/12/14/south-bron-food-co-op-closes-its-doors/, accessed Mar. 1, 2011. Students who wanted to join the South Bronx team paid a $60 membership fee and worked one three-hour shift per month. The co-op rented from a community center for $60 per month. A topic of much debate has been whether co-ops can thrive in inner cities. See http://www.cooperativegrocer.coop/arti cles/2004-01-09/can-we-help-build-inner-city-co-ops, accessed Dec. 2, 2010.

13. http://www.columbiaspectator.com/2009/04/09/affordable-sustainability-found-down-south, accessed Nov. 7, 2010.

14. http://www.columbiaspectator.com/2009/04/09/affordable-sustainability-found-down-south, accessed Nov. 7, 2010; http://www.columbiajournalist.org/www/39-a-healthy-sop-in-the-south-bronx/story, accessed Nov. 9, 2010.

15. http://upsidedownworld.org/main/venezuela-archives-35/2441-chavez-fuels-the-south-bronx, accessed Nov. 8, 2010. For more information about the Green Worker Coopera-tives and other cooperative efforts, see http://www.yesmagazine.org/issues/the-new-economy/ worker-co-ops-green-and-just-jobs-you-can-own, accessed Nov. 9, 2010.

16. http://urbanmogullife.com/2010/06/28/for-a-healthier-bronx-a-farm-of-their-own-swipe/, accessed Nov. 30, 2010; http://motthavenherald.com/2010/12/14/south-bronx-food-co-op-closes-its-doors/ accessed Mar. 29, 2011.

17. Berk received the Robert Redford Center's Art of Activism Award for his work with the co-op. See http://www.mandelafoods.com/html/about.html, accessed Nov. 11, 2010; http://www.sfbg.com/pixel_vision?2010/06/04/mandela-food-cooperative-gets-redford-nod, accessed Nov. 8, 2010.; http://www.sfbg.com/2012/05/16/our-2012-small-business-awards?page=0,2, accessed Sept. 9, 2012.

18. http://sfbayview.com/2009/soul-food-co-op-an-interview-wit-co-owner-yasser/, accessed Nov. 7, 2010.

19. http://indianalivinggreen.com/local-foods-a-wine/co-op-crqzy, accessed Nov. 2, 2010. In addition to the well-known Bloomingfoods, there are food co-ops in Fort Wayne, Rich-mond, Goshen, Paoli, and Evansville. New ones are starting in Indianapolis, Mooresville, South Bend, Lafayette, and Terre Haute. Indianapolis residents opened Pogue's Run Co-op in 2011. It will not only provide healthy foods but pay a living wage to producers. A corner grocery store in a poorer neighborhood, the co-op hopes to educate the community about nutrition and eating better through cooking classes. It also wants to get involved with urban farming and community gardens. See http://indianalivinggreen.com/local-foods-a-wine/co-op-crqzy, accessed Nov. 2, 2010; http://www.nuvo.net/indianapolis/pogues-run-grocer-now-open/Content?oid=1985286, accessed Sept. 9, 2012.

20. http://www.organicconsumers,org/articles/article_12097.cfm,accessed Dec. 2, 2010.

21. http://www.cooperativegrocer.coop/articles/2009-01-20/new-developments-food-co-op-500, accessed Nov. 2, 2010; http://lostrivercoop.com/bopard.html, accessed Nov. 4, 2010; http://www.bloomingtonalternative.com/articles/2005/10/02/7838, accessed Nov. 2, 2010; http://www.wvpubcast.org/newsarticle.aspx?id=1261, accessed Nov. 2, 2010.

22. http://www.cooperativegrocer.coop/articles/2009-01-20/new-developments-food-co-op-500, accessed Nov. 2, 2010; http://www.organicconsumers.org/articles/article_12097.cfm, accessed Oct. 28, 2010; Aug. 2008, Apr. 2008 newsletters; Feb.-Mar. 2010 newsletter; http:// www.lostrivercoop.com/, accessed Sept. 9, 2012.

23. http://wwwbloomingfoods.coop/index.php?option = com_content&task=view& id=104&Itemid=37, accessed Nov. 2, 2010; May, 2009 newsletter; http://lostrivercoop.com/

254 NOTES TO PAGES 196–201

about.html, accessed Oct. 30, 2010; http://lostrivercoop.com/community2.html, accessed Oct. 28, 2010; *Lost River Market & Deli Newsletters* (Nov. 2007, Apr. 2008, Aug. 2008).

24. *Lost River Market & Deli Newsletter* (Oct. 2008) and (Summer 2010).

25. http://www.denverpost.com/news/ci_11047297, accessed Nov. 8, 2010; http://www.people/archive/article/0,,20271120,00.html, accessed Nov. 8, 2010. This example defies the idea that large startup budgets and feasibility studies are necessary. See http://www.cooperativegrocer.cvoop/articles/2010-10-15/changing-face-co-op-development, accessed Nov. 7, 2010.

26. Fresh Connections, *The Scoop Newsletter* (Mar. 2009); http://www.freshcon nectionscoop.com/producers, accessed Nov. 8, 2010; http://www.freshconnection-scoop.com/news/, accessed Nov. 8, 2010. Demographic information is found at http://en.wikipedia.org/wiki/Algona,_Iowa, accessed Sept. 9, 2012.

27. http://www.mooncoop.com, accessed Dec. 2, 2010; http://www.mooncoop.com/downloads/newsletters/MoonNewsletterMay08, accessed Dec. 2, 2010; Phone interview, Tana Richards, Store Manager, Moon Co-op, Sept. 9, 2012.

28. http://locals-thefilm.blogspot.com, accessed Nov. 8, 2010. http://www.realfoodnet-work.org/real-food-coop.html, accessed Nov. 8, 2010; http://www.realfoodnetwork.org/school-garden.html, accessed Nov. 8, 2010.

29. http://www.littleoncoop.org/about_2010.php, accessed Nov. 8, 2010; http://www.chathamrealfoodcoop.net/Co-op%20Newsletter.04.12.pdf, accessed Sept. 9, 2012; http://www.littletoncoop.org/about.php, accessed Sept. 9. 2012.

30. http://www.troyfoodcoop.com/benefits.php, accessed Nov. 12, 2010; http://www.timesunion.com/local/article/Food-co-op-goes-under-2221306.php, accessed Sept. 9, 2012.

31. http://www.fiddleheadsfood.coop/location.htm, accessed Nov. 8, 2010; newsletter (Winter 2011), http://www.fiddleheadsfood.coop/, accessed Sept. 9, 2012.

32. http://eaglerockcoop.org/index.php?section=10, accessed Nov. 8, 2010; http://www.eaglerockcoop.blogspot.com, accessed Nov. 8, 2010.

33. http://www.cooperativegrocer.coop/articles/2010-10-05/harvest-moonrise, accessed Nov. 9, 2010.

34. http://www.greatbasinfood.coop/content/view/32/49/, accessed Nov. 11, 2010.

35. http://www.oregonlive.com/foodday/index.ssf/2008/09/coop.html, accessed Nov. 11, 2009; http://www.albertagrcoery.coop/about/, accessed Nov. 4, 2010.

36. Alberta Cooperative Grocery, Annual Reports 2008 and 2009, are available at http://www.albertagrocery.coop/about/reports/, accessed Dec. 2, 2010. According to their 2009 Annual Report, the co-op is a "sustainable" business in terms of environmental, social, and economic wellness.

37. The co-op now has 700 members. Like other co-ops, the Dill Pickle Food Co-op supports local farmers, such as Genesis Growers from Kankakee, Illinois. http://dillpickle foodcoop.org/newsletter, accessed Nov. 12, 2010; http://dillpicklefoodcoop.org/member also a blog: http://dillpicklefoodcoop/blogsopt.com, which accessed Oct. 22, 2010; http://homes.point2.com/Neighborhood/US/Illinois/Cook-County/Chicago/Bucktown-Demographics.aspx, accessed Nov. 29, 2010.

38. http://www.cooperativegrocer.coop/articles/2004-01-07/suggestion-co-op-survival, accessed Nov. 7, 2010. On Park Slope Co-op's sense of community, see also http://www.crainsnewyork.com/article/20100418/REG/304189959, accessed Dec. 2, 2010.

39. Schudson, "The Troubling Equivalence of Citizens and Consumer," p. 200.

40. Elkinton, Hailes, and Makower, "The Green Consumer," p. 334. Green consump-tion still relies on the traditional economic market, based on supply and demand, and growth in sales. Some consider this "ecologically dangerous" because no consideration is

given to the environmental impact. Smith, *The Myth of Green Marketing*, pp. 72, 77, 91. John Button puts it this way: "Green consumerism means much more than just changing products. It means questioning both the nature and the volume of consumption. It means reassessing our roles as individuals in reinforcing or transforming the fundamental inequalities in today's world economy." Button, quoted in Smith, *The Myth of Green Marketing*, p. 93. See also Durning, "An Environmentalist's Perspective on Consumer Society," pp. 78–81; and http://www.nytimes.com/2011/02/09/opinion/09Little.html?-r=1&emc=eta1&pagewanted, accessed Mar. 22, 2011.

41. Guthman, *Agrarian Dreams*, pp. 2, 14, 21; Pollan, "Naturally," pp. 30–37, 58, 63.

42. http://www.cooperativegrocer.coop/articles/2008-12-27/3-billion-sales-2020-what-does-it-take?, accessed Nov. 7, 2010.

43. http://www.cooperativegrocer.coop/articles/2009-07-02/all-atwitter-seattle, accessed Nov. 7, 2010. One co-op, Ellensburg Food Co-op in Kittitas County, Washington, is an online store that is incorporated and subscribes to the Rochdale principles. Online co-ops might offer more accessibility but how can they help to build and sustain community? And how is it different from a CSA? http://dailyrecordnews.com/top_story/ellensburg-food-co-op-offers-chance-to-buy-grow-and/article_e72c232c-32fb-11e0-8ff3-001cc4c03286.html, accessed Mar. 6, 2011.

Bibliography

ARCHIVES

Adamant Food Co-operative, Adamant, Vermont
    Private Records
Amherst College, Special Collections
    Theses Collection
Chicago History Museum
    Annabelle Prescott Papers
Cornell University, Ithaca, New York
    Ithaca Consumer Co-operative Society Records
Hanover Consumer Co-operative Society, Hanover, New Hampshire
    Hanover Consumer Co-operative Society Records
History Center, Ithaca, New York
    Community Activism Collection
    James L. Gibbs, Southside Community Center Collection
    Ithaca Consumer Co-operative Society Collection
    Sprouts! Collection
La Montanita Coop, Albuquerque, New Mexico
    Private Records
Lake Erie College, Special Collections
    Lake Erie College Collection
Minnesota Historical Society, St. Paul, Minnesota
    Chris Olsen Papers
    Minnesota Food Co-operatives Records
    North Country Co-operative Records
    Powderhorn Food Community Co-operative Records
Newberry Library, Chicago
    Cooperative Trading Company, Twenty Years of Cooperative Trading
        in *Waukegan, Illinois, 1911–1931*. Waukegan: Cooperative Trading Company,
        1931.
    Northern States' Co-operative League, *Yearbooks*, 1925–1928
North Coast Co-operative, Arcata, California
    Private Records
Putney Food Co-operative, Putney, Vermont
    Private Records
Seattle, Washington Public Library
    Business Archives
State Historical Society of Iowa, Iowa City
    Blooming Prairie, Inc., Records
    New Pioneer Co-operative Society Records
University of Chicago, Regenstein Library
    Central Cooperative Wholesale, *Yearbooks*, 1937–1956
University of Chicago, Special Collections
    Chicago Foreign Language Press Survey Records

Hyde Park Co-operative Society Papers
Julius Rosenwald Papers
Henry C. Simons Papers
University of Washington, Seattle
Charles R. Coe Papers
Irwin R. Hogenauer Papers
Waukegan Historical Society, Waukegan, Illinois
Cooperative Trading Company, Waukegan, Papers
Wisconsin Historical Society, University of Wisconsin, Madison
Pamphlet Collection

JOURNALS AND MAGAZINES

Consumers' Cooperation
Co-operation
Cooperative Grocer (http://www.cooperativegrocer.coop/cg_sub.html)
Northern States Co-operator

Primary and Secondary Sources

"1,000 Co-operators at Cloquet." *Co-operation* 12 (July 1926): 142–143.
Anders, Jentri. *Beyond Counterculture. The Community of Mateel.* Pullman: Washington State University Press, 1990.
Anderson, Henry P. *The Bracero Program in California.* New York: Arno Press, 1976.
Anderson, Mary Siler. *Whatever Happened to the Hippies.* San Pedro, CA: R & E Miles, 1990.
Anderson, Oscar Edward, Jr. *Refrigeration in America. A History of a New Technology and its Impact.* Princeton: Princeton University Press, 1953.
Anderson, Ryan K. "Lumbee Kinship, Community, and the Success of the Red Banks Mutual Association." *American Indian Quarterly* 23 (Spring 1999): 39–58.
Anderson, Terry H. *The Movement and the Sixties.* New York: Oxford University Press, 1995.
Angevine, Erma. "The Development of Consumer Education in the Classroom." In *Consumer Activists. They Made A Difference. A History of Consumer Action Related by Leaders in the Consumer Movement,* ed. National Consumer Committee for Research and Education, 259–264. New York: Consumers Union Foundation, 1982.
——. "The Roots of Consumer Cooperatives in the U.S." In *Consumer Activists. They Made A Difference. A History of Consumer Action Related by Leaders in the Consumer Movement,* ed. National Consumer Committee for Research and Education, 19–30. New York: Consumers Union Foundation, 1982.
——. "Florence C. Parker—A Beacon Light." In Joseph G. Knapp and Associates, *Great American Cooperators. Biographical Sketches of 101 Major Pioneers in Cooperative Development,* 379–382. Washington, DC: American Institute of Cooperation, 1967.
Angevine, Erma, with Sarah H. Newman. "The National Consumers League: New Directions, 1940–1980." In *Consumer Activists. They Made A Difference. A History of Consumer Action Related by Leaders in the Consumer Movement,* ed. National Consumer Committee for Research and Education, 361–365. New York: Consumers Union Foundation, 1982.

Arra, Esa. *The Finns in Illinois.* Trans. Andrew I. Brask. Waukegan: Finnish-American Historical Society of Illinois, 1971.

Auerbach, Jerold S. "The La Follette Committee: Labor and Civil Liberties in the New Deal." *Journal of American History* 51 (Dec. 1964): 435–459.

Baker, Jacob. "Self-Help Cooperatives and the Consumer Movement." *Consumers' Co-operation* 21 (Mar. 1935): 66–68.

Baker, James C. "The International Infant Formula Controversy: A Dilemma in Corporate Social Responsibility." *Journal of Business Ethics* 4 (1985): 181–190.

Balch, Emily Greene. "Why Co-operation Is Not Enough." *Co-operation* 10 (Nov. 1925): 208–210.

Barclay, Wade Crawford. "Cooperation Advances in a Mid-West Community." *Consumers' Cooperation* 23 (Apr. 1937): 56–60.

Bari, Judi. *Timber Wars.* Monroe, ME: Common Courage Press, 1994.

Bathory-Kitsz, Dennis. *Country Stores of Vermont.* Charleston, SC: History Press, 2009.

Beach, Patricia. *A Good Forest for Dying. The Tragic Death of a Young Man on the Front Lines of the Environmental Wars.* New York: Doubleday, 2003.

Belasco, Warren J. *Appetite for Change. How the Counterculture Took on the Food Industry.* 2nd ed. Ithaca: Cornell University Press, 2007.

Belasco, Warren, and Roger Horowitz, eds. *Food Chains. From Farmyard to Shopping Cart.* Philadelphia: University of Pennsylvania Press, 2009.

Belasco, Warren, and Philip Scranton, eds. *Food Nations. Selling Taste in Consumer Societies.* New York and London: Routledge, 2002.

Benson, Anne Giles, and Frank Adams. *To Know for Real. Royce S. Pitkin and Goddard College.* Adamant, VT: Adamant Press, 1987.

Berry, Wendell. *A Continuous Harmony: Essays Cultural and Agricultural.* New York: Harcourt Brace Jovanovich, 1972.

Bloodworth, William A., Jr. *Upton Sinclair.* Boston: Twayne Publishers, 1977.

Bluestone, Barry. "Foreword." In *Beyond the Ruins. The Meanings of Deindustrialization,* ed. Jefferson Cowie and Joseph Heathcott, vii–xiii. Ithaca: Cornell University Press, 2003.

Bolles, Joshua K. *The People's Business. The Progress of Consumer Cooperatives in America.* New York: Harper & Brothers, 1942.

Borsodi, Ralph. *This Ugly Civilization.* New York: Simon and Schuster, 1929.

Bowen, E. R. *The Cooperative Road to Abundance. The Alternative to Monopolism and Communism.* New York: Henry Schuman, 1953.

Bowlby, Rachel. *Carried Away. The Invention of Modern Shopping.* New York: Columbia University Press, 2001.

Bramwell, Anna. *Ecology in the 20th Century. A History.* New Haven, CT: Yale University Press, 1969.

Braunstein, Peter, and Michael William Doyle, eds. *Imagine Nation. The American Counterculture of the 1960s and 1970s.* New York and London: Routledge, 2002.

Brinkley, Alan. *The End of Reform: New Deal Liberalism in Recession and War.* New York: Alfred A. Knopf, 1995.

Brown, Marc. "Building an Alternative: People's Food Cooperative in Southeast Portland." *Oregon Historical Quarterly* 112, no. 3 (2011): 298–321.

Buder, Stanley. *Capitalizing on Change. A Social History of American Business.* Chapel Hill: University of North Carolina, 2009.

Burton, Cynthia, Mike Knepler, Mark Looney, and Joe Wrobel, eds. *Non-Profit Foods Stores. A Resource Manual.* Washington, DC: Strongforce, n.d.

Campbell, Wallace J. "Growth of Cooperatives: The Cooperative League of USA, Co-operatives in Housing and in International Relief." In *Consumer Activists. They Made A Difference. A History of Consumer Action Related by Leaders in the Consumer Movement*, ed. National Consumer Committee for Research and Education, 31–44. New York: Consumers Union Foundation, 1982.

Caplovitz, David. *The Poor Pay More. Consumer Practices of Low-Income Families*. Glencoe, IL: Free Press, 1963.

Cappel, Constance. *Utopian Colleges*. New York: Peter Lang, 1999.

Carson, Rachel. *Silent Spring*. Greenwich, CT: Fawcett Publications, 1962.

Case, John, and Rosemary C. R. Taylor, eds. *Co-ops, Communes & Collectives*. New York: Pantheon Books, 1979.

Caspary, William R. *Dewey on Democracy*. Ithaca, NY: Cornell University Press, 2000.

Chateauvert, Melinda. *Marching Together: Women of the Brotherhood of Sleeping Car Porters*. Urbana: University of Illinois Press, 1998.

Cheel, Mabel. "A Journey of Four Weeks to Some Co-operative Centers in the U.S.A." *Northern States Co-operator* 1 (Dec. 1925): 44–46.

Cohen, Lizabeth. *A Consumers' Republic. The Politics of Mass Consumption in Postwar America*. New York: Vintage Books, 2003.

——. *Making a New Deal. Industrial Workers in Chicago, 1919–1939*. New York: Cambridge University Press, 1990.

Commons, John R., Ulrich B. Phillips, Eugene A. Gilmore, Helen L. Sumner, and John B. Andrews, eds. *A Documentary History of American Industrial Society*. Vol. 6. New York: Russell & Russell, 1958.

Conover, Milton. "The Rochdale Principles in American Co-operative Associations." *Western Political Quarterly* 12 (Mar. 1959): 111–122.

"Consumer Co-op Progress in 1941." *Consumers' Cooperation* 28 (Jan. 1942): 9–14.

"Consumers' Societies in 1929." *Co-operation* 17 (Mar. 1931): 48.

Cooley, Oscar. *Behind the Bricks and Mortar … The Story of the Central Cooperative Wholesale*. Superior, WI: Central Cooperative Wholesale, 1939.

Co-op Handbook Collective. *The Food Co-op Handbook*. Boston: Houghton Mifflin, 1975.

"Co-op Legislation Killed." *Consumers' Cooperation* 23 (Sept. 1937): 140.

Cooper, Donald H., and Paul O. Mohn. *The Greenbelt Cooperative: Success and Decline*. Berkeley: University of California, Center for Cooperatives, 1992.

"Cooperative Supersedes Private Business." *Consumers' Cooperation* 21 (June 1935): 109–112.

Coppin, Clayton Anderson, and Jack C. High. *The Politics of Purity: Harvey Washington Wiley and the Origins of Federal Food Policy*. Ann Arbor: University of Michigan Press, 1999.

Cornford, Daniel A. *Workers and Dissent in the Redwood Empire*. Philadelphia: Temple University Press, 1987.

Cosline, Hugh. *An Adventure in Cooperation. A Brief History of the Cooperative Consumers Society of Ithaca, 1939–1969. New York*. Ithaca: Arnold Printing Company, 1970.

Cotterill, Ronald, ed. *Consumer Food Cooperatives*. Danville, IL: Interstate Printers and Publishers, 1984.

Cowie, Jefferson. *Stayin' Alive: The 1970s and the Last Days of the Working Class*. New York: New Press, 2010.

Cowie, Jefferson, and Joseph Heathcott, eds. *Beyond the Ruins. The Meanings of Deindustrialization*. Ithaca: Cornell University Press, 2003.

Cowling, Ellis. *Co-operatives in America: Their Past, Present and Future*. New York: Coward-McCann, 1938.

Cox, Craig. *Storefront Revolution. Food Co-ops and the Counterculture.* New Brunswick, NJ: Rutgers University Press, 1994.

Crews, C. R. *Can We Establish a Consumer Society?* Minneapolis: State Cooperative League, 1936.

Cummins, Ronnie, Organic Consumers Association. "Hazards of Genetically Engineered Foods and Crops: Why We Need A Global Moratorium." In *Fast Food Nation: The Dark Side of the All-American Meal,* ed. Eric Schlosser, 79–90. Boston: Houghton Mifflin, 2001.

Curhan, Ronald C., and Edward G. Wertheim. "Consumer Food Buying Cooperatives Revisited: A Comparison from 1971 to 1974." *Journal of Retailing* 51 (Winter 1975–1976): 22–32, 87.

——. "Consumer Food Buying Cooperatives—A Market Examined." *Journal of Retailing* 48 (Winter 1972–1973): 28–39.

Daniel, Pete. *Toxic Drift: Pesticides and Health in the Post-World War II South.* Baton Rouge: Louisiana State University Press, 2005.

Daniels, John. *Cooperation—An American Way.* New York: Covici Froede, 1938.

Darling, Arthur B. "The Workingmen's Party in Massachusetts, 1833–1834." *American Historical Review* 29 (Oct. 1923): 81–86.

Dasmann, Raymond F. *The Destruction of California.* New York: Macmillan, 1965.

Davis, Henry. "How Success Followed Failure." *Consumers' Cooperation* 22 (Apr. 1936): 56–59.

Deutsch, Tracey. *Building a Housewife's Paradise: Gender, Politics, and American Grocery Stores in the Twentieth Century.* Chapel Hill: University of North Carolina Press, 2010.

Dieckmann, Jane Marsh. *A Short History of Tompkins County.* Ithaca, NY: DeWitt Historical Society of Tompkins County, 1986.

"Do the A. & P. Stores Make Money?" *Co-operation* 10 (Aug. 1924): 145–146.

Dobson, Andrew, ed. *The Green Reader. Essays Toward a Sustainable Society.* San Francisco: Mercury House, 1991.

Doussard, Marc, Jamie Peck, and Nik Theodore. "After Deindustrialization: Uneven Growth and Economic Inequality in 'Postindustrial' Chicago." *Economic Geography* 85 (2009): 183–207.

Drake, St. Clair. *Churches and Voluntary Associations Among Negroes in Chicago.* Chicago: Works Public Administration, 1940.

Duffey, Patrick. "Oneida Grocery Co-op Boosts Community: Help Keep More Money on Reservation—Oneida American Indian Tribe." *Rural Cooperatives* (Jan.–Feb. 2003). http://www.rurdev.usda.gov/rbs/pub/jan03/boosts.html.

Durning, Alan. "An Environmentalist's Perspective on Consumer Society." In *Consumer Society in American History: A Reader,* ed. Lawrence B. Glickman, 78–81. Ithaca: Cornell University Press, 1999.

Elkinton, John, Julia Hailes, and Joel Makower. "The Green Consumer." In *Consumer Society in American History: A Reader,* ed. Lawrence B. Glickman, 333–337. Ithaca: Cornell University Press, 1999.

Estep, Rhoda Elaine. "The Effect of Interorganizational Ties on the Contemporary Consumer Cooperative Movement in Minnesota." Ph.D. diss., University of Minnesota, 1979.

Eversley, Bradwell, Sean. "Always Room at the Top: Black Students and Educational Policy in Ithaca, NY." Ph.D. diss., Cornell University, 2009.

Fairfield, Paul. *Why Democracy?* Albany: State University of New York Press, 2008.

Farber, David. "The Intoxicated State/Illegal Nation: Drugs in the Sixties Counterculture." In *Imagine Nation: The American Counterculture of the 1960s and 1970s,* ed. Peter Braunstein and Michael William Doyle, 17–40. New York and London: Routledge, 2002.

Feinberg, Samuel. *What Makes Shopping Centers Tick*. New York: Fairchild, 1960.

Fink, Leon. *Workingmen's Democracy: The Knights of Labor and American Politics*. Urbana: University of Illinois Press, 1985.

Floersch, Barbara. "Adamant Co-operative Store Celebrates 50 Years." *CV Magazine* (Winter 1985/1986): 22–25.

Foner, Philip S. *History of the Labor Movement in the United States*. Vols. 1 & 2. New York: International Publishers, 1955, rpt. 1988.

Ford, James. *Co-operation in New England. Urban and Rural*. New York: Survey Associates, 1913.

Fox, Richard Wightman. "Epitaph for Middletown. Robert S. Lynd and the Analysis of Consumer Culture." In *The Culture of Consumption: Critical Essays in American History, 1880–1980*, ed. Richard Wightman Fox and T. J. Jackson Lears, 101–142. New York: Pantheon Books, 1983.

Fox, Richard Wightman, and T. J. Jackson Lears, eds. *The Culture of Consumption: Critical Essays in American History, 1880–1980*. New York: Pantheon Books, 1983.

Frank, Dana. *Purchasing Power. Consumer Organizing, Gender, and the Seattle Labor Movement, 1919–1929*. New York: Cambridge University Press, 1994.

Freidel, Frank. *The New Deal in Vermont. Its Impact and Aftermath*. New York: Garland, 1979.

Freyfogle, Eric T., ed. *Agrarianism. Land, Culture, and the Community of Life*. Washington, DC: Island Press, 2001.

Friedman, Monroe. *Consumer Boycotts: Effecting Change Through the Marketplace and the Media*. New York: Routledge, 1999.

Galarza, Ernesto. *Merchants of Labor. The Mexican Bracero Store*. Charlotte, NC: McNally & Loftin, 1964.

Gamboa, Erasmo. *Mexican Labor and World War II: Braceros in the Pacific Northwest, 1942–1947*. Austin: University of Texas Press, 1990.

Gerstle, Gary. "The Protean Character of American Liberalism." *American Historical Review* 99 (Oct. 1994): 1043–1073.

Glickman, Lawrence B. *Buying Power: A History of Consumer Activism in America*. Chicago: University of Chicago Press, 2009.

———. "The Strike in the Temple of Consumption: Consumer Activism and Twentieth-Century American Culture." *Journal of American History* 88 (June 2001): 99–128.

———. *A Living Wage: American Workers and the Making of a Consumer Society*. Ithaca: Cornell University Press, 1997.

Glickman, Lawrence, ed. *Consumer Society in American History: A Reader*. Ithaca: Cornell University Press, 1999.

Gorman, William. "W. E. B. DuBois and His Work." *Fourth International* 11 (May–June 1950): 80–86.

Gosse, Van. *Rethinking the New Left: An Interpretive History*. New York: Palgrave Macmillan, 2005.

Greer, William, with John A. Logan and Paul S. Willis. *America the Bountiful: How the Supermarket Came to Main Street. An Oral History*. Washington, DC: Food Marketing Institute in Cooperation with Beatrice Companies, 1986.

Gregory, James N. *American Exodus: The Dust Bowl Migration and Okie Culture in California*. New York: Oxford University Press, 1988.

Guthman, Julie. *Agrarian Dreams: The Paradox of Organic Farming in California*. Berkeley: University of California Press, 2004.

Gutknecht, Dave. "Development Directions Part 1: Turning Points and Lessons." *Cooperative Grocer* 18 (Aug.–Sept. 1988). http://www.cooperativegrocer.coop/articles/index.php?id=47.

Hall, John Philip. "The Knights of St. Crispin in Massachusetts, 1869–1878." *Journal of Economic History* 18 (June 1958): 161–175.

Hamilton, Shane. *Trucking Country: The Road to America's Walmart Economy*. Princeton: Princeton University Press, 2008.

Harris, David. *The Last Stand: The War Between Wall Street and Main Street over California's Ancient Redwoods*. New York: Times Book, Random House, 1995.

Harris, Emerson P. *Co-operation: The Hope of the Consumer*. New York: Macmillan, 1918.

Hawley, Ellis W. *The New Deal and the Problem of Monopoly. A Study in Economic Ambivalence*. Princeton: Princeton University Press, 1966.

Hawthorne, Fran. *Inside the FDA. The Business and Politics Behind the Drugs We Take and the Food We Eat*. Hoboken, NJ: John Wiley & Sons, 2005.

Hazlett, Maril. "'Woman vs. Man vs. Bugs': Gender and Popular Ecology in Early Reactions to Silent Spring." *Environmental History* 9 (2004): 701–729.

Henderson, Sidney. "The Co-operative Training School." *Co-operation* 10 (Feb. 1924): 24–26.

Holyoake, George Jacob. *Self-Help by the People. The History of the Rochdale Pioneers, 1844–1892*. 10th ed. London: G. Allen & Unwin; New York: C. Scribner's Son, 1893.

Horowitz, Daniel. *The Morality of Spending: Attitudes Toward the Consumer Society in America, 1975–1940*. Chicago: Ivan R. Dee, 1992.

Houston, Dorothy. "The Teaching of Cooperation in the Public Schools." *Consumers' Cooperation* 24 (July 1938): 103–107.

"How One Cooperative Closed A Chain Store." *Co-operation* 14 (Nov. 1928): 210.

Howe, Frederick C. *Denmark: The Cooperative Way*. New York: Coward-McCann, 1936.

Hoyt, Ann. "The Renaissance of Consumer Food Cooperatives: Sources of Growth, 1960–1980." In *Consumer Food Cooperatives*, ed. Ronald Cotterill, 1–37. Danville, IL: Interstate Printers and Publishers, 1984.

Huber, Bridget. "Walmart's Fresh Food Makeover." *Nation* 293 (Oct. 3, 2011): 22–27.

Hunter, Beatrice Trum. *Consumer Beware! Your Food and What's Been Done With It*. New York: Simon and Schuster, 1971.

Hyde Park-Kenwood Community Conference. *Hyde Park-Kenwood. A Guide to an Unusual Community*. Chicago: Hyde Park-Kenwood Community Conference, n.d.

Imhoff, Dan. "Linking Tables to Farms." In *Agrarianism. Land, Culture, and the Community of Life*, ed. Eric T. Freyfogle, 15–28. Washington, DC: Island Press, 2001.

Jacobs, Meg. *Pocketbook Politics. Economic Citizenship in Twentieth-Century America*. Princeton: Princeton University Press, 2005.

———. "Pocketbook Politics. Democracy and the Market in Twentieth-Century America." In *The Democratic Experiment. New Directions in American Political History*, ed. Meg Jacobs, William J. Novak, and Julian Zelizer, 250–275. Princeton: Princeton University Press, 2003.

Jacobs, Meg, William J. Novak, and Julian Zelizer, eds. *The Democratic Experiment. New Directions in American Political History*. Princeton: Princeton University Press, 2003.

Jacobson, George. "Shall We Establish a Cooperators' College in the Northwest?" *Co-operation* 18 (June 1932): 104–106.

Jenkins, J. Craig. *The Politics of Insurgency. The Farm Workers Movement in the 1960s.* New York: Columbia University Press, 1985.

Kallen, Horace M. *The Decline and Rise of the Consumer.* New York: D. Appleton-Century, 1936.

——. "The Philosophy of Cooperation." *Consumers' Cooperation* 22 (Dec. 1936): 199–201.

Kammen, Carol. *Ithaca: A Brief History.* Charleston, SC: History Press, 2008.

Kane, R. James. "Populism, Progressivism, and Pure Food." *Agricultural History* 38 (July 1964): 161–166.

Keillor, Steven J. *Cooperative Commonwealth: Co-ops in Rural Minnesota, 1859–1939.* St. Paul: Minnesota Historical Society Press, 2000.

Kenner, Robert. "Exploring the Corporate Powers Behind the Way We Eat." In *Food, Inc. How Industrial Food is Making Us Sicker, Fatter and Poorer—And What You Can Do*, ed. Karl Weber, 27–40. Philadelphia: PublicAffairs, 2009.

Kercher, Leonard C., Vant W. Kebker, and Wilfred C. Leland, Jr. *Consumers' Cooperatives in the Northern Central States.* Minneapolis: University of Minnesota Press, 1941.

Kern. Louis J. *An Ordered Love. Sex Roles and Sexuality in Victorian Utopias—the Shakers, the Mormons, and the Oneida Community.* Chapel Hill: University of North Carolina Press, 1981.

Kingsolver, Barbara, with Steven L. Hopp and Camille Kingsolver. *Animal, Vegetable, Miracle: A Year of Food Life.* New York: HarperCollins, 2007.

Knapp, Joseph G. *The Advance of American Cooperative Enterprise, 1920–1945.* Danville, IL: Interstate Printers & Publishers, 1973.

——. *The Rise of American Cooperative Enterprise: 1620–1920.* Danville, IL: Interstate Printers & Publishers, 1969.

Knapp, Joseph G., and Associates. *Great American Cooperators. Biographical Sketches of 101 Major Pioneers in Cooperative Development.* Washington, DC: American Institute of Cooperation, 1967.

Knepper, Cathy D. *Greenbelt, Maryland. A Living Legacy of the New Deal.* Baltimore, MD: Johns Hopkins University Press, 2001.

Knupfer, Anne Meis. *The Chicago Black Renaissance and Women's Activism.* Urbana: University of Illinois Press, 2006.

——. "The Urban and Rural Reform Activities of Lilian Wyckoff Johnson (1864 to 1956)." *Journal of East Tennessee History* 77 (2005): 1–27.

Lasch, Christopher. *The Culture of Narcissism. American Life in an Age of Diminishing Expectations.* New York: W.W. Norton, 1978.

——. *The Agony of the American Left.* New York: Vintage Books, 1968.

Lears, T. J. Jackson. "From Salvation to Self-Realization: Advertising and the Therapeutic Roots of the Consumer Culture, 1880–1930." In *The Culture of Consumption: Critical Essays in American History, 1880–1980*, ed. Richard Wightman Fox and T. J. Jackson Lears, 1–38. New York: Pantheon Books, 1983.

Leikin, Steve. *The Practical Utopians. American Workers and the Cooperative Movement in the Gilded Age.* Detroit: Wayne State University Press, 2005.

"Letter from the Acting Chairman of the Federal Trade Commission." In *Chain Stores. Final Report on the Chain-Stores Investigation*, 8–9. Washington, DC: US Government Printing Office, 1935.

Levenstein, Harvey A. *Revolution at the Table: The Transformation of the American Diet.* New York: Oxford University Press, 1988.

Lewis, E. St. Elmo. "A Critique of Consumer Cooperative Theory and Practice." *Annals of the American Academy of Political and Social Science* 191 (May 1937): 192–201.

Lipsitz, George. "Consumer Spending as State Project: Yesterday's Solutions and Today's Problems." In *Getting and Spending. European and American Consumer Societies in the Twentieth Century*, ed. Susan Strasser, Charles McGovern, and Matthias Judt, 127–148. Cambridge: Cambridge University Press, 1998.

Lloyd, Susan McIntosh. *The Putney School. A Progressive Experiment*. New Haven, CT: Yale University Press, 1987.

Lopez, Ann Aurelia. *The Farmworkers' Journey*. Berkeley: University of California Press, 2007.

Lutts, Ralph H. "Chemical Fallout: Rachel Carson's Silent Spring, Radioactive Fallout, and the Environmental Movement." *Environmental Review* 9 (Autumn 1985): 210–225.

Lynd, Robert S. "The Consumer Becomes a 'Problem.'" *Annals of the American Academy of Political and Social Sciences* 173 (May 1934): 1–6.

Mack, Adam. "'Speaking of Tomatoes': Supermarkets, The Senses, and Sexual Fantasy in Modern America." *Journal of Social History* (Summer 2010): 815–842.

Mackey, John. "Walmart for the Granola Crowd." *Economist* 376 (July 30, 2005): 60.

Mayer, Charles S. "Requiem for the Truth-in-Packaging Bill?" *Journal of Marketing* 30 (Apr. 1966): 1–5.

McGerr, Michael. *A Fierce Discontent. The Rise and Fall of the Progressive Movement in America, 1870–1920*. New York: Free Press, 2003.

McGovern, Charles. *Sold American. Consumption and Citizenship, 1890–1945*. Chapel Hill: University of North Carolina Press, 2006.

——. "Consumption and Citizenship in the United States, 1900–1940." In *Getting and Spending. European and American Consumer Societies in the Twentieth Century*, eds. Susan Strasser, Charles McGovern, and Matthias Judt, 37–58. Cambridge: Cambridge University Press, 1988.

McWilliams, Carey. *Factories in the Field. The Story of Migratory Farm Labor in California*. Hamden, CT: Archon Books, 1939, rpt. 1969.

Mikva, Zorita. "The Neighborhood Improvement Association: A Counter-Force to the Expansion of Chicago's Negro Population." MA thesis, University of Chicago, 1951.

Miller, Timothy. *The Hippies and American Values*. Knoxville: University of Tennessee Press, 1991.

Milliman, Thomas E., with Frances E. Sage. *The GLF Story, 1920–1964: The History of the Cooperative Grange League Federation Exchange, Inc*. Ithaca, NY: Wilcox Press, 1964.

"Minneapolis and Its Many Co-operatives." *Co-operation* 12 (Oct. 1926): 182–185.

Myers, James. *Labor and Co-ops: The Value of Consumer Cooperative to Organized Workers*. 3rd ed. Chicago: Cooperative League of the U.S.A., 1944.

Nahmias, Rick. *The Migrant Project. Contemporary Farm Workers*. Albuquerque: University of New Mexico Press, 2008.

National Consumer Committee for Research and Education, ed. *Consumer Activists. They Made A Difference: A History of Consumer Action Related by Leaders in the Consumer Movement*. New York: Consumers Union Foundation, 1982.

"Negro Co-operative Store." *Co-operation* 13 (Nov. 1927): 212–213.

Neptune, Robert. *California's Uncommon Market: The Story of the Consumer Cooperatives, 1977–1981*. Richmond, CA: Associated Cooperatives, 1982.

Nestle, Marion. *Food Politics: How the Food Industry Influences Nutrition and Health*. 2nd ed. Berkeley: University of California Press, 2007.

Nilsson, Henry. "Get into Groceries—Why and How?" *Consumers' Cooperation* 28 (June 1942): 91–95.

O'Leary, Rosemary. *Environmental Change: Federal Courts and the EPA*. Philadelphia: Temple University Press, 1993.

Packard, Vance. *Hidden Persuaders: Businesses Lured Buyers to Purchase Things They Didn't Need, Using Motivation Research*. New York: David McKay, 1957.

Parker, Florence E. *The First 125 Years: A History of Distributive and Service Cooperative in the United States, 1890–1954*. Superior, WI: Cooperative Publishing Association, 1956.

Parker, Robert Allerton. *A Yankee Saint: John Humphrey Noyes and the Oneida Community*. New York: G.P. Putnam's Son, 1935.

Pattillo-McCoy, Mary. *Black Picket Fences: Privilege and Peril among the Black Middle Class*. Chicago: University of Chicago Press, 1999.

Pendleton, P. Kathryn, and Howard U. Heller. "The Relocation of Families Displaced by an Urban Redevelopment Project." MA thesis, University of Chicago, 1952.

Perelli, Nancy, and William Ronco. "Boston Food Co-op." In *Non-Profit Foods Stores: A Resource Manual*, ed. Cynthia Burton, Mike Knepler, Mark Looney, and Joe Wrobel, 3–16. Washington, DC: Strongforce, n.d.

Pesticide Action Network North America. "Fields of Poison: California Farmworkers and Pesticides." In *Fast Food Nation: The Dark Side of the All-American Meal*, ed. Eric Schlosser, 143–149. Boston: Houghton Mifflin, 2001.

Plotkin, Wendy. "Deeds of Mistrust: Race, Housing, and Restrictive Covenants in Chicago, 1900–1953." Ph.D. diss., University of Illinois at Chicago, 1999.

Pollan, Michael. *In Defense of Food: An Eater's Manifesto*. New York: Penguin Press, 2009.

Pringle, Peter. *Food, Inc. Mendel to Monsanto—The Promises and Perils of the Biotech Harvest*. New York: Simon & Schuster, 2003.

Putney. World's Best Known Small Town. Putney: Putney Historical Society, 2003.

Randall, Harlan J. *Consumers' Cooperative Adventures. Case Studies*. Whitewater, WS: Whitewater Press, 1936.

Ransby, Barbara. *Ella Baker and the Black Freedom Movement: A Radical Democratic Vision*. Chapel Hill: University of North Carolina Press, 2003.

Raphael, Ray. *Cash Crop: An American Dream*. Mendocino, CA: Ridge Times Press, 1985.

Reddix, J. L. *The Negro Seeks Economic Freedom Through Co-operation*. Chicago: Central States Co-operative League, 1936.

——. "The Negro Finds A Way to Economic Equality." *Consumers' Cooperation* 21 (Oct. 1935): 173–176.

Report of the Inquiry on Co-operative Enterprise in Europe, 1937. Washington, DC: US Government Printing Office, 1937.

Robbins, William G. *Landscapes of Conflict: The Oregon Story, 1940–2000*. Seattle: University of Washington Press, 2004.

Rodale, Jerome I. *How to Eat for a Healthy Heart*. Emmaus, PA: Rodale Press, 1955.

Rodgers, Daniel T. *Atlantic Crossings: Social Politics in a Progressive Age*. Cambridge, MA: Harvard University Press, 1998.

Rodriguez, Arturo, with Alexa Delwiche and Sheheryar Kaoosji. "Cheap Food: Workers Pay the Price." In *Fast Food Nation: The Dark Side of the All-American Meal*, ed. Eric Schlosser, 123–142. Boston: Houghton Mifflin, 2001.

Ronald, Pamela C., and Raoul W. Adamchak. *Tomorrow's Table: Organic Gardening, Genetics, and the Future of Food*. New York: Oxford University Press, 2008.

Ronco, William. *Food Co-ops: An Alternative to Shopping in Supermarkets.* Boston: Beacon Press, 1974.

"Roseland in Chicago." *Co-operation* 10 (July 1924): 123.

Rossinow, Doug. "'The Revolution Is about Our Lives': The New Left's Consciousness." In *Imagine Nation: The American Counterculture of the 1960s and 1970s,* ed. Peter Braunstein and Michael William Doyle, 99–124. New York and London: Routledge, 2002.

Rothenberg, Daniel. *With These Hands: The Hidden World of Migrant Farmworkers Today.* Berkeley: University of California Press, 2000.

Roy, Ewell Paul. *Cooperatives: Today and Tomorrow.* Danville, IL: Interstate Printers & Publishers, 1969.

Sackman, Douglas Cazaux. *Orange Empire: California and the Fruits of Eden.* Berkeley: University of California Press, 2005.

Satter, Beryl. *Family Properties. Race, Real Estate, and the Exploitation of Black Urban America.* New York: Metropolitan Books, 2009.

Saunders, Kenneth. "Toyohiko Kagawa: The St. Francis of Japan." *Pacific Affairs* 4 (Apr. 1931): 308–317.

Savele, Syrjala. *The Story of a Cooperative: A Brief History of United Co-operative Society of Fitchburg.* Fitchburg, MA: United Co-operative Society, 1947.

Scanlon, Jennifer, ed. *The Gender and Consumer Culture Reader.* New York: New York University Press, 2000.

Schlink, F. J. *Eat, Drink and Be Wary.* Manchester, NH: Ayer, 1992.

Schlosser, Eric, ed. *Fast Food Nation: The Dark Side of the All-American Meal.* Boston: Houghton Mifflin, 2001.

Schlosser, Eric. "Reforming Fast Food Nation: A Conversation with Eric Schlosser." In *Fast Food Nation: The Dark Side of the All-American Meal,* ed. Eric Schlosser, 3–18. Boston: Houghton Mifflin, 2001.

Schudson, Michael. "The Troubling Equivalence of Citizens and Consumer." *Annals of the American Academy of Political and Social Science* 608 (Nov. 2006): 193–203.

Schulman, Bruce J. *The Seventies: The Great Shift in American Culture, Society, and Politics.* New York: Free Press, 2001.

Schulman, Bruce J., and Julian E. Zelizer, eds. *Rightward Bound: Making America Conservative in the 1970s.* Cambridge: Harvard University Press, 2008.

Schuyler, George S. "Consumers' Cooperation: The American Negro's Salvation." *Co-operation* 17 (Aug. 1931): 144–145.

Shapin, Steven. "Paradise Sold." *New Yorker* 82 (May 15, 2006): 84–88.

Shapiro, Laura. *Something from the Oven: Reinventing Dinner in 1950s America.* New York: Viking, 2004.

——. *Perfection Salad. Women and Cooking at the Turn of the Century.* New York: Farrar, Straus & Giroux, 1986.

"Should Cooperatives Sell Beer?" *Co-operation* 19 (July 1933): 131–132.

Showalter, Elaine, ed. *These Modern Women: Autobiographical Essays from the Twenties.* New York: Feminist Press, 1978.

——. "Alice Mary Kimball." In *These Modern Women: Autobiographical Essays from the Twenties,* ed. Elaine Showalter, 52–57. New York: Feminist Press, 1978.

Sinclair, Upton. *The Autobiography of Upton Sinclair.* New York: Harcourt, Brace & World, 1962.

Smith, Michael B. "'Silence, Miss Carson!' Science, Gender, and the Reception of Silent Spring." *Feminist Studies* 27 (Autumn 2001): 733–752.

Smith, Toby M. *The Myth of Green Marketing: Tending Our Goats at the Edge of Apocalypse.* Toronto: University of Toronto Press, 1998.

Sommer, Robert, Franklin Becker, William Hohn, and Jean Warholic. "Customer Characteristics and Attitudes at Participatory and Supermarket Cooperatives." *Journal of Consumer Affairs* 17, 1 (1983): 134–148.

Sonnichsen, Albert. *Consumers' Cooperation.* New York: Macmillan, 1919.

Sorenson, Helen. *The Consumer Movement. What It Is and What It Means.* New York: Harper & Brothers, 1941.

Stage, Sarah, and Virginia B. Vincenti, eds. *Rethinking Home Economics: Women and the History of a Profession.* Ithaca: Cornell University Press, 1997.

Staley, Eugene. *History of the Illinois State Federation of Labor.* Chicago: University of Chicago Press, 1930.

Stampley, James O. *Challenges with Changes: A Documentary of Englewood.* Chicago: n.p., 1979.

Stein, Judith. *Pivotal Decade: How the United States Traded Factories for Finance in the Seventies.* New Haven: Yale University Press, 2010.

——. *Running Steel: Running America. Race, Economic Policy, and the Decline of Liberalism.* Chapel Hill: University of North Carolina Press, 1998.

Stickney, W. M. "The Consumers' Cooperative Movement in Chicago." *Annals of the American Academy of Political and Social Science* 50 (Nov. 1913): 223–228.

Storrs, Landon R.Y. *Civilizing Capitalism: The National Consumers' League, Women's Activism, and Labor Standards in the New Deal Era.* Chapel Hill: University of North Carolina Press, 2000.

Strasser, Susan. *Satisfaction Guaranteed: The Making of the American Mass Market.* New York: Pantheon Books, 1989.

Strasser, Susan, Charles McGovern, and Matthias Judt, eds. *Getting and Spending. European and American Consumer Societies in the Twentieth Century.* Cambridge: Cambridge University Press, 1998.

Stromquist, Shelton. *Re-inventing "The People": The Progressive Movement, the Class Problem, and the Origins of Modern Liberalism.* Urbana: University of Illinois Press, 2006.

Sugrue, Thomas J. "All Politics Is Local: The Persistence of Localism in Twentieth-Century America" In *The Democratic Experiment. New Directions in American Political History,* ed. Meg Jacobs, William J. Novak, and Julian Zelizer, 301–326. Princeton: Princeton University Press, 2003.

——. "Crabgrass-Roots Politics: Race, Rights, and the Reaction Against Liberalism in the Urban North, 1940–1964." *Journal of American History* 82 (September 1995): 551–578.

"The Bohemians in Cleveland." *Co-operation* 16 (Aug. 1930): 142–143.

Tocqueville, Alexis de. *Democracy in America.* Vols. 1 & 2. New York: Alfred A. Knopf, 1948.

Tolbert, Lisa C. "The Aristocracy of the Market Basket: Self-Service Food Shopping in the New South." In *Food Chains. From Farmyard to Shopping Cart,* ed. Warren Belasco and Roger Horowitz, 179–195. Philadelphia: University of Pennsylvania Press, 2009.

Topping, Helen. "Kagawa and Cooperation in Japan." *Consumers' Cooperation* 21 (Jan. 1935): 18–20.

Valdes, Dennis Nodin. *Al Norte. Agricultural Workers in the Great Lakes Region, 1917–1970.* Austin: University of Texas Press, 1991.

Voorhis, Jerry. *Cooperative Enterprise: The Little People's Chance in a World of Bigness.* Danville, IL: Interstate Printer & Publishers, 1975.

——. *American Cooperatives: Where They Come From, What They Do, Where They Are Going*. New York: Harper & Brothers, 1961.

Voss, Kim. *The Making of American Exceptionalism: The Knights of Labor and Class Formation in the Nineteenth Century*. Ithaca: Cornell University Press, 1993.

Waldman, Steven. "The Tyranny of Choice." In *Consumer Society in American History: A Reader*, ed. Lawrence B. Glickman, 359–366. Ithaca: Cornell University Press, 1999.

Wallis, Eilenn V. "The Women's Cooperative Movement in Utah, 1869–1915." *Utah Historical Quarterly* 71 (Oct. 2003): 315–331.

Warbasse, J. P. "Cooperation, A Way of Peace." *Consumers' Cooperation* 25 (Aug. 1939): 154–157.

——. "Consumers' Cooperatives and the National Recovery Administration." *Consumers' Cooperation* (Mar. 1935): 63–66.

——. "The Consumers and the National Recovery Act." *Co-operation* 19 (Aug. 1933): 152–153.

Wargo, John. *Our Children's Toxic Legacy: How Science and Law Fail to Protect Us from Pesticides*. New Haven: Yale University Press, 1996.

Warne, Colston Estey. *Consumers' Co-operative Movement in Illinois*. Chicago: University of Chicago Press, 1926.

——. "The National Consumers' Cooperative Association." *University Journal of Business* 4 (July 1926): 230–244.

Weber, Karl, ed. *Food, Inc.: How Industrial Food is Making Us Sicker, Fatter and Poorer—And What You Can Do About It*. Philadelphia: PublicAffairs, 2009.

Weems, Robert E., Jr. *Desegregating the Dollar: African American Consumerism in the Twentieth Century*. New York: New York University Press, 1998.

Westbrook, Robert B. "Schools for Industrial Democrats: The Social Origins of John Dewey's Philosophy of Education." *American Journal of Education* 100 (Aug. 1992): 401–419.

Whelan, Robert R. "The Growth of Consumer Cooperatives in the United States." B.A. thesis, Amherst College, 1946.

Willett, Sandra L. "Consumer Education: An Activist Approach." In *Consumer Activists: They Made A Difference. A History of Consumer Action Related by Leaders in the Consumer Movement*, ed. National Consumer Committee for Research and Education, 288–293. New York: Consumers Union Foundation, 1982.

Wilson, William Julius. *The Truly Disadvantaged: The Inner City, the Underclass, and Public Policy*. Chicago: University of Chicago Press, 1987.

Winne, Mark. *Closing the Food Gap*. Boston: Beacon Press, 2008.

"Wisconsin First State to Require the Teaching of Consumers' Cooperation." *Consumers' Cooperation* 21 (Dec. 1935): 181.

Woodcock, Leslie. "Mary Ellicott Arnold: Creative Urban Workers." In *Great American Cooperators: Biographical Sketches of 101 Major Pioneers in Cooperative Development*, eds. Joseph G. Knapp and Associates, 39–41. Washington, DC: American Institute of Cooperation, 1967.

"The Workmen's of Chicago." *Co-operation* 14 (Jan. 1928): 14.

Zeuch, William Edward. "Rochdale College." *Co-operation* 17 (Apr. 1931): 64–67.

Zwerdling, Daniel. "The Uncertain Revival of Food Cooperatives." In *Co-ops, Communes & Collectives*, ed. John Case and Rosemary C.R. Taylor, 89–111. New York: Pantheon Books, 1979.

Index

Adamant, Vermont: history of, 106–107
Adamant Food Co-operative, 11, 12, 196;
credit problems of, 111, 114, 116; early
history of, 107, 108, 109, 110; financial loss
at, 114, 115–116; isolation of, 109, 110;
and Maple Corner Co-operative, 113, 114,
115, 116; political activism of, 111–112;
traditions of, 109, 113–114, 116, 117
African Americans, 22, 33, 48, 49, 62, 63, 71,
74–76, 77, 81–82, 118; consumer advocacy of, 35, 37–38, 45, 72–73; as co-op
board members, 53, 57, 58, 83, 84; as co-op
members, 36, 40, 54, 57, 69, 76, 81, 83, 139,
178, 189, 199; as co-op workers, 22, 54, 69;
and development of neighborhood food
co-ops, 7, 11, 13, 37–38, 71–72, 80–81,
134, 177–178, 193–194. See also Hyde Park
Cooperative Society; Ithaca Consumer
Cooperative Society; restrictive covenants;
urban renewal
agribusiness, 1, 8, 12, 146, 191; growth in, 43,
44, 46, 201–202; and pesticide use, 44, 46,
132. See also pesticides; migrant workers
Aiken, George: and Adamant Food Co-
operative, 111, 114–115; and Putney Food
Co-operative, 119–120
Alberta Co-op Grocery, 13, 198, 199
Arcata Co-operative, 12–13; boycotts at, 12,
143–145, 147, 150–151; and concern over
Fortuna Co-op, 13, 152–153, 153, 154, 156;
corporate structure of, 13, 138; environmental
activism of, 143–144; founding of, 142–143;
and product selection, 5, 143, 145, 150,
150–151; workers' discontent at, 145–146,
147. See also Eureka Co-operative; Fortuna
Co-operative; North Coast Co-operative

boycotts, 2, 6, 97; of labor unions, 9, 16; lettuce and grape, 8, 10, 11, 44, 46, 48, 59–63,
94–95, 97–98, 122, 129, 137, 144–145,
150–151, 182; against multinational corporations, 3, 12, 46, 59–61, 123, 137–138,
143–145, 147, 150, 154–155, 159–160, 164;
by women consumers, 42, 45. See also Caesar Chavez; consumer activism

Bronx: and food co-ops, 13, 190, 191,
192–193

Carson, Rachel, 12, 44, 58, 93, 131–132, 136.
See also environmental activism
Central Co-operative Exchange. See Central
Co-operative Wholesale
Central Co-operative Wholesale (CCW) (also
called Central States Co-operative League),
20, 22, 34, 38, 73, 80, 175
Chavez, Caesar, 44, 59, 129, 137, 144. See also
boycotts; new wave co-ops; United Farm
Workers conspiracy co-ops
consumer education. See entries for individual
food co-operatives
consumer activism: history of, 1, 6, 8, 9, 14, 31,
89, 105, 134; models of, 7–8. See also
boycotts; strikes; women
Co-operative League of the U.S.A. (CLUSA),
4, 18, 26, 132; collaboration with co-ops, 42,
43, 73, 80, 110, 132, 134; member stores of,
32, 34, 82; political dissent in, 22–23; presidents of, 22, 23, 34, 82
co-operatives: number of, 2, 32, 129, 134,
209n7; types of, 2
Co-op Organization (CO): and participatory
democracy, 189; and takeover of co-ops,
179–183
Cornell University, 21, 37–38, 48, 58, 60, 68;
faculty assistance with Ithaca Consumer
Co-operative Society (ICCS), 10, 48, 50, 51,
53, 55; and student interest in co-op, 50,
60, 64

Dartmouth College, 91; and co-op members,
11; and influence on Hanover Consumer
Co-operative Society (HCCS), 36, 97, 98,
101
Dewey, John, 120; ideas about democracy, 3,
18, 36
democracy: economic, 3, 6, 9, 17, 18, 47, 82,
112, 134, 189; participatory, 3, 4, 6, 8, 12, 15,
23, 46, 200. See also entries for individual
food co-ops
Douglas, Paul, 33, 70, 78